JOSEPH KARO

LAWYER AND MYSTIC

Responsum with signature of Joseph Karo

JOSEPH KARO

LAWYER AND MYSTIC

R. J. ZWI WERBLOWSKY

The Jewish Publication Society of America
Philadelphia 5740/1980

Revised paperback edition

ISBN 0-8276-0090-9
Library of Congress catalog card no. 77-074605
Manufactured in the United States of America

First published 1962 *in Great Britain*
by Oxford University Press

CONIVGI CARISSIMAE

Prov. xxxi. 28

PREFACE TO THE SECOND EDITION

REVIEWERS and critics have been kind and encouraging after the first appearance of this book. So also have the readers, and the book has consequently been out of print for many years. Though not exactly a popular work, the present study of Joseph Karo's *maggid* proved of sufficient interest to students of Jewish history and of sixteenth-century Kabbalah, as well as to historians of religion, to be still in demand and to justify a reprint.

Reviewers and subsequent research have taught me a great deal and enabled me to correct or reassess many points of detail without, however, materially affecting the overall presentation and argument. I am particularly indebted to the reviews of J. Dan (*Tarbiz*, vol. 33 (1963/64), pp. 89–96) and D. Tamar (*Kiryath Sefer*, vol. 40 (1964/65), pp. 65–71), and regret that not all their corrections and suggestions could be incorporated in this reprint edition. A thoroughly revised edition of this book would have been desirable. However, since this would have involved not only considerable rewriting but also new typesetting, it seemed preferable to let the original text stand, merely correcting a few details (mainly dates) and misprints. Some of the references in the footnotes have been brought up to date. A few major points, requiring more ample discussion, are dealt with in the Postscript added to the present edition.

I am deeply grateful to The Jewish Publication Society of America for republishing, with the kind permission of the Oxford University Press, this study of Karo's *maggid* and adding it to their distinguished list.

R. J. Z. W.
Ereb Shabu'oth 5736 / June 3, 1976

PREFACE

THE wish to write a book on Karo's Maggid calls for no apology, though perhaps its execution may. Both the importance of Joseph Karo as one of the most influential halakhists of Judaism and the intrinsic interest of his kabbalistic diary warrant a closer study of the *Maggid Mesharim*. No serious analysis of the document, let alone of its kabbalistic doctrines, has been attempted so far. Historians—whether denying or defending the genuineness of the *Maggid Mesharim*—have treated the subject only in passing and in connexion with their accounts of post-expulsion history in general. Monographs are few and as a rule tendentious and unreliable. The first biography of Karo ever to be written was, unfortunately, never published.[1] Of later writers on Karo some will be mentioned in the following pages, others it may be kinder to ignore.[2]

Joseph Karo did not live in a social or spiritual vacuum. His halakhic activity, his kabbalistic speculations and his intimate mystical life were closely interwoven with the experiences, problems, hopes, and ideals that agitated sixteenth-century Jewry in general and the devout brotherhoods of the community of saints in Safed in particular. An account of Karo's life and work would

[1] Its author was the Italian-born rabbi Solomon Me'ir b. Moses Navarra. From Jerusalem, where he had settled, he was sent again to Italy to collect charities for the Holy Land. On one of his travels (cf. Bartolocci, *Bibl. magna rabbinica*, vol. iv (1693), p. 527: '*saepe* ad colligendas eleemosynas missus fuit') he was accompanied by a fellow emissary, Elisha Ashkenazi, who brought with him the manuscript of the second part of the *Maggid Mesharim*, subsequently printed in Venice, 1649. Navarra appears to have been a prolific author and to have continued writing on Jewish subjects even after his conversion to Christianity. (On his conversion cf. G. Scholem, *Sabbatai Ṣevi: The Mystical Messiah* (1973), p. 77). Of Solomon Navarra alias Prosper Rugeri (for 'die 25 Iunii 1664 ad Sacrum Baptismatis fontem regeneratus, nomen Prosperi Rugerii assumpsit') Bartolocci informs us that 'plura scripsit . . . tam ante tam post conversionem' and lists among his works a *Life of R. Ioseph Karo* 'de quo fabulantur Iudaei, vocem de caelo quotidie eum docuisse mirabilia coram caeteris Rabbinis, qui talem vocem audientes, omnes attoniti videbantur' (loc. cit.)—I owe the reference to Bartolocci to the kindness of Prof. Scholem.

[2] As for H. L. Gordon's *The Maggid of Karo* (1949), cf. my review in the *Journal of Jewish Studies*, vol. vii (1956), pp. 119–21, which absolves every writer on Karo from the necessity of taking note of the book.

have to present a picture of a sixteenth-century kabbalist rabbi; but in order to be a true portrait, it would have to be both typical of its age and, at the same time, express all the distinctive and individual traits of its subject.

As the subject-matter may be of interest to historians of religion beyond the narrow circle of Hebraists and students of Judaism, I have tried to reduce the Hebrew in the text to a minimum, transliterating and translating wherever possible, and relegating the original Hebrew to the notes. The transliteration of Hebrew has been simplified as far as possible, and for names and words with a more or less established English spelling (Kabbalah, Karo, Cordovero, &c.) the latter has been used instead of the philologically more exact transliteration. The chapters in which some Hebrew appeared to be unavoidable (e.g. those dealing with textual and halakhic matters) are marked with an asterisk in the table of contents. But even apart from the question of Hebrew, the writer is aware that he may have fallen between two stools: the kabbalistic scholar will be exasperated by the amount of space given to what are to him commonplaces and would have preferred greater attention to other, more important, questions of detail, whereas the non-specialist will be annoyed by the excess of irrelevant details and technicalities. The author deliberately chose this risk; whether it was a sensible one to take the reader will have to judge.

Unless stated otherwise, quotations from and references to the *Maggid Mesharim* apply to the first complete edition, Amsterdam, 1708. In order to facilitate the finding of references, I have added indications of the paragraphs on each page. Thus '*M.M.* 19b. 4' means '*Maggid Mesharim*, edition Amsterdam (1708), the 4th paragraph on fol. 19 verso'. References to Zoharic texts (*Zohar*, *Zohar Ḥadash*, *Tiqquney Zohar*) are to the editions of Rabbi R. Margalioth. I have not thought it necessary to add references to general literature on the subject of mysticism,[1] psychology of religion, the psychology of para-normal, viz. psychopathological phenomena, &c., though many works in these fields contain valuable discussions of revelations, inspiration, hallucinations, motor automatisms, and the like. Readers interested in these general

[1] e.g. Evelyn Underhill, *Mysticism* (1930), pp. 60 and 266–97.

problems and discussions are no doubt familiar with the relevant literature, produced partly by the mystics themselves and partly by highly unmystical psychologists. Of particular interest to the main theme of the present study are the many attempts made by theologians, mystics, and psychologists to distinguish between the 'personal' and the more-than-personal elements of mystical experiences. These distinctions, as well as the peculiar terminologies in which they are expressed (e.g. natural—supernatural—preternatural, personal and collective unconscious, &c.) are no doubt familiar to the reader and little reference is therefore made to the diverse schools of modern psychology, the writings of Catholic theologians and the discussions concerning *Ilḥam* in Muslim theology.

The present study was begun at the Institute of Jewish Studies in Manchester and owes much to the encouragement of Professor A. Altmann, then Director of the Institute. Both he and my colleague Dr. J. G. Weiss, who succeeded Professor Altmann, have contributed much to the progress of the work; its inclusion in the *Scripta Judaica* series only increases my gratitude to the Institute. The beginning of the work was assisted by a grant from the cultural funds of the Conference of Jewish Material Claims against Germany.

Colleagues and friends at the Hebrew University of Jerusalem have been liberal and unstinting with help and advice. Their wide knowledge, from which I benefited both orally and through their published work, has more than once saved me from my own ignorance. Although it is impossible to acknowledge all debts individually, yet I would not fail to mention Professor Y. Tishby whose erudition and critical acumen have been a frequent source of enlightenment. Mr. M. Benayahu of the Ben Zvi Institute at the Hebrew University has kindly put at my disposal not only his wide knowledge of the history of oriental Jewry, and of the sixteenth century in particular, but also his important manuscript collections; his friendship and generosity have placed me greatly in his debt. Professor E. E. Urbach kindly read the manuscript of chapter 8 on the *halakhah* in the *Maggid Mesharim* and helped me with information and suggestions on many a point where I might otherwise have gone wrong.

Whoever is concerned with kabbalistic studies—under whatever aspect and in whatever capacity—is, almost by definition, a disciple of Professor G. Scholem. In addition to this general indebtedness, inherent *in rerum cabbalisticarum natura*, I also owe him a very special and personal debt of gratitude which goes beyond anything that bibliographical references or footnotes can indicate. If it cannot be adequately expressed, it should at least be formally placed on record.

R. J. Z. W.

Jerusalem
October 1959

CONTENTS

LIST OF PLATES

ABBREVIATIONS

THE abbreviations used for indicating Biblical books (Gen. = *Genesis*, Ex. = *Exodus*, &c.) and tractates of the Talmud (*Ber.* = *Berakhoth*, &c.) are the usual ones and are not listed below.

A.R.	*'Abqath Rokhel*, responsa by Joseph Karo.
b.	Babylonian Talmud.
B.Y.	*Beth Yosef*, Karo's commentary on *Ṭur*.
B.Z.A.W.	*Beihefte zur Zeitschrift für die Alttestamentliche Wissenschaft*.
E.H.	*'Eben ha'Ezer*.
E.J.	*Encyclopaedia Judaica*.
H.M.	*Ḥoshen Mishpaṭ*.
HUCA.	*Hebrew Union College Annual*.
J.A.O.S.	*Journal of the American Oriental Society*.
J.E.	*Jewish Encyclopaedia*.
J.J.S.	*Journal of Jewish Studies*.
J.Q.R.	*Jewish Quarterly Review*.
M.	*Mishnah*.
M.G.W.J.	*Monatsschrift f. Geschichte u. Wissenschaft d. Judentums*.
M.M.	*Maggid Mesharim*.
MTJM.	G. Scholem, *Major Trends in Jewish Mysticism*,[2] New York, 1946.
O.H.	*'Oraḥ Ḥayyim*.
p.	Palestinian Talmud.
P.G.	Migne, *Patrologia Graeca*.
P.L.	Migne, *Patrologia Latina*.
R.E.J.	*Revue des Études Juives*.
Sh.A.	*Shulḥan 'Arukh*.
Y.D.	*Yoreh De'ah*.

JOSEPH KARO

LAWYER AND MYSTIC

1

INTRODUCTION

FOR many centuries the Jewish people has chosen to remember its greatest sons by the titles of their books, if possible every one by the title of his *magnum opus*. Even when authors were referred to by their actual names, these did not so much represent individual personalities as literary figures. Every name, it might almost be said, functioned as a pen-name. Who, after all, was the Ramban if not the author of the talmudic novellae *ḥiddushey ha-Ramban* or of the commentary on the Pentateuch *perush ha-Ramban*? No doubt the book often hid a distinct and unique personality, but the author was never allowed to protrude, as it were, from his work. The Jewish public has, as a rule, been more interested in ideas and doctrines than in biographies.

Joseph Karo is one of the great pen-names in Jewish history. Though a 'master of all Israel', a veritable *Doctor Synagogae*, his name never signified a particular individual, distinguished by outstanding learning and intellectual power, or by saintliness and charismatic gifts, as do, for example, the names of Elijah, the Gaon of Vilna, or of the Baal Shem Tob in the eighteenth century. The name Joseph Karo was, to the scholar, equivalent to 'the author of the *Beth Yosef*'; to the layman it meant 'the author of the *Shulḥan 'Arukh*'. Either way Karo was the *meḥabber*, the author *kat' exochen* of rabbinic Judaism. It was he who wrote the *Summa* of rabbinic orthodoxy, the code that summed up the practice—or, at least, ideal practice—of halakhic, normative Judaism and that became established for centuries to come as the revered and reviled symbol of orthodox rabbinism. But whereas the Church, by canonizing her saints and writing their individual—albeit stereotyped—*vitae*, preserved a semblance of individuality and often very much more than that, the Jewish *meḥabber* is swallowed up by his work. It took some time before the *Shulḥan 'Arukh* came to epitomize rabbinic Judaism as a whole. Both Karo himself and his contemporaries seem to have regarded the gigantic, synthetic survey of rabbinic law *Beth Yosef* as his main claim to fame, and there were certainly critics who wrote rather slightingly of the 'short book'.[1] But whether of *Beth Yosef* or of the *Shulḥan 'Arukh*, Karo was first and foremost *ha-meḥabber*, 'the author'.

Of course everybody knew that the *Doctor Synagogae* was also a *Doctor Mysticus*: Karo was a kabbalist as well, and his scholarly eminence and saintliness were duly rewarded by the nightly visitations of a celestial mentor who revealed to him 'the secrets of the *Torah*' and other mysteries. There was a fairly persistent tradition to that effect right from Karo's own days.[2] The tradition was perpetuated and given publicity by Solomon Alkabets's account of the Maggid's manifestation during the *Shabu'oth* vigil in Karo's house[3] and spread by Isaiah Hurwitz, who quoted this account *in extenso* in his widely read *Two Tablets of the Covenant*, better known by its abbreviated title *SHeLaH*.[4] But whether this story was accepted as a signal though in no way irregular mark of divine favour, or whether it was dismissed as a superstitious legend, it had nothing to do with the role and function of Joseph Karo in Jewish historical consciousness.

Then, in the nineteenth century, came the historians who started to write biographies. Often they found the halakhic teachings of a rabbi less interesting than the character, temperament, political convictions, &c., which the former were supposed to betray. Occasionally an historian disliked an author's theology or the influence he exerted on his age; in such cases it was desirable to

[1] The expression *sefer ha-qaṣer* almost became a synonym of *Sh.A.* Karo himself describes the relation of his *B.Y.* to the *Sh.A.* by implication in an interesting aside in his *Derashoth* (in *'Or Ṣaddiqim* (Salonica, 1799), fol. 58a): לפי שדרך החכמים שעושים ספרים כותבים ספר א׳ בארוכה וא׳ בלשון קצרה כמו זכרון לבד כמו פסקי הרא״ש הארוכים וקצור פסקי הרא״ש... For his otherwise high opinion of his Code compare the references below, ch. 8, p. 187, n. 3. Hostile and denigrating criticism particularly by Yomtob Ṣahalon (*Responsa*, no. 67); cf. also Greenwald, op. cit. (below, p. 4, n. 6), pp. 174–6. The simple inscription on Karo's tombstone ציון הרב יוסף קארו זצ״ל הבעל שלחן ערוך most probably dates from a later period when the *Sh.A.* was already well established as Karo's main claim to popular fame. See Plate 1.

[2] Cf. below, pp. 15 f.

[3] Cf. below, pp. 19–22.

[4] Edn. 1, Amsterdam, 1649, and many subsequent editions. Quotations and references are to edn. 3, Amsterdam, 1698.

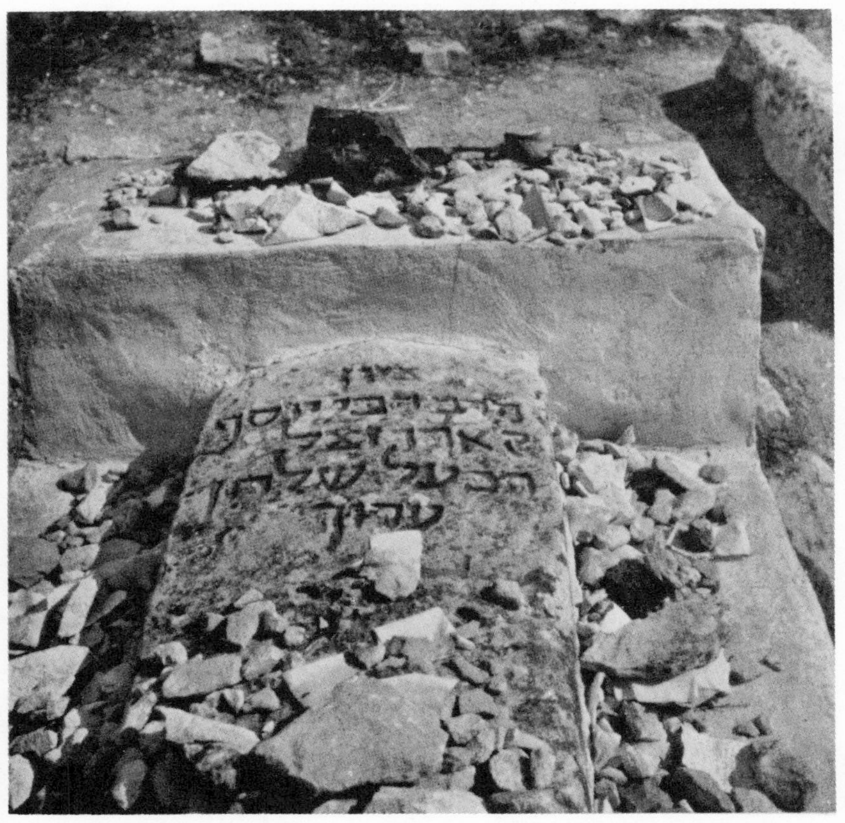

1. The tomb of Joseph Karo, showing the inscription on the tombstone

use the biography, as far as possible, as a stick with which to beat both the man and his work. This, at least, is what seems to have happened with Graetz.[1] As a devout liberal rationalist and a fervent believer in enlightenment and progress, he could not but dislike the *Shulḥan 'Arukh*. Admittedly Karo's code had brought unity to a Judaism threatened by increasing variety of legal and ritual practice.[2] The kabbalistic elements in it had mercifully been kept to a minimum[3] and even many beautiful and exalted teachings of the early rabbis were enshrined in its paragraphs.[4] But alas, 'they disappear in an ocean of casuistical detail and mere externals'. In short, the Judaism reflected by the *Shulḥan 'Arukh* was different from that revealed on Sinai or preached by the Prophets; even worse, it was different from that taught by Maimonides.[5] With that sort of medieval author it must not, of course, surprise us that he fell a prey to the blandishments of the Kabbalah. Similar in outlook though even more amusing in its formulations is the opinion of Geiger, who credits Karo with '*Fleiß, Arbeitskraft . . . auch Eitelkeit und Ehrgeiz . . . ohne . . . überwiegende geistige Anlage*'. In these circumstances one must be prepared for the worst, and sure enough—'*flach und eitel ließ er sich auch von der Kabbalah einfangen*'.[6] According to Graetz[7] '*Schwärmerei* is infectious. Karo . . ., who had hitherto busied himself exclusively with the accumulation of talmudic learning, in his turn fell into the same kabbalistic enthusiasm as Molkho; he also had his dream-prompter (*maggid*) who disclosed to him the most absurd (*geschmacklose*) mystical interpretations and revealed the future.' This Maggid, however, was not 'an angel . . . but funnily (*drollig*) enough the personified *Mishnah* who descended on him generally at night-time and whispered revelations because he had devoted himself to her service'.[8] For more than forty years the activity of Karo's mind 'was divided between dry rabbinical learning and the fantastic [ideas of the] Kabbalah'.[9] By this roundabout route via the Maggid, Graetz

[1] *Geschichte der Juden* (edn. 3), vol. ix (1891), pp. 236, 298–301, 401–4, and particularly Note 5, pp. 530 ff. (on Re'ubeni and Molkho).

[2] Ibid., pp. 402–3.

[3] Ibid., pp. 403–4.

[4] Ibid., p. 404.

[5] Ibid.

[6] *Nachgelassene Schriften*, vol. ii (1875), pp. 186–7.

[7] Op. cit., p. 236.

[8] Ibid., pp. 298–9.

[9] Ibid.

finally returned to the *Shulḥan 'Arukh* and concluded[1] that 'religious promptings, kabbalistic enthusiasm, and personal ambition equally contributed to the making of this book'.

Graetz was the mouthpiece of the spirit of his time. For a long time this spirit dominated Jewish historiography and, to judge from the evidence, still does so in certain quarters. Nothing so well demonstrates the triumph of the 'Graetzian' spirit as the history of his interpretation of Karo. It is a remarkable phenomenon that most of Graetz's opponents accept his values and merely dispute his facts. There is no need for us to surmise the psychological motives behind the attempts of S. J. Rappaport (SHIR), D. Cassel, and others to acquit Karo of the charge of having had a Maggid. Rappaport,[2] after proving to his own satisfaction that Karo did not write the compromising *Maggid Mesharim* (henceforth *M.M.*), triumphantly concludes: 'and thus the Rabbi [Karo] emerges guiltless before the Lord and before Israel and he remains an example for all generations'.[3] Cassel too does his best to show that Karo was an honourable man, and challenges Graetz's assessment of the *Shulḥan 'Arukh*: 'religious promptings'—by all means; 'kabbalistic enthusiasm'—definitely no. Concerning 'personal ambition' Cassel suspends judgement.[4] S. P. Rabinowitz[5] belittles neither Karo nor the *Shulḥan 'Arukh*, yet wistfully reflects how much more significant this great man's work could have been for Judaism had he not succumbed to the fantastic vagaries of Kabbalah. But while deploring Karo's regrettable weakness, Rabinowitz had enough good historical sense to admit that even rationalists of the calibre of a Saadyah or of a Ḥofni Gaon could hardly have affected the benighted temper and atmosphere of sixteenth-century Judaism in general and of Safed in particular.

With Rabbi L. Greenwald's *The Life and Times of R. Joseph Karo*[6] Graetz has consummated his triumph. If those who rejected

[1] *Geschichte der Juden*, vol. ix, p. 401.

[2] *'Iggeroth SHIR* (אגרות שי"ר) (Przsemysl, 1885), pp. 207–8.

[3] ובזה יצא הרב נקי מה׳ ומישראל והוא נשאר מופת לדור ודור (cf. *Num.* xxxii. 22); also id. in Kobak's *Jeschurun*, vol. vi (1868), Hebrew part, p. 30.

[4] 'Josef Karo u. das Maggid Mescharim' in *Sechster Bericht v. d. Lehranstalt f. d. Wissenschaft d. Judentums* (Berlin, 1888), p. 9.

[5] מוצאי גולה (1894), p. 233.

[6] הרב ר׳ יוסף קארו וזמנו (New York, 1954).

Karo's Maggid as an unworthy legend and his *M.M.* as a fabrication were, at one stage of the controversy, rationalists, scoffers, and near-atheists to be taught better by the true believers in God and *maggidim*, everything is now the other way round. According to Greenwald it is the scoffers and ungodly historians who are casting aspersions at Karo and who slander an illustrious and revered name in Israel by compromising him with a Maggid.[1] In fact, the championship of the genuineness of the *M.M.* has apparently become so distinctive a feature of heresy that the author was appalled to find it accepted by a religious journal.[2] Greenwald may well be right in his diagnosis of the underlying tendency to ridicule and discredit not just Joseph Karo but *in* him the author of the *Shulḥan 'Arukh* and, by implication, medieval rabbinic obscurantism in general. But unfortunately Greenwald did not stop to consider whether his own apologetic interest held much promise of dispassionate and objective scholarship or whether a *maggid* was necessarily a disgrace. To a generation living in an age of psychology and sociology it has become a truism that even the most theoretical researches may be prompted by very un-theoretical motives and drives; but this recognition in no way lessens the obligation to conduct our inquiries with the minimum of prejudice and maximum of rigour.

Perhaps the whole past controversy about the *M.M.* is less significant for its doubtful intrinsic merits than for the light it throws on the values and tendencies that have shaped Jewish historiography. As regards the problem itself, the questions that were asked were simple. For both sides in the controversy the existence of Karo's Maggid and the genuineness of the *M.M.* were biographical and bibliographical questions. The book *M.M.* was scanned for personal and historical references but hardly anyone has seen fit to study it as what it really is: a kabbalistic text of the sixteenth century. This strange neglect may have been due to the special preoccupations of historians or to a more general dislike or ignorance of Kabbalah. It did not occur to any of the writers on the *M.M.* that even if the 'diary' was not by Karo it might still repay closer study. The demonstration of Karo's authorship does

[1] Ibid., pp. 6 ff., 184 ff.

[2] Ibid., pp. 7–8.

not 'settle' the problem of the book, nor does its refutation dispose of it. Either way it demands our attention as a kabbalistic document of one of the most active periods of Jewish mysticism. In a way the knowledge of the circle from which the book emanated may be of even greater significance than the identification of the author. If the *M.M.* is indeed by Karo, then we can situate it in the Alkabets–Cordovero circle and it may become a valuable aid to our understanding of sixteenth-century non-Lurianic (or pre-Lurianic) kabbalism.

What has made the authorship of the book a matter of such passionate interest, almost to the exclusion of any serious attention to the text itself, was not merely scholarly enthusiasm for correct bibliographical ascriptions. It was sensed—probably rightly—that if Karo really was the author of the *M.M.*, then the existence of this strange and disconcerting diary in the shadow of the *Shulḥan 'Arukh* was, in a way, symbolic of the hidden complexities of rabbinic Judaism. As has been remarked before, Karo's name had come to epitomize rabbinic Judaism as a whole. In his *Shulḥan 'Arukh* the specific ethos that characterized Jewish piety since the days of Ezra had crystallized—or petrified—into its final shape. The idea of a divine law regulating human life in all its manifestations and down to the smallest detail had been the guiding star of Jewish religiosity for many generations. Compared with it, all other religious movements and currents, significant and fertile as they were, were but eddies in a great and majestic stream. Studying the Law was the highest form of human activity because it meant immersing one's intellect in the divine will as revealed to Moses. Performing the Law was not only a matter of acquiring merits or of doing the will of the Father in Heaven; it was the one way of sanctifying oneself and of testifying to God's Kingdom. It was inevitable that casuistry about legal and ritual minutiae should proliferate as time went on and new situations and problems presented themselves. From time to time attempts were made to take stock of the accumulating mass of *halakhah*, yet by and large Jewish life, as it developed in the various centres in Palestine and the diaspora, seemed to have struck a certain balance between variety and uniformity, fluidity and legal fixity. The various codes or collections of laws, liturgical anthologies, &c., all became added source-books in the vast library of Judaism: they were never regarded as final and authoritative statements.

Then, in the sixteenth century, the 'fullness of time' had come. In the atmosphere of chaos and disintegration that prevailed after the expulsion from Spain, and in the profound conviction that some measure of uniformity and order was indispensable if Israel was to be ready for the advent of the Redeemer, Karo wrote his monumental critical survey of the *corpus totius iuris rabbinici*, the *Beth Yosef*. Based on the latter, he next composed his shorter code, the *Shulḥan 'Arukh*. Perhaps the real significance of these two works was not so much religious or legal as social. As a matter of fact the actual influence of the *Shulḥan 'Arukh* on rabbinic law is—theoretically at least—much smaller than appears at first sight to the layman. Disagreement with Karo's code is possible, and for all purposes of rabbinic casuistry Karo's opinion is but one among many that have to be considered when weighing decisions. Yet the social impact of the *Shulḥan 'Arukh* was unprecedented. Its reception by Jewry everywhere,[1] particularly after Moses Isserles of Cracov had added glosses incorporating the divergent practice of the Ashkenazi tradition, meant that for all ordinary purposes one and the same manual was the *de facto* standard of reference. Even more, the *Shulḥan 'Arukh* came to represent the *Summa* of Jewish life; it was *the* valid formulation of practical Judaism that henceforth dominated Israel. Foolishness to the Greeks and a scandal to later liberal Judaism, it told man to love God, how to tie his bootlaces, and what kind of misspellings rendered a bill of divorce invalid. Practically every society and culture have their regulations or 'patterns' for these things, but in the *Shulḥan 'Arukh* they were presented as an integrated religious system of 'serving God'. When the winds of the modern age began to blow through the house of Israel, the war-cry of orthodoxy was faithfulness to the *Shulḥan 'Arukh*; the slogan of liberalism and reform was 'away from the *Shulḥan 'Arukh*' to whatever form of Judaism was considered to be more adequate and authentic. Few literary documents—apart from the Bible, the Talmud, and perhaps the Prayer Book—have

[1] Cf. the testimonies quoted by Greenwald, op. cit., p. 176 ff.

acquired such immense practical and symbolic social value in Jewish history. The fact that Joseph Karo left an intimate diary, recounting a life-time of mystical, if not pathological, experiences thus very understandably provokes more than ordinary interest. Again it shows, if such proof was necessary at all, that a legal code can never inform us of the spiritual outlook of its author and of the —actual or ideal—society for which he wrote. This lesson was already taught by the greatest codifier before Karo, Moses Maimonides. The problems posed by the necessity of determining the relationship between Maimonides's code and his philosophy are still far from being solved, but Jewish historiography has at least had time to get used to them. In the case of Karo, however, it would seem that the question is not so much one of solving problems as of seeing them first.

2

THE MAGGID OF KARO

SOME brief references to the nineteenth-century controversy about the *M.M.* have already been made in the preceding chapter. But the controversy was older than the nineteenth century, and the authenticity of the book known as *M.M.* had been disputed more than once,[1] although, needless to say, on every such occasion Karo's authorship also found staunch supporters. The scholarly apologies are by themselves sufficient evidence for the existence of critical doubts that could not be ignored. It is one of the ironies of our subject that the first defenders of the genuineness of the diary not only coupled their apology to one for the authenticity of the *Zohar*, but actually tried to prove the latter by calling upon the *M.M.* as a principal witness! The first apologist was Rabbi Solomon 'Abi 'Ad Sar Shalom Bazila of Mantua in chap. 27 of his *'Emunath Ḥakhamim* (Mantua, 1730). Bazila's purpose in bringing the *M.M.* into his argument for the authenticity of kabbalistic tradition as a whole was the submission of evidence that celestial revelations were, at all times, well attested phenomena. Admittedly such occurrences, more particularly the appearance of the prophet Elijah in the *beth ha-midrash*, had been more 'usual 'or frequent in former days, yet even in later times it was by no means rare that chosen spirits should be vouchsafed such mystical privileges. After quoting a few sample passages from the *M.M.*,[2] Bazila neatly sums up his alternatives:

And now the enquirer who refuses to believe in our Kabbalah and in the book *Zohar* cannot escape this dilemma: either the Rabbi Karo was utterly wicked like Jeroboam and his associates, and invented these things from his heart, or else he must assume that Rabbi Karo never

[1] According to Scholem, *Encyclopaedia Judaica*, vol. ix (1932), col. 660, 'ohne guten Grund'; cf. also his later utterances on the question in *Sabbatai Ṣevi: The Mystical Messiah* (1973), pp. 19 and 209, n. 28.

[2] All from the Venice edition, which was probably the only one he had seen.

wrote these things but others invented them and attributed them to a great man. The fools who believe everything were taken in and printed them. Similarly the relation of the *Shabu'oth* vigil must be assumed to be a forgery.

As the first alternative must be rejected out of hand, only the second needs to be seriously considered. In order to establish Karo's authorship, Bazila advances what has since become the main argument of all later apologists by drawing attention to a literal quotation from the *M.M.* in Moses Cordovero's *Pardes Rimmonim.*[1] Alas, in one case at least the argument failed to convince. Bazila himself indignantly reports: 'when I expounded these things to a philosopher, he replied that one has to assume that Rabbi Karo invented lies in order to exalt himself—"let the lying lips [of this philosopher] be put to silence",[2] let them be bound, made dumb, and be silenced.'[3]

Bazila's story is instructive because it gives us, in a nutshell, the whole background of the original controversy. The point at issue was not the reliability of certain reports concerning Karo's mystical life, but rather the question whether supernatural revelations were possible or not. In this dispute dogmatic mystical affirmation is opposed to equally dogmatic rationalist denial. The terms of reference of the debate in Bazila's time were significantly different from those of the nineteenth-century controversy, when nobody doubted the possibility and reality of such mystical (meaning, of course, 'pathological') phenomena.[4] In spite of their anti-supernaturalism, the Early Fathers of the *Wissenschaft des Judentums* and their successors were quite prepared to allow revelations and maggidism as 'natural' phenomena. As late as 1913, D. Kahana still solemnly explained how through mortification and solitude Karo's 'imaginative power waxed strong until he began to see all kinds of visions and believed that the voice proceeding from his mouth spoke of itself', not omitting to enlighten his readers that 'of course all these phenomena were merely the products of his imagination and

[1] Cf. below, pp. 193–4.

[2] An obvious reference to Ps. xxxi. 18: 'let the lying lips be put to silence which speak grievous things proudly and contemptuously against the righteous.'

[3] The midrashic elaboration (*Genesis Rabbah* i. 5) of the curse in Ps. xxxi. 18.

[4] Cf. above, p. 3.

nothing else.[1] . . . But the fact that Rabbi Karo had a heavenly Maggid was a great marvel in the eyes of the people of Safed, to whom the laws of nature and psychology were yet unknown'.[2] Already Graetz had refused to be disconcerted by the awkward fact that some of the Maggid's prophecies had actually come true. These revelations were no fraud 'but inspired by the excited times and by an overheated imagination as happens more frequently in the warm luxurious East than in the cold and sober North'.[3] The crucial issue for the nineteenth-century historians was whether to credit Karo with such compromising psychological states, or whether to save his honour and reputation by exonerating him from the responsibility for the *M.M.* Only a few writers were sufficiently romantic in their outlook to admit Karo's Maggid as a fact without at the same time implying that it was a disgrace.[4]

After Bazila the next great defender of the faith in the *M.M.* was David Luria in his erudite and wrong-headed *Ma'amar Qadmuth ha-Zohar*.[5] In this essay D. Luria is trying to make out a case for Aramaic as the special language of revealed heavenly wisdom. Kabbalistic literature consists of directly revealed mysteries, which are preserved in Aramaic, e.g. the *Zohar* and the *M.M.*, and speculative texts written in Hebrew such as, for example, the works of Cordovero and others. The *M.M.* is not only composed in Aramaic like the *Zohar* but actually makes repeated reference to the 'holy *Zohar*' (*zohara qaddisha*). A study of the *M.M.* thus imposes itself, 'since we shall draw on it for proof of the authenticity of the Zohar'. There is a good deal of incidental information to be gathered from D. Luria's polemic. If on the one hand he was more successful than Bazila with the argument from Cordovero's *Pardes*, since

for good be remembered one recently deceased scholar in whose heart the critics had aroused doubts concerning the genuineness of the Maggid

[1] תולדות המקובלים השבתאים והחסידים, edn. 3, pt. i, 1926, p. 13; cf. also id. 'Eben Negef' in Smolenskin's *ha-Shaḥar*, vol. iv (תרל"ג), pp. 75–79.

[2] Ibid., p. 14.

[3] Op. cit., p. 299.

[4] e.g. Fuenn, *ha-Carmel* ii (1873, תרל"ג), pp. 580 f.: ... מצאנוהו מתפעל התפעלות קדש מתרומם ונשא על כנפי הדמיון למרום שחקים עד נוח עליו לפעמים הופעה רוחנית בצורת שכל נאצל העולה ומתעלה מלמוד המשנה...

[5] 1856. Karo's Maggid is discussed in the Fifth Branch, sections 3–4. D. Luria does not so much as mention Bazila, though he uses the same argument.

of the [author of the] *Beth Yosef*; but when I showed him the quotation in Cordovero's *Pardes* he recanted and agreed that the matter was now plain to him,

yet we also learn that there were 'critics' in the plural. In fact, criticism had become articulate in literature, and Luria enters the lists after having 'recently seen in print falsehoods concerning the book *M.M.*'.

In modern Jewish scholarship Rappaport was the first to deny Karo's authorship; he was followed by David Cassel,[1] S. A. Rosanes,[2] and, more recently, by the late Rabbi L. Greenwald.[3] Their arguments will be considered in more detail as we go along, but two points should, perhaps, be made right at the outset.

The first point is purely a matter of method and concerns the prima facie presumption in favour of a traditional ascription of authorship. There is no justification for doubting an authorship that has been maintained since the first appearance of a text, unless there are very specific and cogent arguments to the contrary. If objections are raised, the onus of proof is on the objector. Secondly, it is well to distinguish between two different aspects of the question of Karo's Maggid. The one concerns Karo's possession of (or by) a Maggid, i.e. his proneness to mystical and/or pathological states of a certain kind, the other relates to the published text of the *M.M.* Unfortunately the two questions have not been kept apart by writers on Karo. It is quite possible, theoretically, to maintain that Karo actually had a Maggid and yet did not compose the *M.M.*, and it is not in the least necessary to discredit Alkabets's epistle and other testimonies in order to pronounce the printed diary to be a forgery. On the contrary, it could reasonably be argued that an impostor would hope to palm off his fraud on a gullible public far more successfully if it circulated under a fairly probable name. For whatever reason anyone might wish to produce

[1] Cf. above, p. 4, n. 4.

[2] קורות היהודים בתורקיה וארצות הקדם (thus the title of vols. ii–v of edn. 2 of the same author's דברי ישראל בתוגרמה 1913), vol. ii, Sofia, 1937–8, particularly Appendix i. Also id. s.v. 'Karo' in the Hebrew encyclopaedia אוצר ישראל (edn. 3, 1935), vol. ix, pp. 88–89. Ch. B. Friedberg in his bibliographical lexicon בית עקד ספרים, edn. 2, vol. ii (1952), p. 546, simply states (no. 471) that Rosanes has 'proved' the *M.M.* to be not by Karo.

[3] Cf. p. 4, n. 6.

a pseudepigraph of this sort, he would reasonably expect it to 'sell' better if he could advertise it as the true and correct text of what the well-known Maggid of the great Rabbi Joseph Karo had actually said. It seems advisable, therefore, to open a discussion of the *M.M.* with an examination of the traditions and testimonies concerning Karo's maggidic visitations.

The student of mysticism needs no special proof that maggidism and similar phenomena (mentor angels, guiding spirits, voices, &c.) exist and that in certain periods and in certain groups their manifestations can be fairly frequent and typical, not to say epidemic. If in addition to scholarship and saintliness a rabbi also enjoyed the reputation of being a profound kabbalist, nothing was more natural than to condense this reputation into accounts of heavenly revelations. Of course it is a long way from the rather vague and general statement that legends grow on the basis of popular esteem and veneration to the concrete problem of examining the specific claims made on behalf of certain individuals. Looking, for example, through H. Y. D. Azulay's Dictionary of Names, *Shem ha-Gedolim*, one is surprised not only at the number of scholars and saints credited with a Maggid,[1] but also at the first-hand testimonies adduced. Thus of Moses Zacuto (1625–97) Azulay reports:[2] 'and I have been told that he had a Maggid; and the Rabbi *Gur 'Aryeh*, who wrote glosses to the *Sh.A.* which were printed with the text of the *Sh.A.* in Mantua, testified that he had heard the angel speaking through him.' Among Karo's own contemporaries and near-contemporaries Azulay mentions Joseph Taytazak who 'had a Maggid like Karo; and in the writings of my own grandfather, who was the son of the author of *Ḥesed le-Abraham*, I found a long and awe-inspiring quotation from the Maggid's communications to Rabbi J. Taytazak'.[3] A recently

[1] Cf. *Shem ha-Gedolim* on Aaron Berekhya of Modena, the author of *Ma'abar Yabboq*, s.v.: ושמעתי שהיה לו מגיד; David Ḥabilio, s.v.: והיה אדם גדול וקדוש והיה לו מגיד; the Polish kabbalist Samson of Ostropol, s.v.: והיה לו מגיד. Others who had no *maggid* were said to have seen apparitions of the prophet Elijah, e.g. David ibn 'Abu Zimra, s.v., and Cordovero, s.v. Cf. also Azulay's reference to Samuel of Freiersdorf (s.v. *Isaiah Hurwitz*). Best known of all and widely discussed in literature was the Maggid of M. H. Luzzatto (cf. below, pp. 13–14).

[2] Azulay, op. cit., s.v.

[3] Ibid., s.v. Also Sambari's chronicle דברי יוסף (MS. Oxford, Neubauer 2410,

discovered maggidic communication to Taytazak[1] is probably identical with the one seen by Azulay and supports the tradition that Karo's older contemporary of Salonica led a charismatic life no less intense than that of the author of the *M.M.* In fact, the fame of the *M.M.* appears to be due not so much to the uniqueness of the phenomenon as to the regrettable fact that all comparable testimonies and documents fell victim to the self-censorship[2] of the kabbalists themselves. Azulay also mentions Menahem Azaryah of Fano (1548–1620), one of Italy's leading kabbalists: 'and Rabbi Isaac Lombroso writes near the beginning of his commentary to *Job* that he had heard the Maggid of his master Rabbi Menahem Azaryah.'[3] Also the latter's disciple, Aaron Berekhya of Modena (d. 1639), is credited with a *maggid.*[4] Isaiah Hurwitz[5] reports that Joseph Karo, Moses Cordovero, and Isaac Luria had received visits by *maggidim* from the celestial academies and by the prophet Elijah, but is, of course, merely rehearsing legends already current in Palestine at the time of his arrival.

The many testimonies and reports about *maggidim* and similar phenomena should not be underestimated. In spite of modern attempts—in diverse quarters—to boost the purely 'spiritual' side of mysticism and to play down consistently the significance of the physical, ecstatic, and near-pathological phenomena in the consciousness of the mystics themselves, it becomes increasingly clear that the history of mysticism does not necessarily justify the fashionable tendencies among writers on mysticism. Whether students of the subject choose their 'spiritual' pet mystics and ignore the rest, or whether the mystics themselves keep quiet

fol. 130*a*) says הר׳ יוסף טאייטאיצק בעל ש״ת והיה לו מגיד (communicated by Mr. Benayahu).

[1] MS. Mani in the possession of Mr. Benayahu. (Mr. Benayahu has already briefly referred to this manuscript in his article in *Scritti in memoria di Sally Mayer* (1956), Hebrew section, p. 34, n. 62.) Taytazak's Maggid is also quoted by the prophet Nathan of Gaza; cf. the fragment published by Ch. Wirszubski in *Zion*, vol. iii (1938), p. 232.

[2] A point stressed by Professor G. Scholem; cf. *MTJM.*, pp. 15–16, 147.

[3] *Shem ha-Gedolim*, s.v. Azulay's source can be found in Lombroso's commentary on the Bible (Venice, 1638–9), fol. 397a.

[4] Cf. above, p. 13, n. 1.

[5] In a letter written to his sons from Palestine and first published in שומר ציון הנאמן (תרי״ג—1853, no. 141); cf. now also A. Ya'ari, אגרות ארץ ישראל (1943), p. 217.

about their inner life and merely give us the speculative ideas distilled from their experiences (as did the kabbalists), there can be little doubt that maggidism and similar 'abnormal' manifestations were more widespread and more valued than has been realized hitherto. Practically every new publication on the history of Jewish mysticism brings to light new cases and amply shows that well-known rabbis and writers did have—or at least did seek—maggidic revelations. It may be confidently asserted that the most interesting and fascinating texts on the subject are still awaiting publication and analysis.[1]

As far as Karo's Maggid goes we have solid contemporary evidence.[2] The slightly deprecatory remark in Vital's *Sha'ar ha-Gilgulim*[3] that the Maggid had misled Karo in the matter of the former incarnations of his son's soul at any rate confirms that Karo's Maggid was taken for granted at the time in Safed. In his visionary diary[4] Vital records (1557) that Karo's Maggid had declared that one-half of the world existed through the merits of his (Vital's) father, a pious scribe who wrote '*tefillin* in holiness', and the other half through his (Vital's) own merits. The famous preacher Moses Alsheikh, a disciple of Karo and the teacher of Vital, was also exhorted by the Maggid to do his very best with his illustrious disciple as the latter was destined one day to take Karo's place.[5]

[1] Cf. in particular the fascinating *Sefer ha-Meshib* (see below, p. 47, n. 3), which shows some striking similarities with the manuscript mentioned above, p. 14, n. 1.

[2] Cf. now also D. Tamar in *Tarbiz*, vol. xxvii (1957/8), p. 107, and in ארשת (Jerusalem, 1958), pp. 473–8, for further testimonies.

[3] In the *Liqquṭim* towards the end: וגם מה שאמר המגיד למהר"ר יוסף קארו זלה"ה על בנו שיש לו נשמת בצלאל שקר ענה לו וגם מה שאמר לו על ר' אלעזר שהוא קבור בטבריה מעומד כן הוא האמת; similarly in the *Sefer ha-Gilgulim* (Przsemysl, 1876, f. 87b).

[4] *Sefer ha-Ḥezyonoth*, as it is called in the manuscripts and in Vital's autograph in the possession of Rabbi Dr. A. Toaff, Livorno. The title of the printed editions, *Shibḥey Rabbi Ḥayyim Vital*, is due solely to the enterprise of the first printer (1826), who was stimulated by the success of the hasidic compilation *Shibḥey ha-Besht*; cf. Scholem in *Zion*, vol. v (1940), p. 135, n. 2. All references are to the last edition (*Sefer ha-Ḥezyonoth*, Jerusalem, 1954), which is based on the Livorno autograph.

[5] *Sefer ha-Ḥezyonoth*, p. 2.—Vital's ordination at the hands of Alsheikh may have been thought a step towards the realization of this ambition; cf. Azulay's report (op. cit., s.v. Ḥayyim Vital) גם ראיתי פתקא מכתב יד מהר"ם אלשיך עצמו וכתוב בה שבכח אשר נסמך ממרן מהר"י קארו הוא סומך את מהרח"ו יורה

Among our most instructive and illuminating sources for the knowledge of kabbalistic Safed are the epistles of the garrulous and perhaps somewhat uncritical Solomon Shlomel Dresnitz, subsequently published under the title *The Praises of the Lion*,[1] i.e. of the ARI, the abbreviated by-name of Isaac Luria current among his disciples. This exemplary kabbalistic gossip left his wife and thirteen-year-old daughter in his native Moravia, and set out a complete beggar (his wife's *kethubah* and the provision of a dowry for his daughter left him without a penny) for the Paradise and Mecca of kabbalists. He arrived in Safed in the autumn of 1602. By that time Vital had already settled in Damascus, but Safed was full of his and Luria's disciples and Dresnitz still met Karo's widow.[2] His letters bear eloquent witness to the complete triumph of Lurianism. From the very beginning the Lurianists had adopted the most subtle and deadly method of dealing with rival schools; they did not oppose them but wholeheartedly endorsed their teaching as a lower and incomplete form of kabbalistic revelation. The full light of esoteric truth shone in Luria alone and the non-Lurianic kabbalists comprehended it not. Lurianic legend is full of accounts in which kabbalists of Cordovero's school beg to be initiated, but are rejected because their soul is only fit to receive the lower, non-Lurianic mysteries. Vital, with disarming frankness, reports a dream, three months after the demise of his master, in which he saw Cordovero standing at the entrance of a Safed academy. To Vital's question which Kabbalah was taught in the 'world of spirits', Cordovero's or Luria's, Cordovero replied that both ways were equally true but that his own system was 'exoteric' in comparison with Luria's which was the 'inner and essential'; he himself now studied only according to the Lurianic system.[3] According to Azulay[4] Moses Alsheikh desired to study under

יורה ידין ידין ככל דיין מוסמך והזמן כ׳ אלול שנת הש״ן. Cf. also below, pp. 140 ff., on the relations between Karo and the Luria–Vital circle, particularly below, pp. 143–4, for the disarming *naïveté* with which Vital's unconscious wishes found expression in his dreams.

[1] Printed first in תעלומות חכמה, Bâle, 1629. A critical examination of the value of *Shibḥey ha-ARI* as a historical source is still outstanding.

[2] Clearly Karo's last wife, whom he married in his old age; cf. below, p. 131.

[3] *Sefer ha-Ḥezyonoth*, p. 57.

[4] Op. cit., s.v. Moses Alsheikh; also *Sefer ha-Ḥezyonoth*, p. 8.

Luria but was not accepted. Shlomel has a good deal to say on this subject and is at pains to explain that even the most illustrious among the non-Lurianic kabbalists were inferior to Luria. Thus we are told of Karo that

every time he recited the *Mishnah* by heart, the Maggid appeared to him and people would hear his voice through the door or at the back of the house saying: 'Peace upon thee, Rabbi Joseph Karo. I am the *Mishnah* which thou hast studied. I came forth to teach thee understanding. The Holy One, blessed be His Name, praises thee greatly in the celestial academy, saying, "my son Joseph, such and such are his deeds, such and such are his ways, such his diligence in his studies. Blessed is he and blessed she who bore him and blessed those who sit in his company." I the *Mishnah* have seen the place that is prepared for thee in Paradise. How great are the joys and delights awaiting thee there! Be strong and courageous in the fear of the Lord. And now I have come to reveal the following kabbalistic mystery....' And all the revelations of the Maggid he collected in a book entitled *The Book of the Maggid*[1]—and yet they are like unto nothing when compared with the wisdom of the ARI.[2] He [Karo] wanted to study with him the mysteries of *Torah*, but the ARI refused to teach him, saying that his [Karo's] soul was unfit to receive higher wisdom than that of Cordovero's system.

The Lurianic story[3] is that Karo promptly fell asleep whenever Luria began to discourse on the mysteries—a sure sign that his soul was not fit to receive them. Shlomel then reports what Karo's widow told him of a banquet at Luria's house in celebration of the engagement of their son to Luria's daughter.[4] On returning home from the celebration Karo is said to have gone into raptures over Luria's absolutely unique eminence:

'Oh my dear wife, what shall I say or tell thee of the mysteries and kabbalistic explanations [which I have heard], and how much knowledge have I gained from the holy mouth of Isaac Luria! Even an angel hardly possesses the knowledge he has. There is no doubt but his is the soul of one of the early prophets, for even a Tanna could not teach as he does. But I fear for him on account of our many sins, for this wicked generation will not be able to suffer his exceeding holiness and he will be taken away and lost to them at an early age.' And thus it came to pass.

[1] This, in fact, is the title of most manuscripts of the *M.M.*; cf. below, p. 25.
[2] Similarly also *'Emeq ha-Melekh* (Amsterdam, 1648), f. 10a, col. ii.
[3] As told by Shlomel, op. cit.
[4] Cf. below, p. 132.

This characteristic sample of Lurianic hagiography does, however, make use of what must have been common knowledge in Safed: Karo's Maggid, the kind of messages he was wont to convey, and the title of Karo's manuscript diary. The Maggid's words as reported by Shlomel are so similar to the stereotyped beginnings of the entries in the printed *M.M.*, though not quite identical with them, as to leave little doubt about the essential correctness of the information. Shlomel makes it quite clear that he is not merely reporting a rumour; people in Safed used to hear the Maggid's voice. By the time of Shlomel's arrival in Safed, more than forty years before the *editio princeps* of the *M.M.*, the existence of Karo's autograph entitled *Sefer ha-Maggid* was common knowledge or, at least, common rumour.[1]

Another testimony to the Maggid's revelations should be added to Shlomel's because, though of late date, its wording is again so similar to that both in the *Shibḥey ha-ARI* and in the printed *M.M.* as to suggest an identical origin. Yet the phrasing is also sufficiently dissimilar to indicate different traditions, not mere copying. The Jerusalem Rabbinate in its approbation to Elisha Ashkenazi's edition of the *M.M.*[2] writes as follows:

'And the Lord was with Joseph and he was a prosperous man' [Gen. xxxiv. 2], reading and studying the six orders of the *Mishnah*, so that the spirit of the Lord moved within him and he heard the voice speaking through the *Mishnah* itself: 'begin and conclude, be strong and of good courage, let not thy hand be weak to save me "for I am ready to halt and my sorrow is continually before me" because of "a servant [i.e. the power of evil] when he reigneth and an handmaid that is heir to her mistress [i.e. the female principle of evil is usurping the place of the divine *Shekhinah*]". For I am *in exile among Slavonians and Serbs*[3] as

[1] The identity of this manuscript diary with our *M.M.* is, of course, a different problem to be discussed in the next chapter. Mr. M. Benayahu kindly drew my attention to another early reference to manuscripts of Karo's *Sefer ha-Maggid*. Immanuel Aboab, in his *Nomologia o discursos legales* (Amsterdam, 1629, p. 309), states in connexion with Joseph Karo: 'Yo he visto escritos de mano, muchos aduertimientos, y reuelaciones de altissima doctrina, que dizen le fueron enseñados de lugar soberano.'

[2] Venice, 1649.

[3] I am proposing this questionable translation with all due hesitancy. The Hebrew text ואני בתוך הגולה בין סלונים וסרבים obviously echoes, and perhaps merely means the same as, Ez. ii. 6, סרבים וסלונים ('though briers and thorns be with thee'). Still, I cannot help feeling that the phrase here refers to the specific

the lily among thorns, and my sorrow is stirred. But thou, blessed of the Lord, hast holpen me and comforted me by the melody of your voice with which you recite and study the *Mishnah*' . . . and much more of this kind is written in the papers of the Maggid who spoke to him *mighty promises and the revelation of kabbalistic mysteries*[1] without end or number.

The passage is illuminating in many ways. First of all it confirms the general pattern of the entries in the *M.M.*: 'mighty promises' of a more personal nature and the 'revelation of kabbalistic mysteries'.[2] Secondly the quotation exhibits many of the stylistic features and typical turns of phrase of the Maggid. Finally the message quoted by the rabbis of Jerusalem in 1649 obviously goes back to a written source and not to an oral tradition since it clearly dates from Karo's European days, i.e. from before 1536. The *Mishnah–Shekhinah*'s complaint 'and I am in exile among Slavonians and Serbs' most probably refers to Karo's residence in Nicopolis.[3]

It has already been mentioned in passing[4] that Alkabets's epistle, printed in the *SHeLaH* and subsequently in most editions of the 'Order of Service for the *Shabu'oth* Vigil' (*tiqqun leyl shabu'oth*), was responsible more than anything else for popularizing Karo's Maggid. There is no reason at all to doubt the authenticity of the epistle[5] which has come down to us in three, ultimately in two,

briers and thorns by which the *Shekhinah*, resting upon Karo and his circle, is surrounded as the lily among thorns, i.e. by the Slavonian and Serb population of the Balkans. Karo lived at the time in Nicopolis; cf. below, ch. 5. To validate the proposed translation it would, of course, be necessary to adduce more examples of such punning use of the expression סרבים וסלונים. For the time being no such examples are known to me. I am assured by an expert in Slavonic philology, my colleague Dr. M. Altbauer, that the terms Slavonian and Serb were certainly in use at the time and no doubt current also among the Jews living in Bulgaria (Nicopolis).

[1] My italics.

[2] Cf. below, p. 79.

[3] Cf. below, p. 92 f.

[4] Above, p. 2.

[5] As is done by Rosanes, op. cit., pp. 219–20. Greenwald, op. cit., pp. 197–9, though pronouncing the *M.M.* to be a fabrication, admits the genuineness of the Epistle. Rosanes's arguments are easily disposed of, though he is undoubtedly right in drawing attention to the unusual signature אלקוויץ. 'The *ḥasid*' may well have been an honorific bestowed upon Karo by the circle of his disciples and admirers. (Cf. also the quotation from Cordovero, below, p. 193, n. 3.) The best witness here is Alkabets himself who addresses a kabbalistic *responsum* (preserved in many manuscripts and printed at the end of his commentary on the Passover *Haggadah* (*Berith ha-Levi*, Lemberg, 1863)) to Karo in this style: שאלת ממני החכם ה ח ס י ד האשל האדיר צדיק יסוד עולם מוהר"ר יוסף קארו

versions. It first appeared in the *editio princeps* of the *M.M.* (Lublin, 1646) and apparently quite independent of it again in the chapter entitled *massekheth shabu'oth* in Isaiah Hurwitz's *SHeLaH* (Amsterdam, 1649). A slightly divergent text is given in *Ḥemdath Yamim* (Constantinople, 1735–7),[1] but a careful analysis leaves little doubt that we are dealing here not with a different tradition but with a tendentious rewriting. The changes and omissions are too significant and systematic to be accidental, and as they relate more particularly to the Maggid's exhortations to proceed forthwith to the Holy Land and to his description of the sufferings of the *Shekhinah* 'which lieth in the dust' and needs to be raised up, the particular Sabbatian bias is evident enough. The author of *Ḥemdath Yamim* gives himself away in his own manner and as much as admits that he produces a 'doctored text' when he introduces the Epistle with the words: 'And in the hidden treasures of my master's writings I discovered an epistle of the kabbalist Rabbi Solomon Alkabets, who was a companion of Rabbi Joseph Karo,

נר"י לערוך לפני זוהר חכמתך כוונת האלהי רשב"י ע"ה . . . יען שמעתי מפי קדושת חסידותך . . . וכאשר נסתרתי מאת פני יפעתך הקדושה והטהורה גמרתי עלי להאריך אהלי אפדנו . . . כי גולה אני ממקומי לעלות אל הר ה' ארץ הצבי תוב"ב. The *responsnm* ends (ibid. 43b) הנה כתבתי המושג אצלי במאמר הזה ואם כי גולה אני ממקומי לעלות אל הר ה' ואני מטולטל . . . ואין לי ספרים . . . ואל שדי אתחנן יאיר עיני ועיניך במאור תורתו וייחדנו בהר הקדש לעבדו בשכם אחד אכי"ר. נאום הגולה ממקומו לעלות אל הר ה' והדומו . . . This proves that (*a*) Karo's reputation was one of saintliness in particular; (*b*) he and Alkabets met long before they both settled in Safed; (*c*) Alkabets went to Palestine before Karo, and the Maggid's promises to the latter 'to unite thee again with Solomon my chosen one' refer to Alkabets. (This was already perceived by Schechter and others.) The final paragraph of the *responsum* incidentally uses a phrase which also occurs at the end of the *Shabu'oth* Epistle but is not found elsewhere, to my knowledge, in contemporary epistolary style. Obviously the phrase ואל שדי אתחנן (based on Job viii. 5) was a favourite one with Alkabets. That Adrianople can very well be described (*contra* Rosanes) as עיר הגדולה, עיר ואם בישראל, exactly as in the *Shabu'oth* Epistle, is borne out by Alkabets's introduction to *Berith ha-Levi*, which begins: אמר הצעיר שלמה בכמהר"ר משה זלה"ה בכמהר"ר שלמה הלוי אלקבץ תנצב"ה ברצות ה' דרכי מבית אבי לקחני ולעלות אל הר ה' לבי נשאני וכעלותי ההרה אל עיר הגדולה לאלקים נהלני הקריה אדריאנופולי . . . There follows a eulogy on the exemplary piety of the scholars and saints there: הן כל אלה ראתה עיני מחסידותם וקדושתם and Alkabets concludes: כי עתה בתוך הגולה ומיטב ספרי הנה היום בארץ תוב"ב ואני מטולטל וגולה אל הר ה' עולה . . . ואני תפלה לאל להתאחד עמכם בהר ה'.

[1] Professor Y. Tishby kindly drew my attention to this version.

in which he recounts a marvellous event [that befell] in the academy of Rabbi Joseph Karo during the *Shabu'oth* vigil.' As Professor Tishby[1] has convincingly shown, this 'master' or 'teacher' is a purely fictitious personality invented to cover the author's own ideas. Quotations from the writings or papers of the 'master' are therefore—by definition—always suspect.[2]

Although the subject-matter and preoccupations of the Epistle are different from those of the *M.M.*, they both share the Maggid's typical turns of phrase[3] as well as his tendency to indulge in excessive praise of maggidism as if the very fact of receiving revelations mattered more than their contents.[4] There is thus sufficient evidence to show that Karo had a Maggid both in Europe (i.e. in Nicopolis)[5] and in Safed. According to the sources quoted so far this Maggid seems to have been identical with both the *Mishnah* and the *Shekhinah*,[6] although in one or two statements,[7] taken in isolation, he need not necessarily be more than simply a kind of messenger from the celestial academy. The messages appear to have consisted mainly of exhortations, spiritual counsels, flattering praise, 'mighty promises', and the communication of kabbalistic explanations on points of doctrine or on the Scriptures. The Maggid never appeared to Karo in any form of vision but spoke through his mouth[8] so that others, present in the same room or behind the door,[9] could distinctly hear his words.[10] Karo was neither a 'roller' nor was he 'speaking tongues'; his Maggid was a genuine case of well-ordered, lucid, but automatic speech. The fact that all descriptions agree in speaking of 'a voice in the mouth of the *ḥasid*' may

[1] לחקר המקורות של ס׳ חמדת ימים, partly published in *Tarbiz*, vol. xxiv (1954/5), pp. 441 f., and partly still awaiting publication.

[2] According to Professor Tishby this instance is merely one typical example of the author's method of treating his sources throughout his work.

[3] e.g. והנני המשנה האם המיסרת את האדם באתי לדבר אליכם... לכן... התחזקו... באהבתי בתורתי ביראתי...

[4] e.g. וחזור לשבח בענין הלימוד כחצי שעה ואמר ראו השמע עם קול ככם שאל אביך וכו׳... אם זה כמה מאות שנה שמעו או ראו הדבר הזה ואתם זכיתם. Cf. also below, p. 264.

[5] Cf. also the explicit statement in the title of MS. C 1 (below, Appendix B).

[6] Cf. below, pp. 266 ff.

[7] e.g. Vital's references to Karo's Maggid, above, p. 15, n. 3.

[8] Cf. *Epistle*: ונשמע את הקול מדבר בפי החסיד נר״ו קול גדול.

[9] *Shibḥey ha-ARI*, quoted above, p. 17.

[10] בחיתוך אותיות (Alkabets, *Epistle*).

indicate that it was a different voice and that listeners did not recognize it as Karo's own. There is, at any rate, no compelling reason to assume with Schechter[1] that 'the listeners recognized in the strange sounds of the Mentor Angel Caro's own voice'. The Maggid's promise to Karo[2] that one day he would be vouchsafed revelations of a still higher order and that then

> I shall grant thee to behold Elijah, for the Ancient of Days will be clothed in white garments and will sit facing thee and will speak unto thee as a man speaketh unto his friend and thine eyes shall behold thy teacher; and although thy wife and other men and women will be in thy house, he will speak with thee *and thou shalt behold him*[3] but they shall not see him and the voice of his speech shall appear to them as if it were thine

may well refer to what would occur at a later stage. It does not imply that during the usual maggidic visitations Karo spoke with his normal voice but rather suggests the opposite. For the time being Karo only enjoyed the *charisma* of automatic speech; he hoped for the gift of vision plus audition. If we assume the Maggid to have spoken with a different voice from Karo's normal one, then the phenomenon attains even greater resemblance in its salient features to normal mediumistic states and trances.

We may safely assume that many of the recorded instances of maggidism were cases of automatic speech, though, of course, the term *maggid* is used to cover a very wide range of charismatic experiences. Often it means a messenger, angel, or other dream-figure appearing during sleep and not, as in the case of Karo and others, after waking. Actually, automatic writing too could be described as a 'maggidic' manifestation.[4] Of particular interest in this respect is the testimony of one of the greatest and most moving figures in the history of Jewish mysticism, Moses Ḥayyim Luzzatto (1707–47 (1744?)), who seems to tell of a subjective experience of automatic speech (i.e. no mere audition) which was, however, inaudible to bystanders. Luzzatto's own account states:[5]

[1] 'Safed' in *Studies in Judaism* (2nd ser.) (1908), p. 214. Also Scholem seems to assume the voice to have been different; cf. *Sabbatai Zevi*, vol. i, p. 65.

[2] *M.M.* 34b. 2.

[3] My italics.

[4] As, apparently, in the case of Taytazak, if we may judge from the manuscript mentioned above, p. 14, n. 1.

[5] Letter to Rabbi Benjamin ha-Kohen; see S. Ginzburg (ed.): אגרות רמח"ל (Tel-Aviv, 1937), p. 39.

> This is a short account of the event: On the first of Sivan 5487 [= 1727], whilst I meditated a certain meditation, I fell asleep. When I awoke I heard a voice saying, 'I have descended to reveal unto thee the hidden mysteries of the Holy King'. For a while I stood trembling, then I collected myself but the voice did not cease . . . until one day he told me that he was a *maggid* sent from heaven.

Though this account suggests a normal case of audition, the information is supplemented on one essential point by Luzzatto's disciple Yequthiel Gordon, who writes:[1] 'he was visited by a *maggid*, a holy and awe-inspiring angel,[2] who revealed to him marvellous mysteries . . . and this is the [usual] procedure: this angel speaks *out of his mouth*,[3] though we, his disciples, do not hear anything.' It is possible, of course, that Yequthiel's wording is not meant to be pressed literally and merely reflects a conventional *cliché* or figure of speech established by the earliest literary references to maggidism in general, which are none other but those referring to Karo's Maggid. Nevertheless, we should not overlook the possibility that Luzatto may present yet another variation on the theme of maggidism; in addition to dream-figures, auditions, automatic speech, automatic writing, &c., we may have here a case of *endophasia*.

Returning to Karo, we may conclude that the question of his having had a *maggid* must be answered in the affirmative.[4] We may now turn to the related yet distinct problem of the authenticity of the *M.M.*

[1] Ibid., p. 19.

[2] The *maggid* is thus considered to be an angel! Cf. below, pp. 78–79, 81.

[3] My italics.

[4] It is worthy of note that the news of Karo's maggidic visitations, though well known to his contemporaries in Safed, was not automatically broadcast to all the congregations of Israel—at least not until the Lurianists began their intensive propaganda-barrage from Safed. This is, of course, quite in accordance with the traditional self-imposed silence of kabbalists concerning their mystical or charismatic states (cf. *MTJM.*, pp. 15–16, 121–2). When the news of Karo's death reached Turkey, Rabbi Moses Albelda chose as a text for his memorial eulogy the verse Num. xxiv. 4, 'He hath said which heard the words of God, which saw the vision of the Almighty'. The reader who after this promising opening expects a reference to the Maggid will find himself grievously disappointed, for Albelda continues his oration הרב הגדול הזה שהחיינו וקיימנו בספרו הגדול בית יוסף, וכבר הודיע הרב ז״ל במדרגת הנבואה בסוף ח״ב (i.e. Maimonides in pt. ii of his *Guide for the Perplexed*) שעשות ספרים וחיבורים הוא ממדרגת הנבואה (*Darash Moshe*, Venice, 1602, fol. 103b).

3

THE TEXTUAL EVIDENCE

WHICHEVER side one chooses to take in the controversy about the authenticity of the *M.M.*, there is no doubt but that our extant text presents something of a literary puzzle. More than seventy years after Karo's death, in 1646, a Lublin printer by the name of Kalonymos (Kalman) Yaffe brought out a book which the title-page describes as 'the Book *Maggid Mesharim*, in which there are explanations of the luminous, exalted, and great mysteries that were revealed to "the plain [i.e. perfect] man dwelling in tents [i.e. in the house of study]", the great scholar, the spark of light, father in wisdom and prince in the Law', Rabbi Joseph Karo. The printer contributes a short Preface in which he praises God for providentially making this publication possible by so disposing that a certain Isaac Bingo of Jerusalem came his way with the precious manuscript: 'And he [God] made me meet the noble and exalted Rabbi Isaac of Jerusalem . . . who had with him a pearl without flaw.' Bingo himself, in his lachrymose and rather wordy Introduction, is not particularly helpful. He has much to tell about his griefs and sorrows but omits to give an exact account of the history or provenance of his manuscript. It is useless to try to extract positive information from his obscure and rhetorical references to the

> holy scriptures that were revealed by the holy Maggid to the aforementioned holy and scholarly rabbi, all equally holy . . . enquire ye and behold who hath stood in the counsel of the Lord in such manner as the aforementioned holy scholar and rabbi who was highly exalted, being fed from the table on high, the table of the King of all kings, and entering into the innermost sanctuary of the King of the universe; and these things were hidden . . . covered and concealed in the heavenly treasuries but now they were revealed to the righteous.

The last words, which obviously mean that great and exalted kabbalistic mysteries had been revealed to Karo, are yet sufficiently vague and ambiguous to explain why Rosanes[1] thought he could construe them to mean that certain mystics ('the righteous') had *now* had dreams in which the departed Karo revealed himself (from the 'heavenly treasuries') and communicated the *M.M.* This hypothesis, clearly inspired by Isaiah Hurwitz's account of Karo's apparition in a dream to an anonymous mystic in Safed,[2] can be dismissed out of hand as unsupported by the evidence and as altogether too fanciful. One inference, however, seems to be justified by the Introduction. Bingo says there, '. . . wherefore I have called this book *Maggid Mesharim* and it shall be remembered for all generations'. In other words, he himself gave the book its title.[3] The inference is supported by the manuscripts,[4] which, with one exception, do not know this title. They speak of 'the book of the Maggid of the *Beth Yosef*' (B 1 and 2), 'the Maggid of Rabbi Joseph Karo' (B 3), 'the book of the Instruction of the Lord, copied from the MS. of Rabbi Joseph Karo' (C 1), 'the book of the Maggid to the kabbalist Rabbi Joseph Karo' (A 2), 'the Tracts of Rabbi Joseph Karo' (A 3), &c. Only A 1 has the superscription 'the Book *Maggid Mesharim*' and this is probably a later addition inspired by the title of the printed text.

A difficulty raised by the form of the first edition is the obvious discrepancy between its arrangement of the material and what must have been the original sequence of Karo's diary entries. If Bingo found the manuscript in precisely the form in which he printed it, then either the author himself or someone else must have 'edited' the original copy and rearranged the contents so as to convert the diary into a kabbalistic commentary on the Bible. The matter is rendered even more interesting by the second, supplementary edition which appeared in Venice in 1649.[5] The title-page is slightly

[1] Op. cit., pp. 257–8, 266–7. [2] Cf. below, p. 45.

[3] Rosanes, op. cit., p. 267. [4] Cf. below, Appendix B.

[5] The date of the Venice edition has always been a moot question, since the Hebr. שנת השק"ט of the title-page may be equally well interpreted as 5409 and as 5414; cf. G. Scholem, *Sabbatai Ṣevi*, p. 201, n. 4, who inclines to the earlier date. The colophon says that the printing was finished on 17 Elul 'and on that day we began [the printing of] the commentary on the Zohar entitled *Zahorey Ḥammah*'. Also the Introduction states 'we hope . . . to publish the book *Zahorey Ḥammah* . . . the printing of which we have already begun'. Since the latter work was published in the year הת"י = 5410, it stands to reason that the *M.M.* left the press on 17 Elul 5409. However, all considerations of this kind are rendered

shorter than that of the first edition though obviously based on it and adds: 'brought to the press by the learned rabbis Isaac Bingo and Elisha Ashkenazi'. The edition contains nothing that had already appeared in the *editio princeps* and Bingo, in a short Preface, explains that after having published 'half of the book *Maggid Mesharim*' he fervently longed and searched for the rest and that at last there appeared his friend Elisha Ḥayyim Ashkenazi of Jerusalem[1] 'in whose possession there was the rest of the book, comely and well-ordered according to the manner of scribes, and disposed *according to the weekly readings* [of the Pentateuch]'.

There can be little doubt that the manuscripts used by the editors of the first and second editions are complementary. They belong together and actually seem to form one single manuscript, deriving probably from a more complete original. The editor of the third, actually the first complete, edition (Amsterdam, 1708) was not slow to perceive this. In his Preface he points out that the book

was printed in halves [and] on two occasions. The first time some things were missing, whereas the second edition [often] begins where the first left off but the beginning is missing. Occasionally the first edition begins in the middle of a passage with the main part [i.e. the opening] missing as e.g. in the portion *Miqqeṣ*[2] which begins 'Metatron who was transformed from flesh into fire', whereas the real beginning is in the second edition[3] in the passage which ends with the words 'Metatron who was transformed' as it is printed [in the proper sequence in this edition].

superfluous by the precise date given at the bottom of the second page, immediately after the signatures of Ashkenazi and Bingo to their Introduction. The line reads: שנת מחצית השקל בשקל הקדש תרומה לה׳

There can be no doubt here that הקדש means [5]409. The line in question is missing in all copies of the Venice edition that I have seen, except the copy at the National and University Library in Jerusalem; see Plate 4. With the decisive line missing from most copies, the ambiguous השק״ט of the title-page could easily mislead the bibliographers, who all (Steinschneider, Friedberg, Benjacob, &c.) give the wrong date 5414 (= 1654 C.E.) as the year of publication, without as much as adding a question mark.

[1] The father of the notorious prophet of Sabbatai Ṣevi, Rabbi Nathan (Ashkenazi) of Gaza. Elisha travelled much in North Africa and Italy as an emissary collecting charities for the Holy Land; for details see A. Ya'ari, שלוחי ארץ ישראל (Jerusalem, 1951), pp. 154–5, 281–2 (on Bingo, ibid., pp. 271–2); also Scholem, *Sabbatai Ṣevi*, pp. 76–7, for his connexions with Solomon Navarra.

[2] Lublin, 1646, p. 9a.

[3] Venice, 1649, p. 8b; see edn. Amsterdam, 1708, fol. 18b.

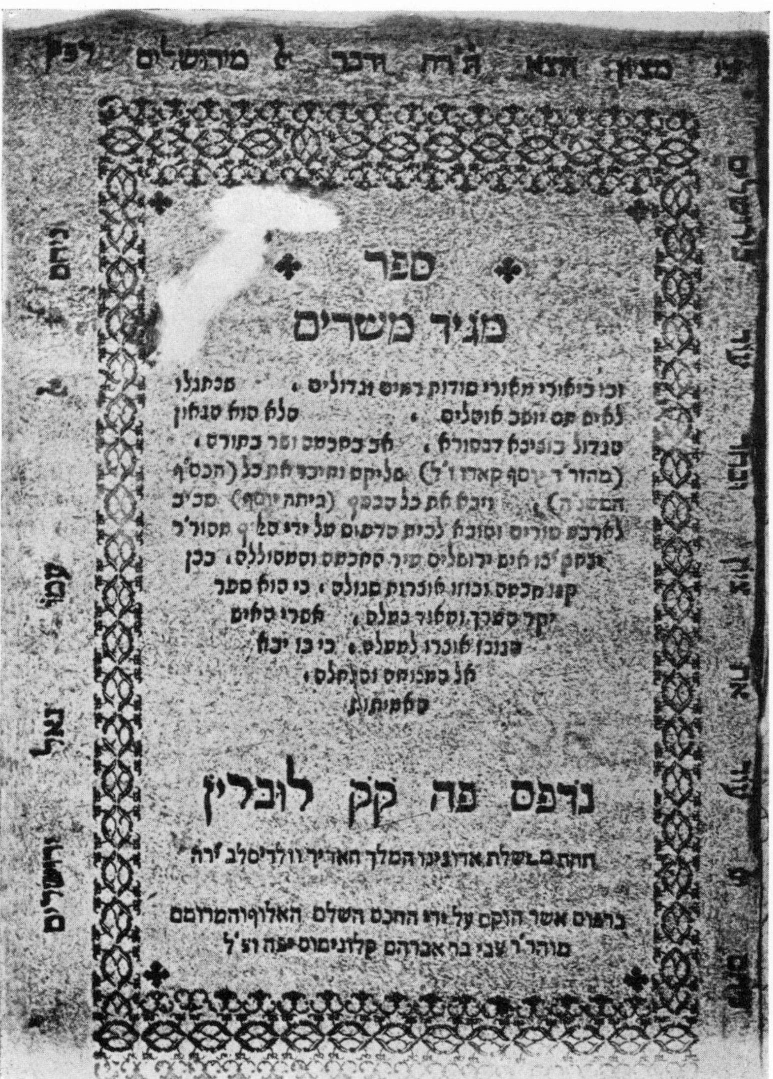

ספר

מגיד משרים

נדפס פה קק לובלין

תחת ממשלת אדונינו המלך האדיר וולדיסלב יר"ה

בדפוס אשר הוקם על ידי החכם השלם האלוף והמרומם

מוהר"ר צבי בר אברהם קלונימוס יפה ז"ל

2. Title-page of the 1st edition of the *M.M.*, Lublin, 1646

כי מציון תצא תורה ודבר ה׳ מירושלם׃

בויניציאה

ספר

מגיד משרים

ביאורי׳ אמרי סודות רמים וגדולים׃
מכתב׳ לאיש תם יושב אוהלים׃
ה״ה הגאון המופלא בוצינא דנהורא׃
אב בחכמה ושר וגדול בתורה׃
הרב הכולל כמוהר״ר

יוסף קארו

זצוק״ל׃

מליקט וחיבר את כל כסף המשנה׃
ובא את כל הכסף

ביתה יוסף

והוכא לדפוס ע״י החכמים כמוהר״ר
יצחק בינגא נר״ו וכמוהר״ר איטע
אשכנזי נר״ו׃ באותיות השר
אנדריאה ויגדרמין׃ שנת השקט
Per Francesco Vieceri. Lic. Sup.

3. Title-page of the 2nd edition, Venice, 1649

The case for an identical source of the manuscripts underlying the two editions is further strengthened by the recognition that there are actually more examples in the text of this kind of dislocation than are mentioned in the Preface of the worthy beadle of the Ashkenazi community in Amsterdam. We may assume that had he noticed these other 'open seams', he would have drawn attention to them and juxtaposed the relevant paragraphs as he did in the case of the Metatron passage. But most of these 'open seams' are so well embedded in their present contexts that they escaped detection. Thus the long communication s.t. *Vayyaqhel* in the first edition which is dated 13 Adar ii very abruptly concludes a long kabbalistic disquisition on the significance of the various dates mentioned in the *Mishnah* for the reading of the *megillah*, with the quite inappropriate phrase 'This has been agreed upon in the Celestial Academy, etc.'[1] The text immediately continues with a different subject: 'Moreover, he [the Maggid] told me . . . .' The second edition, however, also s.t. *Vayyaqhel* (undated), has an even more abrupt beginning. Such abruptness may often be taken as an indication that the passage is a truncated part of a larger text. In this case there is no doubt where the passage belongs, for it begins with the words: 'This has been agreed upon in the Celestial Academy.' In fact, some manuscripts[2] preserve the original order without any break.

It is a remarkable fact that most of the extant manuscripts exhibit a different order of the text from that given in the printed version, which, as said before, has rearranged the Maggid's communications so as to form a kabbalistic commentary on the Pentateuch and on a few verses from the Prophets and Hagiographa. There are, to my knowledge, only two manuscripts exhibiting the latter order. One, MS. 273 of the Badhab collection in Jerusalem (C 2),[3] is described in the catalogue as

Maggid Mesharim by Rabbi Joseph Karo, copied from the Lublin ed. 1648 by a Yemenite Jew, with many notes (possibly from the printed

[1] *M.M.* 33b. 2–34a, line 11; ibid. 36a. 3. [2] All manuscripts of Group B.

[3] The collection itself is still in the old Library Building on Mount Scopus and therefore inaccessible at present, but the manuscript catalogue prepared by Mr. M. Benayahu is available at the National and University Library in Jerusalem.

text). The colophon at the end reads: 'completed on Wednesday, 24th of Ḥeshvan in the year 1927 according to the reckoning of the strange nation [i.e. Seleucid Era], which corresponds to the year of creation [5]436 [= 1675 C.E.].'

The other (C 1), MS. Sassoon 248,[1] seems to be based on the *Vorlage* of the first edition. Although the manuscript is undated, it is improbable that it was copied from the Lublin edition since it contains, apart from a good many scribal errors and corruptions, a fair number of superior readings and actually helps to fill a few lacunas in the editions. Thus the first entry s.t. *Vayyeṣe'* reads:[2] והנה מלאכי אלהים [דהיינו ספירין דאיקרו מלאכי אלהים] עולים ויורדים בו כלומר סליקו עד בינה. The lacuna (חסר) in the first entry s.t. *Vayyishlaḥ* is supplied so that the full text reads: צריך תדיר לאשפעה [שפע ברכאן לקומא דיליה דמבשרי אחזה אלוה דהא ברנש] אתיהיב ביה רוחא חיונא . . . (*M.M.* 12 a. 1). The same chapter *Vayyishlaḥ* has another instance of what appears to be a superior reading rather than a scribal gloss: לארקא בכנסת ישראל [שור וחמור כלומר כל שבע ספירות הבנין כחדא], שור היינו גבורה וחמור חסד . . . (*M.M.* 12 a. 4). The long entry dated 'the night of the Sabbath, the first day of Ḥanukah', s.t. *Vayyesheb*, has a rather confusing lacuna in the middle of a mystical explanation of the prohibition of marital intercourse on the 9th of Ab, the anniversary of the destruction of the Temple, and on the Day of Atonement. As a matter of fact, even the indication of the lacuna is placed wrongly in all editions, since it should obviously come instead of the words in square brackets: דזה להפכו וזה להפכו (חסר חלוקת יום כפורים) דתשעה באב ליכא זיווגא [מרוב עציבו ותקיפו דהנהו סטרי וביום הכיפורים ליכא זיווגא באורח תשמיש] דהא כנ״י אסתלקא לעילא . . . (*M.M.* 15b. 1). Occasionally additions can be made to the printed text even where it is unaware of a lacuna. A good example can be found at the beginning of *Miqqeṣ*[3]: יקרה נפשך בעיני [וראה וצא ולמד אם יקרה נפשך בעיני על אחת כמה וכמה שראוי לך שתיקר נפשך בעיניך] . . .; and again a few lines farther down: ועל ידי כן היו מתעלים ודבקים במדות עליונות [וכאשר היו נותנים עיניהם לטובה באיש הראוי לכך היו משפיעים ברכה על האיש ההוא] וכאשר היו נותנים עיניהם על האיש המחוייב . . . Many of these better readings are

[1] Cf. catalogue *'Ohel David* (1932), vol. i, p. 441.
[2] Cf. *M.M.* 11a, line 14.
[3] Ibid. 16b, line 6.

הקדמת המגיהים

אמר יצחק להמון קראת· כמה הדפקתי דערו עלי כשבתי בשבת מישור ושיבה שלמעלה ותהלה בעיר קדשנו ירושלים תובב״א· אל נחמות הופיע מהר קדשו· להשקיט שאון נפשי מזעף ים יגוניה· ולהשביח נותיה· ויחזק את בדק סדקי בצדקו· ואת חסדי בחסדו· דזכותו אותי להוציא על ידי מחנית ספר מגיד משרים אשר כבר נפשנו ונפוצו מעיינותיו בכל נפוצות ישראל· אז נשאתי את עיני נגד פני ה׳ אלהי יג״ע חשקי לגמור עלי ולזכני לגמור את המצוה· ולכלות את המלאכה כי רבה היא· הן בעודני יושב ומצפה בתוחלת ממושכה· דורש וחוקר בדרישה וחקירה· על שארית הפליטה לדעת איה מקומה· הקרה נא אל חנון ורחום לפני את שאהבה נפשי ביד איש תם וישר וירא אלהים· זה דודי וזה רעי מתושבי עירנו הקדוש׳ החכם הנכבד מהר״ר אישעיה חיים אשכנזי נר״ו אשר נמצא אתו יתר הספר נאה ומתוקן בתיקון סופרים ונכון על סדר הפרשיות. נחמד להשכיל ותאוה לעינים· ויהי בראותי את הדרו ויופי תיקונו עלז לבי בקרבי. כמוצ׳ שלל רב וככל ששון וכל שמחה· תברך נפשי לטוב והטיב אשר לא עזב חסדו ואמתו מעמדי· לצרף מחשבתי הטובה למעשה· ואז תכף ומיד נתועדנו יחד להוציאו מן הכח אל הפועל כי אמרנו עת לעשות לה׳ והשהייה אסורה בכל שהוא· פנינו מכל עסקינו לשים לדרך פעמינו בזריזות וחשבנו לא התמהמהנו. כי חשבנו לחימום המצוה ולא חשבנו על סכנת הדרכי׳ ועל פיזור מעט כ[סף] אשר בכיסנו· ותהלו לאל עליון שהחיינו וקיימנו והגיענו למקום תהלה מקומו של אולם מלכות מלאכת הדפוס· אשר טבע רשומו ניכר בכל הארץ· האותיות הגידו שבחו· והנייר חרש ממש· והפועלים אצילים בזהירותם ואמונת אמונתם· על כן אנחנו קמנו ונתעודדנו לקרבה אל המלאכ׳ ולעשות אותה בתיקון הנאה בכל כחנו· והננו עומדי׳ מצפים לרחמי שמים
ישלח עזרנו מקדש להוציא לאור גם ספר זהרי חמה פירוש יפה ומועלה
על הזוהר אשר כבר התחלנו הדפסתו· ותהי זאת לנו לתזכרת
זכות ושכר מצוה גוררת מלאכות הרבה מעין
המלאכה הזאת· לזכות את ישראל
ולטוב לנו כל
הימים:

כה מתחננים אל יושב בשמים· יצחק בן החבר שמואל בינגא זלה״ה איש ירושלם:

ונאום הצעיר אישעיה חיים בן לא״א החכם השל׳ כמוהר״ר יעקב זלה״ה תושב ירושלם עה״ק תובב״א:

שנת מחצית השקל בשקל הקדש תרומה לה׳:

4. The Foreword to the 2nd edition, Venice, 1649

ספר

מגיד משרים

שמעון כ"ץ

באמשטרדם

יעקב אלואריש סוטו משה אבן יקר בראגדון ובנימין דיונך

5. Title-page of the 3rd (1st complete) edition of the *M.M.*, Amsterdam, 1708

also given in the other manuscripts. They are quoted here from C 1 in order to show that the latter, though exhibiting the order of the printed version, is yet independent of it. This suggests that the rearrangement of the diary to form a running commentary on the Scriptures is not Bingo's work but had been completed in Safed long before. Manuscripts of this commentary-edition seem to have circulated, and Bingo's manuscript as well as C 1 are representatives of the type.

The reading of C 1 s.t. *Shemoth*[1] שפעא דאתי לביתא [והיינו אשר לא ידע את יוסף] דלא ידע הוא כמו והאדם ידע וכו׳ . . . also seems to be original, and it obviously improves on the corrupt text towards the end of the second entry s.t. *Mishpaṭim*[2] when instead of the words *din shemiṭṭah* it reads: וטעמא [דלא מפיק להו] שמיטה אלא שנה שביעית. That the scribe had before him the same type of manuscript as the one in Bingo's hands is shown by the fact that both have many lacunas and 'etcetera's in common. Thus at the end of the second paragraph s.t. *Mishpaṭim*[3] all editions note חסר, but our scribe adds: ונ׳ להמעתיק שאינו חסר ושייך עם זה הדרוש.

Whereas the arrangement of the entries according to the weekly portions of the Pentateuch, though upsetting the chronological sequence, is logical in itself, it is difficult to find any system in the order of the other manuscripts. No principle of either subject-matter or chronology seems to have been operating, although occasionally it seems as if communications relating to certain topics were grouped together. The material in the manuscripts corresponds to both the first and second editions, yet there is not one manuscript which contains our complete printed text. On the other hand the manuscripts do not, with a few exceptions,[4] contain anything that does not appear in the printed editions. The manuscripts thus represent only part of what was actually printed, which, in its turn, is only part of what was actually written.[5] Nevertheless, it is possible to group the extant manuscripts into families. Thus the New York MSS. obviously form one group, though they differ among themselves in length and other details. NY 1 has 40 entries, NY 2 has 35, NY 3 has 31, and NY 4 has 7 only. The

1 *M.M.* 21b. 3. 2 Ibid. 29b. 2. 3 Ibid. 29a. 4.

4 Amounting altogether to a few lines only, apart from the longer passage preserved in the *SHeLaH*; cf. below, pp. 34–35. 5 Cf. below, p. 37.

correspondence to one another of NY 1, 2, and 4 is particularly close, whereas NY 3, the oldest manuscript of them all, being written only nine years after Karo's death,[1] has slightly divergent features. These are due to the fact that a few pages in the middle are by a different hand and actually repeat material already contained in the same manuscript. The British Museum MS. Or. 10109[2] and the Moscow MS.,[3] which are practically identical, also belong to the same group, which I propose to designate as Group A.

The same holds true, *mutatis mutandis*, of the manuscripts in the Bodleian Library in Oxford, which will be referred to as Group B. Thus Oxford 1, 2, and 3 exhibit plenty of variations in their scribal errors, orthography, and corruptions, yet their text, including datings and sequence, is fundamentally the same. Only Oxford 4 stands apart as a class by itself. As it happens these different groups do on occasion have identical sequences, which were, therefore, already juxtaposed in the earlier copies of Karo's manuscript. A schematic representation of the correspondences is set out in the appended table.[4]

Although the manuscript readings are often hopelessly muddled and confused, the scribes clearly tried to copy their texts as conscientiously as possible. This is particularly apparent in MSS. A 3 and B 4, which abound with scribal notes כאן חסר, חסר, &c. On the one hand B 4 supplies the year of the entry for the Sabbath, 22 of Shebaṭ (s.t. *Bereshith*),[5] but lacks the bracketed words ולענין חלב ודם [דאקשית למה החמיר תורה דם בכרת] רזא דמילתא ...; instead the scribe remarks: 'here I found the book torn'. The rather intimate story told in the printed edition s.t. *Beḥuqqothay*[6] appears in this manuscript in a very confused and corrupt state, but the copyist tells us: 'Thus speaks the copyist: I could not make out the script because the paper was erased.' The incident is dated here as well as in *all* other manuscripts in the 'night of *Rosh Ḥodesh* Nisan' as against the printed editions which give 28th of Iyyar. This is

[1] According to the colophon the manuscript was written in 1584; see Appendix B.

[2] MS. Gaster 434; photostatic copy in the Ben Zvi Institute at the Hebrew University.

[3] MS. Ginzburg 334; photostatic copy in the Ben Zvi Institute at the Hebrew University. Both manuscripts were brought to my knowledge by Mr. Benayahu.

[4] Below, Appendix C. [5] *M.M.* 4a. 2. [6] Cf. below, pp. 138–9.

merely one example of the differences in dating between manuscripts and print. These differences are significant because they sufficiently dispose of all arguments[1] based on the incompatibilities of the dates in the *M.M.* with the calendar. The same manuscript leaves out the sixteen words between דרגא דצדיק . . . דיבור ארוך in the entry dated Sabbath, 8 of Shebaṭ (s.t. *Vayyesheb*);[2] the scribe notes: 'I found the writing erased, and what I could copy again begins with the words דיבור ארוך כפעם בפעם.'

Particularly interesting are the cases where the editors of the *M.M.*, or the copyists of the manuscripts used by the editors, 'bowdlerized' the text with a view to removing objectionable or offensive references to living or revered personalities. Thus the first great exposition of the doctrine of sefiroth[3] attributes an erroneous and near-heretical interpretation of it to 'Rabbi X . . . who will have to render account for it and his punishment will be great'. From the manuscripts we learn that the offending kabbalist was R. Ḥayyim Obadyah.[4] In the same discourse the Maggid refutes a malicious kabbalistic statement to the effect that Maimonides was punished for his excessive rationalism by suffering *metempsychosis* into the body of a worm. At one stage in the transmission of our text the offensive word רחשא was deleted and the meaningless דאגלגל וכו׳ left.[5]

Apart from these obvious marks of censorship, there are many lacunas and instances of ordinary textual corruption in the editions which the manuscripts, in spite of their defective state, enable us to correct. Examples have already been given from C 1 and might be multiplied from the other groups of manuscripts. Thus the alleged lacuna (חסר) towards the end of the entry *Bereshith*[6] in the first edition, dated Tuesday, 7 Nisan,[6] appears to be no lacuna at all once we read with B ליחד יתה בהדי ספירין ע״י דההוא קרבנא. Similarly the end of the same entry should read לאחזקא דיבוקא וייחודא טפי and not ויתירא as all editions.[7] Often when the editions or manuscripts say וכו׳ (&c.), it means that at some stage in the transmission a copyist simply left out matter that was in his

[1] Cf. Rosanes, op. cit., p. 266. [2] *M.M.* 13a. 2. [3] Ibid. 37a–b.
[4] Cf. below, p. 203. [5] Cf. below, p. 170, n. 2.
[6] *M.M.* 5b. 2.
[7] Except edn. Lublin, where, however, the word is blurred.

Vorlage. Occasionally one manuscript preserves the full original text, as, for example, in the prophecy concerning the birth of a son in the long entry dated 13 Adar ii (s.t. *Vayyaqhel* in the first edition).[1] No reader can fail to notice that something is missing in the Maggid's instruction to consider the body, provided it is duly mortified, דוגמת [גשר] לזכות ע״י לעה״ב.[2] The bracketed word is supplied by all extant manuscripts. In one of the key passages expounding the Maggid's remarkable doctrine of sefiroth and the three worlds,[3] the middle world is described in all editions as ... עץ הדעת טוב ורע והוא נקרא כלי שראשו טוב וזנבו רע. The obvious emendation is confirmed by the uniform reading of the manuscripts: והוא נקרא תלי. Another such key passage[4] is disfigured by an awkward lacuna at a crucial point. The relation of the *Shekhinah* or 'middle world' to the ten sefiroth of the divine *pleroma* is defined as אחד היא עמהם ביחוד ולא (חסר). All manuscripts as well as Isaiah Hurwitz[5] concur in reading ולא באצילות.

It is, perhaps, in connexion with the aforementioned 'key passages' that the manuscript evidence is most revealing. In spite of the lack of system complained about earlier, there seems to be a tendency to group together the basic expositions of the Maggid's doctrine concerning the sefiroth. Thus A, B 1–3, and BB preserve what seems to be the chronological order of the revelation of the doctrine of sefiroth. The two last entries s.t. *Bereshith* in the first edition are dated Sunday, 4 Nisan, and Tuesday, 7 Nisan, respectively. The latter date should be emended, in accordance with the reading of A 2, to 6 Nisan. In that case the first entry s.t. *Bereshith* in the second edition should really come *between* the two first entries mentioned as it is dated Monday, 5 Nisan. This latter item clearly falls into two parts: the first paragraph, ending with the words ואתה שלום, and the following paragraph, which probably does not belong there at all but should form part of the aforementioned entry of Tuesday, 7 [6] Nisan (first edition s.t. *Bereshith*).[6] Finally,

[1] *M.M.* 34a; cf. below, pp. 119.

[2] Ibid. 70a. 1 (pp. 70–72 in the Amsterdam edition are wrongly numbered 50–52).

[3] Cf. below, ch. 10, particularly pp. 220–1.

[4] *M.M.* 5a. 2; cf. also below, p. 218.

[5] Cf. below, p. 35.

[6] *M.M.* 6a. 1 and 2; 5b. 2. The correct date is surely 6 Nisan; the emendation is supported by one manuscript, though most manuscripts and the editions agree in giving 7 Nisan.

the second edition has a long communication dated 1 Nisan 5296 (1536 C.E.),[1] the second half of which is again concerned with the doctrine of sefiroth and the three worlds. In the manuscripts these passages seem to form one group, together with yet another exposition of the same doctrine which is unknown to the printed editions.[2] A comparison of the first five entries of B 1[3] with the printed text yields the following arrangement:

Date	*Reference*	*Cues*
1. [Thursday], 1 Nisan 5296	Second part of entry s.t. *Vayyaqhel* in 2nd edn.; (Amsterdam 37a–b)	הלא ידעת – מודדין לו
2. No date (Sabbath, 3 Nisan?)	Text not in editions but preserved by Isaiah Hurwitz.	הנה יצאתי – בלי פירודא כלל
3. Sunday, 4 Nisan[4]	1st edn. s.t. *Bereshith* (Amsterdam 5a–b)	הא חזינא דקשה – תדיר
4. Monday, 5 Nisan[5]	2nd edn. s.t. *Bereshith* (Amsterdam 6a)	הלא מאי דאוליפתך – למחטי
5. Tuesday, 6 Nisan[6]	1st edn. s.t. *Bereshith* 2nd edn. s.t. *Bereshith* (Amsterdam 5b, 6a)	הלא הקב"ה – דיבוקא ויחודא טפי, והלא אם תדבק . . .

Our no. 1 begins in the middle of the entry dated *Rosh Ḥodesh* Nisan 5296 and printed s.t. *Vayyaqhel* in the second edition.[7] Whereas the second part of this entry (i.e. our no. 1) stands at the beginning of B 1, the first part appears much later in that manuscript. There it forms the tenth entry and is followed without break by what is in the printed editions the end of the entry dated Sunday, 4 Nisan, s.t. *Bereshith* in the first edition: דא הוא רזא דמילתא – תדיר (Amsterdam 5b). The first part of the printed entry of 1 Nisan is mainly concerned with personal and halakhic matters. Both in chronology and contents it links up well with the

[1] *M.M.* 36b. 6–37b.
[2] Cf. below, pp. 34–5.
[3] B 1 is taken for the sake of convenience; it should be understood that B 2–3 have the same text and order. To some extent this even holds true for Group A, though there these passages come in the middle of the manuscript and not at the beginning; cf. Appendix C.
[4] Date taken from the printed editions; it is not given by the extant manuscripts.
[5] Following the printed editions against the manuscripts, which read Thursday, 5 Nisan.
[6] Cf. above, n. 1.
[7] *M.M.* 36b–37a.

communication dated 13 Adar ii (s.t. *Vayyaqhel* in the second edition),[1] which in fact immediately precedes it in B 1. It has already been pointed out[2] that the long first paragraph (דנא מילתא – לכל עבר) of the entry s.t. *Vayyaqhel* in the second edition (Amsterdam 36a–b) seems to be really a part of the last-mentioned communication of 13 Adar ii. It is only the second half of the communication of 1 Nisan which is concerned with the doctrine of sefiroth.

It is instructive to compare the first entries in B 1–3 with those in BB. The latter manuscript starts in the middle of what clearly corresponds to the first entry in B 1, though the text is broken by a few lines which more or less correspond to B 1, fourth entry. Next there follows the aforementioned doctrinal exposition (= B 1, second entry). There is nothing in BB to correspond to the third doctrinal instruction; the continuation is defective and muddled but roughly corresponds to B 1, entry 5 ff. It thus appears that even in BB these maggidic communications are given more or less as one group. The same holds true of Group A. The first three entries in B have their counterparts if not at the beginning of the manuscripts of Group A then at least in their middle as three consecutive entries. With some qualification this might even be extended to the whole sequence of entries 1–7 in B 1, whose correspondence to the same sequence in the middle of Group A is indicated in the appended chart.[3]

The hypothesis that our manuscripts all go back to a prototype that began with a systematic exposition of the Maggid's doctrine of sefiroth, apparently revealed in a few consecutive nights, gains support from the fact that the second communication (no. 2 in our table), though unknown to the editors of the *M.M.*, was nevertheless printed elsewhere in precisely the same form and context as exhibited by the manuscripts. It can be found in the chapter entitled *Sha'ar ha-gadol* in Isaiah Hurwitz's long introduction to his *SHeLaH*.[4] The manuscript referred to and used by Isaiah Hurwitz evidently belonged to the same class as those discussed so far; most probably it conformed to Group B. Concluding his discussion of

[1] *M.M.* 33b.
[2] Cf. above, p. 27.
[3] Cf. above, p. 33, n. 4, and below, Appendix C.
[4] Ed. Amsterdam, 1698, fol. 34b–35a.

the doctrine of the *Shekhinah*, Hurwitz writes: 'and in conclusion I shall copy the words of the Maggid of the illustrious Rabbi the [author of] *Beth Yosef*, whose papers we were vouchsafed [to have preserved for us]. I shall copy what concerns our present subject and this is the text: [no. 1] Thereafter the Maggid came a second time and said to him as follows: [no. 2] Thereafter the Maggid came a third time and said: [no. 3].' As a matter of fact Isaiah Hurwitz has even more information to give. In the aforementioned letter[1] written from Safed, where he had stopped on his way to Jerusalem in 1621, Hurwitz reports with undisguised satisfaction the compliments paid to him by the local scholars and saints, who invited him to copy from their treasured and jealously guarded manuscripts:

> for they verily love me as themselves and permit me to copy whatever my heart desires . . . and behold, today they honoured me with a great novelty [by permitting me] to copy all the words of the Maggid which he spoke to the Rabbi *Beth Yosef* and which comprise many kabbalistic mysteries, many admonitions, and many ascetic practices, concerning which he [i.e. the Maggid] instructed him, 'this and that you may not eat', prohibiting him various permitted kinds of food as if they were among the ritually forbidden ones.

The manuscript evidence admits of only one conclusion. Karo's diary (or parts of it) became known some time after his death and was copied by kabbalists and pious ascetics who set store either by such mystical instruction from heaven or by the prestige of Karo's name—or by both. There is no need to assume that the diary was ever intended for publication. The evidence suggests the contrary and it is quite possible that Karo's descendants in Salonica did not even know of the existence of the manuscript. In any case Yedidyah Karo's silence on the subject to Conforti[2] proves nothing. We may even doubt whether this 'silence' is a fact. Whatever the exact date of composition of Conforti's *Qore ha-Doroth*,[3] it was certainly written in the second half of the seventeenth century, i.e. *after* the

[1] Cf. above, p. 14.

[2] *Qore ha-Doroth* (ed. Cassel, 1846), p. 35b: ואני הכותב בהיותי בעיר מולדתי שאלוניקי יום אחד בהיותנו החברים בישיבה והיה שם הרב החסיד כמה״ר ידידיא קארו ז״ל בן החכם כמה״ר יאודה קארו ז״ל בן של הרב הגדול מהר״י קארו ז״ל ונתגלגלו הדברים בינינו ובתוך הדברים ספר לנו קצת משבחי הרב זקנו ז״ל ובכלל שבחיו אמר לנו שהרב זקנו אמר בשעת פטירתו שזכה ללמוד התלמוד כולו ג׳ פעמים . . .

[3] See ibid., Cassel's introduction.

M.M. had appeared in print.[1] Conforti would not have troubled himself to quote from Yedidyah Karo as 'exclusive information' what everybody knew anyhow; he was only interested in the less generally known family traditions that Yedidyah might possess of his grandfather. Living in Salonica and Constantinople, Karo's sons may have had no idea of the diary or of the fact that it was assiduously copied in Safed. Somehow, we must assume, part of the diary got into circulation,[2] the contents were copied and re-copied, and the leaves arranged in different orders. The three main types that emerged may, as far as our knowledge goes, conveniently be labelled the New York type (Group A), the Oxford type (Group B), and the *M.M.* type (Group C), the latter being characterized by the arrangement in *parashiyyoth* as in the printed editions and MS. Sassoon. The surmise expressed in one of the rabbinic approbations to the first edition that Karo's notes were 'hidden in the treasuries of the pious disciples of the *ga'on*' and that, finally, in the words of Isaiah Hurwitz,[3] 'we were vouchsafed these papers' seems to get as near to the truth of the matter as is possible in the circumstances. Considering the fact that a large portion of our printed *M.M.* was revealed in a considerably short space of time,[4] it is a fair guess that only a fraction of Karo's notes survived. Unless we assume that the Maggid's visits were rare and irregular—and there is every reason to assume that they were not[5]—the diary must have recorded the experiences and heavenly intimations of some fifty years, i.e. of a whole lifetime. The earliest explicit date given in our printed *M.M.* is 5296 (= 1536 C.E.), the latest is the Eve of the Day of Atonement 5332 (= 1572 C.E.),[6] three years before Karo's demise. There is thus every reason to accept Azulay's

[1] Conforti himself (loc. cit.) of course mentions the *M.M.* and so does already the author of *'Emeq ha-Melekh* (Amsterdam, 1648), fol. 7a, col. i: ספר המגיד הנדפס בק"ק לובלין מקרוב.

[2] An instructive example of how private manuscripts would get copied in kabbalistic Safed is provided by the well-known pirating of Vital's writings during his illness; cf. the account given by Shlomel Dresnitz in שבחי האר"י and also Ph. Bloch, 'Die Kabbalah auf ihrem Höhepunkt u. ihre Meister', *M.G.W.J.*, vol. xlvii (1905), p. 147; Scholem, *MTJM.*, p. 256; id. *Zion*, vol. v (1940), p. 139.

[3] Cf. above, p. 35.

[4] A large number of entries date from 1536, among them many of the passages discussed in this chapter which were revealed in the months Adar–Nisan of that year; cf. also below, Appendix A, § 6.

[5] Cf. below, p. 258.

[6] *M.M.* 46a. 3.

estimate[1] that the printed *M.M.* represents about one-fiftieth part of Karo's diary.

The manuscript and textual evidence in favour of the genuineness of the *M.M.* is greatly strengthened by the internal evidence of the book. There is no need to labour the rather obvious point that a late fabrication by the editor would not have given rise to a 'family tree' of divergent yet related groups of manuscripts. We may thus more profitably turn to the internal evidence of the book and to an analysis of its contents. These are best examined under two heads: first of all the halakhic allusions and references in the *M.M.* and their relation to Karo's explicit utterances in *Beth Yosef* and *Shulḥan 'Arukh*, and secondly the purely kabbalistic parts of the book, which is, when all is said and done, largely a kabbalistic commentary on Scripture. Before, however, addressing ourselves to this analysis, the career and personality of Joseph Karo should be described on the basis of the biographical data provided by the *M.M.* and other sources. And indeed, not only Karo's personality and achievement but also his mystical life has to be seen against the background of his times. We have, so far, established both the fact that Karo had a Maggid and the genuineness of the extant *M.M.* Yet establishing Karo's mystical or 'pathological' states is not, by itself, enough. To understand the phenomenon adequately it is necessary to consider also its sociology, i.e. the significance, value, and function which it had in Karo's group and from which it derived its social sanction. Mystical experience may be a most intimate and individual affair, yet both its content and form are largely conditioned by the traditions, values, symbols, needs, and religious ideals of a particular society. Certain types of enthusiasm are frowned upon, others are accepted, encouraged, and admired; others again would be tolerated from second-class individuals (women, children, unlettered men) but would not be welcomed in a rabbi. It may be useful therefore to survey briefly the mystical life of the circle in which Karo moved and lived and had his being, to analyse the types of contemplation practised there, and to determine the relative 'normalcy' of certain kinds of mystical experience among his associates and neighbours.

[1] Op. cit., s.v. Joseph Karo.

4

SPIRITUAL LIFE IN SIXTEENTH-CENTURY SAFED: MYSTICAL AND MAGICAL CONTEMPLATION

IT is clearly beyond the scope of the present study to attempt even a superficial survey of 'mystical life' in sixteenth-century Safed or to describe the mystical ideals, values, techniques, and experiences that were cherished and cultivated in this remarkable community of saints.[1] Although our understanding of the theoretical and speculative systems evolved by these kabbalists has increased enormously in recent years,[2] the psychological aspects of the lives of the mystics have not yet received the full attention which they deserve.[3] For our present purpose we must confine ourselves to those facts and 'externals' that are likely to throw light on Karo's Maggid. We need not, therefore, go into the various modes of revelation, mystical illumination, or ecstatic rapture known to earlier gnostic and kabbalistic traditions.[4] Of greater and more immediate relevance for our present inquiry is, perhaps, the selection among the many possibilities which later kabbalistic literature seems to have made and the transformations to which it subjected certain older practices and traditions. Thus the pre-kabbalistic, ecstatic technique of the soul's journey and ascent to the vision of the Throne of Glory[5] fell into desuetude, though, as we shall see, a transformed version of it was incorporated in some later systems of meditation. Similarly Abraham Abulafia's method of inducing the 'prophetic' or illuminate state by a technique of permutation and combination of Hebrew letters forming Divine Names was

[1] A popular and still eminently readable account was given by Schechter in his beautiful essay 'Safed in the 16th century', *Studies in Judaism*, 2nd ser. (1908), pp. 203–306.

[2] Cf. the bibliographical indications in Scholem, *MTJM.* (edn. 3, 1956).

[3] Cf. ibid., p. 15.

[4] On the whole subject cf. Scholem, *MTJM.*, ch. 2–4.

[5] Ibid., ch. 2, particularly pp. 43–54.

not adopted by the dominant kabbalistic schools, though it seems to have been practised in some esoteric circles and to have enjoyed something of a major revival in the sixteenth-century. For not only are the Abulafian type of light-experience and the even more suggestive 'prophetic' ecstasy (defined by the kabbalists themselves as the mystic's encounter with his own self[1]) known to Moses Cordovero[2] and Ḥayyim Vital,[3] but many other sixteenth-century ascetic manuals are heavily indebted to Abulafia's writings.[4] Of particular interest in this connexion are Albottini's *Ladder of Ascent*[5] and the unprinted fourth chapter of Vital's *Gates of Holiness*.[6] In fact, Vital's *yiḥudim* are simply the modified and transformed successors of Abulafia's permutations.

One useful way of classifying ecstatic experiences is by means of the well-known distinction between cases where the main emphasis is on the mystic experience itself and its emotional value and those where the stress is on the objective 'mystical' knowledge which it conveys. The distinction corresponds to Rudolf Otto's analysis of mysticism versus theosophy or '*Heilsinteresse*' versus '*Wissenschaft*'.[7] Often the mystical or visionary experience is sought for its own sake as the highest possible spiritual fulfilment. There are minds, however, for whom it is merely a means towards increasing esoteric knowledge; the emphasis remains on knowledge, though it is undoubtedly a saving *gnosis* that is sought. According to this typology it may be said that the kabbalists seem to have found the communication type of mystical experience more congenial. This may be in keeping with the general character of Kabbalah

[1] Scholem, 'Eine kabbalistische Deutung der Prophetie als Selbstbegegnung' *M.G.W.J.*, vol. lxxiv (1930), pp. 285–90.

[2] Scholem, ibid.

[3] Cf. the quotation below, p. 67: ויש אשר נפשו עצמה בהזדככה במאד מאד תתגלה לאדם.

[4] Cf. the paragraph 'Ekstatische Kabbalah' in Scholem's article *Kabbalah* in *E.J.*, vol. ix, cols. 657–8 and the texts listed there, e.g. *Shulḥan ha-Sekhel* (fifteenth century), *'Eben ha-Shoham* (Jerusalem, 1538), *She'erith Yosef* (Jerusalem, 1548), and others.

[5] Written in Jerusalem about 1520; cf. Scholem in *Kiryath Sefer*, vol. ii (1926), pp. 107 and 138–41; ibid., vol. xxii (1946), pp. 161–71; id., כתבי יד בקבלה (1930), pp. 32–33, 225–30.

[6] Cf. below, p. 68.

[7] *West-Östliche Mystik* (edn. 2, 1929).

as a system of theosophical doctrine.[1] Professor Scholem has contended with some force that under the cover of the bewildering and often bizarre theosophical speculations of the kabbalists there hides a genuinely mystical life.[2] The fact remains, nevertheless, that the *discursive* and even dialectical elements are so prominent in kabbalistic literature that we may almost speak of an intellectualistic hypertrophy. It often looks as if the sole difference between talmudic and kabbalistic literature resides in the different subject-matter. As far as form and approach are concerned both are equally dialectical and argumentative, and more often than not kabbalistic literature is less the record of the *cognitio experimentalis dei* than the substitution of a theosophical *pilpul* for the halakhic one of the rabbinic lawyers.

This tendency of kabbalistic literature is borne out by the character of the mystical experiences reported in it. Already the beginnings of Kabbalah are associated with apparitions of the prophet Elijah, that is with the teachings communicated by him.[3] Elijah, as is well known, has had a most chequered career in folklore, apocalypse, and rabbinic and mystical literature. Immortal prophet, precursor of the Messiah, 'Angel of the Covenant' and guardian-witness at every circumcision ceremony, unexpected saviour in moments of need and danger, *deus ex machina*, and celestial teacher and messenger,[4] he acquired the kind of ubiquity and character of mediator that fitted him for the role of mystical instructor. There are some striking resemblances to the *Ḥidr* of Muslim legend.[5] The rabbinic tradition concerning Elijah as the ultimate provider of answers and solutions to all outstanding legal doubts and problems, and as the messenger of the Celestial Academy, ultimately determined his function also for the

[1] *MTJM.*, pp. 11 f., 206. [2] Ibid., pp. 15–16.

[3] Scholem, *Reshith ha-Kabbalah* (1938), p. 16.

[4] Many of these characteristics are already commonplace in Talmud and Midrash. The references have been carefully listed by Friedmann in his introduction to the *Seder 'Eliyahu* (Vienna, 1902)—a late Midrash that was traditionally held to go back to the instruction which Elijah was wont to give to Rabbi Anan, an Amora who flourished about 300 C.E. (cf. b. *Keth.* 106a).

[5] Cf. also *Shorter Encyclopaedia of Islam*, s.vv. 'Ilyas' (p. 164b) and 'al-Khadir' (pp. 232 ff.); also the contributions of J. Stiassny, Y. Moubarac, and L. Massignon to volume ii of *Élie le Prophète* (*Études Carmélitaines*, vol. xxxv), 1956.

kabbalists. His 'revelation', viz. apparition (*gilluy*), was considered one of the superior forms[1] of celestial communication. The Jewish mystic did not, as a rule, aspire to an anticipation of the blessed vision in this life,[2] but rather to authoritative indoctrination by the angel-man Elijah, the Hermes of the kabbalists. Luria, Cordovero, David ibn Zimra, and many others were reported to have had converse with him.[3]

Another, though less exalted, source of information was the dream. There is no need here to discuss the role of dreams in biblical and rabbinic literature.[4] Generally speaking, dreams were supposed throughout the Middle Ages to possess a prophetic, though perhaps only faintly prophetic, character.[5] Of course, dreams are infinitely varied in character and type; as varied, in fact, as mystical experience itself. Consequently all known forms and kinds of mystical experience could be doubled on the dream-level. Thus there are 'sleeping' visions and auditions, and the appearance of Elijah, angels, or departed souls in dreams. As in the case of apparitions of Elijah, the revelatory function of dreams

[1] Cf. *'Emeq ha-Melekh* (Amsterdam, 1648), fol. 10a, and the quotation from Vital, below, p. 76; also the references to Karo's *M.M.* above, p. 22, and below, p. 269.

[2] The usual definition of mysticism in the Catholic Church; cf. E. Krebs, *Grundfragen der kirchlichen Mystik* (1921). Where the ultimate bliss of the soul is conceived in terms of 'study of the *Torah*' in the celestial academies, it may happen that indoctrination by vision or inspiration is rejected precisely because its place is in the Hereafter and not in the human world, which ought to be the scene of strenuous moral and intellectual effort; cf. below, Appendix F, for an example of this point of view.

[3] Azulay, *Shem ha-Gedolim* s.vv.; cf. also above, p. 14. Azikri's account (*Sefer Ḥaredim*, ch. viii), וכן היה פה צפת הרב ר׳ יוסף סרגוסי רבו של הרב ר׳ דוד בן זמרא שהיה משים שלום תמיד בין אדם לחברו ובין איש לאשתו אפילו בין הכותים וזכה לראות את אליהו, seems to refer to the coveted privilege of simply seeing or meeting Elijah without accompanying teaching or communications. This is the traditional ideal of meeting Elijah, saluting him 'Peace' and being returned the salutation 'Peace'; cf. below, p. 269.

[4] The most recent discussion of dreams in the Bible is E. L. Ehrlich, *Der Traum im Alten Testament* (*B.Z.A.W.*, vol. lxxiii, 1953). For dreams in rabbinic literature cf. *J.E.*, vol. iv, pp. 655–7. Cf. also E. E. Urbach, 'When did prophecy cease?', in *Tarbiz*, vol. xvii (1955/6), pp. 5 f.

[5] According to b. *Ber.* 57b 'a dream is one sixtieth part of prophecy'; according to a *Ḥadith*-saying ascribed to Muhammad it is one forty-eighth part of prophecy. The *inspirator* of a dream is not necessarily God or a particular angel or demon (cf. b. *Ber.* 55b); rabbinic literature knows of a rather vague and ill-defined agent called the בעל החלום. On the difference between prophecy and dream cf. also *Zohar*, vol. i. 183a.

is not necessarily mystical or divinatory but may be purely halakhic. Considerable importance was attached to dreams by the German Hasidim[1], and their influence can be detected in some of the great Tosafist scholars. Thus Eliezer ben Nathan (twelfth century) fasted for two days after being told in a dream that in a halakhic decision he had wrongly permitted something he should have prohibited.[2] Rabbi Judah the Pious himself tells how a dream had caused Rabbi Ephraim of Regensburg to reverse a ritual decision.[3] Moses of Coucy, the famous preacher, was prompted by a dream (*'inyan mar'eh baḥalom*) to compose his work *Sefer Miṣvoth Gadol.*[4] Mordekhai[5] refers to a halakhic dilemma of Rabbi Meir of Rothenburg which was answered in a dream. Other instances are reported by Azulay.

The best-known specimen of this kind of dream instruction from heaven is the little booklet *Responsa from Heaven* by Jacob the Pious of Marvège (twelfth century)[6]. Rabbi Jacob's 'dream questions' concerned very definite points of rabbinic law. The '*responsa* from heaven', though cryptic and often obscure, were, nevertheless, usually capable of a satisfactory interpretation.[7] Significantly enough, the one question that remained unanswered

[1] Cf. *Sefer Ḥasidim* (ed. Wistinetzky, 1891), particularly § 382, pp. 116–17.

[2] Cf. E. E. Urbach, בעלי התוספות (1955), p. 154.

[3] Ibid., pp. 174–5.

[4] Ibid., pp. 388–9; also ibid., p. 385, and Azulay, op. cit., s.v. Moses of Coucy.

[5] *Ad* b. *B.Q.* i (beginning).

[6] Cf. *MTJM.*, p. 103. Steinschneider, who deals with the booklet in *Hebr. Bibliographie*, vol. xiv (1874), pp. 122–4, describes R. Jacob as 'der Himmelskorrespondent'. Cf. also Urbach in *Tarbiz*, vol. xviii (1947/8), p. 22.

[7] e.g. *responsum* 10: ונסתפקתי בתשובה זאת ושניתי לשאול כבראשונה. The reply given to R. Jacob by the angel in *responsum* 22 is identical with that of Tosafoth, *Ber.* 55b (s.v. פותרים). One is tempted to suspect that the ר"י of Tosafoth was none other than our dreamer, Rabbi Jacob the Pious of Marvège. Professor E. E. Urbach, however, informs me that the author of the reply quoted by Tosafoth is Rabbi Isaac of Dampierre, whose 'Tosafoth' were written down by his disciple R. Judah Sire Leon of Paris. That the 'Tosafoth of Rabbi Judah Sire Leon' are the immediate source of the aforementioned Tosafoth *Ber.* 55b appears from the text in *Berakhah Meshullesheth* (Warsaw, 1863) ad loc. This little detail is of unexpected relevance to our main argument concerning Karo's Maggid, for it provides further evidence of the extent to which the dream-prompters and *inspiratores* of Jewish mystics reveal mysteries that had already been worked out or even written down either by the mystics themselves or by other scholars. R. Jacob of Marvège was told in a dream what R. Isaac of Dampierre had taught in his school long ago! Cf. also below, pp. 165, 186–7, 256.

was a non-halakhic query about the date of the advent of the Messiah.[1]

These legal oracles were a source of considerable headache to later halakhists since, according to rabbinic tradition, supernatural interventions have no halakhic authority.[2] Neither dreams nor the prophet Elijah can contest, let alone override, the reasoned opinion of a competent scholar. On controversial issues the majority opinion had to be followed—a rule to which, according to a charming legend,[3] even God himself submitted with good grace notwithstanding a previous intervention by *bath qol* or 'heavenly voice' in favour of the minority view. Just as the Tosafists and other writers were at pains to explain why, in spite of this, the Talmud occasionally seemed to allow for a *bath qol*,[4] so later authorities had difficulties with the aforementioned examples from the lives of the hasidic scholars of the twelfth and thirteenth centuries.[5] The main purpose of this halakhic anti-supernaturalism was, of course, the safeguarding of the institutionalized rabbinic procedures for interpreting the Law against the dangers of charismatic anarchy. Consequently the problem was less serious when the dreams or other celestial communications dealt with non-halakhic matters such as moral exhortations, ascetic rules, and counsels of perfection, or when they foretold the future and conveyed other sundry information.

The great value attached by the German Hasidim and later kabbalists to dreams was matched by their frequency. Vital's autobiography[6] is practically a dream-diary. His contemporary, Cordovero's disciple Elijah de Vidas, drives home his great

[1] *Resp.* 70: ועל קץ הגאולה שאלתי כמו כן אך לא מצא התשובה כתובה לפניו.

[2] אין משגיחין בבת קול; cf. b. *Yeb.* 14a, *B.M.* 59b, and parallels, also Tosafoth ad loc. On the whole question see E. E. Urbach's article 'Halakhah u-Nebu'ah' in *Tarbiz*, vol. xviii (1946/7), pp. 1–27.

[3] b. *Yeb.* 14a, *B.M.* 59b, and parallels.

[4] As in the controversy between the schools of Hillel and Shammay; ibid.

[5] Cf., e.g., Azulay, op. cit., s.vv. Abraham b. David (RABED) iii, Eliezer b. Nathan, and particularly Jacob the Pious. The objection weighed so heavily that some scholars tried to give a more innocuous, metaphorical interpretation to the Rabed's claim of possessing supernatural authority for his opposition to two rulings of Maimonides; cf. Rabed's glosses *ad Hilkhoth Lulab* viii. 5, and *Beth ha-Beḥirah* vi. 14, and also Azulay, loc. cit.

[6] Cf. above, p. 15, n. 4.

exhortation to repent before it is too late by telling, as a matter of course, what a departed soul had revealed to him in a dream about the sufferings of hell.[1] Not the direct vision of the harrowings of hell as reported, for example, by many Christian visionaries, but accounts given by the departed souls themselves are the more frequent and typical feature of Jewish moralist writing.[2]

Karo himself seems to have been one of those exalted souls whose apparition in a dream was greatly prized by pious ascetics, particularly when they descended in order to teach some profound kabbalistic mystery. Isaiah Hurwitz[3] quotes a document which he had found in Safed[4] and in which an anonymous dreamer reported how he had learned the proper 'intentions' or 'devotions' (*kawwanoth*) for the *Kedushah*-prayer:

I shall now transcribe a tract which I found in the holy city of Safed concerning a divine vision in a dream, and this is its wording: The devotions for the *Kedushah* according to our Master, the Rabbi Joseph Karo—his soul rests in Paradise—which he communicated in a dream to a member of the Academy. I do not know the identity of the dreamer,[5] but from the awesome contents of the dream it appears that he was a great man in Israel. [The text of the dream:] With the help of God:[6] In

[1] *Reshith Ḥokhmah* (ed. Warsaw, 1875), p. 59: אני הכותב שנת ש"ל בחודש אלול בא לי בחלום הלילה נפש מאותו עולם אחר פטירתו כמו ג' חדשים והייתי מכיר בו שהיה מת והייתי שואל לו על עניני העולם והיה אומר לי שדנים באותו עולם ומענישים על דקדוק הדברים ביותר ממה שאדם יחשוב בדעתו והנשארים ישמעו וייראו.

[2] The most recent example of this type of communication is the little booklet *Spirits are telling* by the kabbalist Rabbi Yehudah Moses Petayah of Baghdad; edn. 1 (in *Minḥath Yehudah*), Baghdad, 1936; edn. 2, Jerusalem, 1954.

[3] In his commentary to the Prayerbook, entitled *Sha'ar ha-Shamayim* (Amsterdam, 1717), fol. 98b. The version in Isaiah Hurwitz's commentary is the only one printed and hence the only one to be generally known or accessible. The text, however, is corrupt. What seems to be a better and more original version is preserved in Jacob Ṣemaḥ's רנו ליעקב (MS. of the Ben Zvi Institute in Jerusalem, fol. 78b; cf. also the MS. of the same work in the Brit. Mus., Add. MS. 27093). I am grateful to Mr. M. Benayahu for having brought the MS. to my notice.

[4] Cf. above, p. 35. Isaiah Hurwitz may have quoted from Jacob Ṣemaḥ's work or directly from the latter's source.

[5] According to Mr. M. Benayahu, a study of Jacob Ṣemaḥ's book as a whole would suggest that the dreamer was none other than Ḥayyim Vital.

[6] From here on I quote Jacob Ṣemaḥ's text and not that given in Hurwitz's commentary to the Prayerbook.

the night of Friday 21 Ḥeshvan, in the year of the creation 5355[1] [= Friday, November 4, 1594], here in Safed, I beheld in my dream our Master the Rabbi Joseph Karo, may the Lord preserve him [!],[2] sitting on a splendid throne, and his hues were resplendent though I do not know of what they consisted.[3] There were present innumerable sages[4] and I soon recognised the Nagid Rabbi Isaac Shulal,[5] may his soul rest in Paradise, our Master Rabbi Jacob Berab of blessed memory,[6] the Sage Rabbi Samuel Sadillo,[7] the Sage Rabbi Mordecai Ḥefeṣ,[8] the Sage Rabbi Jacob Aguilar,[9] and the Sage Rabbi Abraham Zardil.[10] And the Sage

[1] The date is correct. Isaiah Hurwitz reads 'Friday, 1 Ḥeshvan 5365', but 1 Ḥeshvan of that year fell on a Monday.

[2] Isaiah Hurwitz reads 'of blessed memory', which, of course, fits the facts better, Karo having died in 1575.

[3] וגווניו מאירים ולא הכרתי ממה היו. Isaiah Hurwitz reads: ופניו מאירים כזוהר הרקיע.

[4] והיו שם חכמים רבים מאין מספ׳. Isaiah Hurwitz reads: והיו שם חכמים רבני עולם לאין מספר.

[5] Isaac ha-Kohen Shulal, the Nagid of Egyptian Jewry, came to Jerusalem about 1518. He died in 1525; cf. Rosanes, op. cit., vol. i, pp. 194–6.

[6] On Jacob Berab (d. 1546) and his relation to Karo, cf. below, pp. 87–88.

[7] Isaiah Hurwitz adds the words 'may the Lord preserve him', although Sadillo (usually written סדלייו, Hurwitz writes סדיאו) must long have been dead by that time. The person referred to is probably identical with R. Samuel ibn Sid, a contemporary of Karo and fellow expatriate from Spain, author of *Kelaley Shemu'el* (printed at the end of Tam ibn Yaḥya's *responsa Tummath Yesharim*, Venice, 1620); cf. Raphael Aaron b. Simon, *Sefer Ṭub Miṣrayim* (Jerusalem, 1908), p. 30b, and Azulay's biographical dictionary s.v. Samuel ibn Sid had settled in Egypt and seems never to have visited Palestine; the dreamer must have known him in Egypt. Alternatively the name may be taken to refer to his grandson, Samuel ibn Sid/Sadillo (d. 1645) of Jerusalem; cf. Frumkin–Rivlin תולדות חכמי ירושלים, vol. ii (1928), pp. 12–13. However, it seems highly improbable that the seventeenth-century Sadillo should appear together with the Nagid Shulal, Joseph Karo, Jacob Berab, and others in a dream dated 1594 and clearly written down long before Hurwitz arrived in Safed in 1621.

[8] Isaiah Hurwitz reads 'Mordecai Ḥaski', who is otherwise unknown (unless it is a misspelling for 'Mordecai Masnuth'); Jacob Ṣemaḥ clearly has the better reading, cf. below, n. 10.

[9] Jacob Ṣemaḥ reads ר׳ יעקב אלנאגר; Isaiah Hurwitz has כמוהר"ר אלג"ר. The correct reading would seem to be יעקב אגילאר. He may well be a relation (father?) of יוסף באג׳ילאר mentioned in Raphael Aaron's *Ṭub Miṣrayim*, p. 18b, as a rich Egyptian kabbalist who bore all the expenses of Luria's academy in Safed for ten years.

[10] Isaiah Hurwitz reads 'Ziyadal'. The reference is to Rabbi Abraham Zardil (or Abzardil). The dreamer seems to have seen a fairly well-defined circle whose connexions were mainly with Egypt and Jerusalem. Most of the persons mentioned (with the exception of Karo!) were contemporaries and concerned with the same affairs. Abraham Anakawa (in *Kerem Ḥemer*, Livorno, 1871, pt. ii, fol. 23a) prints a document (no. 128) in which Jacob Berab, the Nagid Isaac Shulal, Samuel ibn Sid, and Mordecai Masnuth are mentioned together in connexion with the drafting of certain regulations concerning the

[Rabbi Karo] said: Holy, holy, holy . . . [then follows the text of the kabbalistic 'devotions' for the *Kedushah*].

This dream is a good example of what kabbalists meant when they spoke of the 'souls of the righteous' as being, like angels, a source of supernatural information.[1] Another method, to be described later,[2] was the inducing of unreflected intuitions. We shall discuss angelic revelations at greater length when we come to examine the specific problems of maggidism. But maggidism apart, it may be said that angels are of comparatively little importance in later Kabbalah as messengers of celestial wisdom.[3] Although in earlier periods angels acted more frequently as revealers of mysteries and although examples are not lacking in Jewish literature from the O.T. Apocrypha, the Merkabah writings, and earlier kabbalistic pseudepigrapha down to later kabbalism, for most kabbalists the role of angels was usually restricted to the more 'practical' or magical side of their endeavours. The transmission of heavenly wisdom was monopolized, to a large extent, by the prophet Elijah, and in the sixteenth century to establish contact with the souls of the departed righteous became a major part of Lurianic practice. The desired *rapport* or contact was established by visiting their tombs and by the use of appropriate scriptural verses or formulae constituting 'Divine Names' (*yiḥudim*). Vital's *Book of Yiḥudim* sets forth the theory and practice of this method in full detail.

As the *Book of Yiḥudim* and the *Gates of Holiness* (particularly its unpublished fourth part)[4] amply show, these mystical experi-

rabbinic scholars in Jerusalem. The same work also quotes another document (ibid., no. 129) dated 22 Sivan 269 (= 1509 C.E.) in which אברהם בן בזראדיל, member of the academy of Jerusalem, is mentioned. The dream is therefore internally consistent. The problem that remains unsolved is the relation of the dreamer to the circle of scholars that flourished almost a century before his own time.

[1] Cf. below, p. 76.

[2] Below, pp. 50 ff.

[3] Although in the case of R. Jacob the Pious of Marvège the replies seem to have been conveyed by an angel, this is not typical of later kabbalistic practice (though it does occur not infrequently). The manuscript work *ha-Mal'akh ha-Meshib* (cf. above, ch. 2, p. 15, n. 1) does not introduce an angel as *vox coelestis* since it is really God himself who speaks to the mystic! Cf. Scholem, כתבי יד בקבלה, pp. 85–89. In earlier periods angels acted more frequently as revealers of heavenly mysteries; examples are familiar from the O.T. Apocrypha to the early pseudepigrapha. Cf. also below, pp. 78, 81.

[4] MS. Brit. Mus. P. 9549 (Margoliouth 749. iii) fols. 10b ff.; cf. also below, p. 68.

ences or revelations could be induced by appropriate techniques. Many kabbalistic books and indeed also non-kabbalistic writings in contact with the esoteric tradition[1] recommended or 'revealed' such techniques, which usually consisted of combinations of Hebrew letters, i.e. Divine Names. The interesting manuscript work known as *The Answering Angel*,[2] with its parallel revelations of theoretical and practical Kabbalah (*qabbalah ʿiyyunith—qabbalah maʿasith*) is full of instructions of this kind; one of its most remarkable features is its interest in automatic writing as a channel of revelation.[3] As a matter of fact, also the semi-magical practice of asking dream questions presupposes the existence of well-defined techniques of 'compelling' the dream and the answer. For strictly speaking the traditional term 'dream question' (*she'elath ḥalom*) is misleading; the desideratum was a 'dream answer' to a waking question. The question was accompanied by the proper formulae, which were then supposed to become effective during sleep. The popularity of the method is borne out by the fact that we possess literally 'hundreds of recipes'[4] for it. One such recipe, chosen at random,[5] may illustrate the procedure generally:

Dream question: write this [Divine] Name on [a piece of] parchment, put it under your head, and thus address the Angel of Dreams: 'I adjure you with the great, mighty, and awesome Name [of God] that you visit me this night and answer my question and request, whether by dream,

[1] Cf., e.g. Ibn Ezra's polemical sally in the shorter recension of his Commentary on Exodus (ed. Fleischer, 1926). For in spite of his emphasis that כי בשם אל שדי לא יעשה אותות רק בשם הנכבד (longer recension *ad* iii. 13) and הנה בשם הזה [= הויה] יתחדשו בעולם אותות ומופתים (ibid., *ad* iii. 15), yet he insists (shorter recension *ad* iii. 13) על כן האומרים כי בש"ם יעשו מעשים גדולים לא ידעו הש"ם וחלילה מהאומרים כי השם היה חקוק על המטה ובו בקע הים. Later he admits (ibid.) והנה כח השם מראה אותות ומחדש גופות כנגד המקבל [!] והמבין סוד זה השם ידע נבואת וירא אליו . . . In other words, Ibn Ezra insists, against other contemporary views, that knowledge of the 'Name' confers capacities for *receiving* visionary and prophetic illuminations but no active magical powers.

[2] Cf. above, p. 46, n. 6. The two most important manuscripts of this work are Hebr. 8° 147 of the Jewish National and University Library, Jerusalem, and Brit. Mus. Add. MS. 27002 (Margoliouth 766).

[3] e.g. MS. Brit. Mus., fols. 108a ff.

[4] *MTJM.*, p. 103.

[5] From a collection of סגולות לפתיחת הלב in a Bodleian MS. (Opp. 447, Neubauer 1833), fol. 164b.

by vision, by [indicating] a verse from Scripture,[1] by speech . . . or by [showing me some] writing, in a manner that I should not forget but remember [on waking up] my question and request [together with the answer]. Amen, Selah.' And this is the Name: . . . .

One point that emerges clearly enough from our cursory treatment of dreams and *yiḥudim* should be stressed here although it will be taken up again at a later stage. It is a feature that stands in marked contrast to the basic notions of the mystical theology of the Church.[2] The kabbalistic methods are frankly magical in the sense that they assume 'scientific', albeit esoteric, causal laws regulating our connexions with the 'higher' spheres. These causal connexions can be exploited by the seeker of information and by the mystic who is, in the last resort, also a seeker of information—albeit of a higher and mystical *gnosis*. The manipulation of the hidden, spiritual 'mechanics' leaves little or no room for the free and unpredictable operations of Grace. It is readily admitted that *yiḥudim*, &c., are not quite the same as conjuring up a spirit or jinn. Very often their ultimate purpose is a genuinely mystical one. Yet they are also fundamentally different from the techniques of spiritual preparation, which are designed to make the soul worthy of receiving the mysteries. Of course this latter element too is much emphasized, but ultimately repentance, observance of the Law, ascetic piety, and mortifications are merely preparatory steps to be supplemented by further and more crucial techniques. There is an undoubted tendency to conceive of the efficacy of these kabbalistic techniques as necessary and near-automatic. In more technical language, every *contemplatio* is *acquisita*.

It is very probable that this 'magical' approach to mysticism is due, at least partly, to the medieval, neo-platonic conception of an automatic ascent of the soul to higher, purer, and more divine spheres as it purges itself of matter and of the passions. As is well known, these ideas profoundly influenced medieval Jewish theology and its conception of prophecy. Prophecy was thought of less as a divine *charisma*, freely and graciously dispensed, than as the necessary and almost inevitable result of the right *bios theoretikos*.

[1] Cf. below, p. 53, n. 3.

[2] Cf. on the whole problem the excellent volume *Technique et contemplation* (*Études Carmélitaines*, 1949).

…ıoral) attitude of necessity
…n of the human intellect
…phecy is thus simply the
…ıtellect'. It is instructive in
…heory of prophecy[1] or even
…omas Aquinas's.[2] Medieval
…nonides, tended to efface the
…contemplative life of mystical
… became the ideal and legiti-
… other hand it lost its original
… and message, and became a
…hat seems essential and basic
…phecy appears as an extraneous
…ides. Whereas for St. Thomas
… of anticipation of future bliss or
…nysteries of Faith, is one thing
…cy, with its well-defined message
…ne two are assimilated in Jewish
…tion cuts both ways. Not only is
…l in terms of mysticism but also
…n emotional state of bliss or union,
…e, intelligible, and communicable
…eaves the realm of philosophical
… forms', or similar spiritual realities
…te philosophico-mystical contempla-
tion, and is seen as p… …pecific, albeit 'mystical' information to which discursive logic is applicable, then the metamorphosis of 'prophecy' in terms of mystical theosophy is complete. That this seems to have happened in kabbalism will become clearer as we proceed. At this stage it is sufficient to stress that for the medieval, platonizing Aristotelians prophecy and inspiration, though not *sensu stricto* charismatic, were certainly not magical. They were merely 'natural' in terms of the laws governing the relation of our humanity with that supra-mundane sphere which others prefer to

[1] *Guide for the Perplexed* (Engl. transl. by M. Friedländer, edn. 2, 1904, chs. 32 ff.) and Code, *Yesodey ha-Torah*, vii.

[2] *Summa Theol.* 2a, 2ae, 171: 1, 2; 172: 1–4.

call 'supernatural'. Only the kabbalistic transformation of the philosophic traditions in the climate of late medieval Jewish mysticism gave them that magical character which emerges fully and as it were *idealtypisch* in the writings of the sixteenth-century kabbalistic contemplatives.

In this connexion certain ideas about the apparition of the prophet Elijah assume a novel significance. For whether by accident or design, it seems that the meeting with Elijah was considered, in the main, as an unpredictable charismatic experience. Elijah, it appears, rather like the wind which bloweth whither it listeth, was not amenable to any mystico-magical coercion. To be visited by him, though only in a dream, was a privilege for which a pious ascetic might wait in vain and no techniques are recorded for procuring his presence.[1]

One method of inducing inspirations, less magical in character and of considerable psychological interest, has already been alluded to.[2] It is a peculiar technique of spontaneously producing discursive, intellectual, even highly specialized theoretical and speculative material without any conscious effort or thought. It may perhaps be described as induced intuition or 'automatic thinking'. As a waking alternative to indoctrination in dreams, it is reminiscent of the technique of 'active imagination' cultivated in Jungian analytical psychology as a supplement to or substitute for dreams. The underlying theory obviously assumes that whatever suddenly 'falls' into consciousness is of supernatural origin. The use of the Hebrew verb *nfl* is a beautiful parallel to the suggestive German *Einfall*.[3] The practical problem was how to achieve that vacuity of

[1] Cf. also Vital, *Sha'arey Qedushah*, pt. iv, and the quotation below, p. 74. On Karo's expectation to see Elijah see above, p. 22, and below, pp. 269–70. Cf. also S. Lowy, *J.J.S.*, vol. ix (1958), pp. 36–38.

[2] Above, p. 46.

[3] For a similar use of *nfl* in the writings of R. Dov Baer of Mezrich, who also advances a mystico-psychological theory on the nature of the intuitive *Einfall*, cf. Scholem, 'הבלתי מודע ומושג "קדמות השכל" בספרות החסידית', in *Haguth* (Bergmann Jubilee Volume; Jerusalem, 1944), and S. Hurwitz, 'Archetypische Motive in der chassidischen Mystik', in *Zeitlose Dokumente der Seele* (Studien aus dem C. G. Jung-Institut, Zürich, 1952). The use of *nfl*, however, does not appear to be due to the influence of the German-Yiddish *Einfall*, as it is found in much earlier texts of non-Ashkenazi origin; cf. the Talmudic saying quoted below, p. 53, n. 1.

mind in which alone unobstructed intuition became possible. The method adopted by Moses Cordovero and his teacher and brother-in-law Solomon Alkabets consisted of peregrinations through the Galilean countryside around Safed and fervent prayers at the numerous tombs of Tannaim and Amoraim in the vicinity. These wanderings had nothing in common with romantic notions of communing with nature; they were conceived as symbolic imitations of and participation in the 'exile of the *Shekhinah*'. Hence the opening words of Cordovero's record-book of these 'exile wanderings' (literally 'banishments') or *gerushin*:[1] 'On Friday, the 10 of Shebat in the year 5308 [= 1548 C.E.] we went into the exile of the King and Queen as far as the ruins of the *Beth ha-Midrash* in Nabartin[2] and there I hit upon the following novel kabbalistic idea: for I asked how it was possible, since [the sefiroth] *Tif'ereth* and *Malkhuth* [i.e. the 'King' and the 'Queen'] draw their life from the sides of [the sefiroth] *Ḥesed* and *Geburah* . . .', &c. Participation in the fate of the *Shekhinah* was apparently very close to the heart of Alkabets,[3] as is shown by another entry: 'We went as far as Kefar Biryah, where we entered the Synagogue and devoted ourselves to matters appropriate to *gerushin*; and my master [Alkabets] decided upon the innovation that in the summer months especially we should on occasion walk barefooted in the mystery of the *Shekhinah*: "withhold thy foot from being unshod".'[4] This same ascetic discipline of the 'imitation of the *Shekhinah*' is mentioned elsewhere by Cordovero when he explains:[5]

[1] Both this expression as well as the title and opening words of the *Sefer ha-Gerushin* were misunderstood by Cowley, *Cat. Oxf.* (1929), p. 463, who interpreted them as referring to 'the expulsion of Jews (from Genoa?) in 1548'!. The same mistake was made by earlier bibliographers; cf. Scholem's note in *Kiryath Sefer*, vol. i (1924/5), p. 164.

[2] The Kfar Nabora mentioned in the Talmud. On the tombs there cf. M. Ish-Shalom, קברי אבות (1948), pp. 26, 124.

[3] Cf. above, p. 18. The similar entries in the *M.M.* date from Karo's early period when Alkabets's influence seems to have been particularly strong; cf. below, pp. 108 ff.

[4] Jer. ii. 25. To go barefoot is a sign of mourning; the purpose of the pious exercise was clearly to hasten the advent of redemption and to provide comfort for the *Shekhinah*. This is a good example of one of the most striking and original elements of Safed piety: the liquidation of 'exile' by embracing it wholeheartedly and emptying its bitter cup consciously to the dregs. In mystical terms this meant sharing the exile of the *Shekhinah*; cf. on the subject Scholem, *Sabbatai Sevi*, p. 51.

[5] *Tomer Deborah*, ch. ix.

how to train oneself to the practice of [the divine aspect of] *Malkhuth*: [first of all] . . . another way is expounded in the *Zohar* and it is of great importance. One should wander, as if exiled, from place to place, purely for the sake of Heaven, and thereby make oneself a vessel [lit. *merkabah*, 'chariot'] for the *Shekhinah* in exile. . . . Thus one should humble one's heart and bind it to the Torah, even as Rabbi Simon [bar Yoḥai, the hero of the *Zohar*] and his associates used to wander about and discuss *Torah*. And if one trudges on foot from place to place, without horse or cart, so much the better.

In this practice of *gerushin* we have a good example of one of the most important innovations of Safed spirituality: the parallelism or near-identification of individual ascetic-mystical life on the one hand and the fate of the Godhead, in its female aspect of *Shekhinah*, 'in exile', on the other. The parallelism has not yet become complete identity, but there is a clear correspondence between the mystic's efforts at participating in the suffering and redemption of the *Shekhinah* on the one hand, and at rising himself on the *scala mentis ad Deum* to the state of prophecy or communion, on the other. This correlation comes out very clearly in an important passage in the popular ascetic manual 'The Beginning of Wisdom' (*Reshith Ḥokhmah*) by Cordovero's disciple Elijah de Vidas. There[1] the mystical ideal of *devekuth* or communion is defined as 'cleaving with one's soul and having as one's sole aim the unification of the *Shekhinah* and the separation from her of all *qelippoth* ['shells' or evil, demonic powers] and *similarly*[2] the separation from one's own mind of all alien [i.e. sinful or worldly] thoughts'. The mystic's way towards communion with God thus becomes the human aspect of his theurgic effort to bring about the inner-divine union or *yiḥud*. But whereas this idea is, by itself, a commonplace of earlier kabbalism, it receives an added and novel significance in the parallelism and correlation of the divine *Shekhinah* surrounded by *qelippoth* on the one hand and the mystic's mind beset by 'impure thoughts' on the other. Here the way is opened for the later development of complete identification of the objective, metaphysical evil of the *qelippoth* with the psychological concept of 'impure thoughts'.

[1] Op. cit., p. 51a (*Sha'ar ha-'Ahabah*, ch. 4).

[2] My own italics. The parallelism between the two spheres is an important step towards their identification in later hasidic doctrine.

However, in spite of the eschatological concern with the fate of the *Shekhinah*, the manifest aim of the *gerushin*-peregrinations was intellectual enlightenment in the form of kabbalistic comments on single verses from Scripture. The proceedings were the normal, dialectical ones of the rabbinic academy ('I objected'—'I replied') and the intuition must therefore have consisted of (*a*) the spontaneity with which a particular verse occurred[1] to the 'exiled' kabbalist, and (*b*) the unreflected immediacy of questions and answers. One or two examples may suffice to illustrate both the proceedings themselves and the emotions which they aroused in the participants:

Again we wandered on the 15th day of Shebaṭ, my master and myself alone, and the words of *Torah* were shining in us and the words were *spoken of themselves*.[2] We went as far as the tomb of Rabbi Joseph of Yokrat[3] and on our return we discussed the verse [*Micah* vii. 15] 'According to the days of thy coming out of the land of Egypt will I show him'. For my master asked . . . and replied . . . . Thereupon I commented . . . and my master added to this by saying . . . enlarging very much on the subject because *the words were shining forth of themselves*.

So far the proceedings of that day. Thanks be to God that we were vouchsafed all this, for these things are all *supernal*, *infused without reflection whatsoever*; they are sweeter than honey, *the gift of the Queen to them that wander with her in exile*.

We were still in the study[4] of Rabbi Simon bar Yoḥai in Meron when I concluded my exposition of this subject. Then we fell down [in prayer] in the sepulchre of Rabbi Simon and Rabbi Eleazar, and with my lips still moving[5] I said a short prayer from the depths of my heart. Then my master arose and expounded *Deuteronomy* xxv. 17–19 in a manner different from his previous explanations, and so did some other participants.

[1] Cf. already the talmudic reference to the sudden *Einfall* of verses from Scripture, b. *Ber.* 55b: א״ר יוחנן השכים ונפל לו פסוק לתוך פיו, הרי זו נבואה קטנה.

[2] This brings the phenomenon very close to maggidism; cf. below, pp. 54 and 260–1.

[3] North-east of Meron where the tomb of R. Simon b. Yoḥai and his son Eleazar is situated. From early times it was a popular centre of pilgrimage; cf. M. Ish-Shalom, op. cit., pp. 156–7.

[4] A little structure near the tomb which popular tradition holds to be R. Simon's study where he composed the *Zohar*; cf. Ish-Shalom. op. cit., pp. 173–80.

[5] From the previous 'inspired' automatic speech? Cf. n. 2 above.

Elsewhere,[1] Cordovero speaks of

> what I and others have experienced in connection with *gerushin*, when we wandered in the fields with the kabbalist Rabbi Solomon Alkabets, discussing verses from the Bible suddenly, without previous reflection. On these occasions new ideas would come to us in a manner that cannot be believed unless one has seen or experienced it many times. The gifts which I received and which fell to my part during these *gerushin* by God's mercy upon me I shall set down in a special tract.[2]

Here we have a phenomenon very close to maggidism. No doubt we must not classify it as automatic speech in the sense of a completely autonomous, compulsory, or obsessional activation of the organs of speech. It is probably more correct to describe the experience cultivated in this group as automatic, i.e. uncontrolled, thinking with the conscious control over the speech organs suspended so that the stream of ideas immediately translated itself into speech.[3] It is a tribute to the effectiveness of rabbinic mental discipline and to its power to penetrate the more unconscious

[1] *'Or Ne'erab* (Venice, 1587), pp. 32b–33a.

[2] i.e. the *Sefer ha-Gerushin*.

[3] A very similar though somewhat more 'magical' technique of inspired or 'automatic preaching' is recommended in an interesting manuscript of סגולות וקמיעות in the possession of Mr. M. Benayahu. The autonomous flow of words, chasing each other beyond the conscious control of reason, is well described in our text, which also suggests the ecstatic quality of the experience. The instruction to hide one's hands under one's clothing (in the sleeves?) seems to be a physical expression of the effort at concentration and 'recollection':

לדרשא [!] בחר לך פסוק אחד שתרצה כי הוא יוצא לאור משפט וזה לך האות משעה שתתחיל לדרוש מיד ישתברו כל איבריך ולא תוציא אצבע ולא זרוע מתחת לבושך בעוד שאתה עומד בדרשא ותאמר לכל אות נפשך אשר כמעט תצא נשמתם שאפילו מלך המשיח יהיה לפניך יפתח פיו לדבריך ואשביעך בה׳ אלהי ישראל שלא תראהו לאדם בעולם אלא לבנך היוצא מחלציך בשעת פטירתך וזה תאמר תחלה. . . .

ואתה תעשה עצמך שמח ומיד יבואו כל הדברים לפניך הם מעצמם בלא שום עיכוב בעוד שהדברים האלה בפיך יבואו אחרים וכשתראה הקהל שמחים לדבריך סיים כי ה׳ יהיה בעזרך וישמח לקראתך וחי השם כי אפילו מלאכי השרת מלאכי השלום ישמחו בך ובדברים היוצאים מפיך ודע כי בחון הוא בלא שום ספק, בדוק ומנוסה ועל כן התחזקת בו ותנסהו פעם ופעמים ושלש כי מיום שנחרב בית אלהינו לא נראה כמוהו.

בנ״א מצאתי כתוב שם הדורש כתוב בקלף צבי בשרטוט זה הצרוף הכתוב באחרי הדף ושים אותו באוזן השמאלי, וצריך לכתבו בד׳ שרטוטין כמו שהוא כתוב למעלה. ולא ישיח בעת הדרשה ולא יוציא ידו מתחת בגדו, וצריך תענית וטהרה.

Cf. also M. Benayahu, *Rabbi H. Y. D. Azulay* (1959), p. 131, n. 24.

levels of psychical activity that these kabbalist rabbis always produced from their subconscious perfectly coherent, intelligible, and scholarly disquisitions.

Before turning to other types of illumination or celestial instruction we may establish one preliminary result of considerable psychological interest. As the foregoing examples have shown, kabbalism is not content with guarding, explaining, and transmitting the 'Kabbalah', i.e. the esoteric part of the Mosaic or even pre-Mosaic tradition, which kabbalists considered as a kind of mystic-theosophical *depositum fidei.* On their own premisses the kabbalists could have proceeded much like the halakhists, dialectically developing their teachings from given 'data', i.e. from canonical texts. Instead they appear to thirst for 'new' knowledge, for the revelation of 'mysteries the like of which have never been heard before'[1] and for 'great and mighty secrets of *Torah* whereat all who hear them will marvel'. The logical fact that by definition all Kabbalah must be of hoary antiquity and that consequently even the most startling revelations can of necessity only be the revival, in a wider circle, of the forgotten esoteric knowledge of earlier sages, prophets, and patriarchs does not affect the psychological atmosphere of our texts.[2] Christian and Sufi mystics lived, as a rule, on transhistorical (or suprahistorical) levels; their feelings might be of elation or of gratitude at being vouchsafed glimpses of celestial mysteries. The feeling of the kabbalists was that they were living at a turning-point of history, marked by the revelation of the last secrets of divine wisdom. If this feeling was already strong among the first kabbalists, it was much intensified by the eschatological mood that characterized kabbalism after the expulsion from Spain. In fact, the revelation and spread of kabbalistic doctrines was regarded as an essential feature of the fulfilment of time and of the process of historic growth towards the messianic era. The experience of the kabbalists was not merely one of individual salvation through *gnosis* but definitely that of a *kairos.* Isaac Delattes of Mantua

[1] Similar expressions occur *passim* in the *M.M.* and in kabbalistic literature generally, but particularly in the Lurianic writings; cf., for example, Vital, op. cit. iii. 6: והנה גליתי אליך סוד עמוק כולל עניני המרכבה אשר לא זכו אליה הדורות הקדמונים אלינו, and ibid. iii. 2: ובו יתבאר דרושים לא שערום הראשונים והם סודות נפלאים.

[2] Cf. *MTJM.*, pp. 20 f.

clearly expresses this conviction and mood in his approbation permitting—or rather justifying—the printing of the *Zohar*.

The sixteenth century was a period of intense spiritual and psychological stress and strain.[1] As happens more frequently in the history of mysticism, such periods know no dearth of demoniacal possessions, trances, and other phenomena of enthusiasm 'more interesting to the pathologist than to the theologian'.[2] A particularly instructive example of how powerfully the most debased forms of 'mysticism' and popular superstition affected even leading kabbalists is provided by Vital himself, whose autobiographical *Book of Visions*[3] abounds with reports of visits to soothsayers, palmists, and oil-readers.[4] Possessions, we gather, were not in the least unusual, and the normal procedure in such cases was to call in *mekhashshefim* or 'sorcerers'. Yet however interesting and instructive these phenomena may be to the historian and sociologist, to the student of mysticism they only represent the fringe of what was, at the core, a major upsurge of genuinely mystical life. The kabbalists of the period, particularly those in Safed, earnestly and devotedly sought the immediate presence of God: *devekuth*. For them, as for M. H. Luzzatto in the eighteenth century, the mystical ladder led via the moral and ascetic virtues to the gift of the Holy Spirit; for that reason the so-called 'Baraitha of Rabbi Pinḥas ben Yair'[5] was a favourite text with all moralists and contemplatives.

Penitence, strict observance of the Law, and moral and spiritual perfection, though undoubtedly efficacious in hastening the advent of redemption, were mere preliminaries which 'man should do and live by them';[6] but the life intended here was the *vita contemplativa*

[1] Ibid., pp. 244 f.

[2] Schechter, loc. cit., p. 247; for references see Schechter's notes ad loc.

[3] Cf. above, p. 15, n. 4.

[4] e.g. p. 3: ואשאל ממנה על השמן כמנהג.

[5] 'The knowledge of Torah leads to watchfulness, watchfulness to zeal, zeal to cleanness, cleanness to abstinence, abstinence to purity, purity to saintliness, saintliness to humility, humility to the fear of sin, the fear of sin to holiness, and holiness leads to the gift of the Holy Spirit' (b. *A.Z.* 20b); cf. also the slightly divergent versions *Sheq.* 6a, *M. Soṭah* ix. 15, &c.

[6] For the various rules drawn up by Cordovero, Galante, and others, either for private use or for that of the devout brotherhoods, see Schechter, loc. cit., pp. 299–301.

of communion with God (*devekuth*), which in sixteenth-century Safed acquired an almost erotic quality reminiscent in many ways of Sufi piety. The words of Maimonides[1] on the love of God:

> And what is the proper love? That one love God with a great, excessive, and mighty love until one's soul becomes permanently bound in the love of God like one who is sick of love and cannot distract his mind from the beloved woman but always thinks of her—when lying down or rising up, when eating or drinking. Even greater than that should be the love of God in the hearts of His lovers, meditating constantly upon Him as He commanded us [Deut. vi. 5 'And thou shalt love the Lord thy God] with all thine heart and with all thy soul'. This is what Solomon meant when he said allegorically (*Cant.* ii. 5) 'for I am sick of love', and the whole *Song of Songs* is an allegory on this subject

or the injunctions of Baḥya ibn Pakuda[2] 'he [the lover of God] will not sleep but on the couch of His love, and will not wake up but with the sweetness of His remembrance' were taken up and lived out with an emotional intensity that was enhanced by the corporate life of the kabbalistic brotherhoods. Eliezer Azikri in his ascetic manual[3] accepts all the consequences of violent love: sleeplessness

[1] Code, *Teshubah* x. 3; cf. also ibid. x. 10 and Rabed's somewhat sober gloss ad loc. Maimonides's formulation is remarkable both for its near-erotic conception of the love of God and for the explicit statement that the *Song of Songs* is to be understood as an allegory of the soul's relations with God. According to some writers the understanding of the *Song* as a philosophical allegory of the love of the soul for God, viz. for the active intellect, was first launched by Maimonides; cf. S. Salfeld, 'Das Hohelied bei den jüd. Erklärern des Mittelalters' (*Magazin f. d. Wissenschaft des Judentums*, vols. v–vi (1878/9), particularly vol. vi, pp. 23–38) and A. S. Halkin, 'Ibn Aknin's Commentary on the Song of Songs' (*Alexander Marx Jubilee Volume* (New York, 1950), pp. 389 f. and particularly pp. 396–8). The current belief that the interpretation of the *Song* as a dialogue between God and the soul, fairly common among Christian mystics since Bernard of Clairvaux, established itself in Judaism only in sixteenth-century Safed (cf. Scholem, *MTJM.*, p. 226) may need re-examination for more than one reason. Maimonides may well be dependent on Jewish sources which used the *Song* as the nearest equivalent to the mystical love-lyrics of the *Ṣufis*, though these sources are still unknown. It is significant that elsewhere Maimonides's formulations are more restrained; cf. *Sefer ha-Miṣvoth*, 3rd commandment, and his Code, *Yesodey ha-Torah* ii. 2. On the *Song of Songs* as an allegory of the soul's communion with God, see also *Guide*, iii. 51. Still, it is obvious that for Maimonides the love of God has no real erotic quality; erotic love serves merely as a simile. On the love of God in medieval Jewish thought cf. also G. Vajda, *L'Amour de Dieu dans la théologie juive du moyen âge* (Études de philos. médiévale, vol. xlvi, 1957).

[2] *Duties of the Heart* (*Sha'ar 'Abodath ha-'Elohim*, ch. 5).

[3] *Sefer Ḥaredim*, written *c.* 1583.

('and one should be strong as a lion and arise after midnight and give praise to Him, practise solitude and enjoy His love'),[1] calling God fond names, and singing to the Beloved: 'it is the custom of passionate lovers to sing, and since the love of our Creator is "wonderful, passing the love of women" [cf. 2 Sam. i. 26], therefore he who loves Him with all his heart should sing before Him.' It is true that the love lyrics of the Safed mystics fall short of the literary perfection of Yehudah Halevi and Moses ibn Ezra whom they tried to emulate, but they prove at least that the urge to sing was too powerful to be contained:[2] 'One of the most important expressions of the flame of passion is that the lover should sing songs of love before Him. Therefore I shall place before you some of the love songs that we sang with great joy in the brotherhood of Hearkening Companions [cf. *Cant.* viii. 13].' The best known and, in Schechter's phrase, most 'vividly erotic' of these mystic bards was Israel Nagara, whose hymns have found their way into many a prayer-book.

As has been remarked earlier, the two supreme aims of these mystics were the exaltation and redemption of the exiled *Shekhinah*, and the immediate adhesion to or communion with God—'without any partition whatsoever'. *Devekuth* was possible because of the profound awareness that the mystic's heart was God's true dwelling. This idea is, of course, more at home among Sufis than among theosophical kabbalists, and it is quite obvious that those among the Safed authors who use this kind of language draw heavily upon such writings of earlier kabbalists as have, in fact, absorbed Sufi influence.[3] But the deceptively simple idea of the

[1] Ibid., pt. ii, ch. 1, par. 7. The whole remarkable chapter of the sudden development of the midnight devotion *tiqqun ḥaṣoth* is another example of the combination of purely mystical (the lonely dialogue of the soul with the divine beloved) and kabbalistic-theurgical (sharing and influencing the fate of the *Shekhinah*) motives so typical of Safed. On *tiqqun ḥaṣoth* in general cf. Scholem, 'Tradition and New Creation in the Ritual of the Kabbalists,' in *On the Kabbalah and its Symbolism* (1965), p. 146 ff. For the earlier, purely mystical practice of midnight meditation, cf., for example, Baḥya, op. cit. (*Sha'ar ha-'Ahabah*, ch. 6): ומהם שיתנפל בלילה . . . כי תפלת הלילה היא זכה יותר . . . ומהם שיתיחד בזכר האלהים ויתבודד בו בעת התיחד כל אוהב באוהבו והתבודד כל חושק עם חשוקו . . .

[2] Azikri, op. cit., pt. iii, ch. 7 (end).

[3] Such as, for example, Isaac of Acre (oral communication from Professor Scholem, who also refers to Jellinek, *Beitr. z. Kabbalah*, vol. ii (1852), pp. 45–47) and Abulafia.

heart as God's dwelling is enormously complicated once it is integrated in the context of kabbalistic theories on the relation of the divine sefiroth-macrocosm to the human microcosm. At times it is difficult not to get confused by the bewildering detail in which kabbalists describe the analogous structures in the descending chain of emanations, all identically 'sealed' with the Holy Name YHWH.[1] None the less, the basic idea is frequently expressed in movingly simple words. Azikri[2] repeatedly impresses upon his readers:

And thou, man, know that thy soul is the seat of God . . . the principal dwelling place of the *Shekhinah* is in the heart of the Jew . . . and so also has Rabbi Simon bar Yoḥai[3] explained the verse [Deut. xxiii. 15 acc. to A.V. xxiii. 14] 'For the Lord thy God walketh in the midst of thy camp'—the 'midst', that is the heart which is in the midst of thy 'camp', i.e. the body, ... How much, therefore, should man sanctify himself in body, heart and soul, since he is a temple of the Holy King. . . . 'Prepare to meet thy God, O Israel' [Amos iv. 12], for thy soul is His throne and thine heart is His footstool [cf. Is. lxvi. 1] . . . 'and where is the place of His rest?'—it is in the heart, as the sages have said: God exists in the hearts of His lovers. . . . He who receives a king in his house, would he not sweep it and clean it? Since the hearts of Jews are His house we should sweep from them all the rubble and dust of sinful thoughts.

The royal road to *devekuth* was solitary contemplation and the reduction of all talk, business, and social intercourse to the barest minimum. Even if in the world, one should not be of it: 'The light of the face of the Living King rests on thine head; keep silent in

[1] Cf. de Vidas (*Reshith Ḥokhmah*), Azikri (*Sefer Ḥaredim*), and Vital (*Sha'arey Qedushah*).

[2] Op. cit., pt. vii ('On repentance'), ch. 4.

[3] The reference can only be to *Zohar*, i. 76a or iii. 75a–b, where, however, both wording and meaning are slightly different; there is no trace there of the idea of the heart as God's dwelling. Azikri probably interpreted the *Zohar* in terms of his own favourite conceptions which he had derived from other sources; cf., for example, Scholem's quotation from a manuscript in the British Museum: כי ה׳ אלהיך בקרבך . . . בקרב ממש והמבין יבין (*MTJM.*, p. 110 and n. 97 ibid.). Professor Scholem also draws my attention to a corrupt reading in the *Hekhaloth* manuscripts where one of the most numinous hymns contains the obviously impossible 'immanentist' phrase אתה דר בלב האדם (*Hekhaloth Rabbathi*, ch. 26, in Jellinek, *Beth ha-Midrash*, vol. iii, p. 103). The correct reading, preserved in many manuscripts, is no doubt אתה דר בלבת דינורין ושלהביות. Texts such as these may well have been Azikri's immediate source. See *MTJM.*, pp. 362–3, n. 55.

His fear. And if thou speakest, speak to Him alone and the listener [i.e. your partner in worldly intercourse] may hear. In this way thou wilt practise constant *devekuth*.' The relation to the world and its duties is therefore an indirect, oblique, and external one. The two types of mystical solitude, the seclusion of the hermit and the seclusion 'in' the world, are exemplified by Noah in the ark, and Azikri's interpretation of Gen. vi. 9 on two mystical levels corresponds exactly to the two stages of *Abgeschiedenheit* distinguished by all mystics and so beautifully expressed in one of Tersteegen's stanzas:

> Ich wählte vormals Ort und Zeit
> Zum Beten und zur Einsamkeit;
> Nun bet' ich stets im stillen Sinn,
> Nun bin ich einsam wo ich bin.[1]

Azikri says:

> It is written [Gen. vi. 9] 'and Noah walked with God'. This signifies that he secluded himself with his Creator and avoided human company. Or else it may signify that he was so advanced in the practice of solitude that even when he was among men these did not distract him, for they were as non-existent in his eyes. . . .[2] A man in the company of others is like unto one who has fallen into the sea—unless he swims well he will be drowned; but if he flees society and secludes himself with his Creator, then he is like one in a boat, saved and in communion with God.

The use made here of the image of the sea is extremely significant and suggestive. For whereas in mystical literature generally this commonplace metaphor signifies the Divine Infinite in which the individual soul (the 'drop') loses itself, it here means the world which threatens to swallow the contemplative. He must therefore isolate himself 'in a boat' and fall back on his own, solitary personality, which can then enter into communion with God. The maintenance of the personality as implied by the image of the boat on the infinite sea is an apt illustration of the meaning of *devekuth*

[1] Quoted from *Tersteegen Brevier* (ed. G. Koepper), Berlin 1955, p. 50.

[2] The classical formulation, in Jewish literature, of the idea of absolute communion with God even *in* the world as the highest ascetic achievement can be found in Maimonides, *Guide*, iii. 51. From there it passed as a commonplace into later Jewish literature. For a similar view, though in a very different type of mysticism, cf. Eckhart's *Reden der Unterweisung*, nos. 6, 7, and 23.

as compared with the radical 'annihilation in unification' type of Sufi *unio mystica*.

But solitude is more than withdrawal from the world or society; it is also withdrawal from one's body, i.e. something very near to ecstasy. Prayer is therefore an act of double withdrawal. A man's home should be the House of the Lord, where he can be alone, particularly at night:

> Even as one should make an effort and settle in the Holy Land, so the next step on the spiritual ladder should be the effort to spend the greater part of one's day and night in the Synagogue and the House of Study. There a man should find his rest and peace and joy, as the sages have said: Synagogues and Houses of Study are Paradise for the righteous and a prison for the wicked. A son should offer savoury meat to his father and mother . . . and God delighteth in his creature arising at midnight to practise *devekuth* with him in solitude.

Life is nothing but the reality of God's light shining on man; how could man remain unaware of it? 'The light of God illumines thy face and thus thou livest; when He hides it, immediately man perishes. How then canst thou hide thy face and not contemplate Him always?' This realization is particularly important during prayer, which involves *devekuth* of double withdrawal:

> The Rabbis have taught that at prayer there should be no interception between the worshipper and the wall.[1] This signifies the [immediate communion with the] *Shekhinah*, for which one has to remove all evil thoughts *or even thoughts that are not evil*[2] from one's heart. . . . Another explanation is that the body should not intercept [between the soul and God] but should be as non-existent so that the soul can cleave to the divine soul as a magnet to an iron. . . . You should make an effort to concentrate your mind with *devekuth* whenever you utter the name of God, and this is the meaning of the phrase [1 Sam. i. 15] 'I have poured out my soul before the Lord', removing all partitions. It behoves us to abstract the body from the soul during prayer, as Rabbi Jonah of Gerona[3] has already written.

[1] b. *Ber.* 5b: מנין למתפלל שלא יהא דבר חוצץ בינו לבין הקיר.

[2] Here the mystical quality of Azikri's thought becomes quite apparent. The problem is not a moral ('*evil* thoughts') but a genuinely spiritual one; any thought, of whatever kind, is sufficient to disrupt the intimate communion of the soul with God.

[3] Jonah 'the Pious' or 'the Great' of Gerona (thirteenth century); his short penitential tracts were widely read. I have not come across precisely this formulation

It is interesting to note how the extreme demands of *devekuth* turned solitude into a major virtue in spite of the strong social motives operating in the community. There were not only the devout brotherhoods, banding together in pursuit of redemption and perfection, the corporate visits to the tomb of Rabbi Simon ben Yoḥai and the study of the *Zohar* there,[1] and the habit of mutual confessions of sin. There was also the more general and all-pervading stress on the value of performing all religious ceremonies and divine commandments 'in company'.[2] On the other hand the opposite tendency was no less strongly at work, extolling solitude as a *sine qua non* of the truly perfect state. The stress on solitude had appeared in earlier periods too,[3] but had never combined in such extraordinary fashion with powerful social values and motives. The problem is a well-known one in the sociology of religion: the hermit's cave becomes a monastery, and ascetic contemplatives combine in religious orders to form model social organizations. It seems that the social habits and values of the Safed kabbalists helped to integrate the individual mystic in an ideal, normative community which gave him spiritual security and support, and which provided him with a fund of energy and discipline on which he could constantly draw. But he was never allowed to forget that in seeking God he was always a *monos pros monon*:

How can you fail to practise solitude with God? Behold, most of your time you are alone: alone in your mother's womb, alone when you sleep, the body is lonely and the soul is lonely; the body is solitary in the

in the writings of Jonah of Gerona, but it should be noted that Karo actually enshrined this mystical demand in his Code, *O.H.* 98. 1: המתפלל צריך שיכוין בלבו פי׳ המלות שמוציא בשפתיו ויחשוב כאילו שכינה כנגדו ויסיר כל המחשבות הטורדות אותו עד שתשאר מחשבתו וכוונתו זכה בתפלתו . . . וכך היו עושים חסידים ואנשי מעשה שהיו מתבודדין ומכוונין בתפלתם עד שהיו מגיעים להתפשטות הגשמות ולהתגברות כח השכלי עד שהיו מגיעים קרוב למעלת הנבואה . . .. The wording of the *Sh.A.* here is taken almost *verbatim* from *Ṭur*.

[1] Cf. Azikri's opening remarks: אמר המחבר בהיות חברים מקשיבים אצל ציון רשב״י עוסקין באמרותיו אמרות טהורות כדרכנו פעמים בשנה מעת לעת ומפקידה לפקידה . . ., and also Shlomel Dresnitz's references to this custom.

[2] Azikri, op. cit., Introduction: התנאי הט״ז שישתדל אדם לעשות המצוה בחבורה ולא ביחיד.

[3] Baḥya, *Duties of the Heart* (*Sha'ar ha-Perishuth*), Abulafia, and others; cf. also Maimonides, *Guide*, iii. 51.

grave and the soul is solitary in Paradise, for 'every righteous soul has a [separate] dwelling place according to its dignity'[1] . . . therefore hearken unto my voice, always walk with Him and do not separate yourself [from Him] for a moment, but seek Him and ye shall find Him, He will not part from thee. O how good and how pleasant is His company.

Characteristically enough this exhortation knows of no expectation of life eternal in the happy company of saints (whose counterpart in traditional Jewish eschatology is eternal study in the celestial academies in the company of all the prophets, teachers, and rabbis), but the utter solitude of the soul, transfigured by the bliss of solitude fulfilled in the presence of the divine Beloved. The community is something to be left behind and forgotten: 'I and He, save, I beseech thee'[2]—this means when I and He are alone at the proper times of solitude, as expounded in [Baḥya ibn Pakuda's] *Book of the Duties of the Heart*.[3] Alternatively it can mean that 'even when I am among people . . . no created thing will come between me and you [i.e. God] for compared to Him they are all as nothing, and I and He are quite alone.'[4]

Azikri avers that solitude was the traditional practice of Jewish mystics:[5]

We find in the ascetic writings of the ancients that the pious used to practice ascetic solitude and *devekuth*, which means that when they were alone they withdrew their minds from all worldly things and concentrated [lit. bound] their thoughts on the Lord of all. . . . This is the meaning of the report in the *Mishnah* [*Ber*. v. 1] 'the early *ḥasidim* used to wait [i.e. prepare themselves] one hour before praying [and one hour afterwards]

[1] Azikri's mystical reinterpretation of the rabbinic saying b. *B.B.* 75a.

[2] *M. Sukkah* iv. 5. The enigmatic exclamation אני והו, interpreted here as אני והוא ('I and he'), probably represents an artificial variant pronunciation of the Hosanna Ps. cxviii. 25 אנא ה׳ הושיעה נא 'O Lord, save, we beseech thee'; cf. the commentators to the *Mishnah*, loc. cit., and also C. H. Dodd, *The Interpretation of the Fourth Gospel* (1953), pp. 93–96.

[3] *Sha'ar ha-'Ahabah*, 1 and 6.

[4] Cf. also the beautiful story quoted ibid. (end of pt. iii, ch. 2) of the rabbi who commemorated his escape from a tempest at sea during his voyage to Palestine by instituting an annual day of thanksgiving for all his family, having vowed ששני הימים האלה אצום בהן . . . [ו]שאהא אני יושב לבדי . . . לא אראה אדם אלא מתפלל וקורא כל היום ביני לבין עצמי, וכשם שלא מצאתי בים אותו יום אלא הקב״ה כך לא אראה אדם . . . See also *Duties of the Heart*, x. 3.

[5] Op. cit., ch. 3 (תקנה לחוטא).

in order to concentrate their mind on God'. The commentators[1] explained this to mean that they cleared their minds from all worldly things, concentrating on the Lord of all with fear and love. They thus took off nine hours[2] from the study of Torah[3] and devoted this time to solitary contemplation and *devekuth*. Then they would imagine the light of the *Shekhinah* above their heads as though it were flowing all around them and they were sitting in the midst of the light. So also have I found it [described] in an old manuscript of the ancient ascetics.[4] And while in that [state of meditation] they are all trembling as a natural effect, but [spiritually] rejoicing in trembling as it is written [Ps. ii. 11], 'Serve the Lord with fear and rejoice with trembling'.

The theme is resumed again by Azikri towards the end of his book:

. . . the fifth condition [for the attainment of the state of *devekuth*] is the practice of solitary contemplation as described above. . . . At the appropriate times one should withdraw to a secluded place where one cannot be seen by others, lift up one's eyes on high to the one King, the Cause of all causes, like a mark for the arrow [of the contemplative ascent]; 'as in water face answereth to face, so the heart of man to man' [Prov. xxvii. 19], and similarly as man turns his face to his God so also

[1] Cf. R. Jonah of Gerona ad loc. (in his commentary to Alfasi's talmudic digest). Azikri quotes the wording of the *Mishnah*, to which I have added, in square brackets, the amplification found in the *gemara* b. *Ber*. 32b. There it is said: 'The early *ḥasidim* used to wait one hour, then pray, and then wait another hour.—But if they spent nine hours of the day in prayer, how did they remember the Law (for even if once learned, *Torah* requires constant memorizing and repetition) and how did they do their work (i.e. earn their bread)?—[Answer:] Because they were saintly men, they easily remembered the *Torah* [they had learned], and their work was blessed [i.e. little effort produced sufficient for their needs].' This passage is significant because it implicitly states the 'hasidic' scale of values: prayer and meditation are essential spiritual values; *Torah* is something one should 'know' and remember, not something to be meditated on all the time. It appears that there is value in knowing the *Torah*, but no intrinsic value at all in the activity of studying (i.e. 'meditating') it. For the opposite, more academic and non-hasidic evaluation of Torah and *prayer*, cf. b. *Sab*. 10a as compared with ibid. 33b, j. *Ber*. i. 2 (f. 8a), and *Mekhilta ad Ex*. xvi. 4. Cf. also below, n. 3.

[2] Reckoning one hour for each of the three statutory prayers of the day, plus one hour before and one hour after.

[3] The study of the Law being a central value in Jewish religious life, the very idea of opposing *Talmud Torah* versus contemplation represents a critical development in Jewish spirituality. The problem came to a head in the doctrine of contemplation of the later Hasidim; cf. Scholem, '*Devekuth* or Communion with God,' in *The Messianic Idea in Judaism* (1971), p. 212 ff. and J. G. Weiss, 'Study of the Torah in Israel Baal Shem's Doctrine' (Hebrew) in *Tif'ereth Yisrael* (Israel Brodie Jubilee Volume), 1967, pp. 151–69.

[4] As Scholem has shown (loc. cit., p. 119), Azikri's source is none other than Rabbi Azriel of Gerona.

will He turn to him and they will cleave together [in mystical communion]. This I have heard from my master and teacher, the holy and pious Rabbi Joseph Sagis, and this was also his practice. Similarly I have found in the writings of Rabbi Isaac of Acre that this was the practice of some pious men in his time and you will find the same in the writings of Maimonides, Nahmanides, Bahya ibn Pakuda, and Rabbi Jonah of Gerona.

Here the extreme practice of *devekuth* almost reaches the point where it ceases to be compatible with the traditional Jewish virtues of *Talmud Torah*[1] and of the 'performance of the divine commandments in community'.[2] Azikri's manual recommends a spiritual practice that would lead to the experience of *devekuth*, but does not make it clear to what extent and in what sense this experience is ecstatic or not. We cannot even be sure that Azikri really gives us the whole story. But taking his manual as it is, we should note that it teaches no mystical techniques or formulae[3] beyond the purely spiritual practice of contemplation, prayer, solitude, and the intense yearning of love. There are no indications that the mystic aspires to illumination in the sense of revealed knowledge and celestial indoctrination. All that he seems to seek is the immediate, mystical awareness of the presence of God. For other kabbalists *devekuth* was definitely a more active and, at the same time, more 'revealing' state. At the very outset of their mystical quest they asked for more—and apparently received more. Thus Vital's *Gates of Holiness* was composed because, as the author says,[4]

I saw exalted souls, though but few, desiring to ascend, but ignorant of the [mystical] ladder. They study ancient books to seek and to find the paths of life, the way wherein they must walk and *the work that they must do*[5] in order to raise their soul to its supernal root and make it cleave

[1] See above, p. 64, n. 3.

[2] See above, p. 62, n. 2. In fact, the general social orientation of the Jewish tradition prevented it from developing the more extreme forms of solitary love of God, described as 'self-centred mono-ideism' by Evelyn Underhill or as the 'theopathic condition' by William James.

[3] No reader of the *Sefer Ḥaredim* can help noticing the wide difference between the nature and essence of Azikri's mysticism on the one hand and the kabbalistic theories he shared with his contemporaries on the other.

[4] *Sha'arey Qedushah*, Introduction.

[5] This apparently innocent quotation from Exod. xviii. 20 actually has a magical overtone: there are certain esoteric techniques one has to know if the mystical *opus* is to succeed.

to Him who is eternal perfection, according to the manner of the ancient prophets who were in a state of communion with their Creator throughout their lives.

Here the cat is very quietly let out of the bag in the apparently harmless association of the practice of *devekuth* with prophecy.[1] The notion that the 'prophet' is the ideal type of the perfect man implies that the prophetic *charisma* is the fruit and hence also the necessary concomitant or result of proper *devekuth*: 'By means of their *devekuth* the Holy Spirit rested on them, teaching them "the way where light dwelleth" and enlightening their eyes with the mysteries of the Torah[2] . . . to cleave unto Him . . . for the prophet cleaveth to God by drawing down the influx of prophecy and divine blessing on the nether beings.'[3] The cognitive, intellectual element in contemplation reasserts itself here, since *devekuth* is the means for obtaining the Holy Spirit, viz. the prophetic influx which is identical, to all intents and purposes, with the revelation of kabbalistic mysteries and doctrines.

According to Vital, the original prophetic tradition was continued by the

ancient *ḥasidim* known as 'ascetics' [lit. 'Pharisees'] . . . who retired into the caves of rocks and into the desert, withdrawing from all social intercourse. Some of them were *hermits in their own houses*,[4] living [at home] as in a desert and praising their Creator without interruption, day and night, with the study of Torah and the Psalms of David . . . until their mind cleaved with a mighty force and passion to the supernal lights.[5]

But the mystic tradition was lost and in its stead came dubious attempts to secure illumination by methods that made it difficult to distinguish celestial from demonic inspiration:[6]

in the end despair of ever discovering this wonderful wisdom seized the hearts of men . . . [and as a result] some began to adjure the angels by the power of the Holy Names, expecting light, but behold there was darkness because the angels [that appeared] were very inferior

[1] The indebtedness of this association to Maimonides (*Guide*, iii. 51) is obvious; cf. above, pp. 48–50.

[2] Vital, op. cit., Introduction.

[3] Ibid., vol. iii, p. 2.

[4] Cf. above, p. 60, n. 1.

[5] Vital, op. cit., Introduction.

[6] Ibid.

ones, appointed over worldly affairs [and not over spiritual matters] and composed of good and evil elements so that their revelations too were a composite of good and evil, truth and falsehood and all manner of vanities such as [magical] healing, alchemy, and the techniques of amulets and magical formulae . . . would God that their hearts were set only on [the study of] Torah and [the performance of] the commandments!

The 'Four Travellers' to the garden of mystical knowledge[1] are held up as warning examples. It is true that the four heroes of the talmudic legend risked too much by attempting to attain the highest mystical reaches,[2] whereas

we should be happy to attain the lower manifestations of the Holy Spirit such as the apparition of the prophet Elijah, which, as is well known, was vouchsafed to many, or such as the apparition of the souls of departed saints . . . and *even in our time I have seen holy men who have attained this*. Another form [of charismatic illumination] is that man's own soul, if it is much purified, appears to him and guides him on all his ways.[3] All these methods are within the reach of worthy adepts even in our own time.

In fact,[4] 'we have heard and seen ourselves how choice spirits have in our time attained the degree of [direct inspiration by] the Holy Spirit whereby they could foretell the future.[5] Some of them[6] possessed wisdom that had not been revealed to previous generations.' Nevertheless, the danger of involvement with the demonic world is very real whenever 'prophetic' experience is actively solicited:[7] 'But it requires great discrimination and much experience to find out the truth [about these matters], for perhaps it was an alien, impure spirit that was with him.'

Vital's ladder of ascent begins with counsels of moral and ascetic perfection, and ends with almost magical formulae which so alarmed the publisher of the little book that he left them in manuscript. His pious reticence is an eloquent tribute to the magical character

[1] Cf. b. *Ḥag.* 14b.

[2] Vital, op. cit., Introduction.

[3] Cf. above, p. 40, n. 3.

[4] Vital, op. cit. iii. 7.

[5] On prophecy in the narrow sense of foretelling the future, as an essential part of maggidism, cf. below, p. 79.

[6] This is most probably a reference to Isaac Luria.

[7] Vital, op. cit. iii. 7.

of Vital's mystical instruction, for our printed text ends with the announcement:[1] 'Thus speaketh the printer: this fourth part will not be printed for it is all Holy Names and Secret Mysteries which it would be unseemly to publish.' We may ignore, for the present, the extremely complicated and confusing ontology and anthropology which Vital outlines as the background of his theory of prophecy and inspiration. According to this system of combined anthropology and cosmology, man's ideal nature is such that contact with the highest, divine sphere is possible and even necessary if man is to fulfil his proper function and purpose in the cosmic household. In spite of the proliferation of intermediate, emanated 'worlds' in Lurianic Kabbalah, there is an essential unity to this great chain of being. The 'lower' is always also the 'outer' cover, garment, or shell, surrounding the preceding 'higher', viz. more 'interior', level of existence to which it is related like body to soul. This unity or repeated mystical analogy of infinite cosmic levels is emphatically brought out by another formulation according to which all 'worlds', i.e. stages of emanation, share the same anthropomorphic structure in spite of the vast hierarchical differences between them. From the celestial *anthropos* down to earthly man the same structure infinitely repeats itself. Already the exalted world of divine sefiroth mirrors the even higher sphere of the *Adam Qadmon*.[2] It is thus easy to see how man is in principle fit to attain the state of prophecy. He merely has to establish immediate contact with the highest, that is deepest and most hidden, divine sphere; he can do this by making use of the structure of the cosmos, the chain of being, and the essential identity of his own structure with that of all the higher worlds. The requirements for this ascent are that he purge himself of matter and the passions, sanctify his soul by strict observance of the divine commandments, acquire perfect humility and constant joy,[3] and practise contemplative *devekuth*.

The specifically magical element of Vital's theory of contemplation and prophecy inheres in his refusal to admit that inspiration

[1] Vital, op. cit., pt. iv; cf. also Scholem, *MTJM.*, p. 122.

[2] Vital, op. cit. iii. 2: זה האור המיוחד הנקרא עולם הי״ס בתמונת אדם אחד.

[3] Ibid. iii. 4; also ibid., פתיחה, התנאי הרביעי.

automatically follows *devekuth*.[1] Between the attainment of *devekuth* and the influx of the Holy Spirit there must intervene a specific magico-meditative activity whose effect is to 'trigger off', as it were, the downward movement of the divine influx. A rough outline of Vital's *scala contemplationis* would be somewhat like this:

1. Ascetic purification and sanctification, preparatory to *devekuth* proper.

2. Meditation, preceded by complete withdrawal of the mind from all bodily and material things and sensations, and by absolute mental vacuity due to the absence of sense impressions. In this connexion it is important to note that in Vital's terminology the word *hithpashsheṭuth* does not mean ecstasy. The term is used only in the description of this second stage of contemplation and its connotation is purely negative: withdrawal from material sensations. Actually Vital, like many earlier kabbalists, knows no ecstasy *sensu stricto* because the soul does not leave the body behind except in the lowest form of inspiration, dreams. There is no real ascent or *Himmelsfahrt* of the soul such as was cultivated in some other systems. *Hithpashsheṭuth* means the abstraction of the mind from worldly mental contents so that the imaginative faculty, which continues to function, can exercise itself on other, higher realities. The same imaginative faculty, which usually works on material supplied by the senses, is now free to imagine and contemplate more spiritual things.

3. A purely imaginative[2] ascent of the soul to its individual 'root' or source in the higher world: 'Then the imaginative faculty will turn a man's thoughts to imagine and picture [mental contents] *as if*[3] it ascended in the higher worlds up to the roots of his soul ... until the imagined image reaches its highest source and there the images of the [supernal] lights are imprinted on his mind *as if* he imagined and saw them in the same way in which his imaginative

[1] As the neoplatonic theory of contemplation, followed by Maimonides, implies.

[2] Cf. Vital, op. cit. iii. 5: 'the *hithpashsheṭuth* mentioned in all books dealing with prophecy and the gift of the Holy Spirit is *no real hithpashsheṭuth*, in the sense that the soul actually leaves the body—as during sleep—for in that case we should be dealing not with prophecy but with ordinary dreams.'

[3] The italics in this and the following quotations are, of course, not Vital's but the writer's.

faculty normally pictures in his mind mental contents deriving from the world . . . .'[1] The decisive role attributed here to the imaginative faculty is clearly dependent on Maimonides's theory of prophecy.[2] According to Vital's adaptation of it, the essence of mystical meditation is 'contemplation *as if*'. What makes this contemplative but purely imaginative ascent as seriously real as the less sophisticated and more ecstatic *Himmelsfahrt* of earlier adepts is the underlying doctrine of the 'magical' power of all acts of meditation and concentration, particularly when supported by the right formulae. The meditative ascent, though taking place in the imagination only, thus makes the same real impact on the higher worlds and has the same effects on the soul as would a real ascent through the heavens in which the soul ecstatically left the body. 'This influx and substantial light [which as a result of the contemplative exercise is infused into the mystic's soul] is what is called "Thought" (*maḥashabah*). Understand this well, for it is no vain thing. If this were not so [that imaginative meditation produces these results], then the whole kabbalistic doctrine concerning the right "intentions" and devotions at prayer (*kawwanoth*) and concerning [the mystical significance of] man's good and evil thoughts were as good as nothing. You will now understand why prophecy is not only possible *but necessary*; it is as if a man held fast to the end of the bent down branch of a tree: when he shakes it [his bit of branch] with sufficient strength, then *of necessity* the whole tree is shaken with it.'[3]

4. In his imaginative ascent the mystic contemplates the ten sefiroth. Opening himself to their irradiation, he exalts and raises them to the highest sphere of *En Sof*. From this highest point the light is then 'reflected' and flows back (*'or ḥozer*). The contemplative who draws the light in the reverse direction, down on his own 'soul root', thereby also irradiates the sefiroth themselves, which are now illumined by the reflex light flowing down from *En Sof*. The mystic then proceeds to conduct and direct the light farther downward through the innumerable worlds and stages of the kabbalistic cosmos, down to his rational soul and from there down

[1] Vital, op. cit. iii. 5.
[2] Cf. *Guide*, ii. 36.
[3] Op. cit. iii. 5.

to his animal soul which is the seat of the imaginative faculty[1] and therefore the *locus* where the prophetic, that is spiritual-imaginative, experience takes place: 'and there [in his animal soul] these [heavenly, spiritual] things will be pictured in material images by the imaginative faculty, and then he will apprehend them *as if* he saw them with his bodily eyes.'[2] Occasionally the imaginative faculty may even externalize or project the effects of this 'light', so that the experience becomes one of external sense impressions such as of the apparition of angelic messengers, the hearing of voices, &c. Vital sums up the whole process in the following words:[3] 'The thought of the prophet expands and rises from one level to another . . . until he arrives at the point where the root of his soul is sunk [in the divine world]. Next he concentrates on raising the light of the sefirah to *En Sof* and from there he draws the light down, from on high down to his rational soul and from there, by means of the imaginative faculty, down to his animal soul and there all things are pictured either by the inner senses of the imaginative faculty or by the outer senses.'

So far our brief summary of Vital's *itinerarium mentis* follows the account in *Sha'arey Qedushah*. Practically all its main elements have a respectable ancestry in kabbalistic literature and practice, and regarded in isolation they hardly appear very original. The 'magical' effect of concentration and meditation (*kawwanoth*) is an axioma of kabbalistic tradition, and so is the anthropological-cosmological microcosm-macrocosm doctrine which turns the whole universe into a huge chain of being which can be operated by man, small and insignificant as he may appear to be. That the contemplative ascent was not an actual journey—as, for example, among primitive shamans—was also known among kabbalists, though even as a purely imaginative adventure it required the knowledge and use of Holy Names, formulae, and the like. Obviously every single step during the ascent as well as during the no less dangerous descent had its appropriate and specific formulae

[1] According to the usual teaching of medieval psychology; cf. H. A. Wolfson, 'The Internal Senses in Latin, Arabic, and Hebrew Philosophic Texts', *Harvard Theological Review* (1935), pp. 69 ff.

[2] Vital, op. cit. iii. 5.

[3] Ibid. iii. 6.

and Names. One need but read Abraham Abulafia or the fourteenth-century Spanish work *Berith Menuḥah* to form an idea of the breadth and weight of the tradition on which Vital could draw.

Yet all these elements taken together do not add up to Vital's thoroughly original formulation. His important and decisive innovation resides in the definitely and *necessarily* magical character which he imparts to the contemplative exercise and which depends on his unprecedented and original distinction between 'magic formulae' (*hashba'oth*) and 'mystical formulae' (*yiḥudim*). The crucial point, as far as the magical character of Vital's system of meditation is concerned, is the transition from the contemplative ascent to the reverse movement of drawing the light, i.e. the divine influx, down (*hamshakhath ha-maḥashabah*). This all important reversal can only be effected by special intense meditations and formulae (*yiḥudim, hazkarath shemoth*). The use of 'Holy Names' is indispensable in the Lurianic system of meditation. This fact is indisputable. Its inconsistency with Vital's repeated and grave warnings against the use of *hashba'oth* (magic formulae, literally '*Beschwörungen*') is more apparent than real. It is true that Vital never tires of stressing the dangers inherent in the use of such formulae. Their use can be risked with impunity only by saints in a state of perfect purity; otherwise the adept lets himself in with the demonic powers and is lost. Vital instances the well-known case of Joseph della Reyna[1] and Solomon Molkho (!) as warning examples.[2] This 'practical Kabbalah'[3] is to be eschewed, particularly by the present generation so gravely deficient in purity and saintliness, and living in an age in which only the lowest 'world of *'Asiyyah*' is accessible to *hashba'oth* and can be magically manipulated. The saints of ancient times, whose spiritual lives moved on higher planes than the 'world of *'Asiyyah*' could and did use Holy Names during their mystic ascent in order to unlock

[1] Cf. Scholem in *Zion* (מאסף החברה הא"י להיסטוריה ואתנוגרפיה, תרצ"ג), vol. v, pp. 124–30.

[2] Vital, op. cit. iii. 6.

[3] *Qabbalah ma'asith* because applicable to the *'olam ha-'asiyyah* only! The sages and saints of earlier generations were, of course, capable and worthy of using the formulae and *hashba'oth* appropriate to the higher worlds of *Yeṣirah* and *Beri'ah*. Granted their higher moral and spiritual level, their use of magic formulae was legitimate and also less dangerous to them.

the various celestial gates and to gain access to particular celestial 'worlds', 'stages', or 'mansions'.[1] These formulae were effective because each was appropriately applied to the individual angel or guardian in charge of a particular sefirah, region, or celestial 'gate'. Vital thus completely absorbs the venerable *Merkabah*-tradition of pacifying, exorcizing, and coercing the celestial powers and keepers of the gates. But by prohibiting or at least discouraging its practice he to all intents and purposes also eliminates it. However, what Vital discards is the use of formulae to aid the mystical ascent (*hashba'oth*); what he insists on and actually develops as a major feature of his system are special formulae for reversing the flow of the divine light (*yiḥudim*). Without *yiḥudim* the influx from the highest point in *En Sof* to the lowest terminus in the animal soul cannot be brought down.

It is important to realize clearly the nature of the difference between illegitimate *hashba'oth* and indispensable *yiḥudim*. The former, according to Vital, were never meant as an alternative to *yiḥudim*; the practice of the latter is therefore untouched by the condemnation of *hashba'oth*. The one is concerned with effecting the ascent, the other with bringing about the reverse flow of the divine light and its infusion into the soul. The difference between legitimate and illegitimate use of Holy Names is therefore not one of pure (spiritual) versus selfish (magical) intentions. No doubt, this is how the difference was understood by earlier schools of magical contemplation. Thus according to Abraham Abulafia the same formulae might be used legitimately—if the aim was communion with God and the state of prophetic perfection, or sinfully—if the purpose was the acquisition of magical power. This latter possibility is not even discussed by Vital in the present context; it is too obviously damnable to merit consideration. The distinction, for Vital, is not between unselfish and holy versus selfish and worldly use of the magical power of the Divine Names, but between formulae of ascent and formulae of descent. Originally both were used and taught. The disciples of the prophets of old were

[1] Moses ascended (with certain qualifications) to *'Aṣiluth*; the other prophets, who lived while the temple of Jerusalem was still in existence, to *Beri'ah*; Ezekiel, who prophesied in exile, to *Yeṣirah*.

taught, in addition to the *kawwanoth* and *yiḥudim* that are indispensable even today, also 'certain prayer-formulae and Divine Names to be used against the guardians of the celestial gates . . . and in this way they ascended higher and higher. . . . And concerning the gate-keepers and the Holy Names it is thus: they adjured [the gate-keepers] with the power of the appropriate Holy Name.' In fact, the whole *Merkabah*-vision of the prophet Ezekiel is nothing but an account of such an ascent by means of *hashba'oth*. But today it behoves the adept to sanctify himself to such a degree that he can pass the gates without special incantations. However, once 'inside', viz. 'high up'—whether aided by formulae or not—the mystic still has to meditate, to raise the lights to *En Sof*, and finally to reverse their flow and direct it downward.

The possibilities of pneumatic life are clearly stated by Vital:

> Concerning the manner of attaining the Holy Spirit I have already explained[1] . . . that there are five manners: the Holy Spirit [in the narrow sense], the souls of departed saints, angels of the type called *maggidim*, Elijah, and dreams. Every one of these can be mediated through Elijah and without resorting to any [magical] act, purely as a result of a man's saintliness and his devotion to the Law. It is also possible to attain all these by means of specific actions, but one must be worthy for this and well-prepared for illumination.

The rejection of *hashba'oth* consequently only means that formulae employing power over angels and ministering spirits should be excluded from the mystical exercise and that the initial ascent should be effected solely by means of ascetic discipline, piety, and contemplative *devekuth*. In a way, the half-heartedness of Vital in this matter comes out in the fact that in spite of his grave warnings he did write down the practical method of *hazkarath shemoth*; if the technique remained largely unknown, this was due to the printer's discretion and not to Vital's.[2] But in any case we must fall back on the method of *yiḥudim*, for without it there is no attainment of prophecy: 'for this drawing down of the influx (*hamshakhath ha-maḥashabah*) certainly never comes about by itself but [is effected] solely by the *kawwanoth* and *yiḥudim* transmitted to the disciple by the prophet who taught him the art of prophecy.

[1] Cf. below, pp. 75–76.

[2] Cf. above, p. 68.

. . . By these *yiḥudim* he was then enabled to draw down the light and the influx according to his wish, and this is the ultimate purpose of the whole subject of prophecy.'[1]

Vital himself summarizes the procedure to be followed in this way. The adept begins by preparing himself by 'four purifications', the first two of which are of a more general nature, whereas the other two are specific preparations for the reception of the Holy Spirit. They are (*a*) repentance for all sins of omission and commission, (*b*) scrupulous observance of all commandments positive and negative, particularly of prayer and the love of one's fellow man, (*c*) material purification, i.e. ritual immersions and the wearing of clean garments, (*d*) silence and solitude, preferably after midnight. Thus prepared, the adept should

close his eyes, withdraw his mind from all worldly things *as if* his soul had left the body and he was insensible like a dead corpse. Thereafter he should make an effort to meditate with great passion on the higher [spiritual] world and to cleave there to the roots of his soul and to the supernal lights. He should imagine in his mind *as if* his soul had left him and was ascending on high, and he should picture the higher worlds *as if* he actually stood there. And if he performs any *yiḥud* he should intend thereby to draw the light and the influx down on all the worlds and also intend to receive his own share in the end.[2]

His 'own share' is, of course, the measure of illumination or prophecy which is due to the adept. If nothing happens in spite of all his spiritual exercises, it is a sure sign that the adept is not yet worthy; he should, therefore, continue his preparatory discipline.[3]

If the contemplative effort is successful, the prophetic experience or influx of the Holy Spirit can take one of five forms:[4]

1. The adept draws down upon himself the supernal light from his 'soul root'. This is the Holy Spirit in the narrow and correct sense.
2. The diligent study of the Law and the performance of the divine commandments brings about the creation of a new

[1] Vital, op. cit. iii. 6. 'Thought' or *maḥashabah* here means the pneumatic influx; cf. also iii. 5: וזה השפע והאור הוא ענין הנקרא מחשבה.

[2] Ibid. iii. 8.

[3] Vital: ואם לא ירגיש מאומה, נראה כי עדיין איננו ראוי ומוכן.

[4] Cf. the quotation above, p. 74.

angel.[1] 'From these a new angel is created and this angel then reveals himself to him. This is the matter of the *angels that are called maggidim* which is mentioned in some books. However, if the divine commandment is not performed perfectly, then the [corresponding] *maggid* will be composed of good and evil, truth and falsehood.' A *maggid* is thus an angel who appears to his human 'creator' or progenitor and reveals mysteries to him.

3. The apparition of the prophet Elijah.[2]
4. The 'greatest of all'[3] is the apparition of a departed saint whose soul stems from the same supernal 'root' as the adept's.
5. A dream. This is the lowest form of inspiration.[4]

All five forms are equally unexceptionable, provided they come of themselves after the appropriate preparation. As long as there is no magical coercion they are all good, 'for, since man does not adjure or coerce the higher powers except through his good deeds and saintliness, it is certain that a pure and Holy Spirit will rest on him, without any admixture of evil. It is different, however, when one uses coercion or seeks magical methods through the use of certain acts, prayer formulae, and *yiḥudim*.'[5] There are various such methods 'for drawing down one of the five abovementioned forms, even if they do not come of themselves. But they require great purity and holiness so that they should not contain any admixture [of evil].'

[1] This is the kabbalistic reinterpretation of the rabbinic saying (*M. Aboth*, iv. 11), כל העושה מצוה אחת קונה לו פרקליט אחד. It is interesting to note that the later interpretation really reverts to the original meaning of the vb. *qnh* 'create'.

[2] שע״י חסידות כנ״ל יתגלה אליו אליהו ז״ל.

[3] הד׳ היא גדולה מכולם.

[4] Lowest because in it the rational soul really leaves the body, ascends to the higher worlds, and returns with the impressions of its vision, which it then communicates to the animal soul and the imagination. In this case, however, the co-operation of another faculty, memory, is required in order that the dream may be remembered. Vital, op. cit. iii. 5: נמצא שהנבואה הוא כדמיון החלום שנפשו השכלית יוצאת ממנו ועולה למעלה ממדרגה למדרגה ושם צופה ומביט ואח״כ חוזר ויורד ומשפיע זה האור עד הנפש החייה אשר בה כוח המדמה ושם מצטיירין ומתגשמין יותר אותן הדברים. . . . והרי התבאר ענין הנבואה וענין החלום כי זה בעוד הנפש בגופו וזה אחר צאת הנפש. Cf. also id., *Sefer ha-Ḥezyonoth*, p. 232.

[5] Vital, *Sha'arey Qedushah*, loc. cit.

Once attained, the prophetic state is still far from perfect. First the adept has to examine himself very carefully to make sure that his inspiration is pure and uncontaminated by evil or falsehood. 'This can be tested by the contents of the revelation, whether all his words are true . . . or whether his words contain empty things about the vanities of this world or things that are not in accordance with the Law and such like.' In the second place he has to cultivate this contemplative and prophetic habit or state, so that his prophecy can deepen and develop:

Know that at first the Spirit will come upon him as if by accident, on rare occasions only, and also the contents of the revelations will be slight, not profound, and moreover little in quantity. But as he continues his power will increase. . . . The basic principle [of the mystical life] is to purge oneself to the utmost of matter, to eradicate all [worldly] thoughts and the [activity of the] imaginative faculty [with regard to them], and to adhere with the closest possible adhesion to the higher worlds.[1]

Vital's classification of the five types of prophecy shows, among other things, that revelations 'by angels called *maggidim*' were an acknowledged phenomenon in his time and had to be considered in any comprehensive manual of mystical practice. Though Vital's theory of the nature of *maggidim* is only briefly adumbrated in the *Gates of Holiness*,[2] enough is said to show that the *maggid* is in some way essentially different from the other types of revelation. The idea of *maggid* does not even quite conform to what is usually understood by angelic revelation or apparition. For whereas in the other four types of prophecy the agents of revelation are quite independent of man, the *maggid* is man's own creature. The 'Holy Spirit' and dreams are mechanisms or vehicles by which the supernal light communicates itself to the rational and animal souls of man; Elijah and the 'souls of the righteous' are obviously independent, personal agents. It is true that angels too are distinct, individual agents, but none of the theories surveyed so far makes any allowance for angels in general as the normal celestial messengers

[1] Ibid. iii. 8.

[2] The subject is discussed more systematically in Vital's other writings such as the *Sha'ar Ruaḥ ha-Qodesh* and *Sha'ar ha-Yiḥudim* (i.e. pts. 7 and 8 of his *Shemonah She'arim*) and the *Sefer ha-Gilgulim*.

of the good things of the spiritual world.[1] If angels as independent beings or powers are mentioned in the contexts discussed so far, it is in their role as gate-keepers and the like and they are, more often than not, connected with the 'practical' Kabbalah of magical formulae so vehemently disapproved of by the spiritual manuals. Now, quite unexpectedly, the angels come into their own again in the guise of *maggidim*; but they are angels born of the words of *Torah* and of pious deeds—provided, of course, that these were accompanied by pure intention and the appropriate *kawwanoth*. They are a kind of hypostasis of the moral and spiritual level reached by man, and they come as near to a 'psychological' theory of revelation as the 'projecting' thought of sixteenth-century kabbalism could formulate. The dependence of the *maggid* on the nature of the human action that produced him easily accounts for the mixture of 'good and evil, truth and untruth' which he may exhibit. Vital's opinion of Karo's Maggid[2] is thus in perfect keeping with his general theory, which is based, like most kabbalistic speculation, on a really terrifying conviction of the potency and significance of every human act:

And now let us explain the subject of prophecy and the Holy Spirit. . . . *It is impossible* that anything that comes out of man's mouth should be in vain and there is nothing that is completely ineffective . . . for every word that is uttered creates an angel. . . . Consequently, when a man leads a righteous and pious life, studies the Law, and prays with devotion, then angels and holy spirits are created from the sounds which he utters . . . and these angels are the mystery of *maggidim*, and everything [i.e. the quality and dignity of these *maggidim*] depends on the measure of one's good works.[3]

There are *maggidim* which deceive a little, for though they are holy and their root is in the side of holiness, yet [the imperfection of] the human act [that brought them into existence] caused them [to be imperfect].[4]

Everything depends on the quality of the human act. Sometimes the *maggidim* are true and sometimes there are such as tell lies. Therefore it is said of Samuel [1 Sam. iii. 19 'and the Lord was with him] and did let none of his words fall to the ground'; this is the case when he [the

[1] Cf. above, p. 46.
[2] Cf. above, p. 15.
[3] *Sefer ha-Gilgulim* (Frankfurt, 1684), p. 32b.
[4] Ibid. 33a.

maggid] can substantiate his words. . . . Another criterion is that all his words be for the sake of heaven [i.e. conducive to perfection] . . . another criterion is that he expound kabbalistic doctrines and mysteries. But the reason that an angel can tell lies is this: since his creation results from the actions of man, therefore his nature will be in accordance with these actions. If someone studies the Law with pure intent and without ulterior motives, then, correspondingly, the angel created thereby will be exceedingly holy and exalted and true in all his words; similarly if one reads the Law without making mistakes.[1]

The rank and dignity of the angel thus created depend on the quality and kind of the human action. Good works without the proper devotions and *kawwanoth* only give birth to angels of *'Asiyyah*, whereas the right devotions produce an angel of *Yeṣirah*, and the highest type of activity, *Talmud Torah*, even begets angels of *Beri'ah*. The final test of a *maggid*'s reliability is 'to see whether he substantiates all his words, that all his words should be conducive to perfection and that he should say nothing to the contrary, and that he should be able to expound kabbalistic mysteries'.[2] The last criterion again takes up the intellectualist motif in Jewish mysticism.[3]

Every meritorious action begets an angel, but not every angel thus begotten reveals himself in *maggid*-like fashion: 'These angels that are created by the utterances of man are the mystery of the *maggidim* mentioned in the *Sefer Ḥasidim*[4] and they reveal the future and expound kabbalistic mysteries. However, there are people to whom these created angels reveal themselves and foretell the future, and there are others to whom they do not reveal themselves.'[5] The pattern of personal prophecies and the revelation of kabbalistic doctrines laid down by Vital is that which we have already found characteristic of the communications of Karo's Maggid.[6] With the victory of Lurianism, Vital's theory of maggidism was canonized and subsequently appealed to whenever maggidic manifestations had to be judged.[7] But Vital's theory was not

[1] *Sha'ar ha-Yiḥudim*, ch. 2. [2] Ibid.
[3] Cf. above, p. 41. [4] Cf. above, p. 43, n. 1.
[5] *Sha'ar ha-Yiḥudim*, ch. 2. [6] Cf. above, p. 19, and below, p. 277.
[7] e.g. by Emden in the controversy about Luzzatto's *maggid*; cf. his 'Enquiry concerning Maggidim' in זאת תורת הקנאות (Altona, 1752), pp. 47 f., also מטפחת סופרים (Altona, 1768).

the only one current in Safed. Cordovero, in his *Enquiries concerning Angels*,[1] systematically discusses the nature and function of angels and their role in charismatic or pneumatic life. There are supernatural realities like the Holy Spirit, angels, and demons, which, given the right conditions, can enter the human soul. In fact, this is the essence of charismatic life, whether it be a negative charisma as in the case of Saul who was troubled by an evil spirit from the Lord,[2] or the less spectacular, positive charisma of kingship and authority in general.[3] In addition to the divine spirit that descends on a prophet, there is also the entry of other souls (*'ibbur*—'impregnation') or angels into the human soul, possession by demons or possession by a *maggid* manifesting himself through automatic speech:

> For the Holy Spirit can rest upon man . . .and this was the case with all prophets . . . and the opposite [of this positive charisma] is [the case of Saul where] 'an evil spirit troubled him'. Similarly man can be entered by another soul—a holy or an evil one—and similarly we have seen demons or evil spirits entering men and troubling them. . . . Similarly an angel may enter man *and speak within him words of wisdom and this is what is generally called maggid.*[4]

The identification of *maggid* with automatic speech is evident. Cordovero explicitly states that it is man himself who fits or unfits his soul for receiving the various charismatic influences, but nowhere suggests that the spiritual agent is man's own creation. The angels that manifest themselves as *maggidim* are therefore angels of the normal kind, though, of course, the angelic influence need not necessarily work in this particular way. Much depends on the specific part or faculty of the soul that receives the influx (*nefesh*, *ruaḥ*, or *neshamah*), and much on the hierarchical rank of the angel concerned.[5] Cordovero makes some very instructive and

[1] דרישות בעניני המלאכים, printed as an Appendix in R. Margalioth, *Mal'akhey 'Elyon* (Jerusalem, 1945). Cordovero's dissertation on angels is, as a matter of fact, part of his commentary on the *Zohar Shir ha-Shirim*; cf. the extract already published by Scholem (כתבי יד בקבלה, pp. 230–6) under the title פרקים על הקבלה המעשית מפירושו של ר׳ משה קורדובירו לזהר שיר השירים.

[2] 1 Sam. xvi. 14.

[3] Cordovero, loc. cit., p. 64: . . . כי דרך התלבש רוח אלהי באדם להיותו שר או מלך או נביא הכל ה״ס רוח אלהי יתלבש בו.

[4] Ibid.

[5] i.e. whether he is one of the Cherubim, Ḥayyoth, Ofannim, &c.

illuminating distinctions between various kinds of possession, inspirations, and intuition:

The angelic agent may enter his *neshamah*, coming from the sphere of the Seraphim, and influence his *ruaḥ*, *nefesh*, and body, and act on the latter and force it to speak words of wisdom. Then, when the angel departs, he will remember these things as if they had been told him by someone else.[1] This is so because they are [really] not his own but from a source beyond his own soul. Similarly the angelic agent, coming from the sphere of the Ḥayyoth, may enter his *ruaḥ* . . . or, coming from the sphere of the Ofannim, may enter his *nefesh*. . . . The manner by which the angel imparts his information is by compelling the body to speak these words; after his departure he [the recipient of the revelation] will understand them. . . . [Another type of illumination is by] Elijah entering the intellect of man and teaching him hidden things. In that case it will appear to man as if he had hit upon these things by himself, for the new insight will suddenly come into his mind. These angelic communications may be concerned with religious truths as well as with worldly matters, foretelling 'this shall happen and that shall not happen' and the like. It [the last mentioned type of manifestation of Elijah] comes in a hidden way, without the feeling of heaviness in the head[2] or ringing of the ears or ecstatic experience [?] as happens when the communication comes through a *maggid*, but it is as if one said something oneself. But the types of *'ibbur* depend on a man's moral and spiritual state, whether his soul is entered by a good soul (because he has done some good work) or an evil soul (because he has committed some sin) . . . or whether his *ruaḥ* is entered by a *ruaḥ* . . . or his *nefesh* by a *nefesh*. . . . The upshot of our enquiries is this, that it depends on man's actions whether he attains a very high level so that all divine influences descending upon earth rest upon him, according to the mystery of Metatron, the Prince of the World.[3]

Azikri and Vital are two contrasted and perhaps two extreme examples of sixteenth-century Safed spirituality, yet they may serve to indicate the variety and range of mystical life possible

[1] This seems to be an exact description of Karo's Maggid. The difference between this type of angelic revelation and illumination by Elijah (see below) thus appears to be in the degree of 'dissociation' of the manifestation of the objective psyche: a *maggid* is a message from the beyond, whereas Elijah is an intuition, viz. *Einfall*.

[2] Cf. below, p. 259.

[3] 'Prince of the World' does not, of course, have the pejorative connotation it has in the N.T. and Christian literature. On Metatron as the *Shekhinah* and agent of inspiration, cf. below, p. 271.

within the prima facie limited and homogeneous group of kabbalist saints. From a sufi-like abandon to the love of God, more reminiscent of Baḥya's *Duties of the Heart* than of the *Zohar*, to the thoroughly magical conception of *devekuth* as an active stimulation of the Holy Spirit, sixteenth-century kabbalism had room for the silent dialogue of the soul with the divine Beloved, and for the 'prophetic' illumination of the intellect with theosophical *gnosis*. The phenomenon of maggidism had a well-defined place in this context. It was a phenomenon frequent, not to say commonplace, enough to solicit the attention of every writer on mystical practice. Maggidism was not just a matter of occasional ecstatic or trance-like states; whole books and kabbalistic treatises were composed under such maggidic or prophetic inspiration.[1] Even writers of great speculative and theoretical powers were aware that other authors composed their works by different and more 'inspired' methods. Moses Cordovero records his conviction that the 'very awkward book'[2] *Berith Menuḥah* was inspired by the Holy Spirit,[3] and in his great work *Pardes Rimmonim* repeatedly quotes a 'book that speaks according to the mouth of the *maggid*'.[4] Cordovero may refer to a book written down, like Karo's *Maggid Mesharim*, after having been uttered first in automatic speech, or else he may have in mind a text composed through automatic writing.[5]

But whereas the phenomenon itself was generally known and accepted, the theory of maggidism varied slightly among different authors and groups.[6] Thus, as we have seen, for Cordovero it was a matter of divine or supernatural inspiration, whose nature and degree depended on the purity, holiness, and spiritual preparation of the recipient. According to Vital, *maggidim* are the spirits to

[1] Cf. above, p. 47, on the *Mal'akh ha-Meshib* and also above, p. 14, and below, p. 118, on Taytazak's *maggid*.

[2] Scholem, *MTJM.*, p. 146.

[3] Cordovero, loc. cit., pp. 9–10.

[4] Cordovero, *Pardes Rimmonim*, שער אבי"ע פ"ג, שער השמות פ"ב, שער פרטי השמות פ"ה.

[5] Are the quotations referred to in the previous note from the *Mal'akh ha-Meshib* or a similar source? Automatic writing seems to have been practised more than has been realized so far; for an interesting later example cf. M. Benayahu, *Rabbi H. Y. D. Azulai* (1959), pp. 289 ff.; also ibid., p. 563.

[6] For a later kabbalistic discussion of maggidism cf., for example, Elijah ha-Kohen ha-Itamari's *Minḥath Eliyahu* (Salonica, 1824), col. 4a ff.

which man himself gives birth by good works and holy thoughts. Since they are spirits and at the same time human creations, the degree of perfection, truthfulness, and dignity of these *maggidim* is relative and may vary from case to case. Their communications are mainly of an informative, discursive, and intellectual nature: foretelling the future and revealing kabbalistic teachings. The *Maggid Mesharim*, though ostensibly the record of communications by a typical *maggid*, contains no clearly defined theory of maggidism. Its underlying conception of maggidism seems to be vague and fluctuating. Yet, as we shall see, it fits in well with the general tenor of the more precisely elaborated theories of Vital and Cordovero, and constitutes a further interpretation, in kabbalistic terms, of a phenomenon that began to manifest itself with increasing frequency among Jewish mystics. Joseph Karo's Maggid was one of the first and certainly one of the most famous *maggidim* in the history of Jewish mysticism. Since both the modern psychologist and the Lurianic kabbalist would agree in regarding Karo as the creator and author of his Maggid, we may now turn to the life and history of the great kabbalist whose maggidic experiences form so puzzling and disconcerting a part of his biography.

5

THE LIFE AND TIMES OF R. JOSEPH KARO

I. EXILE

THE biographies of famous Jewish rabbis are rarely more than a thin cloth of hazardous combinations of guesses, wrapped round a meagre skeleton of assured fact. The 'literary' attitude in religious and spiritual matters that made for the prevalence of the book over its author[1] leads to the result that the historian who wants to reconstruct a medieval rabbi's *vita* is engaged on a jig-saw puzzle made up of occasional letters, stray indications, and incidental personal references in the writings and *responsa* of his hero and his contemporaries. In the circumstances great gaps are the rule rather than the exception, and contradictions abound. In the case of Joseph Karo the problem is both complicated and simplified by the *M.M.*, and much depends on whether the biographical information contained in the diary is accepted or not. In what follows the genuineness of the *M.M.* will be regarded as definitely established, and firm, albeit cautious, reliance will be placed upon the data it furnishes. It will be our endeavour to show that the biographical data contained in the *M.M.* are not only consistent with our other evidence but can actually be integrated with it, amplifying and illuminating the rest of our information. It goes without saying that the *M.M.* cannot simply be used as a source of historical and biographical information, for, however illuminating, it yet stands in need of illumination itself. As Mr. M. Benayahu has rightly stressed,[2] mystical diaries such as the *M.M.* or Vital's dream-book do not *report* facts but rather *interpret* them mystically for their authors. Very often, therefore, it is not so much a matter of culling facts from their pages, but of laboriously discovering the facts to which they allude.

[1] Cf. above, p. 1.

[2] 'R. Ḥayyim Vital in Jerusalem', *Sinai*, xv (vol. 30), תשי"ב, p. 69.

Joseph Karo was descended from a learned rabbinic family. Whether the family goes back to R. Joseph Kara of Toledo, who flourished about 1100, is doubtful.[1] However, the names of Joseph Karo's immediate ancestors are known to us, thanks to the signatures and other incidental allusions of his uncle Isaac Karo.[2] Isaac was the brother of Joseph's father Ephraim and not Joseph's grandfather as falsely stated by the printers on the title-page of the edition published at Amsterdam (1708) of the former's *Toledoth Yiṣḥaq*.[3] In a *responsum* printed at the end of his nephew's *Responsa ad E.H.*[4] Isaac signs his name as 'Isaac the son of Rabbi Joseph the son of Rabbi Ephraim Karo'. Since Joseph Karo usually signed his name Joseph b. Ephraim Karo, his grandfather Joseph must have had at least two sons: Isaac and Ephraim.[5] Of R. Ephraim we have little knowledge except for the fact that he was a scholar of standing, since both his brother Isaac[6] and his son Joseph[7] quote him in their writings.[8] It seems that Isaac survived his brother by many years. There was much halakhic correspondence between uncle and nephew,[9] and not only does Joseph Karo respectfully refer to his uncle as 'my master and uncle',[10] but the latter addresses his nephew with particular affection as 'my beloved son'

[1] Karo's descent from Joseph Kara, though mentioned by most authors, seems to have nothing but association of sound to support it.

[2] His most valuable biographical information is given in the Introduction to his *Toledoth Yiṣḥaq*; cf. n. 5 below.

[3] First edition, Constantinople, 1518. The mistake in the title-page of the edition published at Amsterdam, 1708, was then taken over by bibliographers; cf. Benjacob, *'Oṣar ha-Sefarim* (1880), p. 619, no. 140.

[4] Fols. 148a–152b. (All references are to edn. 1, Salonica, 1597.)

[5] According to Rosanes (op. cit., p. 242, n. 4) Joseph Karo quotes his grandfather once, in *B.Y. ad O.H.* 688: וראיתי להר׳ יוסף אבי אבי; but Greenwald (op. cit., p. 56, n. 16) shows that this is an error. The correct reading, as given in edn. 1 of *B.Y. ad O.H.* (e.g. Venice, 1550, f. 454a), is: וראיתי לר׳ יוסף אביו ז״ל. He is, however, quoted by Isaac Karo, *Toledoth Yiṣḥaq*, towards the end (portion *Vezoth ha-Berakhah*): ואבא מרי החכם הר׳ יוסף קארו זצ״ל אמר.

[6] e.g. *Toledoth Yiṣḥaq* (end of portion *Vayyesheb*): והשיב החכם ר׳ אפרים קארו אחי זצ״ל. Other references in Greenwald, op. cit., p. 56. On Isaac Karo see also Rosanes, op. cit., vol. i, pp. 95–100.

[7] References in Greenwald, loc. cit.

[8] According to Rosanes (cf. *'Oṣar Yisra'el*[3], vol. vii, p. 70, s.v. Nicopolis) he died as rabbi of Nicopolis; according to Sambari's chronicle he went to Palestine from Constantinople. There is no evidence for either statement.

[9] Cf. *A.R.*, nos. 47–48.

[10] מורי דודי; for references cf. Greenwald, loc. cit.

and the like.[1] Isaac Karo, who had lost all his children,[2] may well have looked on his nephew Joseph as another son.

From Isaac's introduction to *Toledoth Yiṣḥaq* it appears that the family hailed from Toledo in Castile, where Isaac stood at the head of an academy. Isaac moved his academy to Portugal a few years before the general expulsion from Spain. When Jews were forced to leave Portugal as well in 1498 he fled to Turkey. Sambari[3] mentions him among the Spanish Jews who settled in Constantinople. Even if Sambari's information is correct, it does not imply that Isaac stayed there permanently or that his nephew Joseph was with him. In the year 277 (= 1517 C.E.) Isaac Karo hurriedly prepared his book for print, as he was eager to depart for the Holy Land.[4] Whether indeed he got there[5] or where he lived and how long he lived we do not know. Rosanes's statement[6] that Isaac Karo was settled in Jerusalem by 1518 is based on a curious misinterpretation[7] of a quotation from Nahmanides in Isaac's *Toledoth Yiṣḥaq*.

The date of Joseph Karo's birth is usually inferred from the year of his death when, according to a family tradition reported to Conforti by Joseph's grandson Yedidyah Karo,[8] he was eighty-seven years old. Karo died, according to the postscript added to the Venice edition (1576) of Maimonides's *Mishneh Torah* with Karo's commentary *Kesef Mishneh*, on Thursday, 13 Nisan, 335, corresponding to 24 March 1575.[9] This makes 1488 the year of his birth. Whether he was born in Toledo[10] is not certain; it is, after all, possible that his father had moved to Portugal before the general expulsion just as Isaac had done.

The next certain date is provided by Karo himself, who states at

[1] See above p. 85, n. 9 (החכם הנעלה הבן יקיר לי . . . ודע בני היקר . . .).
[2] *Toledoth Yiṣḥaq*, Introduction.
[3] Op. cit., ch. 29.
[4] Author's postscript to *Toledoth Yiṣḥaq*: ולא היה לי פנאי עכשיו לעיין ולפשפש בזה כי היה דרכי נחוץ לילך לארץ ישראל אם יגזור ה׳ בחיים.
[5] Isaac Karo's settlement in Palestine is taken for granted by Rosanes, vol. i, p. 96, and vol. ii, p. 244; cf. *contra* the editor (E. Rivlin) of Frumkin's תולדות חכמי ירושלים, vol. i, p. 91.
[6] Op. cit., vol. i, p. 96.
[7] Ibid., n. 16.
[8] *Qore ha-Doroth* (ed. Cassel), p. 35b: ראשו כתם פ״ז.
[9] Conforti's date (ibid.) is 334 (= 1574 C.E.); cf. Azulay, *Shem ha-Gedolim*, s.v. Joseph Karo.
[10] Conforti, Azulay.

the end of his commentary *Beth Yosef* (*ad Y.D.*) that the work was begun in the year 282, i.e. 1522 C.E., in Adrianople.[1] The first thirty-four years of his life are thus a blank to be filled by conjectures. His early years were undoubtedly spent in the Iberian peninsula. The precocious child may still have seen and heard the great R. Isaac Aboab (1430–93) in Lissabon, and some lingering childhood memories may well be at the back of *B.Y.*'s references to the latter as *rabbenu ha-gadol*, 'our great master'. But whereas Karo's discipleship of Aboab is, at best, a figure of speech only, his relation to Aboab's most important disciple, Jacob Berab (*c.* 1474–1546), is more significant but also more obscure. Berab is always referred to as 'my master', but Berab was never in Turkey and came to Palestine via Fez and Egypt. When Karo settled in Safed about 1537, he was already a scholar of high repute and authority, and would hardly have entered into a 'disciple' relationship to Berab, though he might have begun to address him with the complimentary title *mori* in view of the ordination he had received at Berab's hands in 1538.[2] But Berab is already styled *mori* and *rabbenu ha-gadol* in early parts of *B.Y.* Unless we assume that these honorific phrases were added during the revision of the work (1542–54), Berab must sometime have been the principal teacher of the young Karo. The Maggid too once refers to Karo's 'teacher' in a communication that must be dated in the winter 1533 or 1536, i.e. before he settled in Palestine.[3] This teacher, it appears from the context, did not reside at the time in Palestine and it is therefore unlikely that the reference is to Berab; there is no way of knowing for certain whether it might apply to R. Joseph Fazi.[4] We do not know when Joseph Karo's family left Portugal, but Berab left at the age of eighteen (*c.* 1492)[5] to become rabbi of Fez. Afterwards he

[1] כי התחלתיו באנדרינופלי בשנת רפ"ב.

[2] This is Azulay's suggestion, loc. cit. On Berab's ordination cf. below, pp. 123 f.

[3] *M.M.* 68b, line 2: 'and if you write to Constantinople or to your teacher or to the sages in Palestine . . . .'

[4] On R. Joseph Fazi cf. Rosanes, op. cit., vol. i, pp. 82–83. Moses di Trani (*Responsa*, pt. i, n. 180) refers to him as his teacher, but there is no evidence that he was ever the teacher of Joseph Karo.

[5] Cf. Berab's letter printed in the Appendix 'On Ordination' at the end of Levi b. Habib's *Responsa* (Venice, 1565), f. 298.

settled in Egypt, where Jewish life and rabbinic culture flourished under the leadership of the *Nagid* Isaac Shulal.[1] Greenwald[2] suggests a solution of the puzzle[3] by proposing Egypt as the place where Karo became Berab's full-fledged disciple. The clue is provided by Karo himself in his contribution to the famous *shemiṭṭah*-controversy that had begun to shake the rabbinic world at regular intervals of seven years since 1504.[4] Karo's words[5] 'and in Egypt I beheld . . . that they observed the *shemiṭṭah*-year in 271 . . .' seem to suggest that about the year 271 (= 1511) he was in Egypt.[6] We do not know whether he came to Egypt from Turkey, where his family had settled in Constantinople, nor how long he stayed. But he does not seem to have spent the following *shemiṭṭah*-year (278 = 1518 C.E.) in Egypt, so that we may assume him to have been back in Turkey by that time. He may have settled in Adrianople in 1522, when he began work on the *B.Y.*, or earlier. It is generally assumed, however, that for some time at least Karo was settled in Salonica. This is not intrinsically impossible, as Salonica was the greatest and most vital Jewish centre after the metropolis Constantinople, and like a vortex drew scholars and rabbis from other parts of Turkey.

That Salonica was a scholar's paradise, amply provided with well-stocked rabbinic libraries, is confirmed by the Maggid who,

[1] Cf. above, p. 45, n. 5.

[2] Op. cit., pp. 59–60.

[3] Cf. also Azulay, loc. cit., and Rosanes, op. cit., vol. ii, pp. 242–3.

[4] Cf. M. Benayahu: תעודה מן הדור הראשון של מגורשי ספרד בצפת, in *Asaf Jubilee Volume* (1953), pp. 118 f., and the sources quoted there.

[5] *B.Y. ad H.M.* 67: וכן ראיתי במצרים ששנת השמיטה היא מקובלת שם שהיתה שנת הרע"א . . . ונראה שכך עלתה הסכמת כל החכמים הנזכרים שכך נוהגים בא"י ששנת הרצ"ט, שנת ש"ו ושנת שי"ג השמיטו.

[6] Mr. D. Tamar draws my attention to a passage in Joseph Solomon Delmedigo's מצרף לחכמה (Basel, 1629), fol. 25b: ומורי זקני הגאון הגדול כמוהר"ר אליעזר דלמדיגו זצק"ל כשחזר ממצרים ששם למד אצל הגאונים כמהר"ר יצחק בירב וכמהרר"י קארו ז"ל. It is, of course, possible that the reference is not to Joseph but to his uncle, Isaac Karo, for the point discussed by Delmedigo is precisely one upon which Isaac Karo touches in one of his few surviving *responsa* (quoted at the end of Joseph Karo's *Responsa ad E.H.* and in *B.Y. ad O.H.* 31, *s.v.* וחולו של מועד). It is a pity that Delmedigo contented himself with the initials instead of spelling out the full name. Mr. Tamar suggests that Isaac Karo is meant, since 'Isaac Berab' is an obvious misspelling or misprint; instead of writing כמהרר"י [= יעקב] בירב and כמהר"ר יצחק קארו he transposed the names.

while pressing Karo to proceed to Palestine without delay, yet permits him to visit Salonica first 'in order to correct your book'.[1] Definite evidence, however, of a prolonged sojourn in Salonica is meagre and it is always doubtful whether a particular documentary reference alludes to a passing visit or to a more permanent residence. Solomon b. Shemtob Attia[2] mentions Isaac Mar Ḥayyim, Solomon Alkabets, and Joseph Karo among the rabbis 'who had gone to Palestine from Salonica'.[3] A manuscript anthology of rabbinic commentaries and *novellae* by Spanish scholars who had settled in Turkey and Palestine quotes a saying of 'Rabbi Joseph Karo of Salonica'.[4] Salonica being the largest and most important Jewish community in Turkey, it is not impossible that many of the newcomers to Palestine were simply described as 'from Salonica'.

Clearly Karo may have stayed for some time in Salonica, but the corroborating evidence is ambiguous. Tam ibn Yaḥya mentions the '*ḥakham ha-shalem* Rabbi Joseph Karo' in connexion with proceedings before the rabbinic court in Salonica on 29 Sivan (= 1531 C.E.) and again the '*ḥakham ha-kolel* Rabbi Joseph Karo'.[5] Conforti[6] reports that he had documents (*haskamoth*) in his possession bearing the signatures of a number of Salonica rabbis together with Karo's. One of these is dated 293 (= 1533 C.E.). The most important evidence, however, is found on two undated tombstones in Salonica[7] commemorating (1) Isaac Karo and Yehudah Karo, the sons of Joseph Karo, and (2) Buena, the daughter of Joseph Karo. Against all this M. Benayahu[8] has adduced weighty

[1] *M.M.* 70a. 1; on the date of the communication cf. below, p. 106, n. 1.

[2] Commentary on Psalms (Venice 1549), Introduction.

[3] ואלה אשר הלכו משאלוניקי לארץ ישראל.

[4] MS. 219 of the Badhab collection, Jerusalem; cf. above, ch. 3, p. 27, n. 3.

[5] Tam ibn Yaḥya, *responsa Tummath Yesharim* (Venice, 1620), nos. 1 (f. 10a) and 33 (f. 23a).

[6] Op. cit., p. 35a.

[7] I. S. Emmanuel, *Les Grands Juifs de Salonique* (in Hebr.) (1936), nos. 101 and 102 (p. 80).

בני ציון היקרים
בני יוסף קארו יצ"ו
הה' יצחק [ו]יהודה
קארו נ"ע (קארו נ"ע)

מצבת היקרה
מרת בואינה נ"ע
בת מהר"ר יוסף
קארו יצ"ו

Cf. also the author's note, ibid., pp. 80–81.

[8] *Sinai*, xiv (vol. 28), תשי"א, pp. 190 f.

considerations to show that there must have been another Joseph Karo, rabbi in Salonica, to whom Tam ibn Yaḥya refers in his *responsa*. Also the signatures mentioned by Conforti as well as the tombstones are held by Benayahu to refer to this other Joseph Karo. The approbation to Abraham Treves Sarphati's *Birkath Abraham* (Venice, 1552), signed in 1532, is of course by our Joseph Karo, but there is no indication where it was written or signed. Rosanes's contention[1] that it was signed in Constantinople is without any foundation. In spite of Benayahu's reasoning, the evidence of the tombstones is disconcerting, since the *M.M.* contains an explicit reference to the death of Karo's wife, his two sons, and his daughter. Until a few decades ago epidemic diseases (cholera, typhoid fever, &c.) were fairly frequent, almost regular, occurrences in eastern countries. During one of these epidemics the Sabbath seems to have been Karo's black day, for the Maggid reminds him:[2] 'on this day you were punished with your son . . . for he died on a Sabbath, and [also] your older son lost his speech on a Sabbath day [before dying of his illness], and your first daughter [also] died on a Sabbath and likewise their mother died on a Sabbath, so that you have lost four [members of your family] by death.' The evidence is not conclusive, yet it would seem very curious if both Joseph Karos lost two sons and a daughter each. There is thus some probability that the epitaphs at least refer to Joseph Karo, the author of *Beth Yosef*.

There are other indications that Joseph Karo had been to Salonica. He seems to have known personally Joseph Taytazak,[3] Ḥayyim Obadyah,[4] and Solomon Ḥazzan[5]—all of Salonica and all co-signatories of the document mentioned by Conforti. It is, of course, possible that the acquaintances were made elsewhere. Taytazak resided in Constantinople for some time[6] and Karo's acquaintance with him was clearly cursory and probably made on a visit.[7]

[1] Op. cit., vol. ii, p. 251.
[2] *M.M.* 22a. 2.
[3] Cf. below, n. 7.
[4] Cf. above, p. 31, and below, p. 203.
[5] Cf. below, p. 124.
[6] Cf. Rosanes, op. cit., vol. ii, pp. 23–24.
[7] Rosanes, ibid., pp. 251–2. Cf. *A.R.*, no. 50: אחרי שזכיתי לחזות בנועם זיו יקרך . . . In addition to this correspondence with Taytazak (see also below, p. 177) cf. also MS. Ginzburg 322: חידושים ברמב"ם הל' שבועות מהר"י בירב וחידושי שבועות וחידושי חולין ששלח מהר"י טאיטציק להר"י קארו.

If Karo wished to visit Salonica in connexion with his work on *Beth Yosef*[1] he may have done so more than once. There are, in fact, indications in the *M.M.* of prolonged absences from home. On 9 Ṭebeth 296[2] (Sabbath, 4 December 1535 C.E.) the Maggid alludes to the sorrow that Karo's wife had suffered by his exile, i.e. absence from home,[3] and on 22 Shebaṭ 293[4] (Saturday, 18 January 1533 C.E.) the Maggid states that 'this is the first Sabbath since your return home'.[5] The date which I am inclined to assign to the last-quoted entry would agree well with Conforti's chronology based on the signatures of 1533. However, Benayahu's contention that the signatories were the official rabbis of the great congregations of Salonica and not visitors, however distinguished, cannot be lightly dismissed. If the maggidic communications to be discussed later[6] date from 1533, they would indicate a projected visit to Salonica; in that case the aforementioned entries can hardly refer to his recent return *from* there. At any rate Conforti's suggestion that the signature on his document implies that Karo 'passed through Salonica on his way to Palestine'[7] is definitely wrong as Karo was still in Nicopolis in 1535. All that we can safely surmise is that Karo had absented himself for longer periods from home. Whether his absences were due solely to scholastic requirements or whether ascetic piety also played its part is difficult to decide on the basis of the available material.

Apart from short visits to Salonica (and perhaps an early residence there ending with the death of his first wife and children), Karo's main places of residence between 1522 and 1537 were Adrianople and Nicopolis. Attempts to fix precise dates require such arbitrary reading of the available evidence that it is wiser to forgo them altogether. Conforti himself is not sure of the precise sequence and chronology.[8] We can be sure of only very few facts and dates. On Karo's own evidence the work on *B.Y.* was begun

[1] Cf. above, p. 89.

[2] *M.M.* 14a; the date is not in the text but is my suggestion, cf. below.

[3] הצער שנצטערה ע״י שגלית מאצלה.

[4] My date.

[5] *M.M.* 26b. 6.

[6] Cf. below, pp. 103 ff.

[7] Loc. cit.: ומזה נראה שהרב מהר״י קארו עבר דרך עיר שאלוניקי כשהלך לדור בא״י.

[8] Ibid.

1522 in Adrianople. After some time he moved to Nicopolis and Rosanes has assembled a number of valuable references—most of them, however, undated—to his residence there.[1] Part of Rosanes's evidence is unfortunately worthless, since references to Nicopolis in *B.Y.* do not always and necessarily imply that the text was written there. Karo certainly incorporated the results of his later reading and experience into the final text of *B.Y.* when he revised this *magnum opus* in the years 1542–54. It is thus clearly inadmissible to conclude from the description of certain shrubs as 'like unto those that grew near Nicopolis'[2] that Karo necessarily resided there in 1523.

In the summer of 295 (= 1535 C.E.) Karo was still in Nicopolis. Abraham Sarphati[3] writes that 'a Jew coming from Nicopolis' had brought him Karo's greetings but indicates in the same letter that Karo had previously been in Adrianople, where he, his brother-in-law Samuel Saba, and Sarphati had been in close personal contact. Towards the end of 1535, Karo again spent some time in Adrianople on his way to Palestine. An incidental brief reference to the beginning of his journey[4] makes no mention at all of Nicopolis, but a mere glance at the map shows that one would have to pass Adrianople on the way from Nicopolis to Constantinople, the port of embarkation for Palestine. Karo may well have tarried in Adrianople for a while.

The next certain date is 1538, when the famous Ordination Controversy took place. When Jacob Berab decided to renew ordination, Karo was one of the scholars chosen to be ordained by Berab before the latter had to flee from Safed. Karo probably arrived in Safed some time in 1536.[5] The document dated Sunday, 17 Elul 296 (= 3 September 1536 C.E.)[6] and printed in *A.R.*,

[1] Op. cit., pp. 246–9.
[2] *B.Y. ad O.H.* 215: כמו שגדלים בסביבות ניקופולי.
[3] Cf. exchange of letters in *A.R.*, nos. 12–14.
[4] *A.R.*, no. 73: ובבואי לארץ הלזו צפת תוב"ב מאנדרינופלא עברתי דרך קוסטאנטינה ליכנס בספינה.
[5] Cf. below, pp. 116 f.
[6] The document is quoted in Karo's *responsa A.R.* no. 124 as well as in the *responsa* of David ibn Zimra (pt. i, no. 177; ed. Venice, 1749, fol. 30b). The proceedings referred to took place before the rabbinic court of Safed on a Sunday (*resp.* David ibn Zimra: יום ראשון; *A.R.*: יום א'), but the date 15 Elul, given in the text of both Karo and ibn Zimra, fits neither the year 5296 (= 1536

no. 124, suggests, though it does not prove, as most historians erroneously thought it did, that Karo was in Safed towards the end of the summer 1536. The *responsum* obviously consists of two parts,[1] and the second part, which bears Karo's signature along with that of other Safed rabbis, merely refers to earlier court proceedings that had taken place still in Berab's lifetime in 1536. The judgement concerns a claim of Aaron Berab, 'heir of the late Rabbi Jacob Berab', and Jacob Berab, as we know, still conferred ordination in 1538 and died on the Sabbath, 18 Iyyar, 306 (= 1546 C.E.).

Even if we had no documentary evidence it would go without saying that Karo had married, or rather remarried, long before he moved to Palestine. Not only did rabbinic law insist on the fulfilment of the first biblical commandment 'be fruitful and multiply', but the rabbis left no doubt that the unmarried state was objectionable and ungodly—for halakhic, moral, and mystical reasons. Karo must have married at least[2] three times, for he mentions the names of Ḥayyim Albalag,[3] Isaac Saba,[4] and Zechariah Sechsel Ashkenazi,[5] each with the added honorific 'my master and father-in-law'. The order of marriages cannot now be determined. Rosanes's method[6] of establishing a chronology of marriages is vitiated by the gratuitous and unwarranted assumption of consistency of rule in the forms of epistolary address. If, for example, Samuel Saba is mentioned[7] without the addition 'my brother-in-law', or Zechariah Sechsel is quoted in 1665[8] without the title 'my

C.E.) nor 5301 (= 1541 C.E.), the latter being a possible alternative interpretation of the *gemaṭriah* שנת הצו"ר (cf. D. Tamar in *Tarbiz*, vol. xxv (1956/7), pp. 98–99). Even the misprint 16 Elul in edn. 2 of *A.R.* (Leipzig, 1859, fol. 114a) fits neither date. The correct date is, of course, Sunday, 17 Elul 1536. The mistake arose through the Sefardi habit of writing ט"וב instead of י"ז for the number 17; it is easy to see how this could have become ט"ו'. For a similar instance of corruption of the date ט"וב to ט"ו see Scholem, *Sabbatai Ṣevi* (1957), vol. i, p. 180 (Hebrew edition).

[1] Cf. the review of Rosanes's book by A. Tauber in *Kiryath Sefer*, vol. vii (1930), p. 344, where the signatures are dated 1546, soon after Berab's death.

[2] Cf. below, p. 112 f.

[3] Cf., for example, *B.Y. ad O.H.* 343, 368.

[4] e.g. *ad O.H.* 425.

[5] *A.R.*, nos. 29, 115.

[6] Op. cit., vol. i, pp. 107–9; vol. ii, pp. 38–39, 244–5.

[7] *Resp. E.H.*, end of *resp.* 1 (fol. 3*a*).

[8] Ibid., fol. 61a–b; the argument is even less conclusive if we consider that Karo does not quote a correspondence with his father-in-law but a court order of the Ashkenazi *Beth Din*.

master and father-in-law', this does not necessarily imply that at the time of writing family relations did not yet exist. As Karo was a Sephardi and therefore not subject to the rule of monogamy adopted by Ashkenazi Jewry, we cannot even be sure, though it is highly probable, that he only had one wife at a time. On the other hand it is certain that he married Zechariah Sechsel's daughter in Palestine, as the latter resided in Jerusalem and Safed but never, to our knowledge, in Turkey.

Before proceeding with Karo's career in Palestine we may now try to fill in the details of his life, and of his spiritual life in particular, before 1538.

The mental climate in which Joseph Karo grew up as a child and lived as an adult was determined by the severest trauma that medieval Jewry had suffered hitherto. The expulsion from the Pyrenean peninsula, the unspeakable sufferings that followed in its wake, and the growth of a new centre of Sephardic Jewry in the Ottoman empire have been described at length by chroniclers of the period as well as by later historians. Jewry's spiritual response to the catastrophe was no less profound and far-reaching. Under the impact of the events, kabbalism, hitherto the esoteric preoccupation of a spiritual aristocracy, developed new forms in which it became the dominant pattern of popular religiosity. Messianic expectations suddenly sprang to life and in combination with the new Kabbalah created a 'universe of discourse' in which extreme halakhic piety, ascetic mysticism, and a mystico-magical discipline for hastening the advent of redemption merged. The outlines of this development have been drawn in a masterly fashion by Professor G. Scholem;[1] the more practical and social side of it has been engagingly described in Schechter's perceptive essay on 'Safed'.[2] Yet it is important to realize that many of these accounts, focused as they are on sixteenth-century Safed, fail to do full justice to the gathering strength and impetus of mystical piety in the large centres of the Turkish empire. It is no doubt true that Safed was the flower and fruit of sixteenth-century Judaism; yet the budding growth took place in Salonica, Adrianople, Nicopolis,

[1] *MTJM.*, pp. 244 ff., and *Sabbatai Ṣevi*, p. 18 ff.

[2] Cf. above, p. 38, n. 1.

and perhaps also Constantinople. The pious brotherhoods that cultivated both mystical experience and kabbalistic speculation did not arise in Safed. They began to flourish in Turkey as the first symptoms of a religious and messianic revival of which the trek to Palestine was already a first result.

The intensity and urgency of the messianic yearning that animated the 'spirituals', stood in a strange contrast to the social chaos and disruption of the Jewish community. Diversity of ritual or of communal organization had presented no serious problem in the natural habitat of the Spanish communities; the strife of factions was a troublesome yet none the less permanent and perfectly normal part of the dynamics of group life. When the balance was upset by the general expulsion and the disorganized community had to try and readjust itself to new and strange surroundings, new tensions would arise and old ones would at times be felt more keenly. The disruption of the traditional organization did not do away with conflicts, parties, and factions, though it did do away with many of the established patterns of dealing with them. We must not be surprised, therefore, at finding contemporary literature teeming with indignant references to scandalous quarrels, conflicts, and jealousies. The exiles of different Spanish communities everywhere grouped themselves according to their places of origin, so that Salonica, Constantinople, &c., each had a number of distinct and independent Sephardi communities called Lisbon, Catalonia, Aragon, Castile, &c. In the circumstances communities could easily split on all kinds of issues, and drastic measures had to be taken to prevent disgruntled individuals from simply leaving their community and requesting admission to another.[1] The prevailing atmosphere of anarchy and chaos must have been particularly painful to those who, for one reason or another, held unity and some measure of ritual uniformity to be indispensable prerequisites for any kind of improvement.

Karo's scheme for bringing about unity of ritual practice was, in a way, more ambitious than any previous attempt at codifying

[1] Cf. Rosanes, op. cit., vol. ii, pp. 34–36, on the great quarrel in Adrianople in which Karo took sides against Aaron of Trani. Similar quarrels and conflicts are found in great number in the *responsa* of all contemporary rabbinic authors.

rabbinic law. He did not want to compose a mere code (like Maimonides), but a complete, critical, and systematic survey or digest of the whole *corpus* of halakhic literature. For this reason he chose to cast his work in the form of a commentary on Jacob Asheri's *'Arba' Ṭurim.*[1] The latter, unlike, for example, Maimonides, had already summarized in his code the most important and relevant conflicting opinions, so that his text could serve Karo as an ideal basis for a thorough and complete survey of the whole rabbinic literature. Karo's reasons for undertaking the work are clearly stated in his Introduction:

As the days passed and we were poured from one vessel into another [i.e. exiled from place to place] . . . and troubles came upon us until, because of our sins, the prophecy was fulfilled 'and the wisdom of his sages shall be lost',[2] and the *Torah* and her students are powerless, *for the Torah is now not like two laws but rather like many laws*[3] because of the many books explaining its rules and ordinances. . . . Everyone writes a book for himself, repeating what someone else had written before or ruling the opposite of what his colleagues have written.[4]

In 1555 Karo could look back with justifiable satisfaction on his achievement, the *House of Joseph* (*B.Y.*), 'in which I have included all laws occurring in halakhic literature . . . with their sources in the Babylonian and Palestinian Talmuds, *Tosefta*, *Sifra*, *Sifre*, *Mekhilta*, commentators, and codifiers . . . and every law fully explained therein.'[5] Throughout the long period of work on *B.Y.* the Maggid repeatedly encouraged Karo, promising him that his *magnum opus*, once finished, would become authoritative in Israel.[6] Karo began work on the *B.Y.* in 1522 in Adrianople,[7] one of the greatest and most flourishing Jewish centres in Turkey. There he also got involved in the violent controversy around Rabbi Yomtob ha-Kohen, as a result of which[8] he left the city and

[1] Cf. Karo's Introduction to *B.Y.*

[2] Ibid. The quotation is from Is. xxix. 14.

[3] Cf. also *M.M.* 59b. 3: ומשום דברבוי השופטים ירבו המחלוקות ונמצאת תורה כאלף תורות ומש"ה כתב כי יפלא ממך דבר וגו'. Here the identity of Karo's motives in participating in the renewal of ordination and in writing the *B.Y.* reveals itself clearly.

[4] Ibid.

[5] From the introduction to *Sh.A.* (*Y.D.*, *E.H.*, *H.M.*) (Venice, 1565), omitted in the later edition.

[6] Cf. *M.M.* 34a, 47b. 2 *et passim.*

[7] Cf. above, p. 87, n. 1.

[8] According to Rosanes; cf. above, p. 95, n. 1.

moved to Nicopolis. At any rate we may assume Karo to have been settled in Nicopolis in the early thirties of the sixteenth century.

During this period two events profoundly and decisively affected Karo's life. The one was the death of Solomon Molkho, the other his meeting with Solomon Alkabets. That Karo was a kabbalist we may take for granted for the simple reason that practically every rabbi at the time was a kabbalist. The line of division must not be drawn between kabbalists and non-kabbalists, but rather between scholars who specialized in kabbalistic speculations and practices and those who simply accepted Kabbalah as the esoteric tradition of Israel but for the rest devoted most of their time and energy to *halakhah*. Yet even the latter would dabble quite frequently in Kabbalah[1] or devote to it at least part of their time.[2] Solomon Molkho was an all-out kabbalist, not of the speculative but rather of the visionary and apocalyptic kind.[3] Molkho's arrival in Salonica seems to have caused a stir, we might almost speak of a 'revival', in the circle of pious scholars and kabbalists around Joseph Taytazak. Molkho's famous epistle[4] written in Monastir and recounting his visions was addressed to Taytazak, and his *Sefer ha-Mefo'ar*[5] was composed in response to a request by 'the brethren in Salonica'. We do not know whether Karo ever met Molkho. The alleged references in the *M.M.* to such a meeting allow of a different interpretation,[6] though there is no inherent impossibility or improbability about the assumption that they actually met. What is beyond doubt is the profound and lasting impression made by the martyr's death. All contemporary records testify to the winning charm of the young visionary enthusiast. The Jewish career of the brilliant young marrano courtier from Lisbon was short and meteoric. Having met the messianic adventurer David ha-Re'ubeni

[1] Cf., for example, below, p. 242, for a kabbalistic explanation by Jacob Berab, whose reputation was certainly that of a halakhist only.

[2] Cf. *M.M.* 20b. 1, 21a, 24b. 2, 33a. 1, 36a. 3, 57b. 2, 58a–b, 64a. 1, 68a. 1, 70b. 4.

[3] Cf. Scholem, *Sabbatai Ṣevi*, pp. 18–19.

[4] Printed under the title חית קנה (Amsterdam, 1658?), cf. ibid. p. 2a: ענין המראה אשר כתבתי מעיר מונישטריאו למוהר"ר יוסף טיטסה יצ"ו.

[5] Salonica, 1529: למען אחי ורעי הנאהבים היושבים בסאלוניקי הדורשים ממני לשלוח להם איזה דרוש על דרך האמת.

[6] Cf. below, pp. 103 f. and 107–8.

in 1525, he performed the operation of circumcision upon himself and was henceforth visited by dreams and visions. As is well known, some of his predictions came to pass exactly at the appointed time, e.g. the overflow of the Tiber in 1530 and the earthquake in Lisbon, 1531. After escaping from Portugal (*c.* 1526) he spent some time in Turkey before proceeding to Italy on his ill-fated mission. Imprisoned by order of Charles V and sentenced to death by the Inquisition, he was burned at Mantua in 1532, eight years before the date that he had predicted for the advent of the Messiah. Molkho's ascetic piety and feverish messianism found a congenial reception in Salonica. It is not impossible that his activity actually inspired the later maggidic manifestations in Taytazak and Karo. In Karo's mind Molkho's death at the stake assumed the significance of a coveted privilege and supreme realization, and throughout the *M.M.* the Maggid repeats the promise[1] 'and thou shalt be privileged to rise as a burnt-offering before me and to be burned for the sanctification of my Name'.[2] The profound psychological roots of this desire of martyrdom become even more evident when we realize its practical improbability. Ambitions of this kind could be entertained with a reasonable chance of fulfilment only under the dominion of the Cross. The prospect of being martyred and burned in an *auto-da-fé* for the 'Sanctification of the Name' was practically nil under the rule of the Crescent.

The dependence of Karo's fantasies on Molkho's fate is borne out by the one passage in the *M.M.*[3] where the Maggid, summing up all Karo's ambitions, explicitly refers to Molkho:

> Behold what thou hast attained and what degree thou hast reached, that [words] are spoken through thy mouth the way I speak in thee. I shall make thee worthy to be *publicly burned in Palestine*, to sanctify my name in public, and thou shalt rise as a burnt offering to my pleasure on my altar and thy sweet savour shall rise as frankincense . . . and thine ashes shall be heaped on my altar to my pleasure. I shall privilege thee also to finish thy book to illuminate thereby the eyes of Israel, for all wise men and scholars and sages shall draw from thy work which is [to be] called the *House of Joseph*; they shall be filled with the fatness of thine house, your springs will flow to all directions . . . and your

[1] On its psychological significance cf. below, p. 151.

[2] *M.M., passim.*

[3] Cf. below, pp. 99–100.

name will be mentioned in synagogues and houses of study. Wherever thou shalt be mentioned in the house of study, the sweet savour of your ashes shall rise like frankincense. Behold what thou hast attained [so far] and what thou shalt still attain by publicly sanctifying my Name. Even so Solomon my chosen one, who is called Molkho, was anointed with a great and supernal anointing and rose on my altar to my pleasure. You likewise shall go up. . . . Lo, I am the Mishnah speaking in your mouth, kissing you with kisses of love and embracing you, for it is in the shadow of my wings that thou restest thy head. 'My glory is on thee and thy glory is on me, my splendour is on thee and thy splendour is on me, I shall not forget thee and thou wilt not forget me, neither in this world nor in the world to come'.[1]

The possible dates of this revealing entry are 1533, 1534, and 1537; the temptation is great to prefer the former date—the year after Molkho's death.

Solomon Alkabets too was an 'inspired' type. A disciple of Joseph Taytazak in Salonica, it is almost certain that he had met Molkho and participated in the revival initiated or at least intensified by the latter. A sufficient quantity of his literary output, homiletic and kabbalistic, has survived to give us an idea of his spiritual outlook. His mystical life, including intuitive revelations of kabbalistic doctrines, has been described by his disciple and brother-in-law Moses Cordovero in his account of their joint *gerushin*.[2] In 1529, after the composition of his commentary on Esther,[3] Alkabets married and left Salonica for Palestine. Part of his belongings he shipped straight to Palestine, but he himself travelled via Adrianople and, probably, Nicopolis, where he tarried for some time.[4]

As the relationship between Karo and Alkabets and the influence of the latter on Karo are of paramount significance for an understanding of the Maggid, it will be necessary to examine the matter in some detail. We may assume with practical certainty that almost all references in the *M.M.* to 'Solomon my beloved one' or

[1] *M.M.* 65a. The last words well illustrate the identification of the *Shekhinah–Mishnah* with the Oral Law (cf. below, pp. 268 f.), since they are taken from the traditional formula recited after finishing the study of an order of the Mishnah or of a tractate of the Talmud.

[2] Cf. above, pp. 51 f.

[3] *Menoth ha-Levi* (printed Venice, 1585); cf. Introduction, ibid.

[4] Cf. below, p. 108 f., and the quotations above, pp. 19–20, n. 5.

'my chosen one' allude to Alkabets.[1] Solomon is mentioned by the Maggid in connexion with kabbalistic speculations of the kind indulged in by Alkabets, Cordovero, and their circle. The corroborating proof-texts are admittedly missing since most of Alkabets's specifically kabbalistic writings, containing his own speculations and liturgical innovations and 'intentions' (*kawwanoth*), are lost. On the other hand we know from the *Sefer ha-Mefo'ar* the type of kabbalism Molkho applied himself to: apocalyptic speculations and eschatological calculations by means of *gemaṭriah* and the like. Whatever Molkho's interest in purely theoretical Kabbalah may have been, it was always mingled with eschatology. Moreover, most of the maggidic communications mentioning Solomon imply that the latter was still alive, yet they also contain the promise of martyrdom on a burning pyre, i.e. they presuppose Molkho's death. On one occasion the Maggid recalls to Karo a prayer formula against evil thoughts which 'my beloved Solomon' had taught him and continues: 'I shall privilege thee to go to Palestine and to be united with my beloved Solomon and the [other] brethren, and thou shalt study and teach [there], and afterwards I shall privilege thee to be burned in their presence.' These and similar utterances evidently refer to Alkabets and to his propaganda for the settlement in Palestine of the kabbalistic brotherhoods that had begun to form in Salonica and Adrianople. He seems to have proceeded to the Holy Land in the early thirties, waiting for his friend to join him there.

The entry from which the last quotation was taken begins with an observation of 'my beloved and pious Solomon' concerning some detail of the doctrine of sefiroth.[2] On another occasion (which I date Saturday, 18 November 1536 C.E.)[3] the Maggid refers to an opinion concerning the *Kaddish*-doxology, advanced by 'Solomon my beloved one'. The point is more fully dealt with

[1] And not to Molkho, as assumed by Graetz throughout (cf. op. cit., p. 546; also D. Kahana in *ha-Shaḥar*, vol. iv, p. 75, n. 6). The one exception is the reference discussed above, p. 97. Already S. P. Rabinowitz (loc. cit.), Schechter (loc. cit.), and others had perceived that 'Solomon' occasionally referred *also* to Alkabets. My contention is that it does so exclusively. [2] Cf. below, p. 198.

[3] *M.M.* 9b; the date is established by the Maggid's promise 'to go to Palestine *this year*' and by the fact that in 5297 Sabbath *Toledoth* fell, in fact, on 4 Kislev; cf. below, p. 179.

elsewhere.[1] Here we are merely concerned with the probability that the Maggid's polemic refers to views expressed by Alkabets in one of his lost liturgical writings, probably his *Shomer 'Emunim* devoted exclusively to expounding the significances of the response 'Amen'. The Maggid concludes his communication with the words[2] 'and if thou writest to Solomon my chosen one, inform him of these teachings [i.e. criticisms of his view]'. Elsewhere the Maggid discusses the mystical intentions (*kawwanoth*) to be meditated when reciting the *Shema'*,[3] and criticizes Solomon's views on the subject. What appears to be an instance of repressed jealousy of Alkabets's inspiring and almost charismatic kabbalistic authority emerges incidentally and quite by the way when the Maggid promises to Karo that his wife would bear him a son 'whose heart will be more open to kabbalistic wisdom than [that of] my beloved Solomon,[4] so that everyone will marvel at his wisdom'.[5]

There are, as a matter of fact, also a number of definite and demonstrable points of contact between the teachings of the Maggid and Alkabets's extant writings.[6] Mention has already been made of Alkabets's *responsum* to Karo,[7] who had asked his friend for an interpretation of a passage in the *Zohar* dealing with the question why Jacob and Joseph died outside the Holy Land yet were buried in it, whereas Moses was not even buried there. The relation between the lengthy *responsum* of Alkabets and the Maggid's short indications on the same subject[8] is evident: both present the same interpretation of the *Zohar* and Rekanati.[9] An even more

[1] Cf. below, p. 179.

[2] *M.M.* 10b. 1.

[3] *M.M.* 69a. 1: ומאי דאוליף לך שלמה בחירי. The most probable date for this communication is 1536.

[4] The scribe of B 1, obviously at a loss about the identity of this Solomon, adds הוא רש"י (*sic*).

[5] On the passage and its psychological context cf. below, p. 119; and also the quotation below, p. 126.

[6] This, of course, is an obvious truism for those who hold, with S. J. Rappaport (cf. reff. above, ch. 1, p. 4, n. 2), that Alkabets was the real author of the *M.M.*

[7] Preserved in many manuscripts and printed at the end of Alkabets's commentary on the Passover-Haggadah *Berith ha-Levi*, Lemberg, 1863.

[8] *M.M.* 65a, 65b–66a.

[9] Cf. *Zohar*, vol. i, pp. 21*b*–22 and also Moses de Leon's *responsum* on the same subject in 'Kabbalistic *responsa* of M. de Leon', ed. by I. Tishby, in *Kobez Al Jad*, vol. v (xv) (1950), pp. 24–30.

striking example is provided by Alkabets in his commentary on the Passover-Haggadah.[1] In the course of his exposition of the proper *kawwanoth* of the ritual of the Passover night, Alkabets discusses the contradiction between the views of Rabbi Yiba in the *Zohar* (iii. 95b) and of Baḥya b. Asher concerning the mystical significance of the statutory four cups. According to the *Zohar* they symbolize the four sefiroth *Neṣaḥ*, *Hod*, *Yesod*, and *Malkhuth*, whereas Baḥya holds them to indicate the Tetragrammaton, i.e. the sefiroth *Ḥokhmah*, *Binah*, *Yesod*, and *Malkhuth*. Alkabets in his commentary quotes the solution proposed by 'the greatest sage of our generation, the *ḥasid* Rabbi Joseph Karo', and it is only by reference to this quotation that the Maggid's cryptic remarks on the same subject[2] become intelligible. Incidentally Karo's solution clearly betrays its dependence on his specific teaching concerning the procession of the sefiroth.[3]

Combining our assumption that in the early thirties Karo was settled in Nicopolis with our certainty that Alkabets had left Salonica for Adrianople, on his way to Palestine, at about the same time,[4] we may further assume that the two either met or renewed their former acquaintance in Nicopolis. The evidence for this assumption is of wider significance than may appear at first sight, for it may throw new light on the development of the kabbalistic community in Safed and of the devout brotherhoods there.

[1] Fol. 24b.

[2] *M.M.* 40b. 3

שלום רב לך ששמת שלום בין הסברות דכסא קמא רמיז ליו"ד דאיהי בחכמה דמשפע בחסד ומניה לנצח, וכסא תניינא רמיז לה"א דאיהו בינה דמשפע לגבורה ומיניה להוד, וכסא תליתאה רמיז לתפארת המתעלה בכתר ומשפע ביסוד, וכסא רביעאה רמיז בה' אחרונה דאיהי מלכות.

Berith ha-Levi, 24b

וגדול הדור החסיד מהר"ר יוסף קארו נר"ו הסכימם באופן אחר, ידוע כי הנצח הוא ענף מהחסד וחסד נמשך מחכמה, והוד ענף מפחד ופחד נמשך מבינה, ויסוד ות"ת אחד באחד ידובקו, ולפי"ז הר' בחיי נקט ראש ור' ייבא נקט סוף, וא"כ יש לכוין בכוס ראשון בחכמה ולהמשיכה עד נצח, ובשני לבינה ולהמשיכה עד הוד, ובג' לת"ת ולחברה ביסוד ובד' במקומה זהו דעתו.

[3] Cf. below, pp. 193 f.

[4] Cf. above, p. 99.

On Tuesday, 30 Adar i (1533 or 1536 C.E.)[1] the Maggid communicates the following message:

How glorious is this day, 'God, terrible out of thy holy places' [Ps. lxviii. 35], which is in the great city whither thou hast written concerning my beloved Solomon, so that they shall be as one in my hand *they and the brethren in Salonica.* You are all exalted before God and He is sanctified by you. And through you the *ekklesia Israel* [a kabbalistic technical term for the *Shekhinah*] will be raised and lifted up. This is the meaning of Scripture [Am. v. 2] 'the virgin of Israel [i.e. the *Shekhinah*] is fallen, she shall no more rise', signifying that she will not rise of herself but through [the efforts] of those who raise her up and unify her with her Beloved [i.e. with God under the aspect of the sefirah *Tif'ereth*]. Wherefore write unto them 'let your hands be strong'. And all that he [they?] have written to you in the name of the Redeeming Angel is true; for although you were not supposed to leave during the first year after your absolution [from what?], yet why did you not proceed to Israel [immediately] afterwards? For although there were wars at the time, *you might have stayed at Adrianople* until they were over and you would have benefited the community there. Nevertheless, your guilt is not heavy, nor is it for that reason alone that the blessing of children was withheld from you, though it was a contributory cause. Yet also here [you did some good, for] you taught the Law, and moreover people are ashamed of sinning in your presence. Concerning that which was said to the Redeeming Angel that it [what?] must needs be done at the specified time and place, [this does] not [imply] that you should tarry there on any account, but merely that on your way to Palestine you should pass there and stay there for a short while, *and many will repent from their sins through you* and thereafter you shall proceed to Palestine. And if you want to go to Salonica first in order to correct your book, do as you please, for it is not with regard to this that it [the aforementioned message] was given to the Redeeming Angel but only that you should not settle there. Likewise I charge you to be careful not to settle anywhere but to proceed to Palestine.

Even a cursory reading of this remarkable text permits a number of important conclusions.

1. Karo was still in Turkey at the time, but neither in Salonica ('if you want to go to Salonica first') nor in Adrianople ('you might have stayed in Adrianople for some time'). We may, therefore,

[1] *M.M.* 70a. 1. The only possible years fitting this date are 5293 and 5296, which were both leap years.

assume the maggidic message to have been communicated in Nicopolis.

2. Karo wrote letters of recommendation introducing Solomon to the 'great city'. This great city is certainly not Salonica, for 'they [of the great city] *and* the brethren in Salonica are all exalted before God'. That Adrianople deserved the title of a 'great city' and even of a 'metropolis in Israel', and was in fact so described, has already been proved from Alkabets's *responsum*.

3. The communication is mildly eschatological in its tenor, inasmuch as its message concerns the fate of the divine *Shekhinah*, who is to be redeemed and exalted and reunited with her divine Bridegroom by the pious exercises of the kabbalistic brotherhoods.

4. The text implies the existence of such brotherhoods in the great centres of Salonica and Adrianople. It appears that Karo was in contact with both and, more particularly, that Solomon was one of the prime movers of their mystical enthusiasm. We may venture the guess that Solomon Alkabets, after leaving the kabbalistic circle round Taytazak in Salonica, proceeded to Adrianople via Nicopolis.[1] Karo provided him with letters of introduction to the kabbalists in Adrianople where Alkabets's arrival seems to have occasioned a wave of revivalist enthusiasm with all the concomitant charismatic manifestations ('God, terrible out of thy holy places'). The *Shekhinah* herself now confirms the benefits she derived from the concerted efforts of the two distant yet spiritually united brotherhoods of ascetic mystics.

5. Some choice members of these brotherhoods used to receive celestial messages and revelations. Taytazak's *maggid* will be discussed later.[2] In our text the agent of revelation is described not as a *maggid* but as the 'Redeeming Angel'.[3] This angel, appearing to Alkabets or some other member of the Adrianople group,

[1] Cf. also below, p. 107.

[2] Below, p. 264.

[3] The identification of the agent of revelation (*maggid*) with the *Shekhinah* is discussed below, pp. 266 f. As this identification is almost a matter-of-course from a kabbalistic point of view, we need not be surprised at the appearance of the Redeeming Angel here, since the latter had been identified with the *Shekhinah* since the beginnings of Spanish Kabbalah; cf., for example, the commentary of Nahmanides *ad Gen.* xlviii. 16.

transmitted messages concerning Karo which were passed on to him in Nicopolis.[1] Karo's Maggid confirms the general tenor of the Redeeming Angel's instructions.[2]

6. Karo had contemplated going to Palestine at an earlier date but had postponed his journey. On his way he would have had to pass through Adrianople, where he might have tarried for a while. The wars referred to are probably not so much Sultan Soliman's campaigns to capture Vienna (1529–30 and 1532) as the Venetian attacks on the Turkish and Greek coast during that period. Exploiting Soliman's fighting elsewhere, Venice embarked on an active maritime warfare, capturing such coastal centres as Patras and Lepanto (1532). Sea communications were extremely perilous and plans to sail to Palestine from Turkey would obviously have to be abandoned in view of the attendant danger. Already Rosanes[3] suggested that Karo's first, abortive attempt to go to Palestine should be dated 1531–2. Forced by the wars to give up his plans, he proceeded to Salonica (1532–3)[4] and then returned to Nicopolis. Even if we do not accept the detail about the visit to Constantinople, it stands to reason that the Maggid refers to events in 1532. This would also agree well with the dates of Alkabets's movements. Alkabets's visit, some time between 1529 and 1530, aroused Karo's desire to go to Palestine. His failure to implement this decision even after 1532[5] and his continued stay in Nicopolis provoked the Redeeming Angel's censures. The following tentative chronology of events suggests itself: Alkabets arrives in Nicopolis probably in 1530 and causes a kind of 'conversion' in Karo,[6] who decides to go to Palestine after one year ('though you were not supposed to leave during the first year after your absolution'). By the time the year was over, in 1532, travelling had become dangerous, yet Karo should have begun implementing his decision by at least moving to

[1] The printed editions read וכל מאי שכתב לך, meaning Alkabets or some other correspondent; some manuscripts read מאי שכתבו, referring to the brethren in Adrianople generally.

[2] וכן אני אומר לך.

[3] Op. cit., pp. 250–1.

[4] Rosanes accepts the evidence for Karo's sojourn in Salonica at that time, since his sole interest is to prove that he could not have been there during Molkho's lifetime.

[5] היית מתעכב . . . עד עברם.

[6] Cf. the quotation below, p. 107.

Adrianople ('for although there were wars, &c.'). But now the time had come for finally striking his tents. The Maggid's words prove that Karo was toying with the idea of (again?) visiting Salonica.[1]

7. For the last years Karo had been childless. The question why his children had died[2] and why God did not grant him new offspring kept him busy more than once.[3] The tenor of the Maggid's words suggests that childlessness was a thing of the past and that —at the very least—Karo was now entitled to expect offspring.[4]

8. The Redeeming Angel also seems to have charged Karo with a mission, the nature of which our text does not disclose. Something had to be done at a specified time and place 'and many will repent from sin' as a result of it. Here one cannot help thinking of Molkho, who proceeded, like Nathan of Gaza in the seventeenth century, on a mysterious and mystical mission to Rome and of whom it was also said that 'he made many repent from sin'.[5] Karo, it appears, was supposed to discharge his task on his way to Palestine; where (Constantinople? Egypt? Rome?) it is impossible to say.

The essentials of the entry of 30 Adar i, as analysed here, are also borne out by a communication dated only four days later, Sabbath, the 4 Adar ii.[6] The opening words of this maggidic communication will be quoted in another context;[7] they sufficiently

[1] Of the two possible dates of this entry, 1533 and 1536, the former has the apparent advantage of being closer to the events referred to. On the other hand the Venetian war was not over until 1534 at least (Battle of Lepanto), so that Karo could be justly reproved for not proceeding to Palestine only as from 1535. My own feeling is that Karo's final resolve (1536) to leave Nicopolis and to travel, via Adrianople, to Palestine, stirred up memories of the beginning of his friendship with Alkabets and the first formation of their joint plans. This would account for the contents of the maggidic messages at this particular moment.

[2] Cf. above, p. 90.

[3] Cf. *M.M.* 70a. 1; cf. also below, pp. 113 f.

[4] שגרמה in the past tense.

[5] Cf. the remark in the diary of the famous sixteenth-century *shethadlan* Joselman of Rosheim (in 'Journal de Joselman', *R.E.J.*, vol. xvi (1888), p. 91): בשנת רצ"ב . . . בא האיש לועז גר צדק המכונה ר' שלמה מולקא נ"ע בדעות חצוניות . . . והוליכו [הקיסר] עד עיר בלונייא שמה נשרף על קדוש השם דתות ישראל ורבים הסיר מעון. The same is also said by Azikri (op. cit., pt. vii, ch. 2) of Isaac Luria.

[6] *M.M.* 68a. 3 ff.

[7] Below, p. 187, n. 2.

prove that Karo was residing at the time neither in Palestine nor in Constantinople. The three major centres of Turkish Jewry being ruled out by the joint evidence of the three entries, all the odds are in favour of Nicopolis. In the course of his exhortation the Maggid refers to a serious illness that might have been fatal[1] but for the intercession, on Karo's behalf, of the great scholars in heaven whose works Karo discussed and expounded in his *B.Y.* Turning to more specifically kabbalistic matters, the Maggid quotes 'Solomon my chosen one',[2] but later reverts again to more personal affairs:[3]

Heaven watches over you for your good. At the time when you were ill many [celestial] advocates but also many accusers rose against you, as I already told you;[4] for on that night of *Simḥath Torah*, when you were very ill, your [death-]sentence was passed, but the Ancient of Ancients [i.e. God in his highest aspect of pure mercy] revealed himself in the splendour of his whiteness [i.e. mercy] and had compassion on you, because of the merit of the *Mishnah* that you had studied during your illness. Thereafter you were enlightened as to how to come close to His fear, and *He made Solomon my chosen one come across your path to see whether you would recognize him.* Verily it is accounted to you as a merit that you made his acquaintance and learned from him to fear me.[5] You also wrote good things concerning him to the great city where he went, so that the holy brethren [there] were stirred to return to their Lord, and this merit is imputed to you for he [Solomon] acted on your initiative.[6] Because they studied *Torah* from your mouth they [now] illuminate you and you illuminate them and [both of] you [together] illuminate the holy brethren in the metropolis of Israel and they [of the metropolis] illuminate [both of] you . . . and I shall privilege you to be burned for the holiness of my Name, so that you will be shining and radiant in the world to come.

It is easy to see why the last reference to Solomon should have been misunderstood as an allusion to Molkho:[7] somebody is providentially crossing Karo's path, he is 'recognized' as a vessel of

[1] Cf. below, p. 149.
[2] Cf. above, pp. 99–100.
[3] *M.M.* 69a. 2.
[4] Cf. below, p. 149.
[5] This is probably a reference to Karo's 'conversion'; cf. above, p. 105, and below, p. 150.
[6] Here the translation is not quite certain; perhaps it means 'acted with your help and co-operation': דאתערו דילך עביד.
[7] Cf. Graetz, op. cit., p. 546.

grace, teaches Karo the 'fear of the Lord', is provided with letters of recommendation, and causes a spiritual revival in the 'Great City'. However, in spite of the applicability of some phrases to Molkho, there is nothing in the whole entry militating against the assumption that 'Solomon' signifies Solomon Alkabets. Alkabets, one of the most 'inspired' members of the Salonica circle of kabbalists, came to see Karo on his journey to Palestine and found him recovering from a severe illness and possibly from a no less severe spiritual crisis. The meeting produced a kind of 'conversion' in Karo: an intensification of his mystical life and the resolve to participate fully in the kabbalistic-ascetic revival propagated by Alkabets. The eschatological character of Alkabets's propaganda is evident from his pre-occupation with the fate of the *Shekhinah* and from his urgent calls to proceed forthwith to the Holy Land.

What is quite certain is that already at that time three different kabbalistic centres were in existence, illuminating one another in a kind of mystical communion. The one is the place of Karo's residence (Nicopolis), the other the 'great city' to which Solomon repaired with Karo's recommendation (Adrianople), and the third is the 'metropolis in Israel' (Salonica). Whatever the ultimate verdict on the identity of Solomon, it is beyond any doubt that Solomon did *not* go to Salonica but travelled *from* Salonica, via Karo's place of residence, to Adrianople.

The discovery of the existence in Turkey of organized or at least gradually crystallizing devout brotherhoods on the pattern known to us from Safed, sharing common ascetic practices and entertaining similar mystical and eschatological ideals and expectations, permits us to see in a new light certain statements contained in Alkabets's famous *Shabu'oth* Epistle,[1] to which insufficient attention has been paid so far.

The epistle presents the closest possible identification of the *Shekhinah* with the Maggid. The celestial voice speaking through Karo introduces itself in unmistakable terms as the very *Shekhinah*. She praises her pious sons for raising her up from the depths of abject exile by their devotional and ascetic exercises. Exactly as in the communication preserved in the approbation of the Jerusalem

[1] Cf. above, p. 19 f. and notes ibid.

rabbinate[1] or in the aforementioned entry in the *M.M.*,[2] the *Shekhinah* expresses her satisfaction with the efforts of her sons and responds, on her part, with 'mighty promises and the revelation of esoteric teachings',[3] viz. with 'many more [revelations] of this [esoteric] Science and many great promises'.[4] The brethren are greatly moved by excessive joy on the one hand and by pity and sorrow for the *Shekhinah* on the other, bursting into tears at hearing her plaintive voice 'like the voice of a sick woman beseeching us [to help her]'.[5]

In the Jerusalem approbation the *Shekhinah* actually refers *to* the *Mishnah* and speaks *through it*. In the Epistle (as in the *M.M. passim*) the identity is brought out even more explicitly:

> Hearken, my pious friends, my dearly beloved, peace be with you, blessed are ye and blessed are they that bore you, both in this world and in the world to come, for that you have taken upon yourselves to crown me in this night. It is many years since the crown fell from my head and there is none that comforteth me; I am thrown in the dust, embracing dunghills. But now you have restored the crown to its former glory. Therefore be strong my friends, be of good courage, my beloved, rejoice and be glad, and know that you are of the exalted few that are privileged to belong to the 'Palace of the King'.[6] . . . *Behold I am the Mishnah that correcteth man,*[7] *I have now come to speak to you . . . and you have been exalted* [*this night*] *and I have been exalted* [*likewise*] *this night through you and through the brethren in the great city, the metropolis in Israel.*

The analogy with the communication in the *M.M.* is evident. Not only is the *Shekhinah* exalted, but also 'you and the brethren in Salonica are all exalted before God'.[8] The Epistle too bears out our contention that similar kabbalistic circles or brotherhoods existed in the various Turkish centres. The *Shabu'oth* vigil in Karo's house was not the first of proceedings of this kind. On the

[1] Cf. above, pp. 18–19. [2] Cf. above, p. 103.

[3] הבטחות עצומות וגילוי רזי תורה (cf. above, p. 19).

[4] Epistle: רבות כהנה וכהנה מעניני החכמה וכמה הבטחות גדולות.

[5] Ibid.: וכולנו געינו בבכיה מרוב שמחה וגם בשמענו את צרת השכינה בעונותינו וקולה כחולה המתחננת אלינו.

[6] A common kabbalistic metaphor for high mystical achievement.

[7] A favourite phrase with the Maggid; cf. below, p. 267.

[8] Cf. the quotation above, p. 103.

contrary, we must assume that Alkabets and his circle had already established this liturgical innovation in Salonica and that Alkabets subsequently introduced it wherever he came. The significant feature of the vigil in Karo's house is the keen awareness of the participants that they were in full spiritual communion with the brethren in Salonica, engaged on the same liturgical and mystical devotion.

The Epistle is obviously addressed to Salonica. Alkabets's main complaint to the addressees is that they had kept the vigil only during the first night of *Shabu'oth* whereas in Karo's house they had watched both nights of the feast:

> Awake ye, my brethren, be strong and of good courage, rejoice in the service of our Creator. But behold, it appears from the Maggid's words[1] in the first night that all or some of you also foregathered [in the same fashion], for thus you were mentioned. But in the second night you were not mentioned [by the Maggid], wherefore . . . take these things to heart.

The Epistle next holds Karo's decision to join Alkabets's project of settling in Palestine as a tempting bait in front of the Salonica brethren: 'for it was promised in the last vision that the *ḥasid* [i.e. Karo] and I shall merit to dwell in the [Holy] Land.' Alkabets indicates that he does not intend to return to Salonica again; the Epistle therefore ends with the hope that he and the brethren would meet again on 'holy ground', i.e. in Palestine, there to serve God with united strength.[2]

Although the general tenor and message of the Epistle is apt to rouse the suspicion that it is a typical fabrication of the kabbalistic propaganda that emanated from Safed,[3] yet both the internal evidence and the agreement with the *M.M.* strongly argue in favour of its genuineness. It remains true, of course, that the Epistle is propagandistic in its intentions. Alkabets sent it to Salonica in order to encourage the brethren to follow his example; he did not

[1] Incidentally we learn that Alkabets already described this type of charismatic manifestation by the technical term *maggid*; cf. below, p. 265–6.

[2] ויזכני להתאחד עמכם על אדמת הקדש לעובדו שכם אחד.

[3] Liturgical innovations (ותקנו תקנות רבות) with the purpose of sharing the exile of the *Shekhinah* and thus hastening redemption, appeals to leave the diaspora and settle in the Holy Land, &c.

include in the Epistle the actual kabbalistic revelations of the Maggid which, as he indicates, he set down in a special tract to be forwarded separately.[1]

The date of this extraordinary public manifestation of the Maggid presents an interesting problem. There is a strong presumption in favour of an early date, soon after Alkabets's departure from Salonica. The Epistle mentions manifestations on the two nights of *Shabu'oth*, and a third manifestation on the following Sabbath.[2] As *Shabu'oth* never falls on Thursday–Friday, the manifestations cannot have occurred on three consecutive days. If we assume *Shabu'oth* to have fallen on Wednesday–Thursday,[3] we can easily imagine the mood of enthusiasm and exaltation to have persisted to the following Sabbath. The only years that would fit this scheme are 1530 and 1534, with the balance of probability perhaps in favour of the earlier date.

One further point emerges from a comparison of the Epistle, the Jerusalem approbation, and the *M.M.* The strikingly emphatic and emotional urgency with which the *Shekhinah* is mentioned, the solicitude for her fate, and the appeal to come to her rescue are typical of Alkabets's mysticism and of those early maggidic messages that betray Alkabets's influence: the Epistle and the *M.M.* entries quoted above. We are, I think, entitled to reckon the Jerusalem approbation as belonging to the same group. The internal differences between the three texts are of minor importance. In the Jerusalem approbation and in the Epistle the *Shekhinah* speaks in the first person; the Epistle also has the explicit identification *Shekhinah–Mishnah*. In the *M.M.* the Maggid speaks *about* the *Shekhinah*, as elsewhere he speaks about the *Mishnah*, in spite of the fact that he is identical with both *Mishnah* and *Shekhinah*.[4] Even the Epistle is not quite consistent in its usage, for the manifestation of the second night is reported as follows: 'hearken my beloved . . . blessed are you that exalt *me*; how greatly are ye exalted . . . blessed are you and blessed they that bore you, fear ye not the reproach of men, neither be ye afraid of their revilings,

[1] Alkabets mentions a קונטרס and refers the brethren to it: ובקונטרס ההוא תראו.

[2] וגם ביום השבת חזר הדיבור אל החסיד.

[3] There is, of course, no compelling reason to do so.

[4] Cf. below, pp. 266 f.

for ye are raising *Keneseth Yisrael*' (i.e. the *Shekhinah*, but now referred to in the third person). This is again very similar to the wording in the *M.M.*: 'through you *Keneseth Yisrael* shall arise and be lifted up.' Alkabets's preoccupation with the fate of the *Shekhinah* and his habit of inventing devotional practices for her sake have already been illustrated by examples from the 'Book of Exile-wanderings', particularly by Cordovero's report of the sudden, i.e. 'inspired', innovation of walking with bare feet as a token of participation in the exile of the *Shekhinah*.[1]

We may now return to the salient events of Karo's inner and outer life as reflected in the *M.M.*

On the Sabbath, 9 of Ṭebeth (probably 1536 C.E.), the Maggid reveals to Karo the secret of the *gilgul* of his *two former wives* (!). The revelation itself is lost but it is referred to again by the Maggid one week later, on Sabbath, *Vayyeḥi*, 16 Ṭebeth (s.t. *Vayyesheb*):[2]

I have revealed to you on the last Sabbath the secrets [of the incarnations] of your two former wives and I now come to reveal to you the secret of this your third wife. You must know that in her past [transmigration] this woman was a male,[3] a virtuous rabbinic scholar but stingy with money—not spending it on charity—and also stingy with his wisdom, refusing to teach others. Therefore he was punished to transmigrate into a female, measure for measure: he did not want to pour out blessing [material and spiritual] on others . . . therefore he is now incarnated in a female [which is the purely receptive principle]. . . . Therefore you will also observe that she is very charitable [i.e. unconsciously engaged on the *tiqqun* of her soul][4] and also greatly loves you because you spread *Torah* to others both by writing books and by teaching. Because these things are her *tiqqun*, therefore she loves you.

There are good reasons for dating this entry in Karo's Turkish period.[5] The inference is that Karo had married for a third time

[1] Cf. above, p. 52.

[2] *M.M.* 14b. 2; the ascription to the portion *Vayyesheb* does not correspond to the true date which is Sabbath *Vayyeḥi*; cf. Appendix A, § 2.

[3] Psychoanalysts would think here of latent homosexual tendencies.

[4] Cf. below, p. 240.

[5] Cf. the following entries of 23 Ṭebeth, 1 Shebaṭ, 15 Shebaṭ, &c. (pp. 114 ff.), with their references to Nicopolis, going to Palestine, &c. Since Graetz (op. cit., p. 299) it has been customary to identify the three wives indicated by this entry with the three wives known to us from Karo's halakhic writings (cf. above, p. 93). But if my analysis of the dates is correct, then this view is no longer tenable.

still *before* he went to Palestine. The reference to writing and teaching clearly has in mind the *B.Y.* and Karo's well-attended *yeshibah* in Nicopolis.[1] Moreover, it appears from the sequel that Karo had been married to this (third) wife already for some time, but had not been blessed with offspring although his wife had borne children in a former marriage. Now, apparently, his wife was pregnant. According to kabbalistic doctrine souls too are male and female, though it is not necessary that they also inhabit bodies of the same 'sex'. However, procreation requires the co-operation of two souls, as of two bodies, of the opposite sex. We may now follow the Maggid's further exposition:

Since she is a male soul she is not really your mate;[2] you received her as 'ownerless property' [i.e. not as your true, predestined partner]—like the daughters of Shilo to the children of Benjamin.[3] Because her soul is essentially a male soul [and so is yours], she could not produce offspring for you. If you object [and ask] how then could she bear children to her first husband, know that his soul contained female sparks; since [in that case] both the male and the female principles were present, they could have children although it was the wrong way round. . . .[4] And this is the reason for the delayed pregnancy of your wife, for both your souls are male and only now have female soul-sparks been added to her [soul] so that she can conceive of you. She merited this by her good works and *by the anguish she suffered whilst you were away from her*[5] and also by the anguish she suffered when nursing you during your illness.[6]

The only question that remains is whence, i.e. from which 'soul' or 'root', derived the feminine sparks that had now descended on Karo's wife. The Maggid has an answer also to this problem:

Behold, these sparks have now come to her from the soul of your [real, predestined] mate [which is, by definition, an essentially female soul]. However, until now it was not possible [for your real mate to emit soul-sparks of her own soul into that of your present wife] because

[1] Cf. *A.R.*, no. 14: כי אין לי פנאי בסבת למוד החברים יצ"ו בבקר ובערב וקביעות למוד לעצמי כי עתותי ורגעי ספורים יום ליום ולילה ללילה ואיני יכול להתעסק בדבר אחר כי אם כמתעגב.

[2] The real, predestined mate obviously has a soul of the 'opposite' sex. On the question of the 'real' mate in cases of multiple marriages (widows or widowers remarrying) cf. *Zohar*, vol. ii, 102b.

[3] Cf. Judges xxi.

[4] There follows the application of this doctrine to the stories of Judah and Tamar and of Ruth, as well as to the initial barrenness of Sarah; *M.M.* 13b–14a.

[5] Cf. above, p. 91.

[6] *M.M.*, 14a.

she [i.e. your real mate] was married to another man and was widowed only now. By her [i.e. your wife's] aforementioned merits some sparks emanated from her [i.e. from your real mate, recently widowed] to your wife . . . and therefore she can [now] bear you male children as I have promised you.

This amazing revelation raises more psychological problems than it can possibly answer. It appears that although Karo was married for the third time, he 'knew' that not his present wife but another, only recently widowed, woman was his real, mystical mate. His unconscious and repressed relationship to this woman is such that he ascribes to her influence the occurrence, at last, of the long-hoped for pregnancy of his wife.

The same subject is taken up again by the Maggid one week later, on Sabbath *Shemoth*, 23 Ṭebeth, s.t. *Lekh Lekha*:[1]

On the previous Sabbaths[2] I revealed to you the secret of the *gilgul* of your [former] wives, but now I shall reveal the secret of this [your present] wife, who she is, so that you may recognize God's mercy and lovingkindness in dealing with you and in giving you so worthy a wife. For I have already informed you [last week] that she was a virtuous rabbinic scholar; but once you know *who* she was in her former existence you will be overawed. You will honour her greatly and be ashamed of having intercourse with her for carnal pleasure. You should know, you should know—and thus he [the Maggid] continued for more than an hour, pausing and then repeating 'you should know', as if he hesitated to tell me. Finally[3] he said: The Holy One Blessed be He has sent me to inform you and to let you know how great a gift he has bestowed upon you.

The following lines are so obscure (or corrupt?) that they defy an intelligible rendering. This awkward and possibly intentional obscurity need not surprise us, as the Maggid solemnly enjoins on Karo:

You must not reveal this matter . . . to any man but to whom I shall give you permission, neither must you write it down in such a manner that others can read [and understand] it. You already know that she has

[1] *M.M.* 7a. 1; Sabbath *Shemoth* is the correct date. The ascription to *Lekh Lekha* is misleading; cf. below, Appendix A.

[2] Reading שבת״יא for שנ״יא.

[3] On the Maggid's hesitant stammering cf. below, pp. 261–2.

lived twice before[1] and that in her second existence she was a miser . . . transmigrated this time in order to receive punishment and to be perfected through you. You are fortunate in that through her you will be privileged to have male children and to teach *Torah* orally and in writing. She too will acquire merits, for through the money that she brought you and through her serving you you will be privileged [enabled?] to teach *Torah*. . . . You are fortunate that you were found worthy of using such a holy vessel.[2]

The Maggid seems to be mainly interested in increasing Karo's reverence and esteem for his wife. The other themes touched on in the earlier entries are again hinted at, but in a way that deliberately leaves everything in the dark. Karo's treatment of this whole intimate subject incidentally throws much light on the psychological background of the composition of the *Sefer ha-Maggid*. Karo's revelations came to him as *speech* and not as *automatic writing*. Nevertheless, he committed all maggidic communications to paper and the Maggid repeatedly enjoined upon him 'be careful to write down everything I tell thee',[3] or 'be careful to write them down in a book'.[4] Karo seems to have neglected this injunction at times, for we find the Maggid upbraiding him 'and write down everything I tell thee and do not neglect it as thou hast done'.[5] 'He reproached me for not writing down everything I was told.'[6] The special instructions given in the entry of 23 Ṭebeth show that, although Karo's intimate diary was not meant for publication, yet the writer reckoned with the possibility (or probability?) of others reading it. If certain matters concerning his wife were to be kept secret, then they had to be veiled beyond the comprehension of outsiders, but they could not be omitted altogether: everything had to be written down.

On the next Sabbath, 1 Shebaṭ, s.t. *Va'era*[7] the Maggid continues the same theme when opening his communication with the words: 'I have informed you of the mystery of your *gilgul* and that of your wives, as well as of the mystery of your present

[1] Cf. below, pp. 239, 244, on the kabbalistic idea that three *gilgulim* are the normal rule.

[2] This is a talmudic idiom for the widow of a saintly scholar; cf. b. *B.M.* 84b.

[3] *M.M.* 70b. 4. [4] Ibid. 16a. 5. [5] Ibid. 61b. 4.

[6] Ibid. 6a–b, 29b. 2.

[7] This time the attribution to the weekly portion is correct.

virtuous wife, so that you should know how greatly to honour her.' If our assumption that his wife was pregnant is correct, then we can understand not only why the subject of his wife's personality and of her relation to him loomed large in Karo's mind, but also why the Maggid now goes on to remind Karo of the death of his first wife and her children.[1] By now, however, all Karo's sins, even those of previous existences, were atoned for and forgiven, 'and by this woman with which I favoured you, you will have saintly sons'. In the same communication the Maggid informs Karo: 'You see that this city of Nicopolis is condemned, etc. [to be destroyed or to suffer in some other way?], because she lacks in charity and the study of *Torah*. Therefore arise and remove your home from that place and also advise your father-in-law[2] to remove his home and his possessions from there.' Rosanes[3] refers to troubles in Nicopolis about 1536. The Maggid's words 'you see' seem to indicate that in fact some kind of trouble had broken out. If my dating of the whole series of entries in 1536 is correct, then we have further confirmation of our proposed chronology: in spring or summer 1536 Karo left Nicopolis with Palestine as his ultimate destination. On the way he tarried a year or so in Adrianople and then boarded ship in Constantinople.[4] Perhaps we may also assume that the troubles in Nicopolis were regarded as a 'sign' which precipitated the decision to move to Palestine.

Another maggidic communication of the same period may be the entry of Sabbath *Beshallaḥ*, 15 Shebaṭ.[5] The entry contains the Maggid's longest and most systematic exhortation to persevere in a life of extreme mortification and is as such a valuable contribution to Karo's moral and ascetic theology. We incidentally learn that Karo enjoyed wide authority and general popularity, a fact that caused him much spiritual anxiety because it rendered the practice of humility more difficult: 'And above all He [God] gave thee favour in the eyes of all the people so that they praise thee; therefore

[1] Cf. above, p. 90.

[2] Graetz, op. cit., p. 545, who misinterprets 'son-in-law', wrongly dates the entry before 1522, and emends to 'Adrianople'. All this is, of course, unnecessary; cf. below, p. 121.

[3] Op. cit., pp. 74–75.

[4] Cf. the quotation above, p. 92, n. 4.

[5] That the entry can be dated on a Sabbath *Beshallaḥ* is proved by the phrase בפרשתא קדישתא דא; cf. Appendix A, § 2.

humble thyself exceedingly. . . .' Again the Maggid promises 'and I shall privilege thee to go to Palestine and be united with Solomon my beloved and with the brethren; thou shalt study and teach . . . and make many repent from sin[1] and thereafter I shall favour thee to be burned for the sanctification of my Name as already promised'.[2] A few weeks later, Sabbath, 20 Adar i,[3] the Maggid again confirms that 'I shall privilege you to ascend the Mount of Glory'.[4]

The last entries, with their reference to an impending departure from Nicopolis and their mention of Solomon, the brethren, and Palestine, are a kind of prelude to the communications of Tuesday, 30 Adar i, and of Sabbath, 4 Adar ii, already discussed earlier.[5] We may conjecture that the decision to leave Nicopolis and to proceed to Palestine stirred up precious memories in Karo's mind of one of the most decisive and significant encounters of his life. The arrival of Alkabets, the revival that followed it, the original plans to go to Palestine abandoned because of the Venetian war—all these became real again as Karo set out to be 're-united with Solomon and the brethren . . . on the Mount of Glory'.

In the circumstances it should not surprise us that the following weeks witnessed a spurt of intensive maggidic activity, embracing halakhic, kabbalistic, and personal interests. Unfortunately many entries are badly dislocated in the extant text, and even parts of single communications have been torn apart in the course of transmission. The text has to be pieced together again before we can hope to interpret it correctly. On the Sabbath *Vayyiqra*, 11 Adar ii,[6] the Maggid expounds the superiority of being burned to all alternative forms of martyrdom.[7]

Two days later, on the Fast of Esther, the significance of this fast and of the reading of the Scroll of Esther on *Purim* are explained.[8] The Maggid goes on to praise Karo's mystical life, for 'I come to delight myself with thee and *to speak in your mouth*, *not in*

[1] Cf. above, p. 106.
[2] *M.M.* 25b (last lines).
[3] Sabbath *Ki Thissa'*; the full text of the communication is given *sub* 2 Sam. x (*M.M.* 66a–b). A fragment of the beginning is repeated s.t. *Vayyaqhel* (*M.M.* 35a. 3); for the second paragraph ibid., cf. below, p. 132, n. 6.
[4] i.e. to go to Palestine; a favourite metaphor with Alkabets.
[5] Above, pp. 103 f.
[6] *M.M.* 38a. 4; the year is probably 1536, though it may well be 1533.
[7] Cf. below, p. 153.
[8] *M.M.* 33b–34a.

a dream but as one speaketh to one's friend'[1] and then discusses Karo's halakhic studies of the previous day.[2] The next communication,[3] probably a day or two later, again harps on the subject of martyrdom at the stake, continues the previous halakhic discussion,[4] and reverts to some of the themes that we already found to have been uppermost in Karo's mind at the time: the fall of the *Shekhinah*,[5] the promise to go to Israel ('and I shall privilege you to go up to Palestine and to study and to teach . . . to distinguished disciples who will be there craving your instruction . . . and you will also be privileged to make sinners repent . . .'), and the praise of his maggidic manifestations: 'You have attained that which only the chosen few attain, that you should be spoken to *in this fashion*. As for the great man in Salonica—his name is Rabbi J. T. —one [i.e. the celestial messenger] does not speak to him *in this fashion* because of his covetousness.' Later[6] the Maggid takes up the same theme again:

Consider the privilege granted to you, for the great man Rabbi J. T. is not spoken to [by a *maggid*] as you are, because of his covetousness and lust for authority. For although by virtue of his scholarship and saintliness, as well as for having deserved well of his community by raising many disciples, he should have merited maggidic speech and to attain what great sages have not attained for many generations, yet his covetousness prevents it. And if you see him, you may tell him so in order that he may repent.

Rabbi J. T. of Salonica seems to be none other than Joseph Taytazak,[7] and I have already suggested[8] that the latter's *maggid* may have been a case of automatic writing and not of automatic speech. Karo is assured that maggidic speech, i.e. divine words spoken 'face to face' ('*in this fashion*'), is superior to the charismatic phenomena of others. The final suggestion 'and if you see him'

[1] Cf. Ex. xxxiii. 11, Num. xii. 6–8; the Maggid clearly echoes some of the most highly regarded attributes of the prophecy of Moses. Cf. below, p. 269.

[2] i.e. his commentary *B.Y. ad Y.D.* 198; cf. below, pp. 170–1.

[3] *M.M.* 34a–b.

[4] *Ad Y.D.* 199; cf. below, p. 171.

[5] Again referred to, here, by the Maggid in the 3rd person!

[6] *M.M.* 34b. 2.

[7] The identification was already proposed by S. R. Rabinowitz, op. cit., p. 234; cf. also below, p. 264.

[8] Above, p. 14; cf. also above, p. 82.

may serve as further confirmation of our surmise[1] that during those weeks Karo was toying with the idea of visiting Salonica, where, of course, he would have met Taytazak.

The Maggid also discusses family affairs:

> You have done well to marry a virtuous and good wife who is a scholar's daughter. But know that your son will have a somewhat ugly face and bad eyes. He will be very poor, but his heart will be open to study *Torah* [i.e. he will be a great scholar]; for that reason he will not be completely blind, so that he should be able to study *Torah*. In kabbalistic knowledge he will far exceed my beloved Solomon, so that all the world will marvel at his great wisdom, and his heart will be prepared to fear me. And as for thy wish, etc.,[2] [that he should have good eyes . . . and be rich, I am prepared to grant it to you; but know that in that case he will be dull of understanding and utterly incapable of studying *Torah*. . . . . I know that you would rather have him be a sage, though it involve ugliness and bad eyes. If you really want him to be beautiful and rich, say so at night at the time of prayer; but if you choose wisdom for him you need not say anything].

Karo, in spite of his profound conviction of his own greatness, seems to have given up all hope of equalling Alkabets as a kabbalist. But the son would realize his father's ambitions. With our deficient knowledge of all personal details concerning Karo, Alkabets, and their respective families and circle it is idle to speculate on the significance of the price of wisdom, to be paid in terms of ugliness and bad eyes.

A few days later the Maggid again discusses halakhic matters.[3] On [Thursday], 1 Nisan 1536, the Maggid signifies his approval of Karo's last additions to *B.Y.*[4] and begins the important series of kabbalistic expositions in which Karo's doctrine of sefiroth is expounded.[5] The communication contains a polemical reference to Ḥayyim Obadyah,[6] adding 'if you meet him, tell him to retract'. As in the case of the similar reference to Taytazak,[7] the advice may be connected with Karo's plans of visiting Salonica. The next

[1] Cf. above, pp. 88–89, 90–91.

[2] All editions merely have 'etc.'. The original text, given in square brackets, is preserved in the Group B manuscripts (cf. Appendix B).

[3] *B.Y. ad Y.D.* 201; cf. below, pp. 172 f.

[4] Cf. below, pp. 175.

[5] Cf. below, ch. 9.

[6] Cf. above, p. 31, and below, p. 203.

[7] Cf. above, p. 118.

kabbalistic communication[1] may be dated Sabbath *Tazri'a*, 3 Nisan; it is followed by more revelations on the same subject on Sunday, 4 Nisan,[2] Monday, 5 Nisan,[3] and Tuesday, 6 Nisan.[4] In fact, the last five entries appear as one continuous series in some manuscripts.

There is no means of deciding whether the communications of *Rosh ha-Shanah*, dealing with one of Karo's most significant dreams,[5] should be ascribed to the New Year days of 5297 (= Saturday–Sunday, 16–17 September 1536 C.E.). If we accept this date, then the Maggid's promise that 'for the sake of your fast on that holy day you shall be favoured with a male son *this year*, and I shall privilege you to go up to my holy mountain' may refer to the aforementioned pregnancy as well as to the now final plans to go to Palestine. On Sabbath *Toledoth*, before embarking on his polemics against Alkabets's teaching concerning the *Kaddish*-doxology,[6] the Maggid again impresses on Karo the magnitude of God's grace, 'for although there are also others who know the six orders of the Mishnah [by heart?], yet He does not speak to them as he speaks to you, even though you know that you have committed graver and more serious sins than they', and promises him 'and I shall favour you to go up to Palestine *this year* to be united there with the *Torah* and to rejoice with the brethren . . . and whatever shall be doubtful to you [in your studies], four-winged angels shall [visit you and] teach it to you'.

By now Karo was probably already in Adrianople and the preparations for his journey were well under way. On Friday, 19 Adar, the Maggid assures him, after the usual exhortations and promises of martyrdom, that 'I shall favour you to go up to Palestine, for *there is no hindrance and no danger* . . .'. In fact, the wars with Venice had completely subsided and sea routes were safe again.

On Friday, 4 Nisan, the wedding took place of Karo's daughter, Tammah.[7] As a result of the celebrations Karo overslept the

[1] Preserved by *SHeLaH* only; cf. above, p. 34. [2] *M.M.* 5a–b.
[3] Ibid. 6a; the entry also contains a further reference to *Y.D.* 201.
[4] Ibid. 5b. 2. [5] Cf. below, p. 183. [6] Cf. above, p. 100.
[7] *M.M.* 77b.

following morning (Sabbath *Vayyiqra*) and is upbraided but also forgiven by the Maggid, who reassures him: 'I shall privilege thee to go to Palestine, to be united with the brethren . . . to raise many disciples and make many repent. Thereafter I shall favour you to be burned for the sanctification of my Name.' We may remember that an earlier entry[1] had mentioned the death of two sons and 'your first daughter'. Karo's other daughter thus married in Turkey shortly before her father left for Palestine. The most probable date for this entry is 1536 (Nicopolis). In the former case Karo would have had a son-in-law in Nicopolis, and Graetz's emendation of 'your father-in-law' (*hothankha*) to 'your son-in-law' (*hathankha*), though unnecessary, is at least not impossible.[2]

Some time in 1536 Karo went to Palestine, arriving in Safed just in time to be involved in one of the most interesting, albeit abortive, rabbinic enterprises of the sixteenth century.

[1] Cf. above, p. 90. [2] Cf. above, p. 116, n. 2.

6

THE LIFE AND TIMES OF R. JOSEPH KARO II. THE HOLY LAND

By the time Karo arrived in Safed,[1] this insignificant Galilean village had developed into a flourishing Jewish centre and was on the verge of becoming the Mecca of Jewish piety. Scholars and saints from Salonica, Adrianople, and other centres of the Sephardi diaspora were joined by pious men from Ashkenazi countries—Germany, Poland, Moravia, &c. Messianic expectation was rife. The traumatic shock of the expulsion had yielded the vision of Israel's suffering as merely a reflection of the sufferings of the divine *Shekhinah*, and the firm resolve to atone for all sin and imperfection by penitence, mortification, and mystical meditation. By exemplary ascetic piety Israel would render itself worthy of the advent of the Messiah, and the *Shekhinah* too would be raised from the dust.[2] One of the fruits of this religious fermentation was the bold attempt of R. Jacob Berab, the leading halakhic scholar of the age and Karo's teacher,[3] to renew rabbinic ordination.

According to rabbinic *halakhah*, as in most developed legal systems, knowledge of the law is not sufficient to administer it. The jurist has to be invested with due authority, in virtue of which his power formally derives from the ultimate source of sovereignty recognized by his society. Jewish law had evolved the notion of a kind of 'apostolic' succession beginning with Moses, who was invested by God himself and who subsequently laid his hands on Joshua. Every ordained 'judge' could pass on ordination to others, and only ordained judges could constitute a 'Synhedrion' or any other kind of valid court. The chain of succession was imagined to pass through Joshua, the Judges and Prophets, the 'men of the Great Assembly',[4] and the rabbinic teachers of the mishnaic and

[1] Cf. Schechter's essay referred to above, p. 38, n. 1.
[2] On the eschatological character of the new Safed piety cf. above, pp. 58 f.
[3] Cf. above, pp. 87–88.
[4] Cf. *M. Aboth* i. 1.

talmudic periods. Some time, in the early Middle Ages, this chain had broken off. Knowledge of the Law remained unimpaired,[1] and even the practical application of the Law was, to some extent, unaffected, since Jews everywhere voluntarily accepted rabbinic jurisdiction. The practical integrity of rabbinic jurisdiction in the diaspora was actually safeguarded by most governments, who granted a large measure of internal autonomy to the Jewish minority group. But from a formal point of view the Law was, as it were, floating in the air, without the ideal legal basis for its administration. Moreover, certain parts of the Law can, in fact, only be administered by properly ordained judges. In theory at least, though not in practice, the situation was somewhat similar to that in which the Church would find itself if all bishops were to drop dead at once. The hope of living again the full life of *Torah*, with all that this implied in terms of the new kabbalistic mysticism, gave a very precise meaning to the prophetic promise[2] 'I will restore thy judges as at first . . . *afterwards* thou shalt be called the city of righteousness, the faithful city'. The prophecy clearly meant the restoration of ordination, and ordination itself was now seen in an eschatological perspective. In fact, it appeared as a necessary condition for the advent of the Messiah.

How could ordination be renewed, *ex nihilo* as it were, without divine intervention and by purely human initiative? The great Maimonides had suggested a possibility:[3] if all rabbis assembled in Palestine would unanimously decide on renewing ordination, their decision would produce the desired legal effect. There can be little doubt that ultimately Maimonides's suggestion (for it is a suggestion only and no ruling) is based on his legal rather than sacramental or charismatic conception of the nature of ordination. It was on Maimonides that Berab and his circle based their decision to renew ordination.[4] The eschatological motives of this revolutionary

[1] Cf., for example, b. *Sanh.* 14a.

[2] Isa. i. 26.

[3] Code, *Sanh.* iv. 11, and Commentary to the *Mishnah*, *Sanh.* i. 3.

[4] The most important sources are collected in the appendix to Levi b. Ḥabib's *Responsa* (Venice, 1565), entitled *Semikhath Zeqenim* (ibid., fol. 277*a*) but popularly known as *Quntres ha-Semikhah*. On the ordination controversy see J. Katz's important and illuminating article, 'The Ordination Controversy between R. Jacob Berab and R. Levi b. Ḥabib', in *Zion*, vol. xvi (1951), pp. 28–45.

initiative have already been pointed out by Graetz[1] and later historians. An assembly in Safed 'unanimously' ordained Berab, who thereupon immediately dispatched a letter of ordination to the Chief Rabbi of Jerusalem, Levi b. Ḥabib. The messenger from Safed, Solomon Ḥazzan,[2] soon returned with the dismaying news that Levi b. Ḥabib had not only refused to accept the ordination but had actually contested the legitimacy of the whole undertaking. An acrimonious controversy ensued, whose violence misled Graetz and other historians into thinking that its main motives were personal grievances and jealousies. As J. Katz has shown in a masterly paper,[3] this naïve oversimplification misses the essential factors of what really was a significant historical controversy. But whatever the true nature of the quarrel, its result was obvious: since even according to Maimonides renewal of ordination required absolute unanimity, there was not even a possibility of a victory for Berab's party short of complete agreement on the part of Levi b. Ḥabib and his followers. As this was not forthcoming and other scholars joined the opposition, the movement of necessity petered out, in spite of the fact that Berab still ordained some of his disciples (among them Joseph Karo), who, in their turn, ordained others, and so on.[4] The decisive point[5] is that, lacking unanimity, not even the ordained scholars—even among themselves—ever claimed special authority or validity for their rulings and judicial acts; they never referred to their ordination as in any way a source of prestige or authority.

Reading Joseph Karo's utterances on the subject in his halakhic writings, one would never guess that he was personally involved in this 'messianic' enterprise of the Safed rabbinate. In his commentary *Kesef Mishneh* on the Code of Maimonides (*Sanhedrin* iv) he does not breathe a single word of approval, and in his *B.Y.* he mentions only once and by the way the possibility that 'according to the view of Maimonides ordained rabbis would be thinkable

[1] Op. cit., pp. 291 ff.

[2] *Semikhath Zeqenim*, fol. 278a, col. 1; cf. also above, p. 90.

[3] Cf. above, p. 123, n. 4.

[4] Cf. Azulay, op. cit., on Moses Alsheikh and Ḥayyim Vital (s.vv.); cf. also above, ch. 2, p. 15, n. 5.

[5] Cf. Katz, loc. cit., p. 36; but cf. below, p. 127, n. 2.

even today'.[1] Elsewhere he takes it for granted that 'nowadays there are no ordained courts'.[2]

What Karo thought in his heart about ordination appears in the *M.M.* By way of introduction to the book the printed editions group together a number of maggidic communications that could not be placed in the 'commentary' on the weekly portions of the Pentateuch. The second of these, dated Sabbath *Bemidbar*, 27 Iyyar,[3] was certainly communicated in Palestine, since in addition to the usual exhortations and praises it also contains references to troubles which Karo seems to have experienced with his congregation in Safed. It appears that he had been invited to be spiritual head of two congregations[4] but was forced to leave the *qahal gadol* or *keneseth ha-gedolah*.[5] He is also assured that funds would soon arrive from the diaspora to maintain his academy and his students.[6] His students would multiply and no student who had not attended his *yeshibah* would enjoy academic standing.[7] He would be raised and exalted to be *nagid* ('supreme head') 'over my people Israel'; his *yeshibah* would surpass that of Isaac Aboab[8] and 'your sons will be [members of the] Synhedrion in the chamber of hewn stones[9] and you shall behold them teaching the laws of *qemiṣah* [i.e. meal-offerings]'. Here the messianic hope is manifest. Ordination is merely a step towards messianic fulfilment. His sons would already sit as full-fledged members of the Synhedrion in the restored Temple. The Maggid goes on to say: 'And this son of yours will be a great rabbi and a great talmudic and kabbalistic scholar.

[1] *ad H.M.* 295: 5. [2] For references cf. Katz, loc. cit., p. 36, nn. 77–79.

[3] *M.M.* 3a–b. According to Mahler's chronological tables this combination is impossible; if we emend to 29, 26, or 24 Iyyar various other dates become possible, of which the most probable are the years [5]299, 301, 304, 306, 313, 316, 318.

[4] דהוית מרביץ תורה בתרתי קהלות. On *marbiṣ torah* as a technical term of rabbinic office, cf. M. Benayahu, *Marbiṣ Torah* (1953).

[5] Cf. below, p. 262.

[6] ודע שמהרה יבא לך ממון רב מחוצה לארץ לתת לתלמידיך הספקה.

[7] וכל תלמיד שלא ילמד בישיבתך לא יוחזק ביודע כלל.

[8] Isaac Aboab ('the second') of Toledo, described as 'the last *gaon* of Castile'; b. 1430 in Spain, d. 1493 in Portugal. Many of Karo's contemporaries had been Aboab's disciples; cf. above, p. 87.

[9] *Lishkath ha-Gazith*; according to the Talmud the assembly hall of the Great Synhedrion within the Temple precincts. Cf. *M. Sanh.* vii. 2 and *Middoth* v. 4.

There will be no kabbalist like him . . . for he will attain more kabbalistic wisdom than anyone for the last five hundred years, even ten times more than my beloved Solomon.'[1] Although the expression 'this son of yours' may refer to any son Karo had at the time, it may also imply that the promised son of earlier entries[2] had, in fact, been born.

Karo's ambition to be the chief spiritual authority of Israel expresses itself again in one of the few clearly dated entries. On Sabbath *Vayyiqra*, 5 Nisan 5303 (= 10 March 1543 C.E.), i.e. five years after the abortive renewal of ordination, the Maggid thus addresses Karo:[3] 'Lo, I am the Mishnah speaking in thy mouth, I am the mother who correcteth her children, I am embracing thee. Always cleave unto me so that my glory be on thee and thine on me, etc.,[4] for I shall exalt thee to be prince and *nagid* over the diaspora of Israel in the kingdom of Arabistan.' Arabistan[5] is the whole Jewish orient east of Palestine and Syria. Whereas Aleppo and Damascus, though outside the Holy Land, still fell within the orbit of Palestine, the area eastwards, comprising Kurdistan, Iraq, and Persia, formed a unit of its own.[6] Karo[7] speaks of the congregations of the Holy Land, of Arabistan, and of the Maghreb (North Africa) as three distinct units. The communities of Arabistan regarded Safed as their spiritual capital.[8] After Berab's departure from Safed (1538) Joseph Karo found himself quickly growing into the role of the leading rabbinic personality of Safed. His signature heads those of his colleagues in most contemporary documents (judgements, court orders, etc.) from Safed[9] and it seems that he also acted as chairman of the informal rabbinic council (*Beth ha-Va'ad*)

[1] Cf. above, pp. 101, 119.
[2] Cf. above, pp. 113 ff.
[3] *M.M.* 39a. 2.
[4] Cf. above, ch. 5, p. 99, n. 1.
[5] The difference between the usual spelling (also in Karo's writings, cf. *A.R.*, no. 32) אראביסטן and that in the *M.M.* עראביסטן is obviously insufficient as an argument against the authenticity of the *M.M.* (*contra* Rosanes, op. cit., p. 264).
[6] For what seems a pretty exhaustive definition of Arabistan, cf. תשובות לקהלת עאנה לר׳ יום טוב צהלון (ed. M. Benayahu) (1951), p. 19: כל אותן הגלילות כלל הקהלות מזרח אשר מחלב ולהלן כגון קהלות עאנה ובג׳דאד, והורמוז וכדומה להן וקהלות מדי ופרס וסביבותיהן וקהילות כורדיסטאן וזאגאם [?] והגלוות והנטפלות אליהן.
[7] *A.R.*, no. 32.
[8] Benayahu, loc. cit., p. 11.
[9] Cf. Greenwald, op. cit., pp. 108–9.

of Safed. As the leading rabbinic authority of Safed, he probably quickly discovered that *ipso facto* his authority extended to the whole of Arabistan, which formed part, as it were, of the 'diocese' of Safed. The Maggid's statements in this matter therefore reflect facts and not ambitious hopes. However, the Maggid continues:

> And because you have devoted yourself to the cause of the restoration of ordination, therefore you shall be found worthy to be ordained by all scholars of Palestine and the diaspora. Through you I shall restore ordination. I shall grant you to finish your book . . . and thereafter you will be burned for the holiness of my Name . . . and share in the resurrection of the dead.

The above quotations from the *M.M.* are illuminating in more than one sense. In the first place they show the utter and total inadequacy of the *argumentum ex silentio* for determining any facts or theories about the life and thought of the great rabbinic figures. The appeal to the *B.Y.* and *Sh.A.* has been a favourite argument with all writers who were concerned to prove the *M.M.* a forgery. Is it plausible that Joseph Karo, the lucid, sober, and rigidly logical arch-talmudist who even rejected the rite of *kapparoth*, was a kabbalistic enthusiast who spent part of his life in mystical fantasies and hallucinations? The answer is that were it not for incontrovertible historical evidence the same logic would enable us to deny that the author of *K.M.* and *B.Y.*[1] could ever have been associated with the ambitious messianic attempt to restore ordination. Yet we know—even without the *M.M.*—how deeply Karo was involved in the matter. One cannot help being reminded again of the two faces of Maimonides in his *Code* and in the *Guide of the Perplexed.*

Our second point concerns Karo's messianism. It seems that for many years after Berab's abortive initiative Karo entertained—perhaps unconsciously—the hope of a second, more successful attempt. He would succeed where Berab had failed. The ordination he had received at the hands of Berab was clearly invalid since it lacked unanimous support. But the next time 'all scholars of Palestine and the diaspora'[2] would be united in confirming his

[1] Cf. above, pp. 124–5.

[2] According to the most recent researches of Mr. Benayahu a second attempt was, in fact, made. By-passing the opponents in Palestine, Karo obtained the

ordination so that he could then proceed to lay hands on other scholars, thus becoming the beginning of a new chain of rabbinic succession. But in spite of this hope Karo's eschatological attitude is what we may describe as 'messianism at a remove'. His messianic mood condenses into active yearning and even into 'practical' steps designed to prepare the way of the Lord's anointed. But it is a preparatory, not a properly 'messianic', mood and activity. Karo never sees himself in a messianic world: he may be gratified to rule over Israel or over the Arabistan part of it as its leading rabbinic authority, but only his sons will have a seat in the Great Synhedrion, administering the Law in the rebuilt Temple. This is hope at a remove, and even the promise to 'behold' his sons in their eschatological dignity, even if it refers to eyes of flesh, cannot have been taken very seriously by a man who expected to die a martyr's death at the stake. Whatever the paraphernalia of the messianic age, burning pyres and the blood of martyrs are not supposed, as a rule, to form part of them. The main substance of Karo's personal eschatology is not the sight of the Messiah, but rather his participation in the subsequent resurrection[1] and his admission to unheard-of glory in the hereafter.[2] Here Karo's fantasies approach sublimated and spiritualized megalomania. The Maggid's prophecies assume an almost Dantesque quality in their description of the heavenly host of angels and saints coming out in procession to welcome Karo and leading him to that supreme vision of God concerning which even the Maggid's speech fails. In fact, already in this life a mighty voice rings through all the worlds whenever Karo leaves his house, invisible angelic hosts accompany him, and the denizens of heaven all say, 'who is this man whom the King delighteth to honour? He is the senior scholar of Palestine, the greatest author of Israel.'

After his death at the stake

all the saints of Paradise with the *Shekhinah* at their head will go forth to meet you and receive you with songs of praise.[3] They will lead you

consent of the scholars in the diaspora and was 'ordained' again; cf. M. Benayahu, 'The Revival of Ordination in Safed', in *Yitzhak F. Baer Jubilee Volume*, 1960, pp. 248–269, particularly pp. 251–3.

[1] Cf. the quotation above, p. 127.

[2] *M.M.* 1b–2a.

[3] Cf. b. *Keth.* 104a for this traditional motif.

before them like a bridegroom walking in front [of the bridal procession] and all will accompany you to your canopy.[1] I have prepared for you seven canopies, one within the other, and seven more canopies one on top of the other.[2] And in the innermost and highest canopy seven rivers of goodly perfume flow. . . . They will prepare for you a throne of gold which has seven steps and in which are set many pearls and jewels,[3] and all the saints shall accompany you and sing before you until you reach the first canopy. There they will clothe you with a second vestment of honour and similarly at every canopy so that as you arrive at the last canopy you will wear fourteen vestments of honour. Thereafter two of the saints that escort you will place themselves at your right and left, like the best men of a bridegroom, and they will lift you to your throne. As you begin to mount the throne they will put a fifteenth vestment of honour on the other fourteen that you already wear, so that you will wear altogether fifteen vestments of honour. Thus they will lift you on the throne, take hold of the crown suspended [above the throne], and lower it on your head. You shall sit on the throne with one [attendant] at each side and all the saints shall be sitting around in a circle, discussing with you talmudic questions for hundred and eighty days so as to fulfil [Scripture (*Esther* i. 4)] 'when he showed the riches of his glorious kingdom and the honour of his excellent majesty many days, even an hundred and fourscore days'. Thereafter you will make a feast for all the saints in Paradise,[4] a feast of the Law. For seven days you shall discourse about the words of *Torah* that I have taught you in this world as well as during those hundred and eighty days. Thereupon the saints will arise and escort you . . . and proclaim your glory and say 'render glory to the holy son[5] of the highest King and render glory to the image of the King'.[6]

However, this apotheosis is merely a prelude to even greater things:

They will sing and chant until they bring you to the place of the

[1] Cf. b. *B.B.* 75a.

[2] Combining the two symbolisms of penetrating to the 'innermost' and of rising to the 'highest' place.

[3] Here eschatology is indebted to old legendary descriptions of King Solomon's throne.

[4] Cf. Esther i. 5 'and when these days were expired he made a feast . . . seven days'. The Maggid's promise to Karo of a feast in heaven was known in Safed and occurs in some of the earliest quotations from the diary; cf. D. Tamar in *' resheth*, vol. i (Jerusalem, 1959), pp. 477–8.

[5] A usual Zoharic designation for pious souls.

[6] A usual figure of speech. Man's potential image of God is fully actualized by the righteous.

thirteen rivers of perfume.[1] As you immerse yourself in the first river, they will divest you of the first of the vestments that you wear, and so with the second and third and the rest until, as you immerse yourself in the thirteenth [river], thirteen vestments will have been removed. Thereupon the River of Fire[2] will flow forth and the fourteenth vestment will be removed from you and you will be clothed with a white garment.

After this baptism of fire Karo is ready for the unspeakable mystery:

Then [the archangel] Michael, the [celestial] high-priest,[3] will be ready to lift up your soul into the presence of God. From this point on it is not permitted to reveal anything for 'neither hath the eye seen, O God, beside thee [what He hath prepared for him that waiteth for Him'].[4]

This is the longest and most sustained expression of Karo's self-esteem, drawing together all the strands of traditional individual eschatology. The climax is as amazing as it is moving: suddenly enthronement, apotheosis, celestial banquet, and triumph in the communion of saints give way to the silence of ultimate fulfilment which is the meeting, in utter solitude, of the naked soul with its creator.

I would date this passage some time during Karo's first years in Palestine, between 1541 and 1547, partly because of the various titles bestowed on him by the Maggid, but more particularly because of the promise that he would finish his book, which was therefore still unfinished. The earlier promises concerning the birth of a son[5] seem to have come true since the Maggid now assures Karo that in him and his sons Scripture would be fulfilled (Joshua i. 8): 'this book of the Law shall not depart out of thy mouth', 'and

[1] Cf. p. *A.Z.* iii. 1; also *Zohar*, i. 7a; ii. 146b; and elsewhere.

[2] On the River of Fire (*di-nur*; cf. Dan. vii. 10) cf. b. *Ḥagigah*, 13b–14a; it plays a considerable role in medieval (individual) eschatology. Cf. *Zohar*, ii. 211b; *Tiqquney Zohar*, 4a; *Reshith Ḥokhmah*, bk. i, ch. 13, end.

[3] For Michael as the celestial high-priest cf. b. *Ḥag.* 12b., *Zeb.* 62a.

[4] Isa. lxiv. 4; cf. also *Zohar*, ii. 97a and 146b, where the same verse and the same motif of thirteen rivers of perfume are mentioned in connexion with the final admission of the soul to the 'Palace of Love', there to receive God's paternal kiss. The gradually mounting tension of 'canopy within canopy', &c., and particularly the normal significance of *ḥuppah* as 'bridal canopy', may suggest some faint erotic overtones. Yet it would certainly be going far beyond the evidence to speak of erotic or bridal mysticism, of which there is as little trace in the *M.M.* as there is in the *Zohar*; cf. Scholem, *MTJM.*, p. 226.

[5] Cf. above, pp. 112 f.

in addition I shall give you from this virtuous and modest wife a pious and wise son, for she has merited it by the sufferings which she bore.' The phrasing here is very similar to that of the communications already quoted[1] and one might be tempted to assume that the same wife is referred to again. On the other hand we have seen that Karo's third wife, referred to in the earlier entries, had been married before,[2] whereas the woman spoken of here was a virgin.[3] Only thus can we understand the Maggid's prophecy 'and after her death you will marry two non-virgins one after the other, and this is what I told you [is signified by Ps. xlv. 14—by arbitrarily changing the pauses] "the virgins—her companions *that follow her*—shall be brought unto thee", and you shall beget on them scholarly sons that will fear the Lord'.

Did Karo marry again in 1556? A communication of that date[4] states: 'behold I have made you meet X, she is your companion and mate.' At any rate, he must have married once more in his later years for still in 1567, at the age of seventy-nine, he expresses the hope 'to beget sons who will study the Law' and who will fear the Lord.[5] As we shall see, this prayer was answered two years later, thus confirming Karo's piety as well as his vigour. Shlomel Dresnitz, who arrived in Safed *c.* 1602, tells in his epistle[6] of his meeting with Karo's widow. It was probably this last wife who was the daughter of Rabbi Solomon Sechsel Ashkenazi.[7]

Of Karo's sons only two are known to have survived: Solomon[8] and Judah. The latter was born towards the end of 5329, i.e. summer 1569 C.E. The 15 Elul 5329 is mentioned in the *M.M.*[9] as 'the day of the circumcision of the child' to be called Judah. Judah Karo, who published a posthumous collection of his father's *Responsa* in the week *Vayyeḥi* 5358 (= December 1597 C.E.)

[1] Above, p. 113. [2] Ibid.

[3] Is this the 'young woman' mentioned in the obscure passage referred to above, p. 114? The most natural solution, that the virgin mentioned here refers to Karo's *first* wife and the 'companions that follow her' to the second and third, seems to be precluded by the date of the entry, for the message was certainly communicated in Palestine.

[4] *M.M.* 31a. 3. [5] Introduction to the *Sh.A.* (Venice, 1567).

[6] Cf. above, p. 16. [7] Cf. above, pp. 93–94.

[8] For references to him in contemporary rabbinic literature cf. Greenwald, op. cit., p. 74. [9] *M.M.* 61b. 4.

describes himself in the introduction as twenty-seven years old[1] and refers to his father's death as having occurred 'almost twenty-four years ago', i.e. in 1575. Long ago Graetz pointed out the approximate agreement of this reference to Judah's age with the date of the circumcision as given in the *M.M.*[2] Rosanes's objection that the discrepancy of one year invalidates the argument is easily disposed of if we remember that the introduction to the *Responsa* may well have been written before the volume went to press, i.e. early in 1597. Another son is mentioned, without name, in the *Responsa* of Yomtob Ṣahalon, no. 31.[3] He must have died after his father's death, leaving no issue. Solomon Karo insisted on marrying his sister-in-law in levirate marriage and finally obtained rabbinic permission to do so. Whether this son was the one who according to Shlomel was engaged to be married to Luria's daughter[4] is impossible to determine.

Our examination of the details of Karo's family life again show how incidental and incomplete our information is. If our interpretation of the obscure maggidic communications is correct, Karo married at least five times (whether, at any time, he had more than one wife, it is impossible to say) and had many children, a number of which died. The great number of deaths need not surprise us considering the frequency of epidemics that until quite recently had ravaged the Mediterranean countries at regular intervals. The only cause for wonderment is Karo's own resistance and vigour which he owed, no doubt, in addition to a strong physical constitution, to a rigorous ascetic discipline: mortification, where it does not degenerate into self-emaciating torture, frequently leads to increased physical health and resistance.[5] That not all promises of offspring necessarily materialized is illustrated by a maggidic message of uncertain date.[6] Karo's wife had apparently

[1] צעיר אני לימים כבן ז"ך שנה אנכי היום. [2] Graetz, op. cit., p. 545.

[3] Venice, 1694, fol. 29b: בשנת הש"ם (= 1580) נפשנו בחיים זה היה מעשה בבנו של הרב המוסמך מהרי"ק ז"ל שמת והיתה אלמנתו זקוקה לאחיו ואביה לא היה רוצה לתתה לו.

[4] Cf. above, p. 17. That the widow in question was not Luria's daughter is proved by the reference to her father (cf. above, n. 3).

[5] Also Evelyn Underhill (op. cit., p. 62) comments on the longevity of many mystics, though none of those mentioned by her reached Karo's age.

[6] *M.M.* 71b. 1; a maggidic message of 1536 (?) with its veiled reference to

had a miscarriage or the expected pregnancy had failed to materialize altogether, in spite of the Maggid's grandiloquent promises of a wise, scholarly, and saintly son, &c. How does one justify prophecies that fail? The Maggid explains:

What I told you concerning your wife's pregnancy was true and valid, for you know that 'God's seal is truth'. The explanation of this saying is that although it may appear that there is untruth in his dealings, when you arrive at the 'seal', i.e. at the end of the matter, you will always find that all is true. This is also the case with the present matter: the pregnancy was true and God would not have withdrawn his gift . . . even if your sins would have warranted it. But because you were sentenced to death,[1] God, in the abundance of his mercy, wanted to redeem you and put the pregnancy in your place [as a vicarious sacrifice].

Before turning from Karo's family life to other matters, it may be useful, at this stage, to suggest a few considerations with regard to the erotic and sexual life of an ascetic *ḥasid* in the sixteenth century. It has frequently been observed that Jewish mysticism employs erotic symbolism only in describing the relations of the Divine to itself, not of man and God.[2] In Professor Scholem's felicitous phrase, kabbalism does not aspire to mystical union with the divine (in which case erotic imagery would be appropriate) but to mystical communion or *devekuth*.[3] In classical kabbalism erotic mysticism is therefore limited to the sphere of the inner-divine, i.e. to the realm of the sefiroth. The kabbalist knows no lover who ravishes him, and he does not tell of the kind of experiences known to us from Christian and Ṣufi literature. In more psychological language this state of affairs might be expressed by saying that the problem of unification or 'individuation' has been projected *as a whole* and located in the heart of the divine itself and not in the relation between God and man. The mystery of unification and the erotic symbolism which expresses it exists on two separate though parallel levels. It is a human as well as a divine mystery, analogous in the sense that macrocosm and microcosm are analogous and are linked together by the kabbalistic axiom that the

Abraham's sacrifice of Isaac, may refer to the death of another child (*M.M.* 35a. 4).

[1] For this motif, cf. below, p. 149.

[2] Cf. Scholem, *MTJM.*, p. 235.

[3] Ibid. (index s.v.), and the article quoted above, p. 64, n. 3.

human microcosm is itself a symbol of the mystical reality of the divine macrocosm. Because everything that happens on the human level has a mystico- (or magico-) symbolic value and consequently produces the most significant corresponding changes on the divine level, therefore the 'unification' of man has tremendous repercussions in the sphere of the Godhead. Both in the image of man[1] and in the image of God totality and perfection are represented by the union of the male and female principles. Here we have a good example of how the kabbalists added a new, mystical layer to the traditional Jewish doctrine that perfection was possible only in the married state. In fact, kabbalism seems to have been the first ascetic system to develop a mystical metaphysic of the sexual act.[2] Marriage is not only an honourable estate instituted of God for procreation ('be fruitful and multiply') or as a remedy for otherwise inevitable sins in act or in thought ('better to marry than to burn'), not even a matter of companionship and mutual society, help, and comfort; it is a state of perfection without which man is incomplete. Translated into kabbalistic language this would read: marriage is a state of perfection in which human reality duplicates and thereby promotes the divine perfection which is the union of God-and-his-*Shekhinah*. This latter unity, disrupted by the fall and human sinfulness, is one that has to be realized. Therefore the sexual act in holy matrimony has an almost sacramental quality, for it is a symbol that mystically promotes the analogous divine union. A man without a wife is mystically a cripple; like a surgeon without hands he cannot perform his most essential twofold duty, to commune with the *Shekhinah* and unite her with her husband. One of the accusations levelled at M. H. Luzzatto by his opponents was that as a bachelor he could not be the recipient of the supernatural graces claimed for him.

There exists, of course, also the more usual type of mysticism in which the intense love of the soul for God assumes definitely

[1] Cf. Gen. i. 27; ii. 18, 24, and the rabbinic commentaries.

[2] Against the palpably false statements of Max Scheler, in *Wesen und Formen der Sympathie* (edn. 5, 1948), pp. 121 f. On the relation of eroticism and sex-life to ascetic spirituality in the Jewish tradition cf. in addition to Scholem's remarks in *MTJM*. also G. Vajda's article 'Continence, Mariage et Vie Mystique selon la Doctrine du Judaïsme' in *Mystique et Continence* (*Études Carmélitaines*, 1952), pp. 82–92.

erotic qualities.[1] Where both motives, that of the theurgic unification of God with his *Shekhinah* and that of a personal communion with God in his personal, accessible, i.e. 'feminine', aspect of the *Shekhinah mediatrix*, merge, as they did in sixteenth-century Safed, the result is a mysticism full of dialectical richness. The normal type of exclusive love of God, whether tinged with erotic imagery or not, represents a spirituality whose attitude to marriage and family life is of necessity indifferent if not outright hostile. Love of God must be exclusive and consuming; it severs all attachments[2] and requires, for its fulfilment, sexual mortification. It is obvious that, were it not for the unequivocal demands of Jewish tradition, 'lovers of God' such as Bahya or even Maimonides would have preferred celibacy as the ideal state. To them matrimony was a chore which God in his wisdom had laid on man—and a dangerous one at that, because apt to draw man into the vortex of sensuality. The kabbalists, on the other hand, made a mystical virtue of halakhic necessity. But this mystical transformation of matrimonial life was purely *formal*. The kabbalists did not seek a new type of relationship with woman or a novel conception of love and spiritual intimacy. They were certainly no romantics. They were ascetic in the extreme and could justify the sexual act and praise its mystical significance only if and because it was performed without carnal pleasure. Already Jonah of Gerona had taught[3] that food was a necessity but should not be enjoyed. The application of the same principle to sexual matters is almost a matter of course. Outside the holy bond of matrimony sex is demonic; within the sanctified bounds of wedlock it has a metaphysical significance, provided all lust and pleasure is barred and the act is performed as an ascetic act of devotion as of 'one possessed [i.e. forced against his will] by a demon'.[4]

It should be mentioned in passing that this dilemma is not

[1] Cf. above, p. 57 f.

[2] Even if it does not necessarily imply the murderous and godly satisfaction felt by St. Angela of Foligno at the deaths of her husband and children (so many 'hindrances'!).

[3] *Sha'arey Teshubah*, i. 30–34; iv. 12. Since R. Jonah the idea that saintliness requires the performance of all bodily acts (eating, mating) without experiencing pleasure has been a commonplace in Jewish ascetic literature; cf., for example, *Reshith Ḥokhmah, Sha'ar ha-Qedushah*, chs. 15–16.

[4] So already the Talmud, b. *Nedarim* 20b.

peculiar to kabbalistic asceticism alone. It is apt to produce itself wherever spiritual life takes the form of a 'unitive' attachment to a feminine heavenly principle. In Catholic mysticism the rule of celibacy solved or rather forestalled the problem, though there seems to have been an attempt to encourage a kind of mystical marriage of priests to the Holy Virgin, similar to that of nuns to Christ. Fortunately the movement proved abortive.[1] Definite analogies to the kabbalist's situation can be found among some Protestant representatives of the *Sophia*-mysticism that came *via* Jacob Boehme to such mystics as Gichtel, Jane Leade, Pordage, and others. Gichtel was the most uncompromising in his demand that marriage to the heavenly Sophia be strictly monogamous. Devotion to Sophia precluded carnal marriage. When Gottfried Arnold did marry, Gichtel considered his marriage as nothing short of an adulterous betrayal of Sophia.[2]

The Jewish view on the subject is clearly brought out in such popular sixteenth-century manuals of spiritual life as Azikri's *Sefer Ḥaredim* or Cordovero's *Tomer Deborah*. Azikri,[3] taking as his text the law Deut. xxi. 15 concerning the man who has two wives, one beloved and another hated, explains

> behold the Torah, she is the wife God has given thee . . . and the other wife is of flesh and blood. . . . The King, blessed be He, commanded us to love her [too], but the real love should be for the former . . . 'glorious is the King's daughter [i.e. the *Shekhinah*] within the palace' [Ps. xlv. 14]. The King—that is the King of the universe—and thou art the King's son-in-law.

Cordovero[4] is more explicit in stating the traditional rabbinico-mystic position: 'It is obvious that the *Shekhinah* cannot be with a man as long as he is unmarried, for the *Shekhinah* cometh to man mainly from the female. Man stands between two females: the lower, physical female . . . and the *Shekhinah* who stands above him.'

Cordovero then explains how a pious man can maintain his communion with the *Shekhinah* even during forced separations

[1] See E. Krebs, op. cit., pp. 227–30.

[2] Cf. E. Seeberg, *Gottfried Arnold* (1923), pp. 6–7, 27–28. See also Walter Nigg, *Heimliche Weisheit* (1953), pp. 244–5, 249–50, 332–7.

[3] Op. cit., pt. vii, ch. 4.

[4] Op. cit., ch. 9.

from his 'lower, physical' wife (e.g. during her monthly periods, when travelling, during the six days of ascetic abstinence throughout the week—intercourse being practised only on the Sabbath). However, the real communion is effected through the ascetic's union with his wife after the aforementioned periods of abstinence. 'He who wants to be united with the King's daughter[1] must sanctify himself and, after his mystical marriage, must always give her her [mystical] 'food, raiment, and conjugal rights'[2] exactly as he is required to do, on the physical plane, to his physical wife.[3]

We can now appreciate the peculiar quandaries of Jewish ascetics. Without the positive injunctions of rabbinic tradition they would, most probably, have chosen the path of celibacy. In that case they would merely have had to withstand all the difficulties and temptations besetting the usual ascetic. But marriage was a duty, and the begetting of a maximum number of sons who would study the Law, perform good works, and serve the Lord was a major ideal. They were thus, perhaps, spared some of the worst primary temptations, but were also faced with many new ones. The knowledge that they could marry—outside Ashkenazi Jewry even more than one wife—obviously allowed of possibilities which celibate ascetics would simply have repressed and never allowed to obtrude on their consciousness. The Jewish kabbalist lived with his wife but knew that he should live only in God. He performed his marital duties with mystico-theurgic intentions, but realized that he was not allowed to give himself up either to his partner or to his passion. Transformed, in theory, into a sacramental act, the 'holy union' of husband and wife was in practice an ascetic exercise which admitted of no genuine relationship between the partners because the kabbalist had to identify himself with the mystical intention of the act and not with its actuality. Add to this the markedly patriarchal and masculine character of Judaism, and the

[1] Cf. the similar wording of Azikri in the passage quoted.

[2] Cf. Ex. xxiv. 10.

[3] For an extremely interesting case of uniting the two levels of mystical and physical eroticism, see Professor Y. Tishby's study of M. H. Luzzatto's *kethubah*, 'The Messianic Ferment in the Circle of Moses Ḥayyim Luzzatto in the Light of a Marriage Contract', in *Baer Jubilee Volume*, 1960, pp. 374 ff. The standard example, in Jewish tradition, of complete abandoning of marital life because of the demands of perpetual nearness to God is, of course, Moses.

one-sidedness of married life, even after the kabbalistic revolution, becomes obvious.

Karo's diary is an exemplary illustration of the general rule. The exhortation not to derive pleasure and enjoyment from married life on pain of increasing the power of Satan is repeated with monotonous regularity for about fifty years. It is never a particular woman that matters but 'the wife'; as such, of course, she deserves love, reverence, and gratitude—already the rabbis of the Talmud had insisted on that. Of course, marriages are not accidental but are regulated by the hidden mechanisms of *gilgul* and *tiqqun*. Yet, though marriages are predestined in heaven and there exists a mystical 'sympathy of souls', in the last resort it does not greatly matter that one's present wife is not the 'real mate'[1] or that after her demise she will be succeeded by 'her companions that follow her'. The role of sex and the merely instrumental function of woman in kabbalist life are nicely brought out by a remarkably frank entry in the *M.M.*[2]

On the same day, 28 Iyyar,[3] [walking] with some of the brethren we passed the *tekiye*[4] and they persuaded me to enter there to walk [in the garden?]. At night I had a pollution[5] and was much aggrieved. About an hour later I had intercourse with my wife. Later I rose up and whilst I was studying [the voice came to me and] he said to me, 'Be strong and of good courage, for the Lord is with you . . . only beware of interrupting the communion and adhesion between you and your Creator. Do not turn to idols, neither go after the Baals as you did yesterday. Moreover, it is three days now that you have interrupted the communion

[1] Cf. above, p. 113.

[2] *M.M.* 51a. The whole passage is left out in the 'bowdlerized' edition of Vilna, 1875; cf. below, Appendix D, no. 11.

[3] So the printed editions where the entry appears in the course of a longer passage dated 'Sabbath night, 28 Iyyar'. The manuscripts of Group A read '1 Iyyar', Group B '1 Nisan'; both groups have this intimate confession at the beginning of the entry, *followed* by what is in the printed editions the beginning of the entry. This again is followed in the manuscripts by what is in the printed editions the beginning of a rather long communication (*M.M.* 40b. 4, s.t. *Ṣav*) dated 'the third day of Passover'.

[4] The Turkish term for a monastery of dervishes. The incident evidently happened whilst Karo was still at Adrianople or Nicopolis.

[5] Pollutions, whether accidental or deliberate, are accounted among the gravest and most terrible sins by all kabbalistic moralists, for they add to the power of Satan by producing more demons instead of human beings that could serve the Lord.

[i.e. the practice of the presence of God]. . . . Although I have made you great in order that your heart should be a vessel for my *Torah* . . . and I also promised you to be burned . . . yet you turned your heart away from the words of *Torah* and even turned to idols by entering yesterday into their sanctuary.[1] I have already informed you[2] that seven clouds of glory are accompanying you and they all left you when you entered there. They [even] wanted to depart from you [for good], were it not that the members of the celestial academy had interceded for you. . . . Moreover, they [i.e. your companions] used unseemly language so that you could not help having sinful thoughts. Also afterwards you saw an unclean [i.e. unchaste] thing and [again] you could not help having sinful thoughts, wherefore evil was attracted to you and "plague came near thy dwelling"[3] and you had a pollution that same night. . . . Scripture says [Lev. xxvi. 27–28] "if ye walk contrary[4] unto me" . . . which Onkelos[5] translates "with hardness",[6] meaning the erection [of the *membrum virile*] . . . wherefore take heed and keep your soul diligently, be zealous and careful, for with the pollution that you had they [i.e. the evil powers] have already snatched their share [due to them as a result of your sinful thoughts and lack of *devekuth*] and when you had intercourse with your wife you communed again with the sphere of holiness. . . . Never more enter the house of Baal, but return to your state of holiness.'

The last but one sentence of this quotation clearly shows the 'sacramental' effects of marital intercourse which has the power to re-establish man in his communion with the *Shekhinah*.

Though surrounded by some of the most prominent scholars of his age, Karo was soon recognized as the leading rabbinic authority. Even Moses de Trani, Karo's most persistent 'antagonist,'[7] who

[1] Here the Maggid is punning by saying בית הקדשים, i.e. literally 'house of sodomites'.

[2] In the same entry; also *M.M.*, *passim*.

[3] Cf. Ps. xci. 10; 'plagues' and similar words are kabbalistic idioms for demons and unclean spirits. For the idea that unclean spirits which cause pollutions live in or near non-Jewish houses of worship cf., for example, ***Reshith Ḥokhmah*, *Sha'ar ha-Qedushah***, ch. 16 (p. 333): ועוד יתרחק האדם מכל הדברים הגורמים פגם לנפש . . . ויתרחק מכל דברים המטונפים ומכל המקומות שהמזיקים נמצאים שם . . . וכן מקום כניסיותם.

[4] This is another pun, for the Hebr. *qeri* also means a nocturnal pollution in rabbinic Hebrew, where it corresponds to the biblical *miqreh*.

[5] The author of an Aramaic version of the Pentateuch.

[6] Meaning, of course, with 'hardness of heart' or 'stiff-necked'.

[7] Cf. Azulay, op. cit., s.v.: בר פלוגתיה דמרן. For details about their at times acrimonious debates cf. both Karo's and Trani's *responsa* as well as Judah Karo's introduction to *Responsa ad E.H.*; other references in Greenwald, op. cit., pp. 110–18.

had come to Safed from Adrianople some time before 1525, as much as admits Karo's *de facto* authority in the Jewish world. Karo's disciples held recognized positions as rabbis in the various communities of Safed—much to Trani's displeasure[1]—and always rallied round their master when his rulings were disputed by other scholars.[2] In fact, we may speak of a 'circle' round Karo, consisting of his old friends, colleagues, and disciples (e.g. Alkabets, Cordovero, Alsheikh and others) quite apart from the large number of students attending his academy. His *responsa* show that his authority was not limited to Palestine or 'Arabistan'; his ruling was sought from all parts of Sefardi Jewry. The pressure on his time must have been formidable: the composition of his great works, replies to questions pouring in from all sides, the financial and academic responsibility for his *yeshibah*, attending to public affairs,[3] and the like. The description given by the Yemenite traveller Al-Dahari of the proceedings at Karo's academy,[4] though evidently idealized, yet shows that about two hundred students used to attend his homiletical and kabbalistic discourses on Sabbath afternoons. It was not until his old age, a few years before his death, that a new revival swept Safed and led to the formation of new circles whose attitude to the old-established authorities was, to say the least, ambiguous.

The arrival in Safed of Isaac Luria (*c.* 1569) and the spectacular changes and results which it produced have been described often enough. A small but enthusiastic group of elect disciples gathered round the mysterious and charismatic 'man of God' and made no attempt to conceal from others their unquestioned superiority in

[1] תשובות המבי"ט (Venice, 1629), pt. i, no. 157. Though the *responsum* does not mention any names, it is more than probable that Karo is meant; cf. also תשובות מהרשד"ם *ad Y.D.*, no. 220: זה כמה שנים כתבתי לארץ ישראל תוב"ב לדרישת הרב הגדול כמוהר"ר יוסף קארו זצ"ל שהחכם השלם כמוה"ר משה מטראנה היה מוחה בתלמידיו שלא יורו הוראה, סדרתי פסק ארוך על זה שהדין היה עם הרב כמהר"י קארו זלה"ה שיורו התלמידים היודעים. Cf. also Greenwald, op. cit., pp. 69–70.

[2] Cf. Trani's *Responsa*, pt. ii, no. 46 (cf. 24b and 25a) and Karo, *Responsa ad E.H.* 13b–17a.

[3] Cf. *A.R.*, no. 143: ועם היותי טרוד בלימוד הישיבה ה"י מלבד כמה טרדות מעול הקהלות ע"א; *responsa ad E.H.*, f. 142: ועם טרדות קהילות הקודש יצ"ו טרחם ומשאם עלי.

[4] Cf. A. Ya'ari, מסעות ארץ ישראל (1946), ch. 13.

the mystical hierarchy. Examples have already been quoted[1] of the methods by which the Lurianists established their superiority: their mysteries were profounder, kabbalists of other schools were essentially incapable of grasping their doctrines, even the great Karo himself was always overcome by sleep whenever Lurianic mysteries were expounded, Karo's famous disciple, Moses Alsheikh, who had been appointed to act as Vital's teacher of exoteric (talmudic) knowledge, was not permitted to learn the secrets of Kabbalah from his pupil.[2] Karo's Maggid himself, so we are told,[3] confirmed the unique greatness of Vital. In fact, many of Karo's disciples were drawn into the vortex of Lurianism, which proved the more irresistible in the long run.

The situation that developed is interesting both from a psychological and a social point of view. By the time the Lurianic revival began, Karo was at the height of his fame. The revered octogenarian represented, as it were, in his person the institutionalized halakhic and religious authority of rabbinic Judaism. Whatever his charismatic gifts and the merits and supernatural rewards of his ascetic austerities, these were not, in the traditional judgement of his contemporaries, the basis of his authority, which derived exclusively from his outstanding scholarship. It was as the author of *B.Y.* that Karo held sway over Jewry. Now suddenly a mystical group formed itself which was purely charismatic in character. It could not be rejected, because it did not formally compete with established authority, let alone oppose it. The Lurianists, and Isaac Luria himself, were all distinguished or at least competent talmudic scholars, and no comparison with, for example, the Baal Shem Tob and his circle is possible in this respect. Talmudic studies were diligently pursued in Luria's *yeshibah*.[4] Even the mystical extravagances of their charismatic life did not outrage their colleagues, as it merely realized more fully what all the others too longed for in their hearts. What matters for our present purpose is the fact that a new, 'upstart', and highly exclusive group established itself solely on the basis of charismatic criteria and was

[1] Above, pp. 16 f.

[2] Vital, *Sefer ha-Ḥezyonoth*, p. 8.

[3] Ibid., p. 2.

[4] Cf. Vital's *Diary*, pp. 218–19. An account of the ישיבת האר"י is still a desideratum.

governed by charismatic authority. The reaction was one of mutual jealousy—repressed, perhaps, but none the less real. The Karo–Alkabets group found that they were now outstripped by the pretensions of a new circle of mystics. For many years they had performed their kabbalistic devotions and studied the *Zohar* at the tomb of R. Simon b. Yoḥai,[1] but now the cave of Meron was the headquarters of Luria and his disciples. On 15 Elul 5329 (= 1569 C.E.), the day of the circumcision of his son Judah, Karo is assured by his Maggid that he would 'delve deeper into kabbalistic wisdom than the HEAD[2] of Meron', who would come in the end to be taught by Karo.[3]

However, the Lurianists also, in spite of their sense of superiority, were sufficiently imbued with traditional Jewish social values to regard a man like Karo as the embodiment of religious authority. Vital's ambition, of which his diary gives eloquent testimony, consequently polarized in his relation to Karo. In spite of occasional fits of doubt—soon dispelled by Luria's assurances—Vital is firmly convinced of his superiority and high calling. He dreams rather often about Karo, even long after the latter's death. The dreams leave no doubt that Karo is a great saint,[4] though, of course, inferior to Luria,[5] but there is a special bond between him and Vital. For Karo clearly represented something which Luria did not have and, as a matter of fact, did not care to have. Luria, in the fullness of his charismatic power and in the reality of the personal fascination which he exercised on his disciples could afford to go his way with an almost naïvely autistic self-assurance and charm. Vital, who lacked all the qualities of personal leadership,[6] was a more complicated and contradictory nature. To be assured of his high calling, he needed not only the psychological identification

[1] Cf. above, p. 54, the quotation from the *Sefer ha-Gerushin*; also *M.M.* 48b. 2: 'R. Simon b. Yoḥai and his son were glad when you read the *Zohar* in their cave and in the neighbouring village.' Cf. also above, p. 62, n. 1.

[2] The identification of the 'Head of Meron' with Luria was already proposed by Graetz (op. cit., p. 571). For some time I considered the possibility that Alkabets (cf. also above, pp. 54 f.) and his visits to Meron (cf. *Sefer ha-Gerushin*) were meant, but the date coincides too well with Luria's arrival in Safed and his immediate and meteoric success. The word הרא"ש seems to be an acrostic and its interpretation may well be הרב אשכנזי (and not הרב אלקבץ שלמה).

[3] *M.M.* 61b. 4.

[4] *Sefer ha-Ḥezyonoth*, pp. 22, 90.

[5] Ibid., p. 88.

[6] Cf. Scholem, in *Zion*, vol. v (1940), p. 141.

with his master Luria but also that with Joseph Karo or, at least, with his internalized image of Joseph Karo which stood for the traditionally sanctioned and recognized religious authority in Jewish society. It is, therefore, no surprise to learn that the souls of both derive from one and the same supernal root[1] 'but mine is greater than Karo's'.[2] Vital also reports that the Maggid had indicated that he was destined to be Karo's successor.[3] Here it appears clearly that the unconscious conflict with Karo was a matter of Vital's recognition in terms of institutionalized authority, rather than of personal antagonisms. The younger mystic aspired to the socially sanctioned authority of the great talmudist; his wish was partly fulfilled in his dreams. Karo, long since deceased, appears in Vital's house to honour him[4] and is entertained by Vital with choice delicacies[5] whilst Vital himself eats only his usual austere food. He is thus also the greater ascetic. The account closes with the frank but significant admission: 'I often dream that Rabbi Karo is ill and about to die and that I go to visit him and prepare medicines for him. And I do not know what this means.' At least we have learned that the great Karo is sick unto death and needs the help of Ḥayyim Vital! With the sly subtlety so characteristic of dream symbolism Vital even reassures himself that he harbours no hostile feelings against the great man. After all, he repeatedly visits him on his death-bed and prepares medicines! There could be no better psychological alibi. Vital knows full well that his power is greater than Karo's: the Primal Adam lies helpless and ill near the house of Joseph Karo and wants to be revived by medicines which Vital provides. Here the dream symbolism assumes almost transpersonal significance. Both Karo and (on a more archetypal level) the Primal Adam are father-figures. They are sick unto death and need Vital's medicines. From a psycho-analytic point of view medicines are, of course, an 'ambivalent' symbol, for they may also be a disguise for poison. But whereas the former dream seems to reflect only Vital's personal problem with regard to

[1] *Sefer ha-Ḥezyonoth*, pp. 146, 198.

[2] Ibid., p. 250; both souls stem from the root of Cain! On the kabbalistic evaluation of the soul of Cain, cf. Scholem, 'Seelenwanderung und Sympathie der Seelen in der jüdischen Mystik', *Eranos-Jahrbuch*, vol. xxiv (1955) (Zürich, 1956), p. 102.

[3] Ibid., p. 2.

[4] Ibid., p. 82.

[5] Ibid., p. 75.

institutionalized authority, represented by Karo, the second dream says much more and appears, in fact, to demand a more than purely personal interpretation. Karo and all he stands for, indeed the '*House of Joseph*' (i.e. *halakhah* by itself), is unequal to the great mystical task of reviving the Primal Adam; it is Lurianism only that knows the secret medicine of the cosmic *tiqqun*. In 1561 he dreams of a burial attended also by Alkabets and Karo. The corpse objects to some part of the ritual but meekly submits to Vital's command, not, however, without inquiring first, 'why is *your* power so much greater?'[1]

Perhaps the most outspoken testimony is contained in Vital's dream of Paradise, dated 1566.[2] He is led by the prophet Elijah through a beautiful garden populated by white geese. These are, so we are told, the souls of the righteous who study the Mishnah![3] Mounting a few steps (i.e. in normal dream language: ascending to a higher level), he beholds God on his Throne of Glory, surrounded by the righteous of a superior order (i.e. the kabbalists). Overwhelmed by the sight, Vital falls to the ground, but God raises him and says, 'Sit thou at my right hand, in this empty seat even next to me.' Although nothing had been said so far about the nature of this seat, Vital immediately and as a matter of course replies: 'How can I sit there since it is [the seat] prepared for Rabbi Joseph Karo?' God now reassures Vital: 'So indeed I had planned originally, but then I gave him another place and this place here . . . I have prepared for you.' To the extent that the invitation, echoing Ps. cxi. 1, 'Sit thou at my right hand', has messianic overtones the dream may indicate again, on the more than purely personal level, that in Vital's unconscious the way of redemption lay with the new kabbalism and no longer with traditional *halakhah* as represented by Karo.

The *Book of Visions*, though primarily of interest for an understanding of Vital and his circle, thus also provides valuable information concerning certain *imponderabilia* in the relations between Karo, the symbol of rabbinic Safed (and rabbinic Safed is

[1] *Sefer ha-Ḥezyonoth*, p. 40. [2] Ibid., pp. 42–47.

[3] Cf. b. *Ber*. 57a 'he who sees a goose in his dream may expect wisdom'. Still, there may be a pinprick against Karo here.

kabbalistic too!) and the new charismatic movement. As described in an earlier chapter, the gifts of the spirit had been abundant long before Luria, in Safed as well as in Salonica and Adrianople. But charismatic phenomena, though not necessarily concealed, were handled discreetly. Without wishing to minimize the differences in outlook, historical setting, and eschatological mood, we may compare the paranormal life of men such as Taytazak and Karo with that of the Gaon Elijah of Vilna, the outstanding eighteenth-century representative of extreme, uncompromising rabbinic Judaism.[1] Whatever the personal significance of *maggidim*, visions, and eschatological expectations, they do not touch, let alone influence or modify the completely autonomous sphere of traditional *halakhah* or even *'aggadah*. Karo's non-halakhic, homiletic *novellae*,[2] exactly like those of Joseph Taytazak,[3] show no trace of kabbalistic influence.[4] A comparison of Karo's exoteric aggadic and homiletic utterances with his maggidic revelations is instructive in this respect. The difference in style between the Maggid's communications and Karo's exoteric, homiletic writing is matched by his clear consciousness of the difference in level between these two manifestations of *Torah*. Karo provides examples of his ability to write in the contemporary homiletic style, shorn of all traces of kabbalism, in the few *derashoth* collected in the volume *'Or Ṣaddiqim*, and once or twice in the *M.M.*[5] Thus on the first Sabbath after

[1] With the difference that the sixteenth-century kabbalists cultivated charismatic experiences (albeit in secret), whereas Elijah of Vilna is said to have rejected them for spiritual reasons; cf. Appendix F.

[2] Published as דרשות מרן (on the Pentateuch and *M. Aboth*) in the volume אור צדיקים (Salonica, 1699).

[3] e.g. his commentary on Daniel and on the Five Scrolls (*Leḥem Setharim*, Venice, 1605), and shorter fragments on the Pentateuch and Psalms, printed in Isaac Adrabi's *Dibrey Shalom* (Salonica, 1580) and in Yedayah ha-Penini's *Leshon ha-Zahab* (Venice, 1599), respectively.

[4] That Karo excluded kabbalism from his public teaching and preaching is also borne out by the *M.M.*; cf. below, p. 146. Al-Dahari's account, on the other hand, suggests that Karo discoursed on Kabbalah also in public, cf. above, p. 140.

[5] There is only one case of clear correspondence between the exoteric revelations of the Maggid and Karo's *derashoth* in *'Or Ṣaddiqim*. Commenting on Exod. xiii. 21–22, Karo explains that it was solely by reason of his great love for Israel that God 'took not away the pillar of the cloud by day and the pillar of fire by night'. Otherwise the pillar would only have been necessary whilst the people were actually travelling but not when they slept or rested. As a matter of

Passover, with the beginning of the liturgical summer season when the *Sayings of the Fathers* are read on Sabbath afternoons, Karo reports:[1]

> Thereafter he expounded the whole of ch. 1 of the *Sayings of the Fathers*, saying that he would not expound it kabbalistically but according to the *peshaṭ* (i.e. literal and moralizing sense), so that the people might understand. He began by raising some questions . . . and solved them all . . . and in this manner he expounded the whole chapter and I preached it [in public] and it was well received. . . . Moreover, he taught me a completely new explanation of the other chapters, according to the literal sense, such as I had never heard before . . . and I preached it in public.[2]

Similarly Ps. xix is expounded in the usual moralizing homiletical style[3] and the Maggid concludes: 'Behold the good judgement and knowledge of this Psalm. Although it can be expounded in many ways—for the *Torah* has seventy ways of explanation—yet this is the way which you may preach in public.'[4]

The dichotomy between the exoteric and esoteric spheres seems so complete that we should be overstepping our evidence by suggesting that only kabbalistic mysticism helps us to make sense of the halakhic and moralist attitudes of Karo and his contemporaries. All we can say is that, knowing the kabbalistic background and the mystical life of men such as Karo, Taytazak, Jacob Berab, &c., we are in a position better to understand the motives and drives that inspired their exoteric activities. These activities themselves, however, were conducted without any manifest dependence on mystical, non-halakhic factors. If Karo, or any other contemporary for that matter, does not once mention his ordination in order to add weight to a halakhic decision, why should he permit celestial revelations, important and full of meaning as they are, to bear upon matters that exist in an autonomous and hallowed 'universe of

fact even when travelling they would have no need for a divine pillar except on dark nights when there was no moon, or at cross-roads when divine guidance was necessary. Cf. *M.M.* 26b. 3 and *'Or Ṣaddiqim* fol. 20a.

1 *M.M.* 48a. 3, 5.

2 Preaching it in public (on Sabbath afternoon; cf. Al-Dahari's account referred to above, p. 140) before he could write it down on Saturday evening after the end of the Sabbath.

3 *M.M.* 70a–b.

4 Cf. also *M.M.* 50b. 3: ואח"כ פי' לי כל פ' ב' בדרך פשט מחודש לא נמצא ולא שמעתיו מעולם והוא יפה אף נעים ודרשתיו ברבים.

discourse' of their own? Rabbinic Judaism celebrated its greatest triumph in its most outstanding halakhist—not by suppressing or ousting all other forms of religious life but rather by maintaining its undisputed supremacy, in spite of the most surprising paranormal manifestations, intense charismatic life, and acute kabbalistic 'enthusiasm' in its greatest representative.

7

THE LIFE AND TIMES OF R. JOSEPH KARO
III: THE INNER LIFE

KARO's inner life was, to a large extent, typical of his time. As we have seen, even his maggidic experiences, although unusual, were by no means unheard-of or unique.[1] If we want to understand Karo's mental life more fully, we must take note not only of the general religious atmosphere of his period but also of some of the more specific pressures, strains, and tensions to which more sensitive religious souls were subjected.

The foremost point to be mentioned in this connexion is the profound sense of sin which heavily weighed on all sixteenth-century *ḥasidim*. Sin as the traditional explanation of national disaster obviously loomed large in the consciousness of a generation that had not yet recovered from the shock of the expulsion from the Pyrenean peninsula. The standards of mystical piety, with their extreme demands of utmost purity of mind, constant practice of the presence of God, and perfect fulfilment of all the minutiae of the Law as a necessary preparation for achieving *devekuth*, made a perpetual bad conscience inevitable for the simple reason that it was well-nigh impossible not to fall short of these standards. Consciousness of sin was rendered even more acute by the change which this concept underwent in kabbalism.[2] There was the great primordial sin in which all shared and which all were called to remedy by acts of *tiqqun*. History was the dimension in which this process of *tiqqun* was to take place. Individual sin consisted in failing to do one's share in the work of *tiqqun* or, even worse, to sabotage it actively by more sins of commission. The acuteness of the sense of sin was raised to a further pitch by the kabbalistic theory which taught that the fate of God himself, more particularly in his aspect of *Shekhinah*, was involved in and affected by man's doings. Consequently a single wandering or sinful thought at

[1] Cf. above, ch. 4.   [2] Cf. Scholem, *MTJM.*, pp. 231 ff.

prayer instead of the appropriate meditation (*kawwanah*) was sufficient to make the *Shekhinah* fall still deeper into 'exile' and to strengthen further the power over her of the 'shells' and demonic forces. There must have been many who, like R. Levi b. Ḥabib, had in their youth avoided violent death and bought the possibility of a subsequent flight from Spain at the price of forced sham-baptism. They were now smarting under the lashes of their conscience for having failed to 'sanctify the Name' in martyrdom.

However, with the oppressive sense of sin and guilt assuming the character of a dominant psychological pattern, it becomes both unnecessary and impossible to search for specific sins or transgressions behind the penitential effusions of ascetic rabbis. A long and urgent exhortation to atone 'for your grievous sin' may more often than not only mean that the penitent had enjoyed a morsel of food, or that a fleeting erotic fantasy had crossed his mind before he could suppress it. This does not, of course, exclude the possibility of more serious sins,[1] but should merely serve as a warning that the extravagance of the penitential style does not, by itself, constitute evidence of them.

Indications in the *M.M.* leave us in no doubt that Karo's life was one of continuous mortification and ascetic austerities. Yet practically every communication of the Maggid opens with severe reproof: Karo had eaten too much, drunk too much, slept too much, failed to meditate sufficiently on the *Mishnah*, or to maintain the uninterrupted practice of the presence of God.[2] By his failings he had forfeited the privilege to receive further visits from his Maggid. In fact, he had even forfeited his life. Only the abundant mercy of God and the untiring intercession of the rabbinic scholars whose opinions he so carefully elucidated in his *B.Y.* had repeatedly saved his life and even restored the maggidic manifestations. The fact that Karo was sentenced to death by the celestial court on various occasions[3] and at various dates is by itself sufficient to show that in all probability no one particular sin was meant. But not always is the grace of forgiveness granted without sacrifice.

[1] Cf. the enigmatic reference to 'that great sin' in the quotation, below, p. 151.
[2] *M.M.*, *passim*.
[3] Ibid. 38b. 2, 40b. 4, 58b. 4, 68b, 69a. 2.

Karo was punished for his sins by the death of his first wife and three children,[1] as well as with illness,[2] and more than once the Maggid indicates that he owed his life to the vicarious death of others. We may assume that every time Karo survived one of the frequent epidemics in which some of his fellow citizens died, this kind of explanation immediately suggested itself to him. But the fact that it suggested itself and was promptly taken up by the Maggid both as a reasonable theory and as an argument for further exhortation clearly demonstrates not only the egocentricity[3] of Karo's self-esteem but also the severe anxiety underlying his sense of sin.

On Sabbath, 5 Nisan, 303 (= 1543 C.E.) Karo is reminded that 'you have thought of improper things, wherefore you have been condemned to death. But I, the *Mishnah*, have interceded for you, as also did Jacob Ṭur, Moses Maimonides, Rashi . . . and they redeemed you from death. Your sentence was commuted to illness instead, and also many worthy people were substituted for you.'[4] The same had already happened in Turkey when an earlier death sentence had been commuted 'and a number of people were substituted for you'.[5]

That penitence was one of Karo's main concerns is borne out by the Maggid's repeated assurances that his exhortations and ascetic instructions represented God's answer to Karo's fervent prayers 'to teach you the awesome ways of penitence'.[6] We cannot be sure when and why Karo began to practise penitential discipline.[7] That there was a definite moment of 'conversion' seems to be obvious. In 1536 the Maggid assures Karo that all his earlier sins had been forgiven 'since the time that you repented',[8] i.e. began to adopt penitential practices; a few days earlier he had already referred[9] to 'those former days when you repented'. Whether this first spurt of intense penitence represents merely a conversion from a less extremely ascetic and more 'normal' religious life to one of extreme

[1] Cf. the quotation above, p. 90. [2] *M.M.* 38b. 2.

[3] I am speaking of 'egocentricity' for want of a better term, since the clinical picture of Karo's maggidism does not seem to warrant the use of the term *Beziehungswahn* with its specific psychopathological implications.

[4] *M.M.* 38b. 2. [5] Ibid. 68b.

[6] Ibid. 26b. 6, 38a. 1, 23a. 2, 31b. 1.

[7] Most probably as a result of Molkho's and Alkabets's eschatological and revivalist propaganda; cf. above, ch. 5. [8] *M.M.* 37a. [9] Ibid. 36a. 3.

mortification and discipline, or whether it was a reaction to a particularly grave sin, is difficult to decide on the evidence. On one occasion (towards the end of 1536?)[1] the Maggid reminds Karo of the 'merit of those former days when you repented . . . and the days that had been darkened by *that great sin* [?][2] began to shine brightly as a result of your continuous fasts day and night . . . for you fasted in this manner all those months for more than one year . . . and thereby you have weakened the clouds[3] that darkened the *Shekhinah*[4] as a result of your sin.'

After a period of severe penance and mortification Karo seems to have reverted to a more moderate type of ascetic life and was consequently bidden to return to his former practice:[5]

> Meditate the exceedingly great goodness and love of God who created you *ex nihilo* . . . and though you sinned, He [mercifully] transmigrated you a number of times[6] until your present existence. And though you sinned [also in your present existence], he took you by your right hand[7] and *you repented in those days, but then discontinued your penance.* But now, since you return again to His fear . . . .

Two days before the New Year festival 310, i.e. in the late summer of 1549, the Maggid reminds Karo that he had been sentenced to death for his sins, but that 'by your penance . . . your life was prolonged. . . . But then you forsook your ways and made room for the evil powers through eating and drinking.'[8]

The oft-repeated promises of martyrdom at the stake[9] must be seen against this background of ascetic penance. They are the ultimate expression of the desire for atonement, purification, transformation, and spiritualization. In fact, even Karo's normal ascetic life has to be viewed *sub specie ignis*, as it were, since the Maggid frequently speaks[10] of 'burning all lusts and pleasures' and 'burning

[1] *M.M.* 9a. 2.
[2] Cf. also the quotation below, p. 274, n. 8.
[3] i.e. the demonic powers surrounding the brightness of the *Shekhinah* like a miasma.
[4] The literal wording of the *M.M.* here is *Keneseth Yisra'el.*
[5] *M.M.* 36a. 3.
[6] Cf. below, pp. 239 f., on the number of transmigrations of a soul.
[7] i.e. inspired you with thoughts of repentance.
[8] *M.M.* 58b. 4, and cf. also 68b. for a very similar message.
[9] Cf. above, pp. 98–99.
[10] *M.M.*, *passim.*

all sinful thoughts'. The Maggid never tires of repeating the same pun about the burning of worldly thoughts in the 'strawfire' of meditation on the unity of God during the '*Shema*ʿ-prayer'.[1]

Karo's desire to be burned alive 'for the sanctification of the Name' seems to be unique in the history of Jewish piety.[2] To judge from the appallingly high numbers of Jewish martyrs—though Jewry never insisted on distinguishing sharply between 'martyrs' and victims of persecution—there was no lack of readiness to sanctify the Name, and Jewish liturgy gratefully and proudly remembers this fact. But readiness to be killed, slaughtered, drowned, and burned if God imposes the sacrifice is one thing, the eager desire for it is quite another. The Donatist kind of enthusiasm for martyrdom seems to have been alien to even the most fervent type of Jewish piety—Rabbi Akiba's famous dictum[3] notwithstanding. In pious circles it was recommended to concentrate one's mind when saying certain prayers, more particularly the *Shema*ʿ, and to imagine in one's meditation that one was being martyred for the sanctification of the Name.[4] The purpose of the meditation was the acceptance of the agonies of death with gladness and love. This particular development of Jewish devotional life is of some interest also for the comparative psychology of religion. The similarity with and difference from analogous Christian devotions is obvious. There the various and variegated motives of total abandon, suffering, sacrifice, and self-immolation are organized around one exemplary focus: the passion of Christ as an object of contemplation, imitation, participation, and perhaps even identification. As far as the peculiar type of suffering known as 'exile' went—and it was a type of suffering with particular and acute meaning for the Jew—Jewish piety actually succeeded in developing a somewhat similar

[1] לישרוף . . . בקש דק"ש.

[2] On martyrdom in practice and as an object of meditation cf. J. Katz, 'Martyrdom in the Middle Ages and in 1648–9' (Hebrew), in *Baer Jubilee Volume*, 1960, particularly pp. 322–7.

[3] b. *Ber.* 61b.

[4] Cf. also *M.M.* 4a. 2, 9a. 2, 17a. 4, 34a. For other contemporary statements cf., e.g., Azikri (op. cit., pt. i, ch. 1, par. 16): מצות עשה לקדש את השי"ת אם יאנסוהו להמיר דתו . . . ויחשוב כן בלבו כשקורא ק"ש . . . ויסכים הסכמה גמורה שאם יבוא לידי נסיון יתחוק וימסור נפשו וממונו בשמחה . . . ונחשב לו כאלו נמסר בפועל, and Vital, *Shaʿarey Qedushah*, pt. ii, gate 4, nr. 5: בבוקר ובערב לקדש את שמו ית' במסירת נפשו להריגה בכח בפסוק שמע ישראל.

pattern of *imitatio dei* in the kabbalistic interpretation of the Exile of the *Shekhinah*.[1] But whereas the sufferings of exile could somehow be linked up with the Deity (or at least with one aspect of it), the agony of death could not. Suffering unto death can be turned into a total and sublime sacrifice of oneself of ultimate religious significance. But for this possibility Judaism had no other concrete embodiment and therefore no other symbol than martyrdom for the sanctification of the Name. From a permanent, at some times more and at others less immediate, historical possibility, martyrdom could become a spiritual value to be realized on the imaginative-meditative level. The devotion was both a spiritual exercise in the *readiness* to perform the commandment of loving God 'with all thy soul' and an actual realization of the sacrifice *itself* on a spiritual level.[2] But even those who practised this kind of devotion would have been the first to admit that, given the choice to evade martyrdom by flight, it was one's religious duty to 'choose life'. Karo too must have known that by fleeing from Spain and Portugal to the hospitable shores of Turkey he and his family had evaded martyrdom. Yet his unconscious longing was strong enough to convince him that sometime, no matter where or when, circumstances would arise that would make martyrdom a reality. He was destined to be burned 'so that you should become clean and pure. . . . Consider yourself, therefore, as a perfect burnt-offering and [take care to] be without any blemish that might invalidate the sacrifice.' His martyrdom has no messianic significance or bearing whatsoever; it is a purely personal matter, the *rite de passage*, as it were, by which his sinful, material existence would be finally transmuted into a spotlessly pure and spiritual one. For that reason also martyrdom must be by fire, for[3] 'he who is killed [by the sword] or strangled for the holiness [of God's Name] is like a sin-offering or a trespass-offering [of which part remains and is eaten by the priests],[4] because his flesh remains in this world . . . but he who is burned for the holiness of God is like a burnt sacrifice which rises wholly upwards.' The burning is a process of de-materializing and

[1] Cf., for example, above, p. 51.

[2] Cf. the quotation from Vital above, p. 152, n. 4; see also J. Katz, loc. cit. (above, p. 152, n. 2).

[3] *M.M.* 38a. 4.

[4] Cf. Lev. vi. 19 and vii. 6–7.

a spiritualizing transformation; as such it is actually a rite of ascension, for as the flesh is consumed by the flames 'your smell will rise like frankincense'[1] and 'all your sins and trespasses will be devoured by fire and you will ascend [in radiant whiteness] like pure wool'.[2] Karo's fantasies of martyrdom and the penitential discipline of his ascetic life have a common foundation: an oppressive sense of sin and a fervent desire to rid himself of sin as well as of the material body. What mortification can achieve only imperfectly in this life is triumphantly consummated in death by the purifying flame that annihilates both body and sin. A handful of ashes remains on the altar, whilst a spotlessly pure and white soul is received into glory.

Anxiety is an important feature of this kind of piety. The relation of anxiety and 'fear and trembling' to the confident hope and trust in God that are demanded by certain religious traditions is one of the most interesting problems of the psychology of religion. Quietistic mystics refuse to be disquieted even by their past sins;[3] worldly people are disquieted even by worldly fears. Rabbinic theology had formulated a compromise solution:[4] in worldly matters fear, anxiety, and worry are evil; one should calmly put one's trust in the Lord. In fact, anxiety is tantamount to lack of faith in divine providence. On the other hand where the spiritual life is concerned, constant fear and trembling are indicated.[5] We cannot here pursue this important theological problem further or describe its developments in medieval Jewish thought. For our present purpose it is sufficient to note that Karo adopted this traditional attitude. The part played by anxiety in his life is manifest throughout the *M.M.* Part of this anxiety may be due to childhood experiences in connexion with the expulsion, though anxiety was more a cultural than an individual trait of the time. Azikri,[6] writing in Safed about 1583, asserts that persecutions, expulsions, and exile

[1] *M.M.* 65a.

[2] Ibid. 1b. 6 and *passim*.

[3] e.g. Brother Lawrence and, in a more subtle manner, even Meister Eckhart. Similar utterances can also be found in Ḥasidic literature.

[4] Cf. my study 'Faith, Hope and Trust: A Study in the Concept of *Biṭṭaḥon*', to be published shortly in the *Bulletin of the Institute of Jewish Studies*.

[5] Cf. b. *Beṣah*, 15b–16a, *Yoma* 38a–b, *Ber.* 60a, *Soṭah* 48b, &c.

[6] Op. cit., Introduction.

wanderings were permanently recurring phenomena in Jewish history as long as the people deserved God's wrath, and exclaims: 'woe unto us that this generation was not found worthy [to see the expected advent of the Messiah] . . . and we cannot be certain about further expulsions, the sword of the oppressor, and the cup of trembling of which our fathers have drunk. *And I have seen the great . . . R. Joseph Karo greatly fearing and worrying about this all his life.*' Karo is repeatedly taken to task by the Maggid for worrying too much about financial and other practical matters instead of putting his trust in God:

> . . . and do not be anxious about your sustenance, for I have told you many times that your sustenance is provided for and that you shall not lack anything. . . .[1]
>
> Do not pay attention to the thoughts which Samael [the Devil] and the Serpent put in your heart, to worry about worldly matters . . . for God has been with you; forty years you did not lack anything nor shall you lack anything [in the future], for your sustenance is prepared for you and you need not be afraid of anything. . . . You have seen how on that occasion God sent you as much relief with two hundred zuz as [normally] with five thousand. . . .[2]
>
> . . . and do not think about financial matters except when you are in the privy or in an unclean place [where one must not think of holy things or practise the presence of God]. Thoughts about business do not avail but, on the contrary, harm you. . . .[3]
>
> Do not worry at all about your material needs . . . for I have already promised you that you shall not lack bread and raiment; neither must you worry because of them that have risen against you[4] for they shall not harm you. . . . You must not pay attention to this or any other matter, but only to the fear of the Lord and to his *Torah*, by day and by night, and be exceedingly humble.[5]

In striking contrast to this trustful attitude, inculcated by the Maggid, which commits all cares to God is the unrelenting fear

[1] *M.M.* 47b. 2. [2] Ibid. 9a. 2. [3] Ibid. 32b. 3.

[4] This motif occurs a number of times in the *M.M.*, e.g. 34b. 3, 35a. 5. Though the precise meaning of the allusions is now impossible to discover, they correspond by and large to what one would expect. There is, after all, no reason why Karo should have been exempt from the strife, antagonism, and intrigue that rent communal life everywhere; cf. above, pp. 95–96. Rosanes (op. cit., pp. 39–40, 247–8) tries to show that also in Nicopolis Karo suffered from the unremitting enmity of a local rabbi.

[5] *M.M.* 34b. 3.

that should accompany the spiritual life. After reprimanding Karo again for having succumbed to the devil by drinking more water and eating more food than was strictly necessary, the Maggid repeats his usual ascetic counsels and instructs Karo:[1]

Henceforth be careful to perform worldly actions only so far as strictly necessary for life. If there is any pleasure connected with any such action, do not regard the pleasurable side of it but be perturbed, and strongly desire to be able to perform the action without feeling any pleasure. When you eat consider yourself as if a sword were held over your head and hell were gaping under your feet. For if you eat and drink more than necessary or even if you eat the right amount but intend to derive pleasure from it, then you will be punished. Consider in your heart that you are standing before the King of all kings, the Holy One, blessed be He, whose *Shekhinah* is constantly above your head . . . wherefore all pleasures should be repulsive to you . . . and all your thoughts should be focused on me, my *Torah*, and my fear. In all your actions you should consider yourself as if a sword was held over your head and hell gaping under your feet—even when engaged on good works. . . . For you should always fear that some unworthy or foul thought spoil the [good] action . . . or that you do not perform it to perfection. . . . Particularly at the time of prayer discard all thoughts which the Evil Inclination [i.e. the devil] and his hosts, together with the powers that are above him, namely the Serpent and Samael and their host, put into your heart. Unify [i.e. concentrate] your heart at all times and at every hour and minute to think of *nothing but me, my Torah, and my worship*. This is the mystery of the union in which man is verily united with his Creator, for the soul adheres and unites itself to Him, whilst the body and the limbs become a true dwelling of the *Shekhinah* . . . .

In this passage Karo gives us his theory and practice of *devekuth*. It is a law of nature 'that the soul adheres to the place [i.e. sphere or object] of a man's thoughts and meditations'.[2] Those whose thoughts are directed to wordly lusts and ambitions bind their souls to the corresponding 'lower' powers—whether angelic or demonic—and after their death are for ever caught in the vortex of their ambitions and desires, between which they are slung out 'as out of the middle of a sling'.[3] Those, on the other hand, who practise the

[1] *M.M.* 25a–b. [2] Ibid. 25b. [3] Cf. 1 Sam. xxv. 29.

presence of God, are 'bound in the bundle of life'; for if already in this earthly life they unite their hearts to God in *devekuth*, then how much closer must this union be once they are rid of the material body: 'since all your thoughts were exclusively turned to me, you shall of necessity cleave to the place on which you have always been meditating.'

Devekuth must be reviewed under a double aspect. On the one hand it is the mystical *elevatio mentis ad deum*, or, in the kabbalistic phrase also used by Karo, 'the raising of the thought to its supernal source'.[1] The burnt-offering is a symbolic representation of this ascent, for by cleaving with his spirit to the sacrifice the sacrificer (viz. his soul) rises heavenward together with the smoke from the altar.[2] The corollary is that the essentially spiritual part of *devekuth* can be realized also without animal sacrifice but by the spiritual offering of ascetic mortification on the altar of the *summum bonum*.[3] On the other hand *devekuth* also converts the duly mortified body into a vessel or tabernacle for the *Shekhinah*.[4] This indwelling of the *Shekhinah* in man also accounts for such mystical phenomena as maggidism. Charismatic gifts of this kind are already hinted at by Scripture in Exod. xx. 24: 'in all places where I record my name, I will come unto thee and I will bless thee.' For those who are united to God in perfect *devekuth* ('in all places') will realize that when they think that they are speaking or recording God's name it is really He who speaks in them, 'for you will be a dwelling of the *Shekhinah*, and the *Shekhinah* will speak in your mouth'.[5]

The outline of the theory of *devekuth* in the *M.M.* is thus fairly simple. It does not, as it stands, betray any awareness of the basic problems or principles of *devekuth*. For our immediate purpose we may begin by referring to two alternative views concerning the nature of *devekuth*:[6] the one which regards it as a leisure-time occupation, and the other which demands continuous and uninterrupted contemplation. The former is the 'classical' approach,[7] based on the realization that worldly activity, involving as it does the diversion of attention to the matters in hand, is incompatible

[1] להעלות מחשבתי אל מקורה.
[2] *M.M.* 38a. 3.
[3] Cf. ibid. 29a. 1.
[4] Ibid., *passim*.
[5] Ibid. 29a. 1.
[6] Cf. above, pp. 60 ff. and p. 64, n. 3.
[7] Cf. Scholem, loc. cit.

with the full practice of the presence of God. Since it is generally impossible to forgo all social intercourse, work for a livelihood, family responsibilities, &c., all that the mystic can do is to reduce these unavoidable distractions to an absolute minimum. The other possibility consists in evolving a technique which would allow the ascetic to be engaged on all sorts of practical activities without, however, mentally participating in them. In this mental state the contemplative lives with a double personality: his mind is all focused on things divine, whereas outwardly he appears to hold social intercourse and to be engaged in secular activities. According to Maimonides[1] this was the type of contemplation practised by the Patriarchs, of whom the biblical narrative seems to suggest that they were mainly engaged in tending flocks, digging wells, arranging for marriages and the like. The same type of contemplation is claimed by Azikri, as we have seen, for Noah and commended as the ideal practice. The somewhat similar dilemmas of Christian mysticism and the problems they have given rise to in the history of quietism and other movements are too well known to require more than a passing reference here. Brother Lawrence, to quote but one famous seventeenth-century example, retired to pray in obedience to the directions of his superiors but failed to see any difference between prayer and other times 'because his greatest business did not divert him from God'.

For Jewish piety the problem was further complicated by the high religious value placed on the study of the Law, that is, in the last resort, of rabbinic casuistry. Study as the greatest of the commandments and as the highest type of human (i.e. intellectual) activity soon came to stand in almost the same dialectical tension to other forms of religious behaviour as did the conflicting ideals of the contemplative versus the active life. But whereas, as we have seen, the demands of contemplation and secular activity can be reconciled, if necessary, by the practice of 'double consciousness', this solution does not work when the competition is between two types of mental activity, viz. of two conflicting mental contents. You cannot meditate on the Law day and night and at the same time be engaged in mystical contemplation. You cannot even study

[1] Cf. above, p. 60, n. 2.

the Law and pray at one and the same time.[1] Real contemplative thinkers, such as Baḥya in the eleventh century, did not hesitate to consider excessive rabbinic casuistry as an unpardonable waste of precious time that had better be devoted to spiritual progress. The conflict came to a head in eighteenth-century hasidic mysticism; it was clearly present, albeit unconsciously, in the minds of the great Safed contemplatives.[2] Karo's Maggid expresses the typically rabbinic view of the matter: the study of the Law can simply be equated with *devekuth*. The *Torah* is God's word, his revealed *logos*, a mystical manifestation of the *Shekhinah*.[3] The blessed man is he whose 'delight is in the law of the Lord, and in his law doth he meditate day and night' (Ps. i. 2), for by studying the *Torah* and making it the object of his intellectual labours and the exclusive (or near-exclusive) contents of his mental life he actually cultivates his communion with God.

Throughout the *M.M. devekuth* means meditating on the Law in general and the *Mishnah* in particular. The oft-repeated reproach of having interrupted *devekuth* and broken the 'union' with God simply means that Karo had interrupted his studies for a short time. He is therefore bidden to cleave 'to me, to my *Torah*, to my *Mishnah*, to my fear', &c. *Devekuth* and *hirhura de'orayetha* are synonymous:

> Be careful not to interrupt the *dibbuq* [i.e. *devekuth*, 'communion'] between you and your Creator . . . for the study of *Torah* strengthens the communion, and grace is infused into him from heaven to strengthen the communion further.[4]
>
> 'This book of the Law shall not depart out of thy mouth' [Joshua i. 8], meaning . . . that when you eat and drink or talk to people and cannot study with your mouth, then think of it [in your heart] all the time.[5]

Karo is bidden[6] to meditate mentally on the Law whenever he is prevented by circumstances from 'studying', i.e. pronouncing, the words he is reading. The only exceptions to this rule are prayer and the times set apart for business of a religious character (e.g. public

[1] Cf. the article referred to above, p. 154, n. 4; also above, p. 64, n. 1, and the references there to the Talmud, b. *Sabbath* 10a (as compared with ibid. 33b), p. *Ber.* i. 2, and *Mekhilta* (ed. Lauterbach, vol. ii, pp. 103–4).

[2] Cf. above, p. 64, n. 3.

[3] Cf. below, p. 268.

[4] *M.M.* 40a. 1.

[5] Ibid. 39a. 1.

[6] Ibid. *passim*.

and community affairs). On one occasion Karo is comforted by the Maggid:[1]

> Be not sorry for the time which you devote to public affairs and lose for the study of the Law, because 'thou shouldst take hold of this, yea also from that withdraw not thy hand [Eccl. vii. 18], for both are alike good' [cf. Eccl. xi. 6], and by all [of them together] man merits [his celestial garments]. . . . For study, prayer, and public affairs should be kept apart, and from all of them together the [spiritual] garments are made with which man is clothed when he leaves this world.

On another occasion[2] the Maggid qualifies his exhortation never on any account to interrupt the study of the Law, by adding: 'but at the time of prayer concentrate on it and do not think of anything else, not even of the words of wisdom [i.e. *Torah*], for the time of study and the time of prayer should be kept apart.'

The significant point about these exhortations is the fact that it was apparently deemed necessary to emphasize the value and importance of prayer and thus to prevent it from being completely dominated by *Torah*. The idea that a pious rabbi might be tempted to gabble off his prayers whilst 'meditating' on a point of casuistry may appear absurd until one remembers that already the Talmud[3] occasionally described the study of the Law as 'life eternal' whereas prayer was classed as 'worldly activity'. Study of the Talmud was the rabbinic equivalent to *la vie d'oraison*. Risking the danger inherent in any overstatement, we might say that the study of the Law, unlike prayer or the performance of good works, was more than the fulfilment of a divine commandment; it was a sacramental activity in which man practised communion with God. When kabbalism had turned the whole practice of Judaism into a sacramental affair,[4] the arch-talmudists among the kabbalists could uphold the superiority of *talmud Torah*—this time on mystical grounds—to all other forms of religious activity. Though sixteenth-century Safed offers few or no analogies to Beshtian Hasidism, we may yet compare Karo's talmudic practice of the presence of God

[1] *M.M.* 21a.
[2] Ibid. 9a. 2; cf. also ibid. 47b. 2, 49a. 2.
[3] b. *Sabbath* 10a.
[4] Cf. Scholem, *MTJM.*, pp. 29–30, and his *On the Kabbalah and Its Symbolism*, p. 122 ff.

with the theory of *devekuth* advocated by R. Ḥayyim of Volozhin,[1] the disciple of the Gaon Elijah of Vilna.

Devekuth, for Karo, does not mean what it meant for the kabbalists whose theories on the subject have been mentioned in an earlier chapter. Positively *devekuth* means the study of the Law (to a lesser extent that of Kabbalah too[2]) and prayer; negatively it means the suppression of all thoughts that might distract attention from study and prayer. On the moral side *devekuth* implies complete and extreme 'indifference'. We cannot here follow the development of the ideal of *apatheia* in Jewish spirituality—from the Stoic imperviousness to all sensations and emotions likely to disturb the tranquillity of the mind and its self-mastery to the genuinely mystical abandon of one's self to the sole action of the divine. This ideal of holy indifference (*middath ha-hishtawwuth*) was propagated in particular by Baḥya in his *Duties of the Heart* and the Maggid quotes with approval[3] an ascetic saying which is actually a Ṣufi anecdote told by Baḥya:[4] 'An ascetic once asked one of his friends, "Do you possess equanimity?" and he replied, "In what respect?". The ascetic then said, "Are praise and insult the same in your eyes?" and he replied, "No". Then the ascetic said, "In that case you have not yet arrived [at the goal]; strive hard, perhaps you may reach this highest of the stages [of perfection] and the greatest of the aims to be aspired to".' Elsewhere the Maggid's demands are even more extreme. The true ascetic should be able to see a naked woman without feeling any affect or temptation whatsoever.[5] One is reminded here of similar views held by some Christian sects

quod non debebat reputari homo vel mulier virtuosus vel virtuosa nisi se

[1] *Nefesh ha-Ḥayyim* (1824).

[2] Cf. *M.M.* 20b. 1, 21a, 24b. 2, 33a. 1, 36a. 3, 57b. 2, 58a–b, 64a. 1, 68a. 1, 70b. 4.

[3] Ibid. 25b.

[4] *Duties of the Heart*, v. 5: וכבר אמרו על אחד מן החסידים שאמר לחבירו הנשתוית אמר לו באיזה ענין אמר לו נשתוה בעיניך השבח והגנות א"ל לא א"ל א"כ עדיין לא הגעת השתדל אולי תגיע אל המדרגה הזאת כי היא העליונה שבמדרגות החסידים ותכלית החמודות. Both the idea of 'equanimity' and this particular story about it were already favourites with earlier mystics; cf. Scholem, *MTJM.*, pp. 96–97 and p. 372, n. 59, also the reference ibid. to Eckhart's usage '*aequaliter se habere*'.

[5] *M.M.* 16b: כי מאחר שלבך תמיד אינו מהרהר אלא בעבודתי, אפילו תפגע באשה ערומה לא תבוא לידי חטא.

possent ponere nudus cum nuda in uno lecto et tamen non perficerent actum carnalem.[1]

Of course, the kabbalists never suggested that perfection in this sphere should be put to the test as some Perfectionist sects seem to have done. The profound difference of the Maggid's teaching from the stoic ideals of *apatheia* or *ataraxia* is as obvious as are the similarities. Complete equanimity and holy indifference are no virtues or moral qualities, but are conceived as aspects of *devekuth*. It is precisely because the mind is so filled with things divine, and consciousness is so exclusively concentrated on God,[2] that no worldly, let alone evil, thought can penetrate. Hence prayer is merely a more intensive form of what should be the permanent, normal life of *devekuth*. *Devekuth* and the *kawwanah* of prayer mean that the mind is directed on God to the exclusion of all other thoughts.

Karo is well aware of the special 'intentions' or 'meditations' recommended by the kabbalists for prayer, and we have seen that at least on one occasion[3] he opposed his own *kawwanoth* to those taught by Alkabets. Nevertheless, *kawwanoth* play a patently minor role, for essentially *devekuth* exhausts itself in the single-mindedness of prayer and study: 'Evacuate all [irrelevant] thoughts from your heart at prayer time and concentrate your mind on what your mouth utters.'[4] That this must not be taken as a radical rejection of *kawwanoth* (unless it represents a different stage in Karo's development) appears from a somewhat more detailed maggidic instruction elsewhere:[5]

> Do not think of anything at all when you pray, but only meditate on that which you know [i.e. on the *kawwanoth* with which you are acquainted]; where you do not know [the appropriate kabbalistic intentions] do as Moses [Maimonides] my elect has said:[6] empty yourself of all thoughts and concentrate on the plain meaning of the words.

Many other passages in the *M.M.* show that in Karo's usage *kawwanah* is synonymous with suppression of extraneous, distracting

[1] Quoted in R. Nell's article 'Les Cathares' in *Mystique et Continence*, p. 143.
[2] כשלבך תמיד מהרהר בתורתי ועבודתי.
[3] Above, p. 101.
[4] *M.M.* 3a. 1.
[5] Ibid. 35a. 1.
[6] The reference is to Maimonides's Code, *Tefillah*, iv. 16. Maimonides's שיפנה את לבו מכל המחשבות = *M.M.* לפנאה כולהו מחשבות. The words ולכוונה בפירושא דמלה are based on *Ṭur*, *O.H.* 98; cf. also *Sh.A.*

thoughts.[1] Its significance, for Karo, is therefore determined by the halakhic and not by the kabbalistic tradition.

It is true that the Maggid occasionally suggests other, supplementary exercises. But these can hardly be described as techniques of *devekuth* since they are rather exercises of the imagination for specific purposes. Thus the act of imagining one's father's image[2] is supposed to increase one's sense of shame and thereby to help prevent sin. The method of always keeping the holy name of God, the Tetragrammaton, before one's eyes[3] might undoubtedly serve the purposes of contemplative or even ecstatic *devekuth*, but the point is that in Karo's case it does not. The function of this imaginative contemplation is purely negative: the constant imagined reminder of God's presence should strengthen the resolve not to admit 'strange' thoughts into one's mind. Other meditations again are designed to increase humility and the distaste for bodily pleasures, e.g. the Maggid's short exhortation, worthy of a Buddhist monk, to

> beware of food and drink and bodily pleasures. Whenever you experience pleasure at eating or drinking, meditate on the repulsiveness of food as it is chewed [in the mouth] and even more on its repulsiveness as it is evacuated from the body.[4]

In fact, everything was grist to Karo's ascetic mill. The Maggid does not even hesitate to hold up Gentiles as shining examples: 'Think of the tortures and mortifications which they suffer. How much more then should you be ready to suffer tortures and mortifications for the true religion in order to be acceptable to your Creator.'[5] The rule to stop eating when you enjoy it most, usually quoted in the name of Rabbi Jonah of Gerona,[6] is repeated more than once by the Maggid: 'Reduce your enjoyment of food and drink to a minimum, and if you feel pleasure at one dish, do

[1] Cf., e.g., *M.M.* 58b. 4, 20b. 1 *et passim*; clearly לבטל הרהורים = לכוין.

[2] Ibid. 39a. 2, 40a. 5; the motif goes back to the legend of Joseph, cf. the midrashic comments on Gen. xxxix. 11 (Midr. *Gen. Rabba* lxxxvii; cf. also below, p. 281).

[3] *M.M.* 39a. 2, 40a. 5.

[4] Ibid. 30a. 2.

[5] Ibid. 38a. 1. The correct text is צא ולמד מהגויים. Later editions (Vilna) have changed this to מהישמעאלים!

[6] Cf. *Sha'arey Teshubah*, Bk. i, sections 30–34, Bk. iv, section 12, and more particularly his *Yesod ha-Teshubah*.

not continue with it but change to another dish which you enjoy less, according to the practice of Al-Constantin.'[1] The identity of Al-Constantin had already puzzled S. P. Rabinowitz.[2] The family had been well known in Spain since the thirteenth century and there are several authors of that name,[3] but it is very improbable that any of them is meant. The traveller Benjamin of Tudela (twelfth century) mentions a 'saint and ascetic Rabbi Abraham Al-Constantin who was one of the mourners of Jerusalem';[4] but it is extremely unlikely that he would be meant. In all probability a contemporary of Karo's by that name was famous among *ḥasidim* for practising this particular form of mortification. At any rate the counsels and practice of Rabbi Jonah as well as of other authors sufficiently prove that extreme ascetic enthusiasm could easily unite with kabbalistic piety but was in no wise dependent on it. In fact, Karo's piety was of the traditional, halakhic-ascetic type recommended by moralist writers since Jonah of Gerona. Its essentially non-mystical, halakhic character is borne out not only by the *Sh.A.*, which, after all, may be said to present a deliberately one-sided picture only, but also—and most significantly—by the Maggid's treatment of *kawwanoth*. Karo's halakhic piety is illustrated by a little incident reported by Azikri[5] which is in many ways reminiscent of the religious *habitus* of Lithuanian nineteenth-century pietism. Observing a man leading a horse and an ass by one rope, Karo ran after him in order to explain that this was an infringement of the prohibition (Deut. xxii. 10) not to plough with an ox and an ass together. He was only satisfied after having devised a method by which the man could lead his two animals without trespassing the divine law. Neither his kabbalistic interests nor his eschatological longings, not even his mystical experiences

[1] *M.M.* 1a. 1, rule 18.

[2] Op. cit., p. 246 note.

[3] Solomon Al-Constantin, author or *Megalleh 'Amuqqoth* and Ḥanokh Al-Constantin, author of *Mar'oth 'Elohim* (the latter the butt of Isaac Abarbanel's sharp criticisms; cf. Abarbanel's commentary *ad Isa.* vi. 1 f. and his *Yeshu'oth Meshiḥo* (ed. Karlsruhe, 1828, fol. 9d)). Cf. also Steinschneider, *Hebr. Handschriften d. Königl. Bibliothek zu Berlin*, p. 56.

[4] Ed. Adler, 1907, Hebr. text, p. 26; Benjamin of Tudela (ibid., p. 50b) also mentions a Moses Al-Constantin of Aleppo. Cf. also Steinschneider, op. cit., p. 63, and H. Y. D. Azulay, *Shem ha-Gedolim*, pt. ii, s.v. נבואת הילד.

[5] Op. cit., pt. iii, ch. 5, par. 75.

could in any way alter, let alone break, the pattern of rabbinic piety. The most extreme penitential discipline of fasts and mortifications could easily be integrated into the traditional halakhic-moralist framework. What Karo owed to the contemporary kabbalistic revival was not his ascetic piety as such but his mystical life, i.e. the maggidic manifestations. Kabbalism provided him with a theoretical background and practical examples[1] of mystical manifestations, celestial messages, demonstrations of special divine election, and the like. This paranormal psychic activity never, so far as our present knowledge goes,[2] produced striking, original insights. The Maggid had nothing to say that went beyond the knowledge, desires (conscious or repressed), and ambitions of Joseph Karo. Perhaps the most striking feature of the Maggid's behaviour is his habit of reproving and humiliating Karo whilst at the same time fostering his sense of unique greatness. The psychological significance of this combination of narcissism with internalized aggression will be discussed later. As far as Karo's sense of greatness goes, the peak is undoubtedly reached with the Maggid's repeated promises that one day he would work miracles like the rabbis of talmudic legend[3] 'and the name of heaven [i.e. God] will be sanctified by you [through these miracles] . . . and all the world will know that there is a God in Israel'. The privilege of working miracles and the value of miracles as a public demonstration of God's existence and power seem to have been standard motifs of the contemporary 'maggidic pattern'. The recipient of the revelations recorded in the amazing *Sefer ha-Meshib*[4] was made the same promises with almost the same wording.[5]

Paranormal manifestations of the unconscious are by no means rare in the history of mysticism. One has to glance only at a book such as H. Thurston's *Surprising Mystics*,[6] not to speak of the

[1] Cf. above, ch. 4 and below, ch. 12.

[2] Cf. below, chs. 8 and 9–11 on the halakhic and kabbalistic contents of the *M.M.*

[3] *M.M.* 1b. 6, 4a. 2, 11a. 2, 16b, 20b. 3, 27b. 2.

[4] Cf. above, pp. 46–47.

[5] MS. Brit. Mus. (Marg. 766), fol. 114a: וכשתדעו המראה הזאת תדעו כי יש אלקים בישראל שעם זה השם הגדול תוכלו לעשות מופתים בשמים ובארץ; also ibid., fol. 96b.

[6] London, 1955.

writings of visionaries such as St. Bridget of Sweden or Swedenborg, to realize that nothing is impossible. There is, however, a widespread prejudice to the effect that these slightly eccentric manifestations of sanctity, bordering on the pathological, are characteristic of a somewhat unbalanced type of personality, distinguished no doubt for its psychic capacities but lacking in higher mental qualities. William James,[1] commenting on the impression of 'extravagance' left by so many saints, pronounced it to be 'on examination, a relative deficiency of intellect'. Many modern apologists and writers on mysticism have gratefully adopted, for their own reasons, James's view. The more respectable saints, they insinuate, are less 'extravagant' in their psychic life and, at the same time, more profound and substantial in their mystical experience and teaching. If the lives of the great mystics too exhibit bizarre and extravagant manifestations, these are gently played down in the interests of an aesthetically more acceptable and spiritually more satisfying picture of pure and exalted mysticism.[2] The one drawback of this idyllic picture is that it is not true. We are here concerned with Karo only and not with mysticism in general, yet Karo's case may serve as an apt illustration. For whatever our opinion of the Maggid, it is quite certain that no intellectual deficiency can be attributed to Karo. His intellectual achievement was impressive by any standard and need hardly stoop to answer the petty sneers of the early fathers of the *Wissenschaft des Judentums* who comforted themselves by unanimously stressing Karo's 'lack of originality'.[3] Yet Karo's intellectual calibre did not prevent his unconscious from expressing itself in the most 'extravagant' and psychologically infantile forms. There is no justification at all for the assumption that Karo's unconscious was in any way essentially different from that of his contemporaries. They were all pious and saintly scholars, earnestly seeking the presence of

[1] *The Varieties of Religious Experience*, lectures xiv–xv.

[2] Cf., for example, Evelyn Underhill, *Mysticism* (edn. 12, 1930), p. 59: 'all true saints . . . detested eccentricity' (!). When psychopathological features are undeniable, then they have to be taken into the bargain, but carefully distinguished from the 'healthy . . . kinds of ecstasy' in the same individual; cf. Underhill, op. cit., p. 362. See also the remarks of H. Delacroix, *Étude d'histoire et de psychologie du mysticisme: les grands mystiques chrétiens*, 1908, pp. ii–iii.

[3] Cf. above, p. 3.

God and desirous of doing his will. It was not their fault that in terms of concrete human life and their concrete historical situation they had to buy their saintliness at the price of repressions and ideals that left a large part of their personalities unconscious and a large part of their unconscious infantile. Karo differed from most of his contemporaries not in his mental and psychological make-up, but merely in his psychic constitution which enabled his unconscious to use the extant kabbalistic patterns of maggidism in order to express itself.[1] The result should not occasion any surprise, since the psychological ravages of repression (of whatever kind) are too well known to call for comment. What does, perhaps, need emphasizing is the truism that psychological jargon, here as elsewhere in historical research, gives us only part of the truth and not always the most important part. To associate the Maggid's revelations with the repressions wrought by halakhic piety is at best a platitude. To assert that they reveal the inevitable results of such piety is not even an illegitimate generalization but merely a meaningless partisan declaration. For the historian of religion the question is simply this: why did halakhic piety tend to produce this increase of psychic-mystical phenomena precisely in the sixteenth century? Was it because sixteenth-century Jewry had been so severely shaken by the catastrophe of the general expulsion? Was it because new and special psychic mechanisms were necessary to impose stability on souls whose old world was broken and whose eschatological mood plainly indicated that what they wanted was a really 'new' world? It is certainly significant that both the *Sh.A.*, the tentative *organon* of religious unity and stability, and the *M.M.* were composed by the same Joseph Karo in the same sixteenth century. The kabbalistic revival was only part of the Jewish response to the great upheaval. Another, no less important, part is to be found in the reassertion of halakhic piety. The final crystallization—or perhaps petrifaction—of rabbinic orthodoxy, and its last great codification were attempts to counter the threat of disintegration experienced as a result of the recent catastrophes. Even more telling than the codification itself—for, after all, such attempts had been made before—was the public response to Karo's *B.Y.*

[1] Cf. above, ch. 4.

and *Sh.A.*, and the general acceptance of these two works after the usual first denigrating criticisms by hostile scholars.[1] It is one of the ironies of history that the author of the *Sh.A.* should also have left us a complementary document, the reverse of the medal whose front side, showing the apparently unproblematic triumph of rabbinic halakhism, has so far been the better known.

[1] Cf. the references in Greenwald, op. cit., pp. 174 f.

8

THE *HALAKHAH* OF THE MAGGID

THE halakhic references in the *M.M.* are few and rather incidental. However, a number of longer and more sustained passages seem to have been written down at one period, during a few consecutive nights. In the present chapter the term 'halakhic' will be taken in the widest sense as including discussions of talmudic passages, and decisions, rulings, or comments of a legal, ritual, or casuistic nature. Incidental references to customs and *minhagim* will be noted too, but no notice will be taken of obvious *halakhoth* or *minhagim* mentioned by the Maggid only in connexion with their kabbalistic interpretation. The motley collection of *halakhoth* in the *M.M.* cannot, of course, be systematized in any way. It seems best, therefore, to discuss the various items in order of their halakhic interest and in comparison with both Karo's Code and, more particularly, his monumental commentary *B.Y.* on Jacob Asheri's Code, the so-called *Ṭur*. As the chapters of *Ṭur* are not subdivided into paragraphs, I am simply applying Karo's own paragraph division in *Sh.A.* to the parallel chapters in Asheri's *Ṭur*.[1]

The entries s.tt. *Vayyaqhel* (Lublin and Venice editions) and *Bereshith* (Venice edition) contain material which even at a first inspection appears to belong together. Disregarding the confused order in which it appears in the printed text, we can easily re-arrange the five passages in chronological sequence. The correctness of the chronology proposed here is confirmed by the fact that the sequence of themes corresponds exactly to the sequence of the self-same halakhic topics in *Y.D.* 198–201. The material should therefore be arranged in the following order:

	Ṭur	*M.M.* (*ed. Amsterdam 1708*)	*Date*
(i)	*Y.D.* 198	p. 35*a*(–*b*)	13 Adar [5]296[2]
(ii)	,, 199	p. 34*a*	[13 Adar ii 5296]

[1] e.g. *Ṭur Y.D.* 188: 31 refers to that part of ch. 188 which corresponds to § 31 of the equivalent chapter in *Sh.A.*, *Y.D.* The cues (opening words) of the paragraphs of the commentary *B.Y.* will be indicated where necessary.

[2] Cf. above, pp. 33–4, where it has been shown that this undated passage from

	Ṭur	*M.M.* (*ed. Amsterdam 1708*)	*Date*
(iii)	*Y.D.* 201: 2	p. 36*b*	?
(iv)	,, 201: 6–7	p. 36*b*–37*a*	1 Nisan 296
(v)	,, 201: 15	p. 6*a*	Monday, 5 Nisan 296

(i) The Maggid[1] refers to something Karo had discussed—orally or in writing—on the previous day. But since *B.Y. ad Y.D.* 198 contains more than one thorough discussion of Maimonides's views[2] (viz. of *Ṭur*'s presentation or alleged misrepresentation of these[3]), it is difficult to dogmatize about the exact meaning of the statement, 'both views are correct'. The Maggid's words, 'and your remarks regarding the statement of Jacob who fears me [i.e. *Ṭur*] that "his father [i.e. R. Asher] did not draw this distinction" are

the Venice edition really belongs to the entry dated 13 Adar 5296 in the Lublin edition. The continuation of the latter entry, 'moreover, he said unto me: behold you now study the tractate *Qiddushin*', &c., may well be later than 13 Adar, as is also suggested by its correspondence with *Y.D.* 199. The next item (*M.M.* 36b), corresponding to *Y.D.* 201, is evidently later again.

[1] The relevant passage in the *M.M.* runs: כי מה שפלפלת אתמול על הרמב"ם ז"ל ב' הדברים אמת הם והרמב"ם שמח בך על שירדת לסוף דעתו וגם שמח עליך שאתה תמיד מביא דעתו ומפלפל בו ודבריך כנים ואמיתיים זולת בקצת מקומות שאני אעירך עליהם. . . . ועוד במה דאמרת דאמר יעקב דחילי וא"א ז"ל לא חילק יאות כוונת, יפה דנת ומידע תנדע דכל דבעי הרמב"ם על הרוב אינון קושטא בגין דאיהו אדבק גרסאי קדמונאי. . . . כגון ר"ח ורבנו האי דגרסתהון ברירא ולזימנין תוספות מסגיאות פלפולא הוו מקשו על ההוא גרסא ודחו לה ולית קושטא הכי. ופירוש נמי דמפרש הרמב"ם הרוב קושטא אינון. ובההיא דצפורן שפרשת וכתבת שני דרכים חייך דהקב"ה חייך בפלפולא דילך אבל אורחא בתראה הוא ברירו דמלה ומ"מ לא תמחוק קדמאה. . . .

[2] MS. B 1 (fol. 9a) reads רמב"ן throughout the paragraph and once emends a written ם to ן. The same manuscript, however, continues later: ומידע תנדע דכל דברי הרמב"ם אמת וכו׳. Similarly B 2 (fol. 11b) had originally read מה שפלפלת אתמול על הרמב"ם, but emended this to רמב"ן, and finally ends כל דברי הרמב"ם וכו׳. B 3 consistently reads רמב"ם. It is, however, beyond doubt that Maimonides is meant. Nahmanides was never slandered in kabbalistic circles, whereas Maimonides was. The Maggid's defence against malicious kabbalistic calumnies can thus only refer to Maimonides: וכי שכיבת הרמב"ם ז"ל נפיק לקדמותך דמתרצית הלכתיה ועל כן השתא מוליף עליך זכו והא איהו במדרגת צדיקיא ולא כדאמרי הנך חכימי דאגלגל [ברחשא] דנהי דהכי אתגזר עלוי בגין קצת מילין דמליל דלא אתחזו אבל אורייתא אגינת עליה ואוף עובדוי טבין דמארי דעובדין טבין הוה [ע"כ] לא אגלגל [ברחשא] אלא אגלגל בגלגולא ואסתלק ויתיב בהדי צדיקייא. The bracketed word ברחשא has been supplied from the manuscripts, as the printed text, out of sheer respect for Maimonides, merely dares to say דאגלגל וכו׳; cf. above, p. 31.

[3] *Y.D.* 198: 7, 9, 14, 21, 31.

perfectly correct', clearly refer to *B.Y. ad Y.D.* 198: 31 towards the end.[1] When the Maggid further declares that 'in the matter of *ṣipporen* where you suggested two possible solutions, by your life, God was pleased with your discussion; however, the second solution is the correct one', he merely confirms Karo's own conclusion after a very thorough examination of Maimonides's position *re* 198: 21. For *B.Y.* there concludes with the words, 'wherefore I incline to the second solution that I have proposed'.[2] It is a comforting thought that God is on the side of the authors and appreciates sheer intellectual virtuosity for its own sake; for Karo is bidden by the Maggid not to delete the first solution although the second only was true and correct.

(ii) This is the only instance in the *M.M.* where an explicit reference to the *Ṭur* is actually given ('*Ṭur* ch. 199'), though it is not stated that book *Y.D.* of the *Ṭur* is meant.[3] The whole paragraph is a characteristic example of a maggidic message, simply and directly concerned with Karo's immediate interests and preoccupations, and without an eye to a prospective reading public. Again it is impossible to be quite sure which comment in the *B.Y.* is meant when we are told that 'Maimonides was glad that you expounded his opinions'.[4] The statement that 'what you wrote concerning *ḥafifah*[5] is true and well-founded' may refer to 199: 10, where the rulings of Maimonides[6] are defended against

[1] *M.M.*: במה דאמרת דאמר יעקב דחילי וא"א ז"ל לא חילק וכו'.

[2] *M.M.*: ובההיא דצפורן שפרשת וכתבת שני דרכים חייך דהקב"ה חייך בפלפולא דילך אבל אורחא בתראה הוא ברירו דמלה. *B.Y.*: לפיכך נראה לי כדרך שני שכתבתי.

[3] Only B 2 (fol. 12*a*) adds י"ד. The relevant lines in the *M.M.* are these: ועוד אמר לי אתה לומד עכשיו בקדושין קודש קדשים היא שכבר למדת אותה שלשה פעמים, וכן אזכך לגמור כל התלמוד כל מסכתא שלשה פעמים.... כי הרמב"ם שמח במה שגלית ופירשת במה שכתב הטור סי' קצ"ט שלא נתפרש עד היום (MS. Sassoon and ed. Amsterdam transpose: שלא עד היום נתפרש; some manuscripts read נתבאר) וגם כן מקומות אחרים אתה מבאר, וגם הרמב"ם שמח בך על שאתה מפרש דעותיו. וגם במה שכתבת בו על ההיא דחפיפה אמת ויציב, וגם במה שכתבת על יעקב דחילי במוסקת שפיר קאמרת ולכך נתכוון הוא, וגם על שכתבת על יעקב דחילי שאין דבריו מבוארים אמת ויציב הוא, ומה שפלפלת ליישב דבריו קוב"ה שמח בהאי פלפולא אבל הוא לא לכך נתכוון ושלשתם מליצים עליך זכות....

[4] הרמב"ם שמח בך על שאתה מפרש דעותיו.

[5] וגם מה שכתבת על ההיא דחפיפה אמת ויציב. B 1 (fol. 9b) and 2 (fol. 12a) read ההוא דחפיסה; B 3 reads חפיסא.

[6] *Miqva'oth* ii, §§ 16 and 23.

the criticisms of RABaD. The initial remark that 'RaMBaM [i.e. Maimonides] was glad with the way you explained the wording in *Ṭur* ch. 199 which has not been properly explained until now' would be far more intelligible if it read RaMBaN [i.e. Nahmanides][1] instead of RaMBaM, as in that case it could be taken to refer to 199: 1. This proposed emendation is corroborated by the Maggid's concluding assurance that 'all three are pleading for you'. The number three can only be arrived at by adding to Maimonides (RaMBaM) and Jacob Asheri ('Jacob the god-fearing one') the name of Nahmanides. In that case the first reference would be to RaMBaN (199: 1), the second to Maimonides (199: 4 or 10), and the third to Jacob Asheri. As concerns *moseqeth*, viz. *'oregeth*,[2] the reference clearly is to 198: 35 where the question is discussed how to ensure unimpeded access of water to the armpits[3] and similar parts of the body when taking a ritual bath. *B.Y.*[4] has some difficulty with the *Ṭur*'s meaning but concludes his analysis with the words, 'in that way the words of our master [the *Ṭur*] can be satisfactorily explained'.[5] The Maggid's final remark, 'it is also very true what you have written concerning Jacob... that his words are not clear', may still refer to 198: 35, but more probably alludes to *Y.D.* 199 with which the whole paragraph (apart from the question of *moseqeth*) is concerned. The precise reference is difficult to determine as the charge 'his words are not clear enough' or 'his words are obscure'[6] is made more than once against Asheri in the commentary *B.Y.* on this chapter.

(iii) This paragraph, which concerns the validity of a ritual bath when 'the dripping water was more than the flowing water',[7] is of special interest. It refers, of course, to *Y.D.* 201: 2, where Asheri records R. Tam's permission to use rivers for the purpose of ritual immersions all the year round, even in early spring when the thaw would cause the 'dripping water' (i.e. the snow carried by the river) to exceed the 'flowing water' (i.e. water originating from

[1] All manuscripts concur in reading רמב"ם; yet רמב"ן seems to be more correct.

[2] B 1 and 2: ומה שכתבת בההוא דאוגרת; B 3 (fol. 69a) reads אוגרת ומוסקת.

[3] תחת בית השחי.

[4] *B.Y.*, s.v. והשתא.

[5] ובכך דברי רבינו עולים יפה.

[6] דבריו סתומין, אין דבריו מדוקדקים.

[7] נוטפים שרבו על הזוחלים, cf. *M. Miqva'oth* v. 5.

a fountain source) in the river. The stricter view, attributed to R. Isaac of Dampierre and also shared by R. Me'ir of Rothenburg, is followed by R. Asher and by his son, the author of the *Ṭur*. In justifying this ruling, the name of R. Me'ir is mentioned as a supporting authority, but neither Jacob Asheri nor Joseph Karo (in *B.Y.*) in his detailed discussion ad loc. seems to base the stricter decision on R. Me'ir's additional, extra-halakhic reputation as a saint and martyr.[1] It is not surprising, however, that the Karo of the *M.M.*, with his curious passion for martyrdom, should fasten on R. Me'ir as the main protagonist of the debate. Instead of saying that the *halakhah* follows the majority opinion against R. Tam, the Maggid puts the cart before the horse by declaring that 'the law is as stated by my beloved and god-fearing R. Me'ir, the law is everywhere as stated by him for he was perfect; and through his imprisonment—in which he also died—his sins have been atoned for and he remained pure and unblemished, and ascended to a very high sphere among the righteous'[2] and adding, almost as an afterthought, that other authorities too agreed with him. The Maggid then explains that although, in principle, the stricter opinion should be followed, *post factum* one may rely on R. Tam's ruling. This compromise, which is justified at length by kabbalistic arguments, is not mentioned at all in *B.Y.* although it is implicit in *Ṭur*'s wording. The Maggid's approval of Karo's refutation of R. Yeruḥam leads to an unexpected and curious digression on the latter's place in the heavenly company of saints: 'wherever you criticize his views you are right. I call him "Yeruḥam my hidden one" because he is hidden in the Garden of Eden. For there are saints whose merits are not sufficient to allow them to appear publicly in Paradise but only to be there in secret, and he is one of them.' This extraordinary declaration is, however, mitigated by the assurance that 'none the less he has attained a high and precious rank'.

Before proceeding to the next *halakhah* (*Y.D.* 201 : 6–7), it may not be out of place to comment on the two paragraphs in the *M.M.*

[1] On R. Me'ir of Rothenburg cf. Irving A. Agus, *R. Meir of Rothenburg* (2 vols.; 1947), and Urbach, op. cit., ch. 10, particularly pp. 405–28.

[2] It would be interesting to examine the *halakhah* of *B.Y.* and *Sh.A.* with an eye to ascertaining whether R. Me'ir's opinion is, in fact, always followed.

immediately preceding the one just discussed.[1] A careful reading and comparison with the entry in the Lublin edition, dated 13 Adar,[2] will lend much support to the suggestion made earlier[3] that the opening of the communication s.t. *Vayyaqhel* (Venice edition) is really the continuation of the entry of 13 Adar of the Lublin edition; the whole combined passage ends with the words 'shining in all directions'.[4] The following three paragraphs were probably communicated some time between 13 Adar and 1 Nisan, and the same applies to the passage in the Lublin edition beginning with the words 'moreover, he told me' and joined to the abrupt beginning of a new subject: 'This matter has been agreed upon in the Celestial Academy'.[5] I have already argued that this chronological arrangement would fit the order of *Y.D.* It would also explain why the Maggid already deals with the first verse of Leviticus, viz. with Nahmanides's commentary on it.[6] The communication is, in reality, no longer part of *Vayyaqhel* but belongs to the following Sabbath (*Vayyiqra*). If this surmise is correct and there is only a few days' interval between the passage beginning 'moreover, he told me' (Amsterdam edition, 34a) and the paragraphs with a similar beginning (ibid. 36b), then the two references to the tractate *Qiddushin* of the Talmud can be seen in perspective. The earlier passage implies that Karo had recently begun his fourth reading of this tractate.[7] By the time the paragraph immediately preceding our no. iii was written, Karo must already have reached fol. 26a of b. *Qiddushin*. For the cryptic message concerning the deletion of the word *vidduy* can only refer to the mention of first fruits at the bottom of fol. 26a ibid. and to the discussion of the subject among

[1] The two paragraphs are:
עוד אמר לי בדיבור הרמב"ן שבתחילת ויקרא... ובזה ביאר כל הדיבור כהוגן ואמר שזו היתה כוונת הרמב"ן.
עוד אמר בפ"ק דקדושין של ובוידוי מוטעה הוא וצריך להגיה, וגם מי שאין לו קרקע אינו צריך להתוודות ובההיא דר"ג והזקנים האמת כדברי תוספות [*Qiddushin* 26b, s.v. מעשה] ושזה לגבי ביעור היא שנוייה בסוף מעשר.

[2] *M.M.* (ed. Amsterdam), 33b.

[3] Cf. above, pp. 33–34.

[4] מתנציצין לכל עבר (*M.M.* 36b, line 1).

[5] Ibid. 34a: דנא מילתא אסכימו במתיבתא דרקיעא.

[6] Cf. the quotation above, n. 1.

[7] Cf. the quotation above, n. 1. If we may believe Karo's grandson Yedidyah, this promise of the Maggid was fulfilled; cf. Conforti, op. cit., p. 35b (quoted above, p. 35, n. 2).

the talmudic commentators. It should be noted that although Karo accepts the deletion (already proposed by Rashi and Tosafoth), he does not draw the apparently obvious conclusion that therefore a man who possesses no land was none the less required to make the oral declaration (*vidduy*) prescribed in Deut. xxvi. 3 ff. On the contrary, the Maggid, viz. Karo, rules that although the word *vidduy* must be deleted for textual reasons, a person who possesses no land is, in fact, absolved from the duty of making the aforementioned declaration. This is precisely the opinion of Tosafoth, b. *Baba Bathra* 27a.[1]

(iv) The long discussion of *B.Y. ad Y.D.* 201: 6–7 is a major *tour de force*. The maze of confusing intricacies through which Karo takes his readers starts from the 'trough of Jehu' (*M. Miqva-'oth* iv. 5) and the rule concerning the 'hole as big as the spout of a water-skin'. *B.Y.* reviews all the relevant texts[2] as well as the opinions of the commentators and codifiers, and devotes much space to a thorough examination of the positions of Maimonides, Asher, and the *Ṭur*. The upshot of Karo's analysis is this: Asher's ruling is ambiguous; *Ṭur*, who had meant to follow his father's opinion, actually misinterpreted it, viz. gave it a different meaning from the one intended (according to Karo) by Asher. There is, moreover, a patent contradiction between Asher's ruling in his talmudic Digest (*pesaqim*) and the one given in his *responsa* (*teshuboth*). Karo solves the contradiction by maintaining that the disqualification, for purposes of ritual immersion, of a trough fixed in the ground and holding forty *se'ah* of water applied even when the trough had a hole as big as the spout of a water-skin. The rule 'one may not immerse in it'[3] therefore holds unconditionally. The famous 'trough of Jehu' never contained forty *se'ah* of water and was never meant to be a proper *miqveh*-basin in its own right. It was connected by a hole as big as the spout of a water-skin to a ritually unexceptionable basin adjacent to it. The expression 'in it', used in connexion with the trough of Jehu, need not therefore be taken literally. *Ṭur*, on the other hand, so *B.Y.* believes, understood the expression 'in it' literally; he was thus unable to reconcile

[1] s.v. ובוידוי.

[2] *M. Miqva'oth* iv. 5, b. *Yebamoth* 15a.

[3] אין טובלין בתוכה.

the contradiction in his father's writings and had, of necessity, to chose between one of the two rulings. In fact, he decided in accordance with the *responsum* against the talmudic Digest. This leads to an interesting aside .*B.Y.* objects to his own account of Asheri's reasoning an explicit statement in *Ṭur* elsewhere (*H.M.* 72) to the effect that in cases of contradiction the Digest had to be preferred above the *responsa*. *B.Y.* is now hard put to justify his own interpretation of *Ṭur*, according to which the latter disregarded the ruling of the Digest in favour of the *responsum*. Karo solves his difficulty by suggesting that *Ṭur H.M.* 72 did not lay down a general rule but merely stated the considerations relevant to that particular issue. In all probability Asheri happened to know that in that particular instance the Digest was later than the *responsum* and therefore represented his father's mature and considered opinion. The same rule need not apply in other cases, such as that of the 'trough of Jehu'.

After this abstract of the discussion in *B.Y.*, the Maggid's message should be abundantly clear:

והשתא אתוסף אשר קדישי [to salute you] בגין דפלפלת במילוי בפסקים ובתשובות. ומאי דאסיקת במסקנה בין הכא ובין התם קסבר דאין טובלין בתוכה אפילו אם נקב הוא כשפופרת הנוד, ויטבול בה שכ׳ בפסקים לאו בתוכה קאמר אלא ע״י וכמו שכתבת. ומה שדייקת מתשובה יפה דייקת, וכן מה שדייקת מדברי אשר יפה דייקת; ומה שפי׳ בדברי יעקב דחילי האמת כפירו[שך] כי הוא סבר שהתשובה והפסקים חולקים ותפש דברי (התשובה) [הפסקים][1] עיקר משום דידע שכתבו אחר אותה תשובה וכדכתבת אבל בעלמא לא. . . .

Before this enthusiastic confirmation of *B.Y.*'s treatment of Asher the Maggid also reports: 'In your discussion of the words of my chosen Moses [Maimonides] . . . you advanced the correct interpretation. Concerning the three different answers which you suggested in defence of Maimonides's view, the last one is not true; none the less do not delete it.' This seems to refer to Karo's lengthy discussion of Maimonides's ruling in his Code, *Miqva'oth* vi. 3, at the end of which he suggests three possibilities

[1] All editions read תשובות but the emendation פסקים is too obvious to require justification; none the less a slight confusion of the two cases is apparent.

in explanation of Maimonides.[1] The third possibility, suggested by *B.Y.* himself with some diffidence, is completely rejected by the Maggid. It should be mentioned in passing that in the course of his extensive discussion of purificatory immersions in dripping, viz. flowing, water *B.Y.* also quotes a long correspondence with R. Joseph Taytazak of Salonica.[2]

(v) The entry s.t. *Bereshith* (Venice edition) ends with a number of paragraphs all introduced by the words 'moreover, he said' (*'od 'amar*). The preceding paragraph is a completely self-contained communication, rounded off by the Maggid's usual valedictory *ve'attah shalom.* The expression 'moreover, he said' is not very frequent in the *M.M.* but does occur a number of times in the long entries s.t. *Vayyaqhel* discussed previously. This may suggest that these paragraphs really belong there, particularly as they contain a brief reference to a 'well whose water was diverted into many channels'.[3] The Maggid agrees that Maimonides in his commentary on this Mishnah is not very clear and confirms that Karo's interpretation of it was correct, although prima facie Maimonides's wording seemed to suggest a different meaning. In fact, Karo had hit on Maimonides's true intention whereas Nissim of Gerona had missed it. The meaning of this maggidic message[4] becomes clear by comparing *B.Y. ad Y.D.* 201: 15.[5]

[1] *M.M.*: ומאי דפלפלת במילי דמשה ברירי בההוא עניינא יאות כוונת ובהנהו ג׳ תירוצים דתרצת אליביה תירוצא בתראה לאו קושטא ומ״מ לא ... תמחוק יתיה. The three proposed solutions are (*B.Y.* s.v. צריך):
(1) תרי שוקת יהוא הווי וקצת טהרות עשו בזו וקצת בזו.
(2) או דילמא בזמן אחד כולן נעשו בזו ובזמן אחר כולן בזו.
(3) ועוד אפשר דדא ודא אחת היא ולא לענין עירובי מקואות מיתניא אלא לענין נקב המבטלה מתורת כלי וכו׳.

[2] Also printed in *A.R.*, no. 50. This correspondence, as well as the Maggid's utterances on the subject, are referred to by H. Y. D. Azulay in שיורי ברכה (Salonica, 1814), fol. 47a. On the relations between Karo and Taytazak cf. above, pp. 90, 118.

[3] Lit. 'centipede-wise' (Danby, *The Mishnah* (1933), p. 737); see *M. Miqva'oth* v. 3: מעין שהוא משוך כנדל and Maimonides's definition (Code, *Miqva'oth* ix. § 11: מעיין שהיו אמות קטנות נמשכות הימנו).

[4] עוד אמר מאי דפרישית על משה בחירי על מעין שהוא משוך כנדל יאות פרישית לכוונא יתיה שם מאי דכתב בפירוש המשנה ואע״ג דמעייניה לא יאמרון הכי, איהו למאי דפרישית איכוון וכן בכל מה דפרישית בהאי לישנא להכי איכוין, ונסים בחירי לא איכווין במילתיה.

[5] s.v. מקוה.

There is one other possible reference to *Y.D.*, although the passage[1] may equally well have been inspired by Karo's reading of the tractate *Ḥullin*. The maggidic message concerns the precise meaning of the term *hagramah*, one of the five technical faults that render Jewish slaughtering (*sheḥiṭah*) invalid. *Hagramah* means the slipping of the knife beyond the area of the throat contained between the large ring of the windpipe and the upper lobe of the inflated lungs, but the precise limits are a matter of controversy. The discussion hinges on the interpretation of the crucial passage b. *Ḥullin* 18b. According to Maimonides[2] and Tosafoth[3] the slaughtering is still valid if the knife cuts through the arytenoid cartilages of the large ring of the windpipe. According to Rashi the knife should be kept more to the inside and must not as much as touch the arytenoid cartilages. Karo follows the view of Maimonides and in the *Sh.A.* (*Y.D.* 20: 1) simply quotes Maimonides's definition of *hagramah*.[4] This is in complete agreement with the Maggid's communication on the subject.

The other halakhic references in the *M.M.* mostly concern matters pertaining to *O.H.*

1. The Maggid repeatedly assures Karo that he was always accompanied and surrounded by hosts of angels except, of course, when entering a privy. On such occasions he should take leave of the accompanying angels with the traditional formula 'By your leave, you honoured ones' (*hithkabbedu mekhubbadim*). This instruction is eloquent testimony to the esteem in which Karo was held by his Maggid, viz. himself. The beautiful talmudic tradition of taking leave, on entering a privy, of the guardian angels that accompany every man had long fallen into desuetude—if, indeed, it was ever practised at all. Karo himself states the reason for the abeyance of this custom by quoting (*B.Y. ad O.H.* 3) an earlier authority to the effect that 'only a god-fearing and pious man on whom the *Shekhinah* rests should say this, but not an ordinary man because it would appear like arrogance', and suggesting that this might be the reason why the formula was never used.[5] The

[1] *M.M.* 42b.

[2] Code, *Sheḥiṭah* i. 7 and iii. 12.

[3] b. *Ḥullin* 18b, s.v. או.

[4] Commentary to *M. Ḥullin* i. 3 and Code, *Sheḥiṭah* i. 7.

[5] אין לומר זה אלא ירא שמים וחסיד שהשכינה שורה עליו אבל אינש אחריני

Maggid's instruction[1] clearly implies that for Karo himself the use of the formula would not be considered as unbecoming pride, since in fact that *Shekhinah* rested upon him.

2. The correct manner of the congregational response 'Amen' when the reader recites the *Kaddish* is a matter of some confusion in the liturgical rubrics.[2] The ruling of *Sh.A.* 56: 2[3] is not only contested by Isserles in his glosses (who herein follows *Ṭur*), but implicitly also by the Maggid, who insists that 'Amen' should be responded five times during the *Kaddish*.[4] The Sefardi and some other authorities are agreed on the response after *berikh hu*'; but in order to arrive at five responses it is necessary also to say 'Amen' either after *yithbarakh* ('Amram, Maimonides, *Sh.A.*) or after *viqareb meshiḥeh* (*M.M.* and the kabbalists generally).[5] Neither in *B.Y.* nor in his *Sh.A.* does Karo make a special point of the fivefold response. The polemical tenor of the Maggid[6] is obvious, though the precise reference is less clear. It seems as if Alkabets, possibly in his lost treatise on the response 'Amen',[7] had maintained that 'Amen' should not be said after *viqareb meshiḥeh*. The emendation of 'Solomon' to 'Moses my beloved one', though supported by one manuscript,[8] has all the other manuscripts and printed editions against it. It is, moreover, intrinsically improbable because in that case the argument 'but it is necessary to respond "Amen" five times' would be pointless: Maimonides too provides for five responses though he places them differently.

לא דמחזי כיוהרא ע"כ. ונראה שמפני זה נתבטל מלאומרו כלל בדורות הללו. Professor E. E. Urbach draws my attention to a violent and rather unfair criticism of Karo's statement quoted and rebutted by H. Y. D. Azulay in *Birkey Yosef*, iii.

[1] *M.M.* 55b: כי אז אני וכל חיילותי ממתינין לך מבחוץ . . . ולכן תאמר בהכנסך התכבדו וכו'.

[2] Cf. *O.H.* and *B.Y.* ad loc.

[3] כשש"צ אומר יתברך כל העם עונין אמן וכן כשאומר בריך הוא וכן כשאומר ואמרו אמן.

[4] i.e. after שמיה רבא, ויקרב משיחיה, איש"ר, בריך הוא, and ואמרו אמן (*M.M.*9b). The contradiction between *Sh.A.* and *M.M.* was already noticed by R. Jacob Ḥayyim Sofer in his commentary on the *Sh.A.* entitled *Kaf ha-Ḥayyim* (vol. i, Jerusalem, 1929).

[5] Cf. Vital (פע"ח שער הקדישים פ"ו; שער הכוונות, דרוש הקדיש), whose order corresponds exactly to that of the *M.M.*

[6] מאי דאמר שלמה בחירי דאין לענות אמן אחר ויקרב משיחיה לאו קושטא איהו אלא צריך לענות אמן ה' זימנין . . . (*M.M.* 9b. 1).

[7] שומר אמונים; cf. Steinschneider, no. 6895 (*opera inedita*, no. 9); cf. also above, p. 101.

[8] B 4.

Other, albeit minor, discrepancies between *B.Y.* and *M.M.* are apparent in the treatment of *Kaddish*. Both texts refer to an apocryphal *responsum* of Joseph Gikatila[1] on the obligation of joining the word *yithbarakh* (i.e. the first word of the second section of the *Kaddish*) to the long response '*Amen* . . . *'almayya*', and both deal with the question why a prayer of such exceeding holiness and mystical significance was composed in Aramaic and not in Hebrew. *B.Y.* merely quotes a passage from the *Zohar*[2] to the effect that it was the function of the recital of the *Kaddish* to 'break the power of the other [= evil] side' and that this victory would be more complete if the 'other side' was defeated, as it were, on its own ground and with its own weapons. For that reason the language of the 'other side', Aramaic, was used and not the holy tongue: 'we must recite it in the language of the "other side" . . . so as to break its power.'[3] The reason given by the Maggid is different, though it too has something of the daring that so often strikes the reader of kabbalistic texts. According to the Maggid's explanation of the matter, the eschatological character of the *Kaddish* represents an anticipation of the final transformation of the profane and its raising to holiness.[4]

3. Karo is severely reprimanded by the Maggid for having caused a 'fall' of the *Shekhinah* by a slight interruption between the

[1] Cf. G. Scholem, תשובות המיוחסות לר׳ יוסף גיקאטילה, in *Freimann Festschrift* (1937), Hebrew part, pp. 163–70. The *responsa* are also quoted in *B.Y. ad O.H.* 25 and 426. According to Scholem, Karo saw these *responsa* between the first composition and the final revision of *B.Y.* (cf. אח"כ מצאתי). If my dating of the maggidic communications is correct, the *responsa* came to Karo's notice before he left Turkey for Palestine. The reference to *Kaddish* (cf. *O.H.* 56, s.v. ולענין and *M.M.* 9b) is dated Sabbath, 4 Kislev. Judging from the context this was Sabbath *Toledoth*. All this fits precisely the year 5297 and the date is therefore Saturday, 18 Nov. 1536. This date is confirmed by the Maggid's promise to go to Palestine 'this year' (*M.M.* 9a. 2) and by his reference to correspondence with Solomon Alkabets ('and if you write to Solomon' *M.M.* 10b. 1), who, as we know, had preceded Karo to Safed. The Maggid's second quotation from the *responsa* is only a fortnight later; the entry (*M.M.* 72a. 3) is dated Sabbath, 18 Kislev, and it is more than probable that this was Sabbath *Vayyishlaḥ*, 18 Kislev of the same year 5297 (= Saturday, 1 Dec. 1536 C.E.).

[2] *Zohar*, ii. 129b.

[3] ואנן בעינן למימר ליה בלישנא דס"א . . . בגין דיתבר חילא דס"א.

[4] ודא הוא רזא דאמרינן קדיש בלשון תרגום לאחזאה דבההוא זימנא יהא לשון תרגום שקול כלשון הקודש דכולהו יהא יחודא חד (*M.M.* 9a. 1). For another utterance of the Maggid concerning Aramaic, see *M.M.* 69a (bottom).

ʿAmidah-prayer and the preceding benediction on the Exodus (*beyn ge'ullah lithefillah*). The uninterrupted sequence of the two prayers was considered to be so important that even the response 'Amen', obligatory after every benediction, was waived in this case.[1] *Ṭur* is the only authority demanding the response 'Amen' after *ga'al Yisra'el* and for this he is taken to task in one of the aforementioned apocryphal *responsa* ascribed to Joseph Gikatila.[2] *Responsum*, no. 5, as edited by Scholem, prohibits the response and actually qualifies it as the worst type of kabbalistic sin.[3] A juxtaposition of the concluding words of Gikatila's *responsum* and the Maggid's message[4] clearly shows that the latter is quoting literally from the *responsum*:

Responsum	*M.M.*
וחוץ מכבוד רבינו יעקב ז"ל שאמר מצוה לענות אמן ח"ו עבירה גדולה היא ולא מצוה.	אל תפסיק כלל ואפי' בעניית אמן. וחוץ מכבוד ר' יעקב שאמר מצוה לענות אמן אחר גאל ישראל לא ירד לעומקן של דברים, אדרבה עברה היא בידו ולא מצוה ולכן אין להפסיק כלל.

4. The Talmud was well aware that the popular institution of dream-fast (*taʿanith ḥalom*) could easily collide with the Sabbath laws. Fasting was forbidden on a Sabbath, as the commandment to call the day a delight and to honour and hallow it was held to include honouring it also with food and drink. But since evil dreams were generally considered to be premonitory warnings of impending disaster, sent by God in order to prompt men to avert the latter by fasts and repentance, dream-fasting became a kind of urgent and necessary precaution that must not be postponed. A perusal of the relevant halakhic literature suggests that the rabbis compromised for psychological reasons, not because they were convinced of the premonitory or religious character of dreams. They merely noted the fact that the consciousness of having had an ominous dream could in itself be disastrous and that fasting could bring enormous relief to the anxiety-ridden dreamer. They

[1] Cf. *B.Y. ad O.H.* 66 and 111.

[2] Cf. above, p. 180, n. 1. In fact, the reference of 'Gikatila' to Jacob b. Asher is a decisive proof of the spuriousness of the document, composed about 1400; cf. Scholem, loc. cit.

[3] קיצוץ ופירוד.

[4] *M.M.* 72a. 3.

consequently permitted dream-fasting even on a Sabbath—with certain provisos and conditions attached.[1] For the superstitious and the mystically inclined this permission was, of course, merely further proof of the great store to be set by dreams.[2] Altogether, rabbinic law evinced a marked tendency to restrict this dispensation to the gravest dreams only. These were, according to 'old books', three kinds of dreams:[3] a *Torah*-scroll being burned, the concluding service of the Day of Atonement, and the beams of one's house or one's teeth falling out; possibly also reading in a *Torah*-scroll or marrying. This selection, which is of great psychological interest in itself, is codified by Karo (*Sh.A.*, *O.H.* 288: 5) and confirmed by the Maggid:[4]

> You have correctly ruled that one should not fast on the Sabbath except for these three [types of dream]. You have also ruled correctly that one should not fast on a Sabbath for dreaming of having dropped a *Torah*-scroll from one's hand, for one should fast only for those [three]; and though there is a controversy about one of them, one may fast for it none the less, for the three are really four—and you shall still learn the mystery of it.

The phrase 'and though there is a controversy', &c., is actually quoted by *Magen 'Abraham ad O.H.* 288 gloss 7, and means that all dreams about the Day of Atonement, whether of *Ne'ilah* or not, can be counted as one group. The case of a *Torah*-scroll falling from the dreamer's hand is not mentioned in halakhic literature, but may well have been put to Karo as a real or hypothetical problem.

5. The three dreams that justify fasting on a Sabbath gain in interest when it is realized that Karo himself actually dreamed one of them. The diary reports:[5]

[1] For the halakhic discussion cf. *O.H.* 288 and *B.Y.* ad loc.; also *O.H.* 286. On the talmudic view of dreams and dream-fasting see S. Lowy, 'The Motivation of Fasting in Talmudic Literature', *J.J.S.*, vol. ix (1958), pp. 34–36.

[2] For a kabbalistic view of dreams cf. Werblowsky, 'Kabbalistische Buchstabenmystik und der Traum', in *Zeitschrift f. Religions- u. Geistesgeschichte*, vol. iii (1956), pp. 164–9.

[3] *B.Y. ad O.H.* 288.

[4] *M.M.* 36b: יפה הורית שלא להתענות בשבת אלא על אותם ג׳ בלבד, ויפה הורית שלא להתענות בשבת על שחלם שנפל ס״ת מידו שאין להתענות אלא על אותם בלבד ואע״פי שיש מחלוקת בא׳ מהם גם בו מתענים דג׳ שהם ד׳ הם עוד תדע סודם.

[5] *M.M.* 66b, s.t. ישעיה מ׳ כ״ו, אור ליום א׳ של ר״ה.

I dreamed that it was the night of the outgoing Day of Atonement and I could not remember our having recited during the day the Order of the *'Abodah* nor the confession of sins of R. Shem Tob Ardotiel.[1] I was amazed at this and said to myself: perhaps I was sleeping while the congregation recited them, and then I remembered that we had not even said the Concluding Service (*Ne'ilah*). I tried to reassemble the worshippers so that we might still recite the *Ne'ilah*-prayer, saying to myself that although it was already dark there was still time to say the *Ne'ilah*-prayer. Meanwhile I awoke from my sleep and recited *Mishnayyoth* . . . . (follows the manifestation of the Maggid).

This is a genuine anxiety-dream, but it also provides an instructive example of the 'literary' background of much apparently spontaneous and unconscious dream or other symbolic material produced by the kabbalists. The main theme of the dream, the increasingly acute awareness of having irretrievably lost the great spiritual boon of the Day of Atonement (*'abodah*, *vidduy*, and finally the realization that *Ne'ilah* itself had been forgotten), has the anguished pungency, though not the literary perfection, of some of S. Y. Agnon's short stories that revolve round the same experience.[2]

No doubt this was one of those disturbing dreams that would justify a fast even on a Sabbath or feast day. Karo had dreamed it (and apparently others like it) on the first night of the New Year festival (*Rosh ha-Shanah*). From the Maggid's words[3] we learn that many years earlier, in the night of *Rosh ha-Shanah*, Karo had had 'a dream such as for which one ought to fast', but apparently had not been sufficiently upset by it to fast the whole day afterwards. Possibly he did not want to create a precedent for fasting on *Rosh ha-Shanah*, or perhaps he deferred to the opinion of Natronai Gaon, who held that the festive character of the day precluded fasting on it. At any rate Karo is now severely taken to task by the Maggid, who tells him that he would have saved himself much trouble and misfortune if for the last years he had regularly fasted on the *first day* of the feast.[4] The emphasis on fasting the first day only of *Rosh*

[1] The *vidduy* for the *musaf*-prayer of the Day of Atonement according to the Sefardi rite. On Shem Tob Ardotiel cf. Zunz, *Liter. d. synag. Poesie*, p. 503.

[2] Cf. particularly the haunting story *Pi shenayim* in the volume סמוך ונראה (3rd edn., 1955, pp. 128–42).

[3] *M.M.* 67a; another important reference to dreams and fasting, ibid. 83b.

[4] יומא קמא דר"ה.

ha-Shanah constitutes the one major contradiction between the *halakhah* of the *M.M.* and that of the Codes. *O.H.* 597 lays down, after reviewing all the relevant views and opinions, that if one fasts *even once only* on the first day of *Rosh ha-Shanah*, one has to fast on the second day as well and has to go on doing so for the rest of one's life.[1] This contradiction has already been pointed out by critics of the *M.M.*, and it may be readily conceded that this is by far the strongest argument for the spuriousness of the diary.[2] How weak this strongest argument really is should be obvious to anyone who is prepared to admit the autonomy of dream-thinking. What we may derive from this passage in the *M.M.* is further confirmation of Karo's well-known unwillingness to allow kabbalistic considerations or mystical experiences to influence halakhic decisions, which, he felt, should be arrived at exclusively by the traditional methods of rabbinic dialectic.[3]

Although not of strictly halakhic interest it may be mentioned here that the custom of fasting during a certain period in winter (*shobabim tat*) is mentioned twice in the *M.M.*[4] The custom is often described as 'Lurianic' though it appears to be earlier and of Germano-Polish origin. *Shobabim tat* are still missing from the lists of voluntary fasts recommended to the sixteenth-century ascetics, an example of which can be found in de Vidas's *Reshith Ḥokhmah*.[5] Since the maggidic reference to these fasts can be dated before 1536,[5] it provides evidence that *shobabim tat* were already established at the time in the ascetic and kabbalistic circles in Turkey and were not introduced to the Sefardic world after Luria's arrival in Safed.

[1] *O.H.* 597.

[2] Rosanes, op. cit., p. 215; Greenwald, op. cit., p. 207.

[3] Cf., for example, the *responsum* of R. Samuel Vital in Damascus to R. Azaryah Ze'ebi in Jerusalem (in M. Benayahu: רבי חיים ויטאל בירושלים *Sinai*, xv, vol. 30, 1951/2, p. 72), which comments on the fact that all halakhic decisors מהלכם ומעמדם בדרך הפשט לא יופשט...ואחריהם כל ישרי לב תפסו דרכם ובפרט מורנו הרב הגאון כמהר"י קארו זלה"ה... The *responsum* also gives some instructive examples. Cf. also *B.Y. ad O.H.* 25 (s.v. ויברך) and 31 (s.v. וחולו ש"מ).

[4] *M.M.* 25a, 30b. 2.

[5] *Sha'ar ha-Teshubah*, ch. 4 (pp. 192–3).

[6] This is proved by the ending of the entry where Karo is told that he would soon go to the Holy Land to be united there with 'my beloved Solomon [i.e. Alkabets] and the brethren'.

The Livorno edition of the Sefardi prayer book for *Rosh ha-Shanah* enumerates some of the 'augural' foods traditionally eaten on that day as good omens for the new year. The rubric refers to the *M.M.* as its source[1] and gives a list of dishes that is very similar to that in *Sh.A.*, *O.H.* 583, but not identical with it.[2] In fact, our *M.M.* says nothing at all on the subject. The discrepancy was already noted by Rosanes[3] for whom it was, of course, further proof of the spuriousness of the *M.M.* In reality, however, the rubric is based on a somewhat amusing error. The source of most such rubrics mentioning special intentions, kabbalistic customs, and the like is the famous guidebook for liturgical and spiritual life, *Ḥemdath Yamim*. The section dealing with the New Year festival does, in fact, contain a quotation from the *M.M.*, enjoining the utmost frugality (no meat, little wine only) on this holy day whose festive character precludes more extreme forms of mortification. Thereafter *Ḥemdath Yamim* proceeds to list the traditional 'augural' foods.[4] The compiler of the rubric overlooked the full stop separating the two sentences and consequently attributed the list of special dishes to the *M.M.*[5]

With one or two exceptions, therefore, the *halakhah* of the *M.M.* is closely related to *B.Y.* and *Sh.A.* The contradictions and discrepancies, confined exclusively to *O.H.* and mainly to matters of *minhag* i.e. custom, are not of a kind to cause surprise once the difference of background and method of composition of the different writings is considered. But although the analysis of the halakhic contents of the *M.M.* appears to confirm Karo's authorship, the result is disappointing from a psychological point of view. As

[1] בתחילת סעודתו יעשה דברים שיעלו לזכרון טוב לפני ה׳ כמבואר בס׳ מגיד משרים למהר״י קארו ז״ל

[2] Rubric in prayer book: רוביא, קרא, תמרי, סלקא, כרתא, תפוחים בדבש, ראש כבש, דגים, רמון. Apples (though mentioned by *Ṭur*) and pomegranates (though recommended by Mordecai) are not mentioned in the *Sh.A.* but are added in Isserles's gloss.

[3] Op. cit., p. 218.

[4] Ed. Venice 1763, pt. iv, fol. 33b, col. ii: ... ע״כ מס׳ מגיד משרים למהר״י קארו ז״ל ויאחז צדיק דרכו: ובתחלת סעודתו יעשה דברים שיעלו לזכרון טוב לפני ה׳ אשר חכמים הגידו סימנא מילתא היא ולאכול רוביא, כרתי, סילקא, תמרי, קרא. ...

[5] This explanation was suggested to me by Mr. M. Benayahu.

a rule the Maggid's halakhic utterances merely give vent to a repressed but for all that no less smug satisfaction, clothed in the garb of celestial congratulations—or else compensate for doubts and vague fears of inferiority which Karo may have unconsciously harboured. The Maggid clearly pays Karo all the compliments which his ascetic and truly humble *ego* would not permit him to acknowledge in waking consciousness. This self-congratulatory attitude also shows that Karo's halakhic activity was a straightforward intellectual effort without any personal doubts or conflicts accompanying it unless it were doubts about the recognition of his authority. The dreams of the earlier Tosaphists[1] as well as some references to 'compensatory' dream-messages in the Talmud[2] are examples testifying to unconscious conflicts or, at least, unconscious misgivings and uncertainty concerning halakhic decisions. In a dream the 'unconscious' may either provide solutions to halakhic problems or else express objections to decisions that had been reached previously by the usual and correct methods of rabbinic casuistry. Halakhic dreams could thus be either intuitive or compensatory (i.e. manifesting unconscious doubts and conflicting tendencies). Karo's Maggid, however, was different: he confined himself to complimentary confirmations *post eventum*, i.e. to strengthening Karo's self-esteem. In this respect the Maggid definitely promised more than he seems to have kept, for in a long communication[3] he actually assures Karo that 'whatever is doubtful to you, whether it be halakhic decisions or the interpretation of the Talmud and its commentaries, I shall answer you, provided you meditate on your problem and express the desire that an answer be given to you [from above]'. The truth of the matter is that the Maggid rarely taught anything. Even in purely homiletical and non-halakhic matters he would often simply repeat and confirm, perhaps also slightly enlarge on, what Karo had produced the day before.[4] One cannot but agree with Ḥakham Ṣebi's caustic

[1] Cf. above, p. 42. [2] b. *Ber.* 28a, *Hor.* 13b.

[3] *M.M.* 69b. 1.

[4] Ibid. 72a. 2. This significant fact, that the Maggid never taught *halakhah* but merely confirmed the results of Karo's studies, disposes of Dubnow's unfounded and palpably false statement (*Weltgeschichte des jüdischen Volkes*, vol. vi, 1927, p. 56): 'Übrigens bildete sich der mystisch gestimmte Karo auch selbst ein, daß er seine Einfälle auf dem Gebiete der Gesetzeskunde den Offenbarungen

remark that 'Rabbi Joseph Karo was a better scholar than his Maggid'.[1] No doubts, conscious or unconscious, seem to have troubled Karo in his halakhic activity.[2] Sure of himself[3] and of his sovereign mastery over the vast material that he marshalled, he wrote the *Summa* of rabbinic law with full confidence in the sufficiency of his intellectual equipment. His alert mind was always self-critical enough to assess the varying value of his learned feats and to distinguish between mere exhibitions of intellectual brilliance and the true, responsible elucidation of a law or of an author's opinion.[4] Pressing the psychological point of view one might perhaps maintain that Karo did harbour unconscious doubts or fears of inferiority which were compensated by the Maggid's emphatic words of praise.

Of course there were tensions and conflicts in Karo's personality, but these, as we have seen, resulted mainly from his ascetic morality, his mystical ambitions, the historical situation of contemporary Jewry, and, we might add, the unconscious realities underlying them. With regard to this part of Karo's inner world

eines unsichtbaren Genius zu verdanken habe, den er mit der Mischna . . . identifizierte.' After all that has been said, Dubnow's surmise (loc. cit., n. 1) that the *M.M.* ('an apocryphal work attributed to the authorship of Joseph Karo') 'stammt wohl von einem begeisterten Jünger des Karo' hardly requires comment.

[1] Jacob Emden in זאת תורת הקנאות (Altona, 1752, fol. 48a) quoting his father: ואמ"ה החסיד זצ"ל היה אומר הב"י היה למדן יותר גדול ממגיד שלו.

[2] The allusion to doubts and uncertainty to be found in the entry s.t. ישעיה מ"ב (*M.M.* 68b) is exceptional, though it contains valuable evidence of the scholar's habitual self-criticism: וכן מסכימים במתיבתא דרקיעא חי ה׳ כי פסק זה אמת ויציב הלכה למשה מסיני, הלכה כוותך ומטעמך. ואם תשלח לקושטאנטינה או לרבך או לחכמי א"י כולם יסכימו כוותך וגם הוא בעצמו אם ישאל לו כן ישיב אלא לפי שעה נתבהל וגם קצת טינא שעלה בלבו וכו׳ כי אף על פי שאתה תמיד חושד סברותיך וזו מידה טובה היא, מ"מ ניכרים דברי אמת . . .

[3] Cf., for example, *A.R.*, end of no. 28: וכן כתבתי . . . בתוך ספרי היקר הנקרא ב"י; *Responsa E.H.*, fol. 5a: ויהא רעוא דכל כי הני מילי מעלייתא לימרו משמן; ibid. fol. 12b (also 58b): מה שהשבתי כפי אשר הורוני מן השמים; ibid. fol. 34b: ובכן אתחנן אל ה׳ יזכנו תמיד לשפוט משפטי צדק; ibid. fol. 62a: ונמצאת משנתינו שלמה ונכנס[נ]ו בשלום ויצאנו בשלום וכל מן דין סמוכו לנא ויהא רעוא דכל כי הני מילי מעלייתא לימרו משמן. Other utterances showing what Karo thought of his *B.Y.* can be found in his *Responsa ad E.H.*, fol. 78b and 82a. For Karo's opinion of his *Sh.A.* cf. his Introduction to that work (referred to above, p. 96, n. 5).

[4] Cf. the quotation above, p. 170, n. 1.

the Maggid's function, as will appear later, was mainly expressive (i.e. 'revelatory'), normative, and punitive. The Maggid thus exhibits a good many of the characteristics of the classical super-ego; he stands in a precise, compensatory, and inverse relation to Karo's ascetic life. Whenever Karo fell short of the standards set by himself and his circle, the Maggid was there to reprove him; whenever he succeeded in satisfying his own exacting but essentially realizable demands, the Maggid was there to accord that praise and flattery which Karo could hardly bestow upon himself. For a man of Karo's learning and intellectual calibre the essential difference between *halakhah* and ascetic piety reduced itself to this: that in the former he would be less liable to failure and to a continuous sense of insufficiency. In the circumstances, the halakhic communications of the Maggid must have been among the most gratifying to their recipient and author.

9

THE DOCTRINE OF SEFIROTH

UNTIL the advent of Lurianism, the doctrine of sefiroth necessarily formed the core and bulk of almost all kabbalistic writing. Whatever other theories engaged the attention and at times passionate interest of the kabbalists, the mystery of the sefiroth remained the unfaltering centre of their speculations and the absorbing focus of their contemplative exercises. There were the doctrines of metempsychosis (*gilgul*) and of world-cycles (*shemiṭṭoth*); there was angelology and demonology. But nothing could ever compete with the theological significance and compelling fascination of that highly complex and dynamic image of the deity: the sefirotic *plērōma*.[1]

Quite naturally any systematic doctrine of the sefiroth subdivides into a number of well-defined topics. There is, first of all, the question of the relation of the ten sefiroth to *En Sof*, the nature of the process of emanation, the function of the individual sefiroth and their relation to one another as well as to the 'lower worlds', the association and correlation of individual sefiroth with the various 'Holy Names' of the Deity, and many more problems of the kind. In the more systematic expositions of Kabbalah the chapter divisions fairly accurately reflect the many-sidedness of the subject. But the same themes and problems are clearly there in the many unsystematic, in fact, confused and confusing kabbalistic writings whose lack of method and clarity is due, as a rule, to their literary form. Many of these works are written in the form of commentaries or homilies on books of the Bible; both subject-matter and treatment are consequently determined by exegetical accident and homiletical whim.

The *M.M.* belongs, as we have seen, to this class of writings. In spite of the large amount of autobiographical material, Karo's diary easily lent itself to rearrangement and editing as a kabbalistic

[1] Cf. Scholem, *MTJM.*, pp. 207 ff.

commentary on Scripture. But far from presenting a running commentary, our text is rather a collection of shorter or longer homilies, expositions, and comments on single verses or parts of chapters, containing mystical interpretations of ceremonial laws such as, for example, *sheḥiṭah*,[1] *tefillin*,[2] *'Erub Tabshilin*,[3] &c. Most of these expositions are in terms of the traditional doctrine of sefiroth, although on one point—and an important one at that—the Maggid contributes what seems to be an original theory which is found nowhere else, to my knowledge, in kabbalistic literature.

The kabbalistic content of the *M.M.* gains both in interest and significance if we remember that it represents a phase of kabbalism that has so far been less thoroughly investigated than, for example, the classical Spanish Kabbalah or the great systems produced during the spectacular sixteenth-century renaissance in Safed. Not only is our knowledge of the state of Spanish kabbalism immediately before the expulsion less full than it should be, but no attempt has yet been made to analyse and describe the development of kabbalistic thought in the subsequent half-century which, after all, culminated in the great systems of Safed. What we have got so far is, in the main, the names of innumerable kabbalists and the titles of their writings, but no clear picture of the evolution of kabbalism through their work has emerged yet.

Karo's Maggid reflects the problems and ideas that agitated contemporary kabbalism. His quotations, allusions, and polemical sallies must be counted among our most useful sources for a better understanding of the kabbalistic activity that went on in the Turkish empire and that finally produced the great systems and the new creations of Safed. In view of Karo's intimacy with the leading kabbalists of the day, particularly with his friends and disciples Solomon Alkabets and Moses Cordovero, it is only to be expected that the *M.M.* should exhibit many points of contact with their writings without, of course, anywhere approaching the homiletic breadth of the former or the speculative penetration and power of synthesis of the latter.

For our present purpose we may summarize Karo's teaching on the sefiroth under three heads. (A) The vexed question of ten

[1] *M.M.* 42b. [2] Ibid. 24b. 3. [3] Ibid. 40a. 3.

versus thirteen potencies and, in connexion with this, the problem of the origin and procession of the sefiroth. (B) The structure and nature of the sefirotic *plērōma*. (C) The specific functions and relations of the various sefiroth. Of these relations the most significant are undoubtedly those between the sixth and tenth sefirah, as well as those between the tenth sefirah and the 'lower world'. Already in the *Zohar* these receive more attention than the rest of the sefiroth together. The same may also be said of the Maggid's doctrine of the *Shekhinah*.

The similarity, in certain significant respects, of the kabbalistic doctrine of sefiroth with the philosophical concept of divine attributes is a commonplace. One hardly needs the kabbalistic equivocation of calling their 'potencies' among other things also *middoth* in order to realize that we are dealing here with a theosophical substitute for the attributes. This inevitably raises the purely exegetical problem how to reconcile the kabbalist's ten potencies, allegedly taught by the so-called *Mishnah* of the *Sefer Yeṣirah*[1] and indicated by the ten *logoi* of the *Mishnah 'Aboth* v. 1, with the traditional aggadic notion of thirteen[2] divine attributes. Matters were complicated when the kabbalists found themselves confronted with an apocryphal *responsum* attributed to Hai Gaon (939–1038), in which the thirteen *middoth* are defined as the 'branches' of an even more exalted, supernal set of thirteen forces, i.e. the ten sefiroth of kabbalism plus 'three supernal lights' (*ṣaḥṣaḥoth*). Of course both the *responsum* of Pseudo-Hai and the type of speculation which it represents were prompted by the desire 'to solve the contradiction between the ten [kabbalistic] sefiroth and the thirteen attributes of talmudic theology'.[3] However, once formulated, the doctrine of the three supernal lights acquired an independent, genuinely kabbalistic significance by introducing a kind of 'trinity', i.e. an element of plurality and potential differentiation, into the very sphere of *En Sof*. The problem is known to every student of Kabbalah from Cordovero's *Pardes*, where, however, the matter is

[1] Cf. Scholem, op. cit., pp. 75–77.

[2] Cf. Scholem, *Reshith ha-Kabbalah* (1948), pp. 171–4.

[3] Ibid., p. 171. The *responsum* originates in the *'Iyyun*-circle of the early thirteenth century.

further complicated by an additional confusion between the aforementioned notion of three supernal lights (*ṣaḥṣaḥoth*) *above* the sefirah *Kether* and the concept of 'ten brilliant lights' (also *ṣaḥṣaḥoth*) *within* it.[1] Whereas the *responsum* of Pseudo-Hai allows the identification of the 'thirteen attributes of mercy' with the sefiroth-plus-(three supernal) *ṣaḥṣaḥoth*, Cordovero rejects this solution for himself.[2] According to him the differentiated structure of the ten sefiroth is ultimately contained in the first three, which, in their turn, are prefigured in *Kether* even before they manifest themselves. This 'trinitarian' source likewise has its ultimate source in the three supernal hidden lights called *'or qadmon*, *'or ṣaḥ*, *'or meṣuḥṣaḥ*. Cordovero[3] defines the matter thus:

for the [whole sefirotic] Emanation is contained in *Kether* and *Binah*. . . . Also the procession of the sefiroth was such that *Ḥesed* and *Neṣaḥ* were in *Ḥokhmah*, contained one in the other, and all was one; similarly *Hod* was contained in *Geburah* and *Geburah* in *Binah*, and similarly *Malkhuth* in *Yesod* and *Yesod* in *Tif'ereth* and all in *Kether*. Therefore when [the Creator] conceived the will to produce the Emanation, three points took shape in the very root [of things]; these were *Kether*, *Ḥokhmah*, and *Binah*, which contain the whole Emanation. . . . [The actual] *Kether*, *Ḥokhmah*, and *Binah* thus draw [their existence] from their particular source in the [ideal prefigurations] *Kether–Ḥokhmah–Binah* which are within *Kether*, and these again draw [their existence] from the very root, i.e. from [the three supernal lights which are] the primordial light, the bright light, and the brilliant light.

The *ṣaḥṣaḥoth* or 'supernal lights' are thus the hidden archetypes, within *En Sof*, of the three highest sefiroth, which, in their turn, are the source and origin of the three lines forming the sefirotic structure.[4]

The Maggid too cannot escape the necessity of harmonizing the attributes of mercy with the doctrine of sefiroth. But according to him they are neither identical with each other, nor are the thirteen

[1] Cf. Cordovero, *Pardes*, i. 7 and xi; also Scholem's remarks in *Tarbiz*, vol. ii (1930/1), p. 206, n. 17. Cf. also Cordovero, *'Or Ne'erab* (Venice, 1587), 41a–b: צריך עוד שידע שיש למעלה בכתר מציאות כל הספירות הם הנקראות אל המקובלים עשר צחצחות והם כלולות בשלשה כשם שהספירות נכללות בחסד דין ורחמים, והם העלם הענפים בשרשם . . . וכולם בכתר והם סוד כח"ב שבכתר והם נקראות אור קדמון וכו'.

[2] *Pardes*, i. 7.

[3] Ibid. xi. 3.

[4] Cf. below, p. 193.

attributes the ideal prefiguration of the sefiroth in *Kether*. They are, surprisingly enough, all contained in *En Sof*. The Maggid thus says of the thirteen *middoth* what Cordovero would only say of the three supernal lights.[1] Karo locates thirteen lights (!), which are none other than the thirteen attributes of mercy, in *En Sof* itself.

The process of emanation is then initiated by these thirteen lights collectively producing one concentrated light which, on closer inspection, appears to contain three lights (*Kether–Ḥokhmah–Binah*). The latter two, when 'lighting up', emit two further lights each (*Ḥesed–Neṣaḥ*, and *Geburah–Hod* respectively), whilst *Kether* imitates *En Sof* itself by producing likewise three lights (*Tif'ereth–Yesod–Malkhuth*), corresponding to the three lights (*Kether–Ḥokhmah–Binah*) emitted by *En Sof*. The Maggid's own words[2] deserve to be quoted here:

When *En Sof* conceived the will to create the worlds, there sparked from Him thirteen lights which are the thirteen Attributes of Mercy. These thirteen lights are within *En Sof* and are, to all intents and purposes, the same as *En Sof*. From these thirteen lights there sparked another light containing three—*Kether*, *Ḥokhmah*, and *Binah*. Then *Ḥokhmah* and *Binah* emitted two lights each, whilst *Kether* emitted three lights, as I taught you.

This account of the procession of the sefiroth seems to be the Maggid's original contribution, as is also suggested by the repeated and insistent addition 'as I taught thee'. The skeleton of the system is, of course, identical with the conventional diagram of the sefirotic 'tree', and Karo's main contribution may simply be the refinement about the single lights dividing into (or rather emitting) double, viz. triple, lights. The point to remember, however, is that Cordovero, with all his wide knowledge of almost all the accessible kabbalistic sources, expressly quotes this particular doctrine as 'the Kabbalah of my master, the saintly R. Joseph Karo'. It is, in fact, the famous passage in *Pardes*, v. 3, which has been used so often as decisive evidence of the genuineness of the *M.M.*[3] The peculiar doctrine of the Maggid is stated or alluded to

[1] i.e. the צחצחות הנעלמות באין סוף.

[2] *M.M.* 3b. 3.

[3] Cf. above, p. 10; Cordovero's quotation, which is clearly from the Maggid and not from any other teaching he may have received from Karo, reads: קבלת מורי ורבי החסיד כמוהר״ר יוסף קארו נר״י וז״ל והא אתינא לאודעה לך

dozens of times throughout the *M.M.*, but is developed systematically in a few key-passages[1] which, in addition to expounding the manner of the procession of the sefiroth, incidentally also discuss a number of other controversial issues.

Similar to the last quotation from the *M.M.*, but concerned solely with the procession of the sefiroth and therefore omitting all mention of the *ṣaḥṣaḥoth* or thirteen *middoth*, is the following passage,[2] which none the less clearly stresses the ideal prefiguration of the ten sefiroth in *En Sof*:

> The truth of the matter is this: Thou shouldst know that the ten supernal sefiroth lighted up within *En Sof* in the manner I told thee, that is, *En Sof* emitted one light that contained three lights. One of these lights emitted two [further] lights and so did the other, whereas the supernal *Kether* emitted three more lights. Thus the ten sefiroth were completed.

The same point is repeated by the Maggid elsewhere,[3] but this time without even mentioning the prefiguration of the sefiroth in *En Sof*:

> You ought to know that when the Ancient One, *En Sof*, conceived the will to create the worlds . . . there sparked one light consisting of three, that is, of *Kether*, *Ḥokhmah*, and *Binah*. Thereafter each of these lights emitted a further light. *Ḥokhmah* struck a light consisting of two, *Ḥesed* and *Neṣaḥ*; together with *Ḥokhmah* itself they are three. *Binah* also struck a light consisting of two, *Geburah* and *Hod*; together with *Binah* they are three. *Kether* struck a light consisting of three, *Tif'ereth*, *Yesod*, *Malkhuth*; for because it is closer to *En Sof* [than either *Ḥokhmah* or *Binah*] and therefore more similar to it, being likewise extremely hidden, therefore the light which it emitted, like the one emitted by *En Sof*, consists of three.

In this passage the Maggid is satisfied with stating his own system and does not trouble himself to mention the alternative

קושטא דמילתא ורזא דרזין אלו . . . ומשום הכי קאמר אברהם עלה וגם אמנם אחותי בת אבי היא אך לא בת אמי והא אשתלימו להן עכ"ל תאר צדקותו וחסידותו. Cordovero's text corresponds to *M.M.* 37a–b.

[1] Cf. above, pp. 32 f.

[2] *M.M.* 5a. 2; cf. also ibid. 10a: דתפארת ויסוד ומלכות נפקו מבטישותא דכתר כמה דאוליפתך; and ibid. 5b. 2: דכתר בטיש ואפיק תלת נהורין כמו דאוליפתך דאינון ת"ת יסוד ומלכות.

[3] *M.M.* 37a–b.

patterns of a straight line or concentric circles. Cordovero, though he adopts Karo's pattern, yet carefully weighs and examines the alternative accounts. The difference between the two is very striking indeed, as Karo's Maggid is much less intent than Cordovero on getting at the one, ultimate kabbalistic truth. The Maggid is always ready to admit alternative possibilities which he introduces with phrases such as 'or else' or 'it may also be said',[1] much like a Tosafist endeavouring to harmonize contradictory talmudic statements. It does not really matter *how* they are reconciled, provided that they *are*. In this respect the otherwise dubious comparison between Cordovero's *Pardes* and Karo's *B.Y.* almost forces itself on the student, for both works do the same for the kabbalistic and halakhic traditions respectively. Cordovero reviews the whole body of kabbalistic literature in order to arrive at the one true, correct, and orthodox esoteric doctrine. Karo does the same with the much vaster halakhic literature, and his aim is to formulate true, correct, and binding legal decisions. The difference between the two should be equally obvious: halakhic practice requires unequivocal rulings, whereas religious speculation traditionally admitted of greater latitude. None the less an examination of the similarities and differences of *B.Y.* and *Pardes*, as well as of Karo's own method in the *M.M.*, is instructive. It appears that the Maggid easily takes in his stride inconsistencies of a kind which Karo would never have permitted in the *B.Y.* One example may suffice here. When discussing the function of the 'mediating sefiroth' (*makhri'in*) and the absence of any such between *Ḥokhmah* and *Binah*, the Maggid suggests[2] that, according to the view that the first three sefiroth form one straight descending line, the problem does not exist at all; according to the other view that they form a triangle, it might be said that the upper three are considered as one. The former alternative is categorically rejected by Cordovero,[3] who also dismisses the second suggestion as indefensible.[4] Cordovero is, in fact, very emphatic about the necessity of mediating between *Ḥokhmah* and *Binah*. Although he cannot allow an additional sefirah into his system—there must be ten only and *Kether* is one

[1] איכא למימר, אי נמי.

[2] Cf. below, p. 200, n. 2.

[3] *Pardes*, vi. 2, first diagram.

[4] Ibid. ix. 6.

of them—he yet retains *Da'ath* precisely for its mediating function.[1] Even more relevant to our present issue than Cordovero's views is the utter incompatibility of the former alternative with the Maggid's own repeated statements on the process of emanation. But the Karo of the *M.M.*, as distinct from the Karo of *B.Y.*, was apparently undisturbed by inconsistencies of this kind.

The relationship of *En Sof* to its emanation presents a twofold problem in kabbalistic literature. On the one hand there is the relation between *En Sof* and the sefirotic complex as a whole, on the other hand there is its relation to the first emanation *Kether* in particular. The latter difficulty is fairly obvious. So much is said in the *Zohar* and elsewhere about *Kether*, or rather so much, we are told, must not, viz. cannot, be said about it, that in its inaccessibility, transcendent remoteness, and mystical 'nothingness' it becomes practically indistinguishable from *En Sof*. Both are described as the mysterious abyss of the divine *nihil*, and inasmuch as the sefiroth are the self-revelation of the hidden God, *Kether* can hardly be said to be a 'manifestation', i.e. sefirah. Why, then, should it be reckoned as one of the ten sefiroth? A goodly number of kabbalists did not, in fact, reckon it as such and for some time this was quite a respectable view to hold. But during the sixteenth century and particularly in Safed it almost became a heresy.[2] Thus Karo's Maggid says of the kabbalist Isaac Mar Ḥayyim:[3] 'It is correct what Isaac Mar Ḥayyim has written concerning the question of change and number [in the sefiroth]. But when he said that *Kether* was the same as *En Sof* he was in error. He will not be punished, however [for this heresy], since he did not intend to sin.' Karo apparently knew the kabbalistic epistles of Isaac Mar Ḥayyim, and while emphatically agreeing with his solution of the problem of 'change and number' in the Godhead,[4] he takes Isaac severely to task for

[1] Cf. *Pardes*, iii. 8 and ix. 5, 6.

[2] Ibid., iii.

[3] On Isaac Mar Ḥayyim cf. M. Benayahu, *Assaf Jubilee Volume* (1953), p. 117. His kabbalistic views are set forth in two epistles, of which the second was published by Greenup, *J.Q.R.*, N.S., vol. xxvii (1931), pp. 365–75, and the first by Mrs. Y. Nadav in *Tarbiz*, vol. xxvi (1957), pp. 440–58. Cf. also Scholem's remarks in his article לידיעת הקבלה בספרד ערב הגירוש in *Tarbiz*, vol. xxiv (1954/5), pp. 168–9. The Maggid's words (6a. 1) are: יאות כתב יצחק מר חיים אלא במאי דאמר שהכתר הוא הא"ס טעה ואעפ"כ לית ליה עונשא כיון דלא אכוין למחטיה.

[4] Greenup, art. cit., pp. 367–8.

identifying *Kether* and *En Sof*, though, one is glad to learn, he is let off mildly.

Meanwhile another sefirah that could make up the number ten had established itself in kabbalistic texts and was leading a kind of shadow existence. This was the sefirah *Da'ath*. Often identified with *Tif'ereth*, it was on occasion also treated as a sefirah in its own right, viz. *Da'ath* in its independent aspect was distinguished from *Da'ath* as *Tif'ereth*.[1] The whole question of *Da'ath* is of course closely related to the controversy about the nature of *Kether*,[2] and once *Kether* had been recognized as the first sefirah, *Da'ath* inevitably became a stumbling block, since an eleventh sefirah could not conceivably be tolerated. But as *Da'ath* could no longer be extruded altogether, it had to be accommodated in other ways. How this was done can be gleaned, e.g. from Cordovero.[3] Cordovero agrees that *Kether* is so hidden that it can hardly be described as a *manifest*ation. Even *Ḥokhmah*, the first emanation that deserves the appellation 'Beginning' or 'Existence', must be viewed under two aspects: that of 'hidden wisdom' (in its relation to *Kether*) and that of 'manifest wisdom' (in its relation to the lower sefiroth).[4] *Da'ath*, situated as it is on the central line *Kether–Tif'ereth–Yesod–Malkhuth*, is really the ideal, hidden existence of *Tif'ereth* within *Kether*.[5] The stress on the hidden, ideal, or latent character of *Da'ath* is important if we want to prevent the latter from becoming a full-fledged sefirah. Since *Kether* is the first sefirah, Cordovero is obliged to interpret accordingly all earlier references to *Da'ath*, including the famous talmudic utterance[6] to the effect that the high value of knowledge (i.e. for the kabbalists the sefirah *Da'ath*)

[1] Cf. the *'Idra Zuṭa*, *Zohar*, iii. 291a: דעת אחרא; Prof. Scholem was the first to draw attention to this important passage.

[2] On the whole problem cf. Scholem, שרידי ספרו של ר׳ שם טוב אבן גאון על יסודות תורת הקבלה, in *Kiryath Sefer*, vol. viii (1931/2), pp. 397–408, vol. ix (1932/3), pp. 126–34, particularly his brief analysis of the problem ibid., vol. viii, pp. 398–9. Shem Tob ibn Gaon is the direct source of Shem Tob b. Shem Tob, whose statements on *Da'ath* in his *Sefer ha-'Emunoth* (see below, p. 198) are quoted—polemically or in agreement—by all later kabbalists (Scholem, op. cit., pp. 399–400).

[3] *Pardes*, iii. 7–8; cf. also ibid., chs. 3 and 6.

[4] חכמה נעלמת, חכמה מתגלית.

[5] והנה הת״ת לו מציאות נבחר ונעלם בכתר.

[6] b. *Ber*. 33a: גדולה דעה שנתנה בין שתי אותיות שנאמר כי אל דעות ה׳.

may be inferred from its being placed between two names of God.[1] The talmudic statement almost invites the kabbalistic interpretation that the sefirah *Da'ath* is situated between two 'names', i.e. between the two sefiroth *Kether* and *Tif'ereth*. This, at least, is how Shem Tob[2] and others had understood the Talmud. Since Shem Tob himself identifies *Kether* and *En Sof*, the order of sefiroth begins with *Ḥokhmah*[3] and the number ten is completed by *Da'ath*.[4] His full definition is this:[5] 'the highest *Da'ath* . . . corresponds to *Kether* and is hidden in the middle of *Tif'ereth*. It is concerning this mystery that our sages taught. . . .[6] The number of the ten sefiroth thus begins with *Ḥokhmah* and the highest *Da'ath* is one of them.' It is in explicit polemics against this view that Cordovero maintains 'the truth about *Da'ath* is not as imagined by R. Shem Tob, who made it into an independent sefirah. The truth of the matter is that it is the hidden reality of *Tif'ereth* . . . but *Kether* is numbered among the sefiroth.'[7]

The problem could not but solicit the Maggid's attention also. In fact, the passage already referred to earlier[8] concerning the procession of the sefiroth is lifted from a context dealing with *Da'ath* and defining it as a light shining in both *Kether* and *Tif'ereth*, viz. between them. The Maggid appears to be taking up a comment of Solomon Alkabets[9] on the aforementioned statement of Shem Tob. The passage[10] is not quite clear, but we may assume

[1] In 1 Sam. ii. 3: כי אל דעות ה׳.

[2] *Sefer ha-'Emunoth* (Ferrara, 1556).

[3] Ibid. 35b: זה סדרן: חכמה בינה, למעלה מהן כתר עליון בסוד המחשבה עד אין סוף, במקום הכתר למטה הוא הדעת . . .

[4] Ibid. 36b: והמשלים המנין הוא הדעת העליון.

[5] Ibid. 38b: הדעת העליון הוא . . . כנגד הכתר והוא גנוז באמצעות התפארת, ועל הסוד הזה נאמר כי אל דעות ה׳ ואמרו חז״ל גדולה דעה שנתנה בין שתי שמות, הנה מן החכמה הוא מנין הי׳ ספירות ודעת העליון הוא במנין. Cf. also ibid. 37b: ועל התפארת אמר שהיא בית העולם הבא ושהיא היכל להיכל הפנימי הדעת העליון.

[6] i.e. the talmudic saying quoted above, p. 197, n. 6.

[7] ענין הדעת שאין ענינו כמו שחשב הרש״ט שדימה לעשותו ספירה בפני עצמה ואין הענין כן אלא שהוא מציאות הת״ת הנעלם . . . אבל הכתר הוא במנין הספירות.

[8] Above, p. 193.

[9] Orally or in one of his lost writings.

[10] *M.M.* 3b: הלא לך למנדע דמאי דמדקדק האי צדיקא שלמה [אלקביץ] ידידי בספרא [בחכמה?] נעלמת דקאמר ההוא חכימא ש״ט שמיה יאה דקדק.

Alkabets (and the approving Maggid) to have reinterpreted Shem Tob's teaching in a way compatible with the true and correct doctrine according to which *Kether* is the first of the ten sefiroth. Once this is admitted, it is always easy to echo the rest of Shem Tob's exposition and to place *Da'ath*, which is 'hidden' (*ne'elemeth*) in *Tif'ereth*, between the latter and *Kether*. The only difference between the two systems is that according to the final, orthodox version *Da'ath* is so 'hidden' that it need not be counted. The similarity of the Maggid's (viz. Alkabets's) argument with Shem Tob's is patent: 'and this light shining between *Kether* and *Tif'ereth* is called *Da'ath*, and it is called 'hidden' because it is concealed and hidden within *Tif'ereth* like the spirit in the heart. This is also the meaning of the Talmud . . . .'[1] Although *Da'ath* is thus hidden within *Tif'ereth*, it can still be defined as the mysterious light shining between the latter and *Kether*. It is, as it were, double-faced, looking at both sefiroth. This fact, according to the Maggid, accounts for the plural form *de'oth*:

> You should ask yourself why it is written [1 Samuel ii. 3] 'for the Lord is a God of Knowledge'. Since the Talmud understands this verse as referring to 'Understanding' [*de'ah*], Scripture should have used the singular form *da'ath* [and not the plural form *de'oth*]. But the kabbalistic reason of this is because the spark that is called *Da'ath* lights to both *Kether* and *Tif'ereth*; and therefore—although it is only one light—it is called *De'oth* in the plural . . . because it lights in two directions. Therefore Scripture says *'El de'oth YHVH*: *'El* signifies *Kether* . . ., *YHVH* signifies *Tif'ereth*, and *Da'ath* is situated between them to illuminate both of them. It has thus been made clear to you that *Da'ath* is hidden in *Tif'ereth*.

However, the 'topographical' position of *Da'ath* also implies that its double face is turned not only towards *Kether* and *Tif'ereth*, but similarly towards *Ḥokhmah* and *Binah*. The question quite naturally arises why *Ḥokhmah* and *Binah* should not be harmonized by a mediating sefirah just as all the other pairs of sefiroth are. According to Cordovero[2] the provision of a *makhria'* between *Ḥokhmah* and *Binah* is one of the main advantages of the doctrine

[1] Ibid.: והך ניצוצו דמתנוצץ בכתר ות״ת איקרי דעת והיינו שהיא נעלמת משום דבגו ת״ת איהו נעלם ונסתר דוגמת רוחא בלבא והיינו דאמר רבנן גדולה דעה. . . .

[2] Cf. above, p. 196, n. 1.

of *Daʿath*. The Maggid, as we have seen,[1] seems to be less passionately interested in this particular point.[2]

Of greater significance and consequence for speculative Kabbalah was the problem of the general relationship between the *deus absconditus En Sof* and his manifestation in the sefiroth. This is a matter on which ultimately the very essence and meaning of the kabbalistic doctrine of God depends. Two extreme views, defining the sefiroth as either 'very substance of God' (*ʿaṣmuth*) or 'instruments' (*kelim*) respectively, were championed by the kabbalistic schools. There was also the *via media* which conceived the sefiroth under their double aspect of substance *and* instruments—a view which reached its full development in Cordovero's great synthesis. The doctrine, first propounded by Menaḥem Recanati (*c.* 1300), which conceived the emanations as mere 'tools' or 'instruments' through which the Godhead, the ineffable *En Sof*, acted, had one tremendous advantage: it could swallow, without too much choking, the kabbalistic system of sefiroth with its otherwise theologically offensive suggestions of plurality and change in the Deity. The other kabbalists felt that in this way the doctrine of sefiroth lost its essential character and significance; the solution of the theological problem had to be sought in other directions.

As a matter of fact, this controversy of *ʿaṣmuth* versus *kelim* is closely related to the aforementioned discussions concerning the nature of the *ṣaḥṣaḥoth* and the relation of *En Sof* to the first sefirah *Kether*. For only if *Kether* and *En Sof* are *not* identical, i.e. if they are divided by the vast chasm of qualitative difference between the mystical Nothingness of the divine *Ungrund* and the first emanation—only then is there any point in the doctrine that the sefiroth as a whole are distinct from *En Sof* and that they function as the instruments or garments through which *En Sof* acts and manifests itself. The conception of *ṣaḥṣaḥoth* is organically connected with this view. For once we hold the sefiroth to be

[1] Cf. above, p. 195.

[2] *M.M.* 4a: ומאי דאקשי [שלמה אלקביץ ?] למיהוי מכריע בין חכמה ובינה כמו בין שאר ספירין איכא למימר דלחד גוונא דאילנא דכתר חכמה ובינה אינון דא על גב דא (cf. above, p. 195, n. 3) לא קשה מידי, ואוף לאידך אילנא דאינון דוגמת סגולתא לא תקשי בהני תלת אינון יחודא חד דג׳ ראשונות חשובות כא׳.

'vessels' only and not the very substance of the Godhead, then the problem arises whether we should not assume some kind of ideal prefiguration of these vessels within the hidden recesses of *En Sof*. In this way we might account for the emergence of these vessels which the Infinite Godhead produces in order to manifest itself. If, on the other hand, we assume that the sefiroth are *'aṣmuth*, i.e. divine substance, and, concomitantly, that the first sefirah *Kether* is actually identical with *En Sof*, then there is little point in worrying about their ideal prefiguration within *En Sof*. There is thus, originally, a logical interconnexion between the doctrines of *ṣaḥṣaḥoth*, *kelim*, and the distinctness of *Kether* from *En Sof* on the one hand, and the absence of *ṣaḥṣaḥoth*, the concept of *'aṣmuth*, and the identity of *Kether* and *En Sof* on the other. However, kabbalistic speculation is not always characterized by consistency or by excess of logical rigidity, and kabbalists usually succeeded in combining in their systems the most heterogenous and prima facie irreconcilable elements.[1]

An illuminating and instructive example of this kabbalistic controversy can be gleaned from the correspondence of one of its main protagonists. The representative spokesman of the *kelim*-faction is, in most kabbalistic texts, R. Yehudah Ḥayyaṭ,[2] the author of the commentary *Minḥath Yehudah* on the anonymous thirteenth-century work *Ma'arekheth ha-'Elohuth*.[3] It is against Ḥayyaṭ that Cordovero argues when rejecting the view that the sefiroth are mere instruments. Also the Maggid, whilst appreciating the considerations that caused 'the author of *Minḥath Yehudah* to teach that they [the sefiroth] are like the tackle [*kelim*] of a ship, etc.',[4] adds, 'May the Lord save us from such an opinion.

[1] Cf. also the remarks of Y. Nadav, loc. cit., pp. 443–7.

[2] Born in Spain, second half of the fifteenth century; died in Mantua 1509.

[3] Cf. Scholem in *Kiryath Sefer*, vol. xxi (1945), pp. 284–7, and *MTJM.*, p. 385, n. 2.

[4] *Minḥath Yehudah* (Mantua, 1558), fol. 29b: דע כי כל מה שאנו מדברים מן הספירות לא מן הבורא נדבר אלא הספירות הם כמו כלי האומן שהאומן פועל בהם פעולתו. Karo must have confused two passages in *Minḥath Yehudah*, since Ḥayyaṭ nowhere mentions the simile of the ship and tackle in connexion with *'aṣmuth* and *kelim*. For the real context of the simile see below, p. 222. The simile, however, highlights a significant ambiguity of the term *kelim* which may be understood both as 'instrument', 'tackle', or 'tools' through which the divine substance acts, and as 'vessel' in which the substance manifests itself in

Nevertheless, he will not be punished for this doctrine because he did not propound it with the intention to sin.' Yet 'it is a great error'.[1] But the same writer, before embracing the cause of *kelim*, had once addressed a question on this very subject to his master R. Joseph al-Castili.[2] The wording of the question is rather obscure, but the questioner seems to have inquired about the divine nature of the '*middoth* and their garments'. Even more revealing than the question is the reaction of R. Joseph, who, before proceeding to his answer, deems it necessary to paraphrase and reformulate the question. In his paraphrase R. Joseph makes it quite plain that he was going to treat the question about the divine '*middoth* and their garments' as if it referred to the *qelippoth*, i.e. the 'shells' and forces of evil! It could not, so he argues,[3] conceivably refer to the sefiroth themselves since in that case 'it would appear that you doubt the divine force in the Emanation, but this is beyond any doubt. . . . Since the *middoth*, i.e. the Emanation and the Cause of All Causes [*En Sof*] are one in complete unity, how could you possibly doubt whether they contain the divine force.'[4] One cannot help wondering what R. Joseph al-Castili would have said had he known that his disciple was to become the spokesman of the theory of *kelim*.

Similar views were held by Karo's contemporary and (perhaps) acquaintance, R. Ḥayyim ʿObadyah, also known as Ḥayyim ʿObadyah di Bossal.[5] Ḥayyim ʿObadyah is known to us mainly from references in contemporary *responsa*; of his work *Be'er Mayim*

a determined form. The latter sense is close to that of a 'garment' in which the ʿ*aṣmuth* clothes itself. Kabbalistic speculation could take different turns according to the interpretation of *kelim* which it adopted.

[1] This judgement is similar to the one passed on Isaac Mar Ḥayyim; cf. above, p. 196.

[2] Cf. Scholem's article in *Tarbiz*, vol. xxiv (referred to above, p. 196, n. 3), p. 175, question 7, and the answer ibid., pp. 186–7.

[3] Ibid.

[4] נראה שאתה מסתפק אם יש כח [אלהות] באצילות וזה א"א שתסתפק אתה בזה כי גלוי וידוע שהאצילות הוא רשות היחיד ובכל יום אתה מיחד האצילות עד תשלום י"ג מדות, ומשם ולמטה עולם הנפרדים. וכל האצילות בעילת העילות כשלהבת קשורה בגחלת והשלהבת מהתחלת הבנין ולמטה והגחלת מהתחלת אור המצוחצח ולמעלה, והידיעות הנעלמות והאצילות הם אחדות שוה וגמורה.

[5] Cf. Rosanes, op. cit., pp. 32, 73; M. Benayahu, ידיעות על יהודי ספרד במאה הראשונה להתישבות בתורכיה, *Sinai* xiv (vol. xxviii), תשי"א, pp. 186–8.

Ḥayyim only the first two parts, *'Eṣ Ḥayyim* and *Meqor Ḥayyim*, were printed in Salonica, 1546. In the second introduction to pt. i of this book the author also refers to 'my kabbalistic work *Derekh 'Eṣ ha-Ḥayyim* . . . on the relation of the three worlds'.[1] We shall return to this reference in a later chapter.[2] Here it suffices to quote the Maggid, who admits that certain aggadic anthropomorphisms like, for example, 'God rises from his Throne of Judgement and sits on his Throne of Mercy' brought some kabbalists, among them R. Ḥayyim 'Obadyah,[3] to the wrong conclusion that the sefiroth could not be divine *'aṣmuth*. R. Ḥayyim 'Obadyah must expect severe punishment for his heresy: 'wherefore if you meet him tell him to recant, for he will accept [correction] from you. Though he is not of an altogether perfect character, he is none the less a competent kabbalist.'[4]

That R. Ḥayyim 'Obadyah was not an easy person to live with we know from other sources,[5] but here we learn that his reputation as a kabbalist was well established and that Karo could pride himself on exercising some influence over him. For aught we know Karo's influence may have been effective in this case, for in the aforementioned introduction Ḥayyim 'Obadyah speaks of the ten *logoi* through which the world was created and declares that 'they are the unity of the Creator, and the Creator is one within them, and they are the substance (*'aṣmuth*) of the Creator, absolute and simple spirit to which no counting and numbers are applicable'.[6] This is very much like the Maggid's declaration that 'the supernal ten sefiroth are divine substance and absolute unity . . . without any change whatsoever'.[7] Here the Maggid comes down on the side

[1] ספרי דרך עץ החיים אשר חברתי בקבלה על כל הדרושים האלה ועל קשר ג׳ העולמות... The reference is also quoted by Steinschneider, *Cat. Cod. MS.* (Munich, 1895), p. 30, n. 46.

[2] Below, p. 213.

[3] Cf. above, p. 31.

[4] ...הביאו למקצת מקובלייא למימר דלא אינון [הספירות] עצם האלהות ח"ו והא ידעת דר׳ (פלוני) [חיים עובדיה] הכי סבר ועתיד למיהב דינא עליה ועונשא סגיא, לכן אי תשתכח עמיה אמר ליה דיהדר ביה והוא יקבל מינך דאע"ג דאית ביה קצת מדות דלא מכוון מ"מ בהאי חכמתא הא ידע בה קצת.

[5] Benayahu, art. cit., p. 187 and nn. 32 and 33.

[6] הם רמז לעשרה אספקלריאות רוחניות . . . והם אחדות הבורא והבורא יתעלה אחד בהם והם עצמות הבורא יתעלה רוחניות גמור רוחניות פשוטה ולא יפול בהם לא לשון מספר ולא לשון מנין כלל . . .

[7] Cf. the quotation below, p. 204, n. 5.

of *'aṣmuth* without even a shadow of the synthesis proposed by Cordovero. The Maggid also knows the further refinement of the doctrine of sefiroth, according to which all ten sefiroth are present in every single one and so on *ad infinitum*, but 'all are divine substance, like the flame which is bound to the burning coal or like the soul in the human body where all is one.'[1]

The question how, in that case, it was possible to attribute number (ten!), multiplicity, and change to the sefiroth which are very God was answered in a similar vein by most kabbalists of the *'aṣmuth*-school. Already Isaac Mar Ḥayyim[2] had allowed that the doctrine of sefiroth appeared riddled with contradictions 'as when you say that it is divine substance and yet ten sefiroth, unifies and multiplies, is divided and indivisible, changing and without change'[3] and answered that two kinds of emanations had to be distinguished in the sefiroth.[4] We may assume Ḥayyim 'Obadyah's answer in his lost work to have been similar. The same point is made in terms very reminiscent of Isaac Mar Ḥayyim's by the Maggid, who concludes that all manifestations of multiplicity and change are due to the recipients of the divine influx and to the limitations which their nature imposes.[5]

Next to the relations obtaining between *En Sof* and the sefiroth, those between the sefiroth themselves and in particular between the sixth and tenth sefirah form the main subject of kabbalistic speculation. There is no need here to go over ground familiar to

[1] *M.M.* 37b. 1: אשתכך דכל א׳ מהני י׳ ספירין כלול מכולהו י׳ דינקא דהני י׳ סלקין למאה ומק׳ לכמה רבוא רבוון דלית לון חושבן ומנין. וכל הני י׳ ספירין ייחודא חדא אינון ואינון עצם האלהות אינון בא״ס כשלהבת קשור בגחלת דוגמת הנשמה בגוף האדם שהכל אחד וכן הכל ייחוד גמור בלי שום צד פירוד. . . .

[2] Cf. Greenup, loc. cit., p. 367.

[3] יראה בהם דברים סותרים כמו שאמ׳ שעצם האלהות והוא עשר ספירות, מתאחד ומתרבה, מתחלק ובלתי-מתחלק, משתנה ובלתי משתנה. . . .

[4] שיש בעצם הספירות ב׳ מיני התפשטות או אצילות, האחד אקראהו התפשטות הויה, והשני אקראהו התפשטות שפע . . . התפשטות המתפשט מהמקור העליון וכל אחד מהם מצד המקבלים התחתונים כפי עבודתם . . . וזהו סוד השינוי הבא מצד המקבלים. The continuation of this text is less unobjectionable: וזה השינוי לא יכלול זולת הט׳ ספירות כי אין סוף לא נשתנה ולא ישתנה לעולם. . . . This, of course, is the part of R. Isaac's teaching of which the Maggid so strongly disapproves.

[5] *M.M.*, loc. cit.: והי״ס עליונות הם עצם האלהות והם אחדות גמור כמו שאמרתי ואין בהם שום שינוי כלל רק כפי מה שאדם עושה כך מודדין לו.

every student of kabbalism and to describe once more the drama of the holy union and tragic separation of *Tif'ereth* and *Malkhuth*—a drama which forms the climax of the whole sefirotic life. The *M.M.* has very little to contribute to this particular feature of classical Kabbalah. When the Maggid springs his great surprise and reveals his startlingly unconventional doctrine of the *Shekhinah*, it is connected not so much with the divine life of the supernal sefiroth as with another, very complex, theory of Spanish kabbalism. This is the theory of the cosmos as a hierarchically stratified system of three, viz. four, worlds.

10

THE LIVING GARMENT OF THE DEITY: *SHEKHINAH*

THE dynamic process of the unfolding or self-manifestation of the Godhead reaches its climax and fulfilment in the tenth sefirah. The mystery of the Godhead is none other than the movement of the hidden life that takes place between the unfathomable abyss of *En Sof* and the manifestation of the divine in the last sefirah. As befits its complexity and richness of meaning, this sefirah is characterized by a host of names, by-names, and symbols. In addition to her usual name *Malkhuth*, she is also called *Keneseth Yisrael* ('the *ekklesia* of Israel'), *Maṭronitha* ('the Lady'), and *Shekhinah*—to mention a few of the most important only. As the point where the world of the divine borders on the non-divine, and where God and man, viz. creation, meet, *Shekhinah* is, perhaps, the most immediately meaningful of all sefiroth. For it is precisely the nature of God's relation to the world and to the soul and the consequent possibilities of communion—contemplative or otherwise—that matter most to religion in general and to the mystic in particular. It is therefore quite obvious what the kabbalists, with their love for terminological equivocations, have in mind when they echo older rabbinic ideas to the effect that God's 'kingdom' (i.e. *malkhuth*) is his dominion over the created order and that 'the principal dwelling of the *Shekhinah* is in the nether worlds'. It is certainly no accident that the images and symbols of the tenth sefirah are all heavily charged with 'earthly' meanings or associations. In fact, until the kabbalists got hold of the term *Shekhinah* and twisted its meaning to fit their peculiar theosophical usage, it simply denoted —in the terminology of rabbinic theology—the principle of divine immanence.[1] It is through, and by means of, *Shekhinah* that the Godhead is in contact with creation or even immanent in it. In the kabbalistic cosmos *Shekhinah* is a keypoint both in the downward

[1] Cf. J. Abelson, *The Immanence of God in Rabbinical Literature* (1912).

movement of divine self-communication, creation, and revelation, and in the upward movement of mystical ascent. The mystical ladder leads first of all to *Shekhinah*, and none come to the higher aspects of the Godhead except it be through her, the 'Gate of Heaven' and *mater mediatrix*. The tenth sefirah is thus a kind of frontier post, and much of its fascinating manysidedness or multivalence derives from this fact. On the one hand she is the passive, feminine receptacle of the whole sefirotic life, on the other hand she is the divine power that rules the world. *Shekhinah* is the 'last of the upper worlds[1] and the first of the lower worlds'.

Here we have come to the point where philosophical speculations about the possibility of matter proceeding from spirit, the many from the one, or the finite from the infinite, link up with the originally more gnosticizing preoccupations of the kabbalists. The world of ten sefiroth is a kabbalistic variation on the gnostic theme of a divine *plērōma* made up of innumberable *aiones*. But the descending hierarchy of sefiroth-*aiones* is also not much different from the Neoplatonic sequence of emanations ending up in our sublunar, material universe. It is true that some kabbalistic texts seem to want to limit the emanatist doctrine in the interests of orthodoxy. According to this version emanation is a purely inner-divine process and takes place strictly within the sefirotic realm only; the non-divine or lower worlds were then created *ex nihilo*. But as a rule the platonizing tendency got the better of the kabbalists. Sometimes it is expressly stated that the (lower) worlds proceeded from *Shekhinah* precisely as the higher sefiroth themselves emanated from the first sefirah *Kether* or from *Ḥokhmah*.[2] But whether the world is conceived as a non-divine, created substance, or as ultimately a divine emanation in a cautiously qualified semi-

[1] 'Worlds' meaning here sefiroth; the usage goes back to the ambiguous interpretation of *'olam* as (Gnostic) *aion* and as (Neoplatonic) *kosmos*. Cf. Scholem's important study, לחקר קבלת ר׳ יצחק בן יעקב הכהן. (1) פירושו של ר׳ יצחק למרכבת יחזקאל, (2) התפתחות תורת העולמות בקבלת הראשונים, in *Tarbiz*, vol. ii (1930/1), pp. 188–217, 415–442; vol. iii (1931/2), pp. 33–66, from which the opening pages of this chapter are summarized; Scholem's remarks on the meaning of *'olam*, ibid. vol. ii, pp. 416–17, and vol. iii, p. 36.

[2] Cf. Tishby, *Mishnath ha-Zohar*, p. 384. R. Isaac ha-Kohen (Scholem, op. cit., vol. ii, p. 195) speaks of האור הצפון [= מלכות] והיא התחלת ועלת העולם הנבדל.

pantheistic scheme, *Shekhinah* remains the most vital and significant mediating aspect of the Deity.

For systematic Kabbalah this raised the interesting problem of how to square the doctrine of sefiroth-emanations with the current philosophical cosmology which conceived of the universe as a descending series of cosmic strata.[1] Various systems of three, viz. four, worlds were taught by different schools, but the most widely accepted versions were the Neoplatonic and the Aristotelian. According to the former, the division was into Intellect, Soul, and Body, and the formula *muskal, muṭba', murgash* is fairly commonplace in Jewish writings. The Aristotelian tradition preferred to speak of a Higher World (i.e. that of incorporeal beings, angels), a Middle World (i.e. the 'spheres' and celestial bodies), and a Lower (i.e. sublunar) World. It is obvious that a theologically inspired philosophy requires a fourth world above that of the angels. Though the latter inhabit what is technically called the 'Higher World', the sphere of divine existence is evidently higher still. Translated into kabbalistic terms, this problem became a matter of the place of the 'world of sefiroth' in the cosmological scheme. The Jewish Neoplatonist Isaac Israeli (*c.* 850–950)[2] in his *Book of Definitions* considered the three worlds of Intellect, Soul, and Body as mediating between the highest 'Light of the Godhead' and the nether world.[3] In the case of the Aristotelian trias, the superimposition of the World of the Godhead on the 'Higher World' can only mean that the latter, in spite of its name, is no longer highest in the hierarchy.[4] This 'Higher World' is, as we have seen, identical with the world of incorporeal beings and angels. These spiritual substances were customarily defined as separate from matter and hence called 'separate intelligences' (*sekhalim nifradim*); as a result the Higher World as a whole came to be termed *'olam ha-nifradim* or *'olam ha-nibdalim* or even simply

[1] In addition to Scholem's study referred to above, p. 207, n. 1, cf. also Tishby, op. cit., pp. 386 ff., and G. Vajda, *Juda ben Nissim ibn Malka, Philosophe Juif Marocain* (1954), pp. 94–95.

[2] On Isaac Israeli see A. Altmann and S. Stern, *Isaac Israeli, a Neoplatonic Philosopher of the early Tenth Century* (*Scripta Judaica*, vol. i, 1958).

[3] Scholem, op. cit., p. 418.

[4] Ibid., p. 419.

'the separate world' (*'olam ha-nibdal*).[1] As the source of prophecy and inspiration it was also described as *'olam ha-nebu'ah*.[2] It is not surprising that some kabbalistic circles drew the logical conclusion and, exploding the traditional terminology, proceeded to designate the sefirotic *plērōma* as the 'Highest World'.[3] The circle of Gerona combined the Aristotelian, Neoplatonic, and kabbalistic divisions: the ten sefiroth were distributed over the three worlds of Intellect, Soul, and Body, with the result that these became mere metaphorical labels for dividing the sefiroth into groups. The worlds of Separate Intelligences ('higher'), of Celestial Spheres ('middle'), and of sublunar existence follow after, that is under, them. This system can still be found in the sixteenth-century work *Derekh 'Emunah* of Me'ir ibn Gabbay. There[4] it is simply stated that the first three sefiroth constitute the World of Intellect, the fourth, fifth, and sixth the World of Soul, and the seventh to tenth the World of Body. But all these three worlds, being nothing but the sefiroth themselves, are 'the world of unity without any separation',[5] which means that they are followed by the 'World of Separation' and the nether worlds.

Once it was absorbed into the kabbalistic climate, something very strange happened to the 'World of Separation'. It was subjected, as Professor Scholem has demonstrated in a beautiful and convincing argument, to a curious change of meaning which may incidentally serve as a characteristic example of the kabbalistic use or abuse of pre-kabbalistic philosophical terminology. The term, as we have seen, originally meant separation from matter and hence designated the angels as 'separate' intelligences. It denoted the 'higher' world precisely because the latter was 'separate' from 'lower' things, i.e. from material bodies. With the kabbalists the meaning of 'separation' became the reverse: it meant 'separate' from the supernal world of sefiroth which is the sphere of absolute unity and oneness. The kabbalists, as is well known,[6] never tired of stressing the essential unity of the sefirotic *plērōma* and insisted that all appearances

1 R. Isaac ha-Kohen in Scholem, loc. cit., p. 195, ll. 17–18, and Scholem's note ibid., p. 208, n. 28.

2 Ibid., p. 194 and Scholem's note p. 205, n. 12.

3 Ibid., pp. 420–1.

4 Ed. Warsaw, 1889, p. 5.

5 Ibid: עולם הייחוד בלי פירוד.

6 Cf. above, ch. 9.

of 'multiplicity and change' existed in relation to the receivers or perceivers only.[1] In fact, within the world of sefiroth no separation or number is thinkable and all is absolute unity. Only in the next and lower stratum, the world of angels (or of 'prophecy', viz. the 'active intellect'), does separation become possible, because this world is in its very essence 'separated' from the realm of divine unity. The opposite of 'World of Separation' (*'olam ha-perud*) is thus no longer the lower, material world but the higher 'World of Unity' (*'olam ha-yiḥud*)—a term synonymous with 'sefiroth'.[2]

So far no mention has been made of the well-known kabbalistic doctrine of four worlds. This doctrine developed quite independently within the kabbalistic fold though, of course, its growth was prepared by the aforementioned philosophical theories and particularly by the clear distinction drawn between the sefiroth and the (so-called 'highest') world of angels. If we posit a divine realm above the trias of angels, celestial spheres, and sublunar universe, the kabbalistic cosmos becomes a fourfold structure: the world of *'Aṣiluth* followed by the lower worlds of *Beri'ah*, *Yeṣirah*, and *'Asiyyah*.[3] Thus R. Isaac ha-Kohen, in his commentary on Ezekiel's 'Vision of the Chariot', already formulates the famous doctrine of hierarchical worlds, each repeating within itself the tenfold structure of the sefiroth-system.[4] According to R. Isaac there are three such worlds: the world of divine sefiroth (*ha-'olam ha-mithboded*), the world of prophecy (i.e. the world of 'separation' and of separate intelligences), and the world of the celestial spheres (*'olam ha-tekhunah*). These correspond more or less to the first three of the classical kabbalistic quaternity, generally known by the abbreviation *'ABY'A*. The peculiar, specifically kabbalistic, feature of the evolution of this doctrine of worlds was the distinction made between the essentially divine realm of the sefiroth and the next lower world of the divine 'Chariot' or 'Throne'; it was this latter sphere which came to be technically termed *Beri'ah*. At first this highest world in the order of non-divine being, second only to the Godhead itself as manifest in the sefiroth, was identified with the

[1] The kabbalists liked even more than the scholastics to repeat the rule *quidquid recipitur ad modum recipientis recipitur*.

[2] Scholem, loc. cit., pp. 195 and 208, n. 28; also nn. pp. 204 f.

[3] Ibid., vol. iii, pp. 46–47.

[4] Ibid., pp. 194 f. and nn. pp. 204 f.

aforementioned 'Higher World' of the non-kabbalistic, Aristotelian cosmology. As such it was, of course, identical with the 'World of Separation' and angels. For the author of the *Zohar*, things were slightly different; he taught, as we shall see, a doctrine of three worlds. Meanwhile the theory of four worlds, which was finally to become the dominating kabbalistic view, continued to develop. It appeared fully grown in the later portions of the *Zohar* known as *Ra'ya Mehemna* and *Tiqqunin*. Shortly afterwards, in the writings of R. Isaac of Acre, the famous abbreviation *'ABY'A* made its first appearance; since then it has remained the standard kabbalistic symbol for the structure of the cosmos.

One significant change took place with the transition from a system of three to one of four worlds: the original association of the term 'separation' with the world of angels was disrupted. The second stratum of the kabbalistic cosmos (Throne, Chariot, *Beri'ah* or whatever else it was called) continued to be described as the 'World of Separation' (*'alma de-peruda*) because, as has been noted, it is separated from the divine sphere of total unity. But the angels were now moved down to a third and lower level commonly called *Yeṣirah*. In accordance with the Aristotelian scheme, the next level, immediately below the world of angels, should be the Middle World consisting of the celestial spheres. It is, in fact, as an equivalent of *'olam ha-galgallim* that the kabbalistic term *'Asiyyah* is often used.

The doctrine of three worlds and the distinction between *'alma de-yiḥuda* and *'alma de-peruda* occurs a number of times in the main part of the *Zohar*.[1] The most explicit and instructive statement is probably this: 'The Holy One, Blessed Be He, has three worlds in which He is hidden. The first, the highest and most hidden of all, cannot be seen or known but by Him who is hidden within it. The second world is linked to that which is above it, and it is from there that God can be known. . . . The third world is the world beneath it in which separation obtains, and this is the world in which the high angels exist; God is and yet is not in it.'[2] It thus appears that the World of Separation is the non-divine sphere of existence, possibly including in addition to the angels

[1] Scholem, loc. cit., vol. iii, pp. 38–39.

[2] *Zohar*, vol. iii, 159a.

also all lower orders of creation. The two higher worlds both belong to the realm of the divine, the first being none other than the hidden sphere of *En Sof* whereas the second is the world of the manifest Godhead, i.e. the sefiroth. A minor difficulty about this passage is its use of the term 'the Holy One, Blessed Be He', which is generally reserved for the central sefirah *Tif'ereth* but here seems to refer also to *En Sof*. However, terminological latitude of this kind is not infrequent and elsewhere[1] we shall find an example of Karo's Maggid taking the same liberty of referring *qudsha berikh hu* to *En Sof*. As against this triadic cosmology, the full-fledged doctrine of four worlds, which posits three worlds *in addition* to the realm of sefiroth, seems to be implied at least once in the main part of the *Zohar*. The text comments on Isa. vi. 3 and explains that 'the *Trishagion*, referred to in the phrase "and one cried unto another and said . . ." rises to God from three worlds. "And one cried"—this is one; "unto another"—this makes two; "and said" —this makes three. These are the three worlds and corresponding to them three times "Holy".'[2] One world is undoubtedly the material universe in which the earthly Israel praises its Lord. The other is clearly the world of angels. We are probably right in assuming that the third world referred to is *not* the realm of sefiroth, as in that case we should have to think of the sefiroth as joining Israel and the angels in the praise of the hidden *En Sof*. One would rather think that the threefold 'Holy' is addressed to the Deity as manifest in the sefiroth, and that the third world is therefore some intermediate sphere half-way between the sefiroth and the world of angels. It would correspond, therefore, to the sphere generally known as the world of separation, Throne or *Beri'ah*. Here it seems as if the theory of four worlds, which is the explicit doctrine of the *Ra'ya Mehemna* and the *Tiqqunin*, is already adumbrated in the *Zohar* too. Alternatively (though most improbably) the passage could be interpreted as including the sefiroth in the choir of praise to *En Sof*. In that case the second world would then have to be thought of as embracing both the angel-world *Yeṣirah* and the

[1] Below, p. 227. It is not surprising that the more thorough and systematic Cordovero (*Pardes*, v. 4) rejects this looseness in the use of symbols which have, or at least should have, a precise and definite meaning: וזה לנו דוחק גדול שאינו צודק מלת הקב"ה בא"ס . . . אלא בכתר (!).

[2] *Zohar*.

Throne-world *Beri'ah*. The differentiated spheres *Beri'ah–Yeṣirah* of post-Zoharic Kabbalah would thus be treated as one.[1] As it happens, this is precisely what we shall find in the teaching of the Maggid.

Before, however, turning to an analysis of Karo's doctrine of worlds, it may be useful to survey briefly the corresponding views held by some of his contemporaries. It may seem surprising that such a survey is possible at all, since it is generally taken for granted that the doctrine of four worlds (*'ABY'A*) had attained undisputed sway after the fourteenth century and that there was therefore nothing more to be said on the subject. For the fourteenth century Scholem has drawn attention to a characteristically ambiguous co-existence of the two theories. As time went on the three worlds of the triadic scheme were more and more conceived as being outside the Godhead (i.e. outside the ten sefiroth) 'so that, in point of fact, here too the four-world scheme established itself'.[2] Scholem's dictum might well be extended to hold also for the sixteenth century. It is certainly worthy of note that after the Expulsion and up to the middle of the sixteenth century Spanish kabbalists still at times ignored the *'ABY'A*-terminology and continued to talk of three worlds, though the realm of the divine would have to be added to these as a fourth stratum.

In a previous chapter we already had occasion to mention Karo's contemporary, R. Ḥayyim 'Obadyah of Salonica.[3] His work '*The Way of the Tree of Life* which I wrote on kabbalistic subjects . . . [and] on the connection of the three worlds'[4] is lost, but its basic theory appears from the few indications contained in the second Introduction to his *Well of Living Water*.[5] There the author explains that

all the three worlds are closely joined and connected with each other. . . . These three worlds were necessary because the utterly simple spiritual substance cannot pour its effluence into the utterly material . . . without mediation . . . wherefore the *world of angels* was needed. The world of

[1] Cf. Tishby, op. cit., p. 389, from whose discussion of the Zohar passage this argument is summarized.

[2] Scholem, loc. cit., vol. iii, p. 63.

[3] Cf. above, p. 203.

[4] דרך עץ החיים אשר חברתי בקבלה . . . על קשר ג׳ העולמות.

[5] באר מים חיים, Salonica, 1546.

angels too cannot [immediately] influence real matter, wherefore the *middle world* or *world of spheres* was needed. From the world of spheres the low nether world is derived, yet all are one world.

To these three worlds we have to add, of course, the realm of sefiroth: 'the ten *logoi* with which the world was created hint at the ten spiritual lights . . . which are the unity of the Creator. The Creator is One in them and they are the very substance of the Creator.'[1]

Similarly also al-Bottini,[2] perhaps the most important sixteenth-century representative of the Abulafian school of 'prophetic' or ecstatic mysticism. In his unpublished commentary on Maimonides's code *Yad ha-ḥazaqah*,[3] al-Bottini interprets and supplements the cosmology of Maimonides in accordance with kabbalistic views. In the manner of a seventeenth-century English Neoplatonist, he starts by pointing out[4] that there is full agreement between the true Kabbalah of Moses and that of the ancient sages of the Gentiles to the effect that the universe consists of three parts: 'the world of separate intelligences with their ten orders . . . the world of spheres with their ten heavens . . . the nether world with its four elements.' These three worlds, al-Bottini hastens to explain, did not emanate but were created *ex nihilo* and they correspond to *BY'A*. However, all mystics agree that between

the blessed Cause of all Causes[5] and the world of separate intelligences there exists another intelligent, spiritual, and simple being . . . far above the degree of the world of separate intelligences . . . and this intelligent being emanates from the depths of the hiddenness . . . of *En Sof*. This intelligent spiritual existent was called the world of *'Aṣiluth*. . . . [And all the kabbalists] agree that this intelligent existent is the same as the ten holy spiritual degrees from which the ten orders of angels and separate intelligences draw their influx, and the kabbalists called these ten holy degrees the ten sefiroth.[6]

Another variation of this doctrine can be found in the strange and disconcerting mystical work known as *Sefer ha-Meshib* to

[1] באר מים חיים.

[2] Cf. above, p. 40.

[3] M. Benayahu, 'ר' יהודה בן ר' משה אלבוטיני וספרו יסוד משנה תורה', קובץ הרמב"ם, ירושלים, תשט"ו, pp. 240–4.

[4] Ibid., p. 251.

[5] Which must here mean *En Sof*. Kabbalists only rarely bothered about the distinction between the 'Cause of All Causes' (= *Kether*) and the 'Cause Above All Causes' (= *En Sof*).

[6] Al-Bottini, loc. cit.

which reference has already been made.[1] The author does not make use of the *'ABY'A* terminology but speaks of 'the unified world, and the world of separation which is the world of angels, and the mystery of the world of the spheres'.[2] Since he also alludes to the world of angels as *hekhaloth*, it appears that we are dealing here either with an approximate equivalent to the *Yeṣirah* of classical kabbalistic cosmology, or else with a system in which the *hekhaloth* follow immediately on the tenth sefirah.[3] For though the author says that 'in [the section on] the world of separation I shall explain the mystery of the angels which is the mystery of the *hekhaloth* . . . and this mystery of the world[4] of separation is the mystery of the *hekhaloth*',[5] mediating between the Deity and the angels-*hekhaloth*, the passage is preceded by an expression that seems to imply another world, mediating between the Deity and the angels-*hekhaloth*. At any rate the reference to 'the whole mystery of the Godhead and the mystery of the *merkabah*'[6] may be construed as meaning something like the Throne- or *Beri'ah*-world of other systems. For our immediate purpose the crucial feature of this version is the important fact that here the 'world of separation' *remains* the world of angels; the term no longer denotes the kabbalistic Higher World (*merkabah*, throne) immediately following on the realm of the sefiroth. It has already been pointed out how in the kabbalistic systems the world of separation remained the highest of the non-divine worlds, but ceased to be the world of separate intelligences. The angels were moved down to a lower, third level. On this point the *Sefer ha-Meshib* presents an interesting variation: the 'world of separation' as such is moved down so that its original association with the angels remains unimpaired. Instead of saying, with all other kabbalists, that the world of *Beri'ah*, viz. the Throne, intervenes between the sefiroth (= *'Aṣiluth*) and the angels-*hekhaloth* (= *Yeṣirah*), the *Sefer ha-Meshib*

[1] Above, p. 47.

[2] MS. London (Marg. 766), fol. 100b: עולם המיוחד ועולם הפירוד הוא עולם המלאכים וסוד עולם הגלגלים.

[3] Cf. below, p. 223.

[4] Emending the manuscript reading נעלם to עולם.

[5] *Sefer ha-Meshib*, fol. 92a: אח"כ בעולם הפירוד יתבאר סוד המלאכים אשר הם סוד ההיכלות. . . . וזהו סוד עולם הפירוד הוא סוד ההיכלות.

[6] Ibid.: סוד האלהות כולו וסוד המרכבה.

would put it that the *merkabah* mediates between the *'olam ha-yiḥud* (= *'Aṣiluth*, the sefiroth) and the *'olam ha-perud* (= *Yeṣirah*, the world of angels). The addition of the *'olam ha-galgallim* completes the parallelism with the *'ABY'A* system.

Now it is a remarkable fact that in all systematic discussions of the succession, procession, or emanation of worlds no mention is made of the *Shekhinah*, although, according to the theosophical conceptions of the kabbalists, she is the mediating aspect of the Godhead and actually stands at the head of all extra-pleromatic existence. *Shekhinah* is situated at the point of transition from *'Aṣiluth* to *Beri'ah*. In Tishby's felicitous phrase,[1] 'on the one hand she is a connecting link, joining together the two realms, on the other hand she is a kind of barrier separating the "higher" from the "lower" spheres'. As a matter of fact, *Shekhinah* stands at more than one frontier. Not only is she the end of *'Aṣiluth* and the head of *Beri'ah*, yet part of both, but she also borders on the sphere of the demonic and evil.[2] This aspect too will demand our attention in due course.[3] But enough has been said so far to explain why some of the inherent qualities of the symbol of *Shekhinah* almost inevitably led to the latter's being occasionally situated as an independent entity outside the world of *'Aṣiluth*.

This development towards increasing differentiation was helped by another peculiarity in the early kabbalistic treatment of *Shekhinah*. In the *Zohar* and other early classics, *Shekhinah*, viz. *Malkhuth*, is often described as passive, destitute, and poor. She has nothing of her own and functions merely as the vessel receiving —and then transmitting—the influx of the higher, active, dynamic, and hence 'male' sefiroth. As a result the tenth sefirah is sometimes spoken of as if it were not a real sefirah at all but a mere receptacle, a secondary unit made up of the powers of the other sefiroth. This impression is strengthened by the frequent use of expressions like '*Malkhuth* which is made up of ten sefiroth'[4] (though strictly speaking she could be made up of only nine at the utmost!) or '*Malkhuth* and her sefiroth'. The line which this development could take is illustrated by a statement in Shem Tob's *Sefer ha-'Emunoth*:

[1] Op. cit., p. 383. [2] Ibid., pp. 220–1. [3] Cf. below, pp. 219 f.

[4] מלכות הכלולה מי' ספירות.

Malkhuth receives from all sefiroth, she is identical with *Shekhinah* and *Keneseth Yisra'el* as well as with the 'active intellect' present in the angels and lower orders of being; 'all sefiroth are in analogy to the male, whereas *Malkhuth* and her sefiroth are analogous to the female. . . . She is called the 'image of God' and with her there are ten other sefiroth of which she is the first and like the innermost point'.[1] Here *Shekhinah* is to 'her' sefiroth what *Kether* is to the higher sefiroth of *'Aṣiluth*. The ambiguity of these formulations is obvious. On the one hand *Malkhuth–Shekhinah* is the central principle or 'head' of a lower, secondary system of ten potencies; on the other hand she remains part of the original 'higher' *pleroma*. The ambiguity is both mitigated and increased by the classical theory of *'ABY'A* according to which the whole structure of ten sefiroth is repeated in each of the four worlds, each sefirah being identified by specifying the level to which it belongs: *Malkhuth* of *'Aṣiluth*, *Malkhuth* of *Beri'ah*, of *Yeṣirah*, &c. A good summing up of the whole scheme is given at the very beginning of the *Tiqqunin*:[2]

> Blessed is he who clothes the King and the Lady with the ten sefiroth of *Beri'ah* . . . because on Sabbath and Holy days He [i.e. the King] clothes himself in royal garments—these are the ten sefiroth of *Beri'ah*—and on weekdays He clothes Himself with ten orders of angels[3] who serve the ten sefiroth of *Beri'ah*. As for the ten sefiroth of *'Aṣiluth*, the King is in them, He and His Substance is one within them, He and His Life is one within them,[4] which is not the case with the ten sefiroth of *Beri'ah* which are not one with their life or with their substance. And the Cause Above All [i.e. *En Sof*] shines in the ten sefiroth of *'Aṣiluth*, and in the ten [sefiroth] of *Beri'ah*, and it shines in the ten orders of angels[5] and in the ten celestial spheres,[6] but nowhere changes [itself].

The explicitness of this passage could hardly be bettered. It reaffirms—if reaffirmation were necessary—the validity of the symbolic equation: tenth sefirah = *Malkhuth* = *Keneseth Yisra'el* = *Shekhinah* = *Maṭronitha*. It is not *Shekhinah* which 'clothes' the higher sefiroth, but *Beri'ah* which clothes 'the King and the Lady', i.e. the whole world of *'Aṣiluth*.

[1] Shem Tob, op. cit.

[2] *Tiqquney Zohar*, fol. 3b.

[3] i.e. the ten sefiroth of *Yeṣirah*.

[4] This is nothing but a long-winded description of the *'olam ha-yiḥud*.

[5] i.e. *Yeṣirah*-Metatron.

[6] i.e. *'Asiyyah*.

This is the point at which Karo deviates in a surprisingly novel manner: *Shekhinah* and *Maṭronitha* are the same, but they are not identical with the tenth sefirah *Malkhuth*. After expounding his doctrine of the procession of the sefiroth, terminating with the emanation of the central line *Tif'ereth–Yesod–Malkhuth* from *Kether*, the Maggid continues: 'but the *Shekhinah* is the garment of them all because she proceeded from them all, and each of the supernal ten sefiroth lighted one light in her and she is made up of them all.'[1] The ambiguity of *Malkhuth–Shekhinah* comes out in the next sentence:[2] 'wherefore you find that in one of the diagrams of the sefiroth-tree there is a path from every single sefirah to *Malkhuth*'—as if *Malkhuth* and *Shekhinah* were identical after all. But the truth is that *Shekhinah* 'is one with them [i.e. the sefiroth] in respect of unity but not in respect of emanation'.[3] The process by which *Shekhinah* emanated or was produced belongs to a distinct, secondary level.

This process is described as identical with the 'Diminution of the Moon'. For 'the matter of the moon's complaint is this: the [secondary] light that proceeded from each and every sefirah complained that [it was superfluous because] there was no need for two lights in each sefirah. . . . Then God, that is *En Sof* [!], said to her "go and make yourself small"—meaning that all these [secondary] lights that had proceeded from the sefiroth should coalesce into one and thereby constitute the *Maṭronitha* in order to govern the world of separation.'[4]

This account closely resembles the one usually given of the procession of the *Beri'ah*-world.[5] But at any rate the last two quota-

[1] *M.M.* 5a. 2: אבל שכינתא היא מנא דכולהו דמכולהו נפקת וכל חד מעשר ספירין עילאין נהר בה חד נהירו ואיתכליל' מכולהו.

[2] Ibid.: ולהכי תשכח בכתבא דחד מאילניא דאית ביה מכל ספירה וספירה שבילא חד למלכות לרמזי רזא דא. As a matter of fact, this diagram of the sefiroth is nowhere found, but similar views (e.g. that certain sefiroth such as *Neṣaḥ* and *Hod* communicate directly with *Malkhuth*) are emphatically rejected by Cordovero, *Pardes*, vii. 3. *Malkhuth*, we are repeatedly assured, receives everything through *Yesod* only.

[3] *M.M.* 5a. 2: אחד היא עמהם ביחוד ולא [באצילות]; cf. also above, p. 32. Curiously enough Yehudah Ḥayyaṭ (*Minḥath Yehudah*, Mantua, 1558) repeatedly quotes a dictum of Nahmanides' according to which the relation of *Malkhuth* to the other sefiroth is described in exactly the opposite way: כי היא עמהם באצילות ולא באחדות.

[4] See below, pp. 226–7.

[5] Cf. below, pp. 227–8.

tions in conjunction prove beyond doubt that for the Maggid *Shekhinah* and *Maṭronitha* are identical; they are a secondary emanation of the ten sefiroth. But instead of each secondary light remaining attached to its own sefirah and source, the ten lights coalesce, as it were, to form a complete secondary system, surrounding, enveloping, and 'clothing' the primary sefiroth. The relation of the secondary sefiroth to the higher sefiroth is analogous to that of the latter to *En Sof*: they are described as a garment, sheath, or cocoon.[1] The function of this secondary system is to govern the 'World of Separation'. The Maggid's cosmology thus resembles some of the aforementioned schemes in requiring a middle world to mediate between the sefirotic 'World of Unity' and the lower angelic 'World of Separation'. These two terms are explicitly used by the Maggid, whereas the *'ABY'A*-terminology is conspicuously absent from this particular context.[2] The Maggid winds up one of his major communications on the subject of the procession of the sefiroth by declaring:

All these ten sefiroth are one unity and very substance of the Godhead . . . and all is complete unity without any aspect of separation . . . in complete union with *En Sof* . . . and this is the World of complete Unity and from then onward begins the World of Separation, for although all worlds subsist by the word of God, yet they are not of his very substance as are the ten sefiroth. But between the World of Complete Unity and the World of Complete Separation there is another World which has an aspect of unity (as it is made up of all ten sefiroth) and an aspect of separation (as it is a kind of sheath for the ten higher sefiroth, like a larva spinning its own cocoon), and it is called the World of the Name. . . . This world between the World of Unity and the World of Separation is Metatron, which comprises the ten sefiroth . . . and there also is the point at which the Princes of the Gentiles [i.e. the demonic powers] can attach themselves, for no such Power can approach the higher sefiroth . . . there also is the poison with which the Serpent infected Eve and it is thither that the sins rise and separate the World of complete Unity from [the lower world] . . . but no taint whatsoever can reach the higher ten sefiroth . . . 'and from thence' [Gen. ii. 10]—i.e. from this world—'it was parted and became into four heads'—these are the four camps of the *Shekhinah*. Between this world and the four camps of the *Shekhinah* there is the Tree of the Knowledge of Good

[1] לבוש, נרתיק, כהדין קמצא דלבושיה מניה.

[2] Cf. below, p. 232.

and Evil . . . which is called *teli*,[1] because its head is good and its tail is evil . . . and this mystery was indicated to you by Solomon Ḥazzan by the analogy of the shoe, etc.'[2]

This highly interesting passage deserves close and detailed analysis. Here it must suffice to note that neither *Shekhinah* nor *Maṭronitha* are mentioned in the Maggid's specific sense. Instead the name of the intermediate world is the 'World of the Name' (*'olam ha-shem*). This world is identified with Metatron and described as the sphere to which evil can penetrate and with which the 'Tree of the Knowledge of Good and Evil' (i.e. the kabbalistic concept of the Fall as a mingling of good and evil) is associated. Unfortunately all that is left in the extant text of Solomon Ḥazzan's[3] kabbalistic hint on the subject is a mere 'etcetera', but the reference to the 'shoe' (*na'al*) makes it probable that it referred to Metatron, one of whose symbols is 'shoe' to distinguish him from Sandalfon who is called 'sandal'.[4]

The extent to which this kind of problem exercised the kabbalistic circle to which Karo belonged may be illustrated by one or two quotations from the writings of his friend Solomon Alkabets. In *Berith ha-Levi*, his parting gift to the kabbalistic brotherhood in Salonica, Alkabets writes:[5] 'In the first place I must ask you not to expect me to discuss in this treatise matters of *'Aṣiluth* and *Beri'ah*, nor the subject of *Malkhuth* of *'Aṣiluth* and *Malkhuth* of *Beri'ah*, since these matters are exceedingly deep.' *'Aṣiluth* and *Beri'ah*, and the sefirah *Malkhuth* in these two worlds—this is clearly the problem of *Shekhinah*. Part of the problem was how to reconcile the exalted and divine nature of the tenth sefirah with its association with evil.[6] The Maggid himself, as we have seen,

[1] 'Dragon' or 'serpent'. Originally an astronomical term referring to the constellation of the Dragon (cf. *Yeṣirah*, vi. 1), *teli* had acquired a mystical significance by the time of the *Bahir* (cf. edn. R. Margoliouth, §§55, 101, 106); cf. A. Epstein, 'Recherches sur le Sefer Yesira', in *R.E.J.*, vol. xxviii (1894), pp. 63–64, and Scholem's note, *Das Buch Bahir* (1923), p. 66, n. 6.

[2] *M.M.* 37b. 1.

[3] Solomon Ḥazzan is well known to us as a contemporary of Karo. He was the messenger of the Safed Rabbinate who brought Berab's *semikhah* to the rabbis of Jerusalem, who rejected it; cf. above, p. 124. Ḥazzan is also mentioned by Conforti, op. cit. 37a; cf. also above, p. 90.

[4] Cf. also *M.M.* 47b–48a.

[5] *Berith ha-Levi* (Lemberg, 1864), fol. 9a.

[6] Cf. above, p. 216.

speaks of the Tree of the Knowledge of Good and Evil and of the *teli* when expounding his doctrine of the *Shekhinah*. Alkabets takes up the same problem in his commentary on Ruth,[1] precisely in connexion with the 'shoe' mentioned in iv. 7–8. He is particularly concerned with correcting a serious error of some kabbalistic students who describe the 'last attribute', i.e. the tenth sefirah *Malkhuth*, with all kinds of unworthy epithets such as

> the Tree of Death, the Tree of the Knowledge of Good and Evil, the flaming sword which turned every way. But [in reality] these three are hidden away and removed from her and placed under her feet [i.e. *Malkhuth* is above them]. . . . Therefore I say that these epithets apply to Metatron who is underneath this attribute [i.e. sefirah] and who is good from his loins upwards . . . and bad from his loins downwards[2] when he attaches himself to the sphere of evil (*qelippoth*), wherefore he is called the Tree of the Knowledge of Good and Evil. . . . But he who applies this epithet to the 'Virtuous Woman' [i.e. *Malkhuth*; cf. Prov. xxxi. 10] indeed destroys and cuts off [the divine plantations].

Here we seem to catch a glimpse of the motives that led to the demotion of the *Shekhinah* from *'Aṣiluth* to *Beri'ah* in the circle of the Salonica kabbalists. The interesting feature of the Maggid's exposition is that the intermediate world below *Malkhuth* is generally called *Shekhinah–Maṭronitha*, although the Maggid is well aware of the alternative appellation Metatron. Part of the reason of this surprising demotion of the *Shekhinah* is clearly the fear underlying Alkabets's argument: the classical *Shekhinah* is too closely associated with the demonic sphere of evil and the *qelippoth*. *Malkhuth*, as part of the divine realm of supernal sefiroth must be kept beyond all taint and blemish. Whatever is said to the contrary must therefore refer to a lower stage of emanation, i.e. to Metatron (Alkabets, Karo), viz. *Shekhinah–Maṭronitha* (Karo). This development was made possible by the aforementioned habit of early kabbalistic texts of describing the tenth sefirah *Malkhuth–Shekhinah* as a passive, secondary entity composed of the first nine sefiroth.[3] An interesting example which almost seems to foreshadow the

[1] שרש ישי (Constantinople, 1561), pp. 76b ff. The source of Alkabets's ideas can be traced to certain parts of the *Zohar*; cf., e.g. *Zohar*, i. 27a.

[2] Exactly like the *teli* whose 'head is good and its tail is evil'.

[3] Cf. above, p. 216.

Maggid's doctrine can be found in the writings of Karo's near-contemporary Yehudah Ḥayyaṭ. Talking of *Malkhuth*, he explains:[1]

Once the nine points [i.e. sefiroth] emanated in the form of one normal and two inverted triangles, it was necessary that a power to contain them all, i.e. *Malkhuth*, be added to them. For the divine emanation proceeds to *Yesod* which is the last of the aforementioned nine points, but from these individual [sefiroth] there arose the aforementioned general power which receives them all. For it is known that the whole is composed of parts yet possesses a new power which was not in the parts. This is like a ship where every part, instrument, and tackle has its specific function for the purposes of navigation . . . but only after all parts have been joined together does the assembly produce a new activity which is her purpose, i.e. her sailing to her destination. . . . Nevertheless, she [*Malkhuth*] is an independent sefirah like all the others, and therefore it is said[2] 'ten and not nine'.

Elsewhere Ḥayyaṭ describes *Malkhuth* as an 'independent entity'.[3] Ḥayyaṭ clearly tries to have the best of both worlds. In a quotation from Shem Tob's *Sefer ha-'Emunoth* we found that the sefiroth emitted by *Malkhuth* constitute the world of *hekhaloth*. A very similar view of the world of *hekhaloth* is given by Me'ir ibn Gabbay,[4] but its genesis is described in words almost identical with the Maggid's account of the emanation of *Shekhinah*. Ibn Gabbay says: 'The kabbalists have a tradition that after the first emanation there emanated a second emanation, meaning that from each of the supernal attributes [i.e. sefiroth] another attribute emanated underneath the "headstone" [i.e. *Malkhuth*; cf. Zech. iv. 7].'

Enough has been said to show that the Maggid is drawing on traditional kabbalistic material from diverse, occasionally even divergent, sources. There is the doctrine of *Shekhinah* as somehow outside the realm of supernal sefiroth and as manifest in the form of Metatron. There is also the dichotomy 'World of Unity' and 'World of Separation' with an intermediate world in between. To these can be added a number of other expressions and ideas tending to strengthen the notion of *Shekhinah* as an entity standing over and against the other sefiroth and constituting a 'world' of its

1 *Minḥath Yehudah* (Mantua, 1558), p. 10b.
2 *Yeṣirah*, i. 4.
3 Op. cit., p. 12a: חתיכה בפני עצמה.
4 *'Abodath ha-Qodesh*, i. 16 (ed. Cracow, 1577, fol. 17b).

own. Among the expressions which testify to the highly complex character of *Shekhinah* in the mind of the kabbalists we should also count the use of *'olam* in connexion with *Shekhinah*, as distinct from its usage as a synonym of sefirah in general. Expressions such as *'alma de-'ithgalya*, &c., tend to confirm *Shekhinah* in her position as a complete 'world' over and against the *'olam* of the other sefiroth. Moreover, in the *Zohar* itself the *Shekhinah* is sometimes spoken of as the 'Throne of Glory' and described in images suggesting a position *below* the realm of sefiroth.[1] Tishby[2] quotes Geronese sources according to which the 'Throne' is situated in the seventh *hekhal*, and points out that 'this *hekhal* is the dwelling of the *Shekhinah* and the locus of her union with *Yesod*. . . . However, this *hekhal* is sometimes spoken of as if it were the *Shekhinah* herself.' Karo boldly combines these different strands, though there remains some doubt whether for him the term 'World of Separation' still denotes the world of angels and *hekhaloth*. It will be remembered that for some authors[3] the secondary emanation is nothing but the *hekhaloth*, which, in their turn, are identical with the angels and the *'alma de-peruda*. If we now add the lowest world of *'Asiyyah* (i.e. the celestial spheres)—though the *M.M.* does not mention it at all—then we may perhaps claim the four-world scheme even for Karo: *'olam ha-yiḥud*, *'olam ha-shem*, *'olam ha-perud*, *'olam ha-galgallim*. In that case the *'alma de-peruda* might, after all, include the angels. However, the wording of the passage quoted above[4] rather suggests that *'alma de-peruda* means the lower worlds in general, including the celestial spheres and the sublunar universe.

The relations between the realm of the supernal sefiroth and the 'ten sefiroth of *Shekhinah*' are described by the Maggid in the terminology and with the emotional fervour reserved by earlier kabbalists for 'the Holy One, Blessed be He' (i.e. the sixth sefirah *Tif'ereth*) and his *Shekhinah* (i.e. the tenth sefirah *Malkhuth*). In fact, we now witness a subtle but none the less significant change in the meaning of the supreme mystery of 'union'. All religious acts and intentions are directed and related to this 'new', lower

[1] Tishby, op. cit., pp. 417 f.
[2] Ibid., pp. 420–1.
[3] Cf. also above, p. 215.
[4] Above, p. 219.

Shekhinah 'to unify her with the ten supernal sefiroth. For even as she proceeded from them all, even so we must unite her and meditate on the correspondence of her ten sefiroth with the supernal ten sefiroth. For when they are completely congruent [through the appropriate meditations], then there is perfection and joy in all worlds.[1]

The highly unconventional character of this doctrine becomes fully apparent when we consider its consequences for the anatomy of the kabbalistic cosmos. The classical systems assumed the sixth and ninth sefiroth in particular, but generally speaking all the sefiroth but the last,[2] to represent the male body, whereas *Malkhuth* typified the female frame.[3] The union of *Tif'ereth* and *Malkhuth* symbolizes the holy marriage of the male and female aspects within the Deity. This traditional kabbalistic pattern is significantly modified when we learn the Maggid's view of the divine *anthropos*:[4]

And this is the mystery of 'And God said, Let us make man in our image, after our likeness' [Gen. i. 26]. For 'God' [*Elohim*], which is *Binah*,[5] said to the ten sefiroth [!] 'let us make man', that is: let every one of us produce one light, and through the combination of all ten lights let us make man. 'Man' that is *Maṭronitha* . . . as it is written [Is. xliv. 13] 'according to the beauty of a man, that it may remain in the house'—and it is the woman that remaineth in the house. And this man should be in our image, i.e. he should be a sheath for each of us, and after our likeness, i.e. similar to us by being composed, like ourselves, of ten sefiroth. . . . And when *Binah* had said 'let us make man' these lights coalesced and there emerged this man [*Adam*] who is in the likeness of a female whose limbs are made to correspond to those of the male so that they may unite in perfect union. Even so when the ten sefiroth of the *Maṭronitha* unite with the ten supernal sefiroth, they then correspond to each other and this is perfect union and the joy of all worlds. This is the mystery of union which we have to perform always. And this also is the mystery of God's making a woman of Adam's rib . . . even as the

[1] *M.M.* 5a. 2.

[2] For our present purpose we may ignore the female character of the 'left' side in general and of *Binah* in particular.

[3] Cf. the writer's 'Some psychological aspects of Kabbalah' in *Harvest*, vol. iii (1956), pp. 86, 90–91; cf. also above, p. 217, the quotation from Shem Tob.

[4] *M.M.* 5a–b.

[5] i.e. *Binah* took the initiative in the process that led to the formation of *Shekhinah*.

Maṭronitha was produced by the movement of the ten supernal sefiroth which are the 'male' world. And now behold how 'in my flesh I see God' [Job xix. 26], for precisely as *En Sof* produced the ten sefiroth and the ten sefiroth [then] produced the *Shekhinah*, yet all are one unity, so also in the creation of man God 'breathed into his nostrils the breath of life' [Gen. ii. 7]—which symbolizes *En Sof*—and from this breath of life there came into existence the body—which symbolizes the ten supernal sefiroth—and from the body of Adam was formed the female—which symbolizes the *Maṭronitha*—who was formed from the ten sefiroth . . . for each sefirah gave her one light . . . and all these ten lights combined and became one, and this is the *Shekhinah*, which is like a female that receives and conceives from the male. . . . She also governs the house and distributes sustenance to all worlds.[1] This is the mystery and the true doctrine which the Holy One, Blessed be He, and the members of His academy wanted to reveal to you.

The Maggid seems to be aware that he is propounding a novel doctrine. In the entry *Debarim* (Sabbath, 12 Menaḥem [Ab])[2] the Maggid informs Karo:

this mystery of the lower *Maṭronitha* is very profound and it behoves to keep it hidden. For that reason the works of all the kabbalists mention only the ten sefiroth [including, therefore, *Malkhuth*, i.e. the 'higher' *Maṭronitha*], but this mystery of the lower *Maṭronitha* none would reveal. . . . Yet all of them knew the truth of the matter and all that they wrote concerning *Malkhuth*, without further qualification, really referred to the lower *Maṭronitha*. . . . The lower *Maṭronitha* distributes to each [of the lower worlds and creatures] according to its need[3] . . . and all that Joseph Gikatila, my chosen one, has written concerning the sefirah *Malkhuth*[4] refers to the lower *Malkhuth* [!], for he well knew the mystery but concealed it.

It seems as if the Maggid, in addition to teaching a novel doctrine, was actually undoing here one of the major achievements of the classical, mythological *Kabbalah*. From a psychological point of view one of the great feats of the kabbalistic movement that culminated in the *Zohar* and similar texts was its discovery of a 'female'

[1] This is a standard Zoharic theme in connexion with the *Shekhinah*.

[2] *M.M.* 56b–57a. Either the date or the ascription to Sabbath *Debarim* must be wrong since the latter always falls before (or on) 9 Ab.

[3] This is one of the principal functions of *Malkhuth* according to the classical systems.

[4] In the first chapter of his systematic work on the sefiroth, one of the earliest kabbalistic classics, *Sha'arey 'Orah*.

principle within the Godhead. It was the union of the male and female aspects of the sefirotic *plērōma* that constituted the ultimate mystery of the life divine. The divine *anthropos* was truly one and perfect by virtue of the holy union of these two principles. This union, however, was not with something outside; it was conceived as an inner process of the dynamic forces that constituted the divine Being. With the Maggid we return to a more orthodox and 'patriarchal' image of the divine. The sefirotic realm as a whole is male. Like Adam, it gives birth to an analogous, equally differentiated, but secondary structure, corresponding to it in all details but lower in rank and—strictly speaking—outside the original divine sphere. The mystery of *yiḥud* is no longer the fullness and perfection of the interior life divine, but the close union of the secondary emanation with its source. Israel is called to promote this union by religious acts and intentions, but it is clearly not the Godhead itself which is thus unified (i.e. God and his *Shekhinah* in the old sense) but rather the lower world which is brought into full communion with God:[1]

> I have taught thee the exalted and holy mystery of the ten supernal sefiroth and the *Maṭronitha* which is composed of them all. He who separates the ten supernal sefiroth from the *Maṭronitha* is 'a whisperer who separateth chief friends' [Prov. xvi. 28] and causes destruction of the worlds, whereas he who unites the ten sefiroth with the *Maṭronitha* strengthens all the worlds.

A brief reference has already been made to the old legend of the 'Diminution of the Moon'[2] which the kabbalists transformed into the 'Mystery of the Diminution of the Moon'. Normally when a kabbalist says 'sun' he means, of course, *Tif'ereth*, and when he says 'moon' he means the tenth sefirah *Malkhuth*, viz. *Shekhinah*. The Maggid, however, interprets this mystery in terms of his own system. Karo had inquired, 'Since the *Maṭronitha* consists of the ten lights emitted by the ten supernal sefiroth—each sefirah one light—how could [the moon] say, "Two kings cannot share one crown", and what is the meaning of [God's reply], "Go and lessen

[1] *M.M.* 49a. 1.

[2] Above, p. 218. On the rituals and liturgy connected with this myth cf. Scholem's article (referred to above, p. 58, n. 1), pp. 172–4.

thyself"?'[1] The Maggid replies that this grave discussion had not taken place between any two sefiroth in particular but between *En Sof* and the *Shekhinah* (in the Maggid's peculiar technical sense):

> The complaint of the moon was this, that each light as it came forth from its respective sefirah said that there was no need of two lights [the original and the secondary] in each sefirah. This is the meaning of 'two kings cannot share one crown'. . . . Thereupon the Holy One, Blessed be He, that is *En Sof*,[2] replied, 'Go and lessen thyself', that is to say that all the lights emitted by the sefiroth should coalesce and form one *Maṭronitha* to govern the world of separation. That is its diminution that it should now act as the head of the kingdom of foxes. . . .[3]

When the *Shekhinah* bitterly complained about her degradation, God comforted her: 'Israel shall raise and unite thee again by their good works.'

According to the Maggid it is thus a matter of the secondary lights protesting to *En Sof* about redundancy. The divine answer took the form of the organization and constitution of these lights as a unified structure whose function is the guidance of the lower worlds. The degradation inherent in this function is to be counteracted and balanced by the religious acts of Israel which exalt the *Shekhinah* again to a state of union with the higher sefiroth from which she originated.

For a better understanding of this conception of *Shekhinah* it may be useful to compare it with the fully developed and systematized doctrine of four worlds as expounded, for example, by Cordovero. The Maggid's communications quoted above[4] are by themselves enough to illustrate the close parallelism between Karo's doctrine of *Shekhinah* and Cordovero's definition of *Beri'ah*. Even the connexion with the 'Diminution of the Moon' is there when Cordovero states:[5]

[1] *M.M.* 5b. 2. [2] Here הקב"ה is identified with *En Sof*; cf. above, p. 212.

[3] Echoing the proverb, *M. Aboth* iv. 15, 'Be a tail unto lions rather than a head unto foxes'. *Shekhinah*, originally a secondary appendage to the supernal sefiroth ('tail to lions'), was demoted to form a second, lower sphere which rules over the nether worlds ('head to foxes').

[4] pp. 218, 224–5.

[5] *Pardes*, שער אבי"ע פ"ג. It will be noticed that for Cordovero the emanation of the secondary lights or branches is the result of a preceding 'fall' of the *Shekhinah*, whereas for Karo there is no fall at all and the Diminution consists in the organization of the redundant lights as an intermediate world.

The truth about *Beri'ah* and the Throne is this: when the *Shekhinah* was exiled from her original place and the moon was lessened, God increased her hosts so as to pacify her. And this is the meaning of the increase of her hosts: that every single sefirah produced from itself one branch,[1] and these ten branches united underneath *Malkhuth* to form a throne for her. This is the aforementioned Throne. These ten branches are a palace[2] for the ten higher [sefiroth] . . . and because they are underneath *Malkhuth* they are called by her name. . . .[3]

The close union of the *Shekhinah* with the supernal sefiroth is formulated by Cordovero in these terms:[4]

When the emanation of the ten sefiroth was achieved, God wanted to create a Throne whose ten degrees should serve the ten sefiroth of *'Aṣiluth*. . . . And they were created by the power of the ten letters [i.e. sefiroth] which clothe themselves [with the ten degrees of the Throne] like a larva spinning its cocoon, for the Throne and its wheels are like a garment for the [supernal] Emanation, i.e. the sefiroth. . . . Thus all is one, and therefore it behoves [us] never to separate *Beri'ah* from *'Aṣiluth*.

Also the term *'olam ha-shem* occurs in Cordovero's writings as one of the names of *Beri'ah*:[5] ' "Name" actually means garment. . . . Thus all sefiroth are a garment to *En Sof* . . . and the world of *Beri'ah* is called "Name" because it is a name, viz. garment, to *'Aṣiluth*.' Another name for *Beri'ah* is, surprisingly enough, *Maṭronitha* but not *Shekhinah*. Cordovero, who carefully distinguishes between *Beri'ah* and *Yeṣirah*, is equally careful to distinguish between *Maṭronitha* and *Shekhinah*. The latter is one of the names of *Yeṣirah*,

for *Yeṣirah* is nothing but the ten orders of angels comprised in the name Metatron which corresponds to the six days of the week. Now these ten sefiroth of *Yeṣirah*, which are branches extending from the [supernal] sefiroth, are the *Shekhinah* which is named after *Yeṣirah*, and it behoves [us] to unite the branches with their sources. . . . And because they are branches extending in Metatron, who is called the 'lad', therefore these branches are called 'virgins'.[6]

[1] Cordovero says 'branch' where the Maggid said 'light'.

[2] Cf. above, pp. 222–3, on the connexion of *Shekhinah* and *hekhaloth*.

[3] This is Cordovero's way of accounting for the terminological transition of the original names of the tenth sefirah to denote the lower world of *Beri'ah*.

[4] שער אבי"ע פ"ג. [5] Ibid. [6] Ibid., שער פרטי השמות.

It appears, therefore, that Karo's 'World of the Name'—*Maṭronitha–Shekhinah*—combines the characteristics of both *Beri'ah* and *Yeṣirah*. When discussing a passage in the *Zohar* possibly bearing out a similar meaning, we already had occasion to point out[1] that it would be natural for a three-world system to compress *Beri'ah* and *Yeṣirah* into one, since there was not much that could be done with either the higher world of the divine sefiroth or the nether world, both of which were fixed in their respective places. As Karo's 'World of Separation' seems to embrace the whole of the 'lower' world, including the celestial spheres and the sublunar universe, there is no compelling reason to assume that a fourth world should be added. Doubts may remain, as has already been remarked,[2] about the precise location of the angels. Since in Karo's system *Yeṣirah* is assimilated to *Beri'ah*, the angels probably belong to this middle world (*Shekhinah*, *'olam ha-shem*) which—like *Yeṣirah* in other systems—carries the name of Metatron, who stands as a symbol for the totality of the ten angelic orders. It is just possible, however, that the angels should be placed in the 'World of Separation', of which they originally were the terminological cause. There are no angelological hints or indications in the extant text of the *M.M.* that could shed light on this point.

So far we have stated the basic outline of the Maggid's doctrine without going into more detailed analyses or examining his terminological consistency. We have found that the traditional equation of the tenth sefirah = *Malkhuth* = *Shekhinah* = *Maṭronitha* = *Keneseth Yisra'el* does not seem to be valid for the Maggid and that *Maṭronitha–Shekhinah*, instead of denoting a sefirah in the *'Aṣiluth*-world of the divine *plērōma*, now signifies a second, lower world in union with the first and corresponding more or less to the *Beri'ah–Yeṣirah* worlds of the better-known systems. The remarkable feature of Karo's scheme is the transference of the mystery of *yiḥud* and of the many symbolic overtones of the classical *Shekhinah* to the world of *Beri'ah–Yeṣirah* combined.[3]

[1] Above, pp. 212–13. [2] Above, p. 223.

[3] But cf. this echo of the classical system (*M.M.* 38b): דכיון דת"ת דאינון פגים דספירין עילאין מתייחד בפנים דמלכות הא כולהו ספירן מתייחדא במלכות והוה ייחודא שלים דוגמת בר נש מתייחד עם בת זוגיה...

From the maggidic utterances quoted so far it appears that the main distinction is between the secondary sefiroth of *Shekhinah–Maṭronitha* on the one hand, and the supernal sefiroth on the other. This division is referred to in passing and as a matter of course a large number of times.[1] However, leaving it at that would be simplifying matters unduly. Karo was not primarily a theoretical kabbalist bent on elaborating his system consistently and with intentional disregard of traditional kabbalistic usage. It thus happens that an apparently contradictory and, in fact, more conventional use of these terms keeps on intruding without, however, seriously jeopardizing the original features of the Maggid's teaching. It is quite certain that *Maṭronitha* is always and consistently distinguished from *Keneseth Yisra'el*.[2] It is equally certain that *Keneseth Yisra'el* is the Maggid's favourite term for the tenth sefirah *Malkhuth*.[3] The distinction between *Malkhuth* of *'Aṣiluth* and *Malkhuth* of *Beri'ah* is expressed by the terms higher/lower *Malkhuth* or higher/lower *Keneseth Yisra'el*; the terms seem to be interchangeable.[4] It is hardly surprising that where Cordovero

[1] חיבורא דמטרוניתא בהדי מלכות דספירין עילאין (13b. 1); למיתן לספירין דמטרוניתא דביקא בספירין עילאין (22b. 3); דיתחדו ספירין עילאין בספירין דמטרוניתא (23a. 1); דקישורא [דתפילין] דבעינן לקשרא מטרוניתא עם ספירין עילאין (24b. 3); ספירין עילאין דאינון ממלאין שפע לספירין דמטרוניתא (30b. 3); לוית חן היינו מטרוניתא דכולהו ספירין מתלוין ומתחברין בה . . . וענקים דהיינו ספירין עילאין (31b. 1); לוחי קדמאי רמיזי בת״ת וכ״י בספירין עילאין . . . אבל לוחי בתראי רמיזי לספירין דמטרוניתא (31b. 3); דייחד כולהון ספירין כי היכי דינהרון דהא משה רמיז בת״ת ואת במלכות וכל ביסוד ועדת בני ישראל בספירין דמטרוניתא (33a. 6); דכד יתייחדן ספירייא דמטרוניתא . . . דהיא נאצלה מעשר ספירין עילאין . . . וכד אינהו מתייחדו בכ״י כלומר דספירין דילה מתיחדין בספירין עילאין . . . (39b. 2).

[2] Cf. in addition to the examples quoted above, n. 1, *M.M.* 27a. 3: דגבעה ואבן חדא רמיזא לכ״י עילאה וחדא למטרוניתא.

[3] הצדיק המשפיע גורם ליסוד . . . .שהוא משפיע בברכה שהיא כנ״י (13b. 2); כנ״י לחברא לה עם ת״ת (21a); ארבע רגלי המרכבה דאינון שלשה אבהן וכנ״י (22b. 3); ותשועת צדיקים וכו׳ תשועה היינו כנ״י דיתבא בין שני צדיקים . . . דצדיק וכנ״י בעת צרה כד מתתקפן אינך סטרין לאטלאה זוהמא בכנ״י . . . ומטה אלהים בידי ליחדא לת״ת עם כנ״י . . . ויקחו אבן דרמיזא לכנ״י וישב עליה לאתייחדא טפי בכנ״י . . . דעל ידי כך אתייחד כנ״י בתפארת (26b–27a).

[4] וחזיין למטרוניתא דאתדבק עם מלכות דספירות עילאין בדבקותא וייחודא חדא (6a. 2); כל בשר . . . דכל היינו מלכות דספירין עילאין ובשר היינו מטרוניתא (23a. 1); וכל זה בכנ״י תתאה דאילו בכנ״י עילאה ובספירות שעליה אין שום דבר חיצון יכול לגשת לשם (65b. 2, cf. also 30a. 4); אם אני דהיינו

would say *Malkhuth* of *Beri'ah* the Maggid says *Malkhuth* of *Maṭronitha*.[1] Terminological complications start when we find the term *Malkhuth* (with or without the qualification 'lower') in contexts where it can only mean the *Maṭronitha*-world as a whole.[2] In point of fact the traditional matter-of-course identification of *Maṭronitha–Shekhinah–Keneseth Yisra'el–Malkhuth* fairly often intrudes into the Maggid's formulations. Occasionally the qualifying adjective 'lower' is left out, and it is only by his knowledge of Karo's system as a whole that the reader knows that *Maṭronitha* is meant when the text says *Malkhuth*.[3]

What is true of *Malkhuth* applies also to *Keneseth Yisra'el*. The expression often appears in contexts where it seems to mean the secondary *Maṭronitha*-world, though it may, just possibly, be construed as referring to the tenth sefirah of *'Aṣiluth*.[4] Sometimes the Maggid speaks of the functions of *Malkhuth* with regard to the higher sefiroth in completely conventional terms and as if he had forgotten his own doctrine of *Shekhinah*.[5] The ambiguity of these texts may serve, incidentally, as an illustration of our contention that some of the traditional sayings about *Malkhuth–Shekhinah* provided a natural transition to the Maggid's doctrine of *Shekhinah* as the product, sheath, garment, or 'cocoon' of the higher sefiroth. Depending on whether we interpret *Malkhuth–Keneseth Yisra'el*

מלכות כאן . . . וכשאני לעצמי כלומר כד נקטינן אני . . . לעצמי דהיינו לנטוע שמים . . . וליסוד ארץ היינו לחברא יסוד עם (32a. 3); מלכות תתאה מלכות ולאמר לציון עמי אתה היינו לחבר במלכות תתאה עם ספירין עילאין (54a. 5).

[1] דבית אמי היינו מטרוניתא וחדר הורתי היינו החלק שבה הרומז למלכות (26a. 1).

[2] הציבי לך ציונים דחד ציון איהו מלכות תתאה גופי' וציון תניינא איהו סטרא דאית במלכות תתאה ממלכות עלאה (54a. 5).

[3] מלכות קדישא דהיא כלילא מי"ס עלאין (47b. 4). In this particular text the 'real' *Malkhuth* is referred to as עטרת דספירין עלאין.

[4] מעיל הוא לקבל כנ"י כד איהי מתייחדת עם שאר ספירין דאיהי מנא דכולהו (31a. 1); עריני הם הספירות העליונות, וערי אלהינו הם היכלות כנסת ישראל (35a. 3); דספירין דכנ"י יתייחדו בספירין עילאין (23a. 1). In the same passage the expression ספירין עילאין בספירין דמטרוניתא [לייחדא] seems to be equivalent to כנ"י דספירין עילאין במטרוניתא [לייחדא]. The *shammash*-light of the Ḥanukah-lamp symbolizes לכנ"י דאיהי משמשא לכלהו ואיהי מנא דכלהו (18b. 1).

[5] ואזהר דלא ינקוט בר נש ספירין עילאין דכל מאן דבעי למיעיל לא יכיל למיעיל אלא בה והיינו דקאמר אם אני כאן הכל כאן דהיינו צדיק וספירין דעליה כאן (32a. 3).

of these doubtful texts as the tenth sefirah or as *Beri'ah*, we shall have to understand the expression 'supernal sefiroth' as referring either to the nine higher sefiroth of *'Aṣiluth* or to *'Aṣiluth* as a whole.

Conversely there are indications that the Maggid at times applies the names *Shekhinah* or *Maṭronitha* to the tenth sefirah. We are, perhaps, unduly pressing the phrase 'lower *Maṭronitha*'[1] by concluding that the Maggid must therefore acknowledge a 'higher *Maṭronitha*' (= *Malkhuth*), but certainly the wording is often so vague that it is difficult to decide whether the tenth sefirah *Malkhuth* or the *Beri'ah*-world is meant. Sometimes there is little doubt that the former is the case.[2] Once the secondary *Beri'ah*-world is described, as usual, as *Maṭronitha*, but *Malkhuth* of *'Aṣiluth* is actually called the 'supernal *Shekhinah*'[3]—apparently to distinguish it from the lower *Shekhinah*. It appears that in actual fact the Maggid's terminology is less precise and consistent than his system, from which, in spite of terminological vagaries, he never deviates.

Once only are *'Aṣiluth*, *Beri'ah*, and *Yeṣirah* mentioned by name, but the text does not square too well with the Maggid's system as outlined so far. The passage[4] seeks to give kabbalistic reasons for the strict biblical prohibitions against eating blood and certain animal fats, and makes use of the *'ABY* terminology. However, to equate the *'ABY* of this passage with the Maggid's *'olam ha-yiḥud*, *Shekhinah*, viz. *'olam ha-shem*, and *'olam ha-perud*, though easy, seems to be forcing the meaning too much in the interests of a harmonizing exegesis.

[1] *M.M.* 56b–57a.

[2] דמפריד בין יסוד למטרוניתא . . . דזה היינו יסוד וה״א רמיז לכנ״י (18a. 1; cf. also 40a. 3, 41a); ומלכות שהיא מטרוניתא ושאר ספירות בייחוד גמור עם א״ס (37b. 1).

[3] חדא לרמזי לשכינה עילאה דספירין עילאין וחדא לרמזי למטרוניתא (5b. 2).

[4] ורזא דמילתא דג׳ מיני ספירין אצילות בריאה יצירה ועלמא מתנהג ע״י הנך דיצירה [var. דבריאה] ולית לן תפיסה בהנך דבריאה וכ״ש באצילות. והא הנך דאצילות אינון לובן גמור וחלב רמיז להון. . . . וספירין דבריאה אית בהון קצת דין ודם רמיז להון. . . . ומאן דאכיל חלב בעי לאחדא בספירין דאצילות ומאן דאכיל דם בעי לאחדא בספירין דבריאה ועונשה מדה כנגד מדה, איהו בעי לאדבקא נפשיה באתר גבוה מאתר דחזי ליה עונשיה דיכרת מאתר דחזי ליה (4a. 2).

To sum up, it appears that the Maggid ignores the kabbalistic cosmology of four-world *'ABY'A* and teaches instead a scheme of three worlds, consisting of the divine *plērōma* of 'supernal sefiroth', a middle world or secondary sefiroth-emanation, and the 'World of Separation' which seems to include the lower worlds generally. The elements of this system can all be traced in earlier kabbalistic literature. The original feature of the Maggid's teaching is the explicit identification of the intermediate world, a kind of combination of *Beri'ah* and *Yeṣirah*, with the *Shekhinah*. By making this equation, the Maggid transferred to the intermediate world all the specific emotional qualities and overtones associated with *Malkhuth* as *Shekhinah* in classical kabbalism. The resultant modification of the anatomy of the divine sefiroth and of the conception of *yiḥud* presents what would appear to be unique features in the history of kabbalistic ideas. An added interest attaches to Karo's doctrine of the *Shekhinah* once it is remembered that the instrument of the heavenly revelations, the Maggid, describes himself as being none other than the *Shekhinah*. Karo fails to draw the consequences from this suggestive identification and nowhere tries to unify the two strands of the rabbinic usage of the term *Shekhinah*: as a symbol, name, or hypostasis of God revealing himself in prophetic speech, Holy Spirit, &c., and as a technical term of kabbalistic theosophy. Karo's apparent lack of awareness of the problems posed by his dual usage of the term *Shekhinah* only strengthens the unsystematic and mainly homiletic impression left by the *M.M.*

11

MAN AND HIS SOUL

IF the doctrine of the Godhead is undoubtedly the major and most significant part of kabbalism, its teachings on the nature and fate of man may surely qualify for the second place in the order of interest. The two subjects are obviously interrelated and show many significant points of contact. Yet the relationship is neither all of a piece nor inherently necessary. It is true that by an extraordinary combination of what might be described as Zoroastrian and gnostic motifs the kabbalists linked the *raison d'être* and fate of man with that of the Deity. The theosophical doctrine of the sefirotic *plērōma*, the mystical discipline of its contemplation, and the performance of the *yiḥud* of the divine potencies—all these placed the human soul in a much wider setting than would have been the case if its sole preoccupation were its private celestial bliss. Nevertheless, and in spite of the elaboration of kabbalistic anthropology on the pattern of the divine sefiroth,[1] there is no doubt but that the kabbalistic doctrine of the soul has its own background and origins, and its own autonomous lines of development. As a result, the connexion with other kabbalistic doctrines is often tenuous, artificial, or, at best, incidental.

The most telling illustration of this state of affairs is provided by the main chapter of kabbalistic anthropology: the doctrine of *gilgul* or metempsychosis.[2] This doctrine has achieved a maximum symbiosis with the main kabbalistic tenets, which it fits remarkably well in many respects, yet it clearly has its own origins and its independent foci of interest. As a matter of fact, most theosophical systems, whether ancient or modern, seem to evince a natural

[1] The at times bizarre anthropomorphic 'anatomy' of the world of sefiroth is thus nothing but the kabbalistic application of the medieval macrocosm–microcosm analogy.

[2] On the whole subject cf. G. Scholem, 'Seelenwanderung und Sympathie der Seelen in der jüdischen Mystik', *Eranos-Jahrbuch*, vol. xxiv (1955; Zürich, 1956), pp. 55–118; also id. in *E.J.*, vol. ix, coll. 704–11.

proclivity for linking their particular systems of spiritual metaphysics with the transmigration of souls. Metempsychosis was, of course, a central Manichean doctrine,[1] ultimately derived, according to al-Biruni,[2] from India. The soul was individually pre-existent before birth, as Plato had taught; it could therefore pass through various bodies though (at least originally) only through human ones.[3] Those who lived in a worldly state or were married[4] had to return again into the body. The best fortune that could befall such souls was to be incarnated in food[5] and to be eaten by the Manichean saints—a process which would translate them to their final goal of bliss. These ideas have close analogies with notions developed by later kabbalists and particularly by the Lurianic school in the sixteenth century,[6] but are still foreign to early *Kabbalah*. The earliest texts[7] do not yet know the later commonplace technical term *gilgul*, but speak of *'ibbur* or *ha'athaqah*, the latter being a literal translation of Arabic *tanasukh*. Unknown in Hebrew literature is the original Manichean term *taš̌pikha*, which, like its

[1] Cf. A. V. Williams Jackson, 'The Doctrine of Metempsychosis in Manichaeism', *J.A.O.S.*, vol. xlv (1925), pp. 246 ff., and C. R. C. Allberry, 'Symbole von Tod und Wiedergeburt im Manichäismus', *Eranos-Jahrbuch*, vol. vii (1939; Zürich, 1940), pp. 113–49.

[2] *Alberuni's India* (ed. E. S. Sachau) (1910), vol. i, p. 54.

[3] Cf. Hierokles, *De Providentia et Fato*, quoted by Photius, *Library*, ccxiv (*P.G.*, vol. ciii, coll. 704–5); cf. also the Manichean texts collected by Williams Jackson, loc. cit.

[4] For Judaism, of course, everything is the other way round: to have remained childless is sufficient reason for the soul to be sent back into the world in order to make amends where it had failed in its duty towards God and the cosmos.

[5] In 'cucumbers and melons', as St. Augustine points out with somewhat savage humour (*Contra Faustum*, v. 10, *P.L.*, vol. xlii, col. 226; cf. also ibid. vi. 4–6, coll. 231 f.).

[6] Cf. below, p. 243, n. 4. The earlier kabbalists seem to have known the notion of a soul achieving final perfection and release through the sacrifice of the animal in which it was incarnated, but there is no hint yet of perfection through being eaten by the saints. But even the later kabbalistic theory of the redemption of souls by eating the animals into which they were transmigrated differs from that of the Manichees. The latter did, indeed, admit transmigration into animal bodies (cf. *Contra Faustum*, xx. 20, *P.L.*, vol. xlii, col. 384: *quia humanas animas in ea* [*pecora*] *revolvi arbitramini*; *Contra Adimantum* xii. 1, *P.L.*, vol. xlii, col. 144: *hominum animae . . . revolvi . . . in pecora existimant*), but for this very reason the *electi* abstained from killing animals (*nefas habetis pecora occidi*, *Contra Faustum*, loc. cit.).

[7] Cf. G. Scholem, לחקר תורת הגלגול בקבלה במאה הי״ג, in *Tarbiz*, vol. xvi (1945), pp. 135–50.

Greek translation *metangismos*,[1] conveys the underlying notion of a 'transfusion' or change of vessel, the soul being 'poured' from one body into another. Another Manichean term, however, does seem to have percolated into kabbalistic usage. It is the term *revolutiones*, mentioned by St. Augustine,[2] which later became the standard kabbalistic expression *gilgul*.[3] Exactly as in Manichean doctrine, *gilgul* was originally considered as a kind of purgatory. In fact, one kabbalist actually drew what seems to be the obvious and logical conclusion by declaring that metempsychosis was equivalent to *gehinnom* (hell, or, more exactly, purgatory) and therefore rendered the traditional conception of the latter superfluous.[4] According to the *Zohar* metempsychosis is the punishment for a few specific sins only, such as sexual transgressions or the failure to produce offspring. Other early authors were attracted by the possibilities which the doctrine offered for a satisfactory theodicy.[5] By the sixteenth century *gilgul* into the bodies of animals also was generally accepted,[6] dissenting kabbalists being few and far between.[7]

One obvious question arises. What exactly is the nature, origin, and destiny of the soul, whose transmigrations are so prominent a feature of its fate? The general consensus of Jewish theologians[8] was unquestionably in favour of the Platonic doctrine of the pre-existence of the soul. There are early rabbinic references[9] to a celestial *guf*, a kind of heavenly storehouse or waiting-room in which all souls that will descend to earth and be incarnated in

[1] *Tašpikha denafshatha* (Titus of Bostra); μεταγγίζεσθαι; transfundi.

[2] Cf. in addition to the quotations above, p. 235, n. 6, *Contra Faustum*, v. 10 (*P.L.*, vol. xlii, col. 226): *non resurrectionem sed revolutionem*; *De Haer.* xlvi (*P.L.*, vol. xlii, col. 37): *animas auditorum suorum in Electos revolvi arbitrantur*; *De Civ. Dei*, xxii (*P.L.*, vol. xli, col. 776): *per diversa corpora revolutiones*; and *De Trin.* xii. 15 (*P.L.*, vol. xlii, col. 1012): *de revolutionibus animarum*. The last two passages (which, incidentally, refer to the Neoplatonists and not to the Manichees) are quoted by DuCange s.v. *revolutio*.

[3] Scholem, *Eranos-Jahrbuch*, vol. xxiv, p. 70, n. 23.

[4] Ibid., p. 74; cf. also *E.J.*, vol. ix, col. 708, and Scholem's reference there to Joseph of Hamadan.

[5] Scholem, *Eranos-Jahrbuch*, vol. xxiv, p. 69.

[6] Ibid., pp. 90–92; cf. also above, p. 235, n. 6.

[7] e.g. Yehudah Ḥayyaṭ and Shem Ṭob.

[8] Excepting the more extreme Aristotelians; but on the whole Neoplatonism won the day.

[9] b. *Yebamoth* 63b and parallel passages.

bodies during this *aion* bide their time. At a later date this view proved to be of the utmost significance in linking speculations concerning the soul with eschatological expectations about the end of the present *aion* and the advent of the Messiah.

The cause of the descent of the heavenly soul into the material body was a fundamental problem of Jewish-Platonic anthropology. One way of explaining the 'descent' is to account for it by a 'fall' into matter, but this semi-gnostic answer could not commend itself to the Jewish tradition. It was necessary, therefore, to discover reasons why God sent the pure and spiritual soul into a lower form of existence[1] where, by definition, it was exposed to the gravest dangers. Indeed, according to rabbinic teaching, souls do not 'fall' into the body, but once they have descended into it they tend to fall into sin. The traditional answer of talmudists, philosophers, and kabbalists was that the soul should acquire merit,[2] though one may wonder whether this answer is really very much more than just another way of begging the question. The kabbalists went beyond the traditional rabbinic formulation by taking up a motif known to us mainly from Zoroastrianism—the soul's descent as a mission. Like all military expeditions it is not without its dangers, but in view of God's need of helpers in the struggle against evil the risk involved must be considered as justified. This view was held in combination with the traditional rabbinic doctrine that the soul was sent down into the material world for its own good and ultimate exaltation. This doctrine of 'acquiring merit', especially when absorbed into a kabbalistic context, could assume a highly paradoxical quality. The performance of the commandments of the *Torah* raises the soul to a higher level than that which it occupied before its descent, in its original celestial

[1] See I. Heinemann's important study, 'Die Lehre von der Zweckbestimmung des Menschen im griechisch-römischen Altertum und im jüdischen Mittelalter', in *Jahresb. Breslau* (1926). For our present purpose Heinemann's account, which is concerned solely with the philosophers, should be supplemented by an analysis of the views of kabbalistic authors such as Moses de Leon, Joseph Gikatila, and others.

[2] Cf. the statement at the end of *M. Makkoth* iii. 15. For a convenient anthology of rabbinic sayings concerning merits and reward, see Strack–Billerbeck, *Kommentar zum N.T. aus Talmud und Midrasch*, vol. i, pp. 231–2; vol. iv. 1, pp. 488–90, 492–5, 496–500. This anthology of rabbinic dicta is useful, although the interpretation is usually vitiated by St.–B.'s glaringly obvious theological bias.

state. Commenting on a famous debate between the schools of Hillel and Shammay,[1] whether it were better for man not to have been created at all, the Maggid[2] asserts that souls, though 'hewn from under the Throne of the Divine Glory',[3] do not return thither, but after a life well spent with *Torah* and *miṣvoth* ascend to a higher realm called the 'Bundle of Life'.[4] The old talmudic debate, embodying as it does the eternal opposition between optimism and pessimism, is thus interpreted as posing the alternative—whether the possibility of further ascent justifies the tremendous risk of descent into a material body. It might be wiser, after all, to avoid hell with certainty, even if it meant remaining for ever under the Throne of Glory and forgoing the chance of translation to the Bundle of Life. All that the Maggid can adduce in explanation of the 'ascent' through life in this world is the rabbinic idea[5] that the original, i.e. unmerited, state of heavenly bliss is humiliating to the soul and thus inferior to the spiritual delights vouchsafed by God as merited reward for 'service' rendered. Of course, the notion of 'service' itself hangs, as it were, in mid-air because it does not go beyond the traditional rabbinic conception of simple obedience to the divine commandments as the essence of 'serving God'. It is easy to see that merit can be acquired through obedience, but the more 'metaphysical' fact of actual exaltation of the soul to a higher

[1] b. *'Erubin* 13b.

[2] *M.M.* 4b. 3.

[3] Cf. b. *Sabbath* 152b. This passage and early rabbinic tradition in general only know of the Throne of Glory as the place of reward where the souls of the righteous are 'hidden away'. In medieval literature the Throne of Glory then also became the place of the soul's origin whence it is 'hewn'; cf., for example, the poetic rendering of this philosophico-religious commonplace in Solomon ibn Gabirol's *Kether Malkhuth*.

[4] 1 Sam. xxv. 29; this verse also serves as proof-text in the aforementioned passage b. *Sabbath* 152b. On the 'Bundle of Life' as an eschatological term in early kabbalistic texts, cf. Scholem's brief remarks in his article, לבוש הנשמות וחלוקא דרבנן, *Tarbiz*, vol. xxiv (1954/5), pp. 291–2.

[5] This notion is never stated in so many words in early rabbinic texts, though it implicitly underlies much of what the rabbis have to say on the subject of merit and reward. In the sixteenth century the doctrine is clearly formulated that for a man to enjoy celestial bliss from God's free grace and without having merited it by good works is a humiliation from which God Himself desires to save His creatures. Man should earn his bread and not eat alms like a beggar (נהמא דכסופא; the expression is not found before the sixteenth century but seems to go back to statements like the one quoted by Tosafoth b. *Qiddushin* 36b [s.v. כל מצוה]: מאן דאכיל מחבריה בהית לאיסתכולי ביה).

level is more satisfactorily explained on the broader basis of the kabbalistic doctrine which ascribes a positively transforming and redeeming value to religious acts. The Maggid's failure to link the two themes may serve as another illustration of the haphazard, half-accidental, and purely homiletical character of Karo's speculations.

Both the anthropology and the individual eschatology of the kabbalistic systems are enormously complicated by the tripartite division of man's soul. Sometimes it almost looks as if the soul was not merely tripartite but that man was endowed with three types of soul[1] called—in ascending order—*nefesh*, *ruaḥ*, and *neshamah*. Their origin is described by the Maggid[2] with reference to Gen. ii. 7, where the expression 'breath of life' (*nishmath ḥayyim*) is made to refer to *neshamah*, whose source is in the third sefirah *Binah*, the *magna mater* of the sefirotic system. The divine act of breathing *neshamah* into man turns him into a person, i.e. *nefesh*. Without *nefesh* man would not be a person but merely flesh. The origin of *ruaḥ* is left out in this account. When man dies, *neshamah*, his highest part, returns to heaven followed by *ruaḥ*. In the case of a righteous man *nefesh* cleaves to *ruaḥ* and accompanies it in its ascent, but *nefesh* always remains connected with the earth, to which it may return on occasion.[3] The average of three transmigrations for every soul, which the kabbalists deduce from Job xxxiii. 29,[4] is related to the tripartite psychology, 'for the kabbalistic truth is that every man has to transmigrate at least [!] three times, corresponding to *nefesh*, *ruaḥ*, and *neshamah*. He [man] is like a sapling that is taken out and replanted elsewhere, and in this

[1] According to another division the soul has even five parts; cf. Scholem, *Eranos-Jahrbuch*, vol. xxiv, pp. 81–83, 96–97.

[2] 4b–5a.

[3] Only the patriarch Jacob succeeded in maintaining the connexion of even his *ruaḥ* with the earth; in this respect his *ruaḥ* resembles the *nefesh* of ordinary mortals. (On Jacob cf. also the references in Scholem's article [mentioned above, p. 238, n. 4], pp. 292–3.)

[4] Literally translated: 'Lo, all these things worketh God, two or three times [i.e. up to three times] with man'; cf. also the sequel in verse 30, 'To bring back his soul from the pit, to be enlightened with the light of the living'. On the use of this verse for kabbalistic speculations concerning *gilgul*, cf. Scholem, loc. cit., pp. 73 (n. 31), 74 (n. 34), 80, 83. For another interpretation of this verse compare Vital's *Diary*, p. 192.

way it grows.'[1] *Gilgul* is thus not merely a matter of punishment but of spiritual growth. A fully mature personality is one whose soul is in its third incarnation.[2] Elsewhere the Maggid explains that every *gilgul* produces a fresh *nefesh*: 'The joining together of *ruaḥ* with a body produces a *nefesh*, but this *nefesh*, in its turn, becomes the *ruaḥ* of a[nother] body in its next *gilgul*, and this joining together produces another *nefesh* which then becomes a *ruaḥ* for the third incarnation.'[3]

Both sins and good works are correlated to the three parts of the soul, so that, for example, one sin may defile, hurt, or even kill *nefesh* only, whereas another taints *ruaḥ* or even *neshamah*.[4] As a matter of fact, the kabbalists assumed that *gilgul* could affect *nefesh–ruaḥ–neshamah* jointly and severally, and that both the wicked and the righteous were subject to it.[5] *Gilgul* is not identical with *'ibbur*, the temporary 'impregnation' of a living person by another soul.[6] There is a fundamental difference between *gilgul* as atonement for past sins and transgressions, and *gilgul* whose purpose is to repair omissions and to enable a man to complete his spiritual stature by performing those religious acts which he had left undone or had no occasion to perform in his former existence. The connexion between the complete performance of the *Torah* and the completion of one's spiritual stature is, of course, based on the kabbalistic analogy between the anthropomorphic macrocosm–microcosm on the one hand and the inner structure of *Torah* on the other. Some kabbalists held that in the former case three incarnations were a maximum: he who had not atoned for his past sins by then deserved no further chance. In the case of repairing omissions, however, transmigration may go on indefinitely according to God's word 'which He commanded to a *thousand generations*' (1 Chr. xvi. 15).

[1] *M.M.* 6b. [2] Ibid. [3] Ibid. 18b.

[4] Ibid. 17b. 2. This also accounts for the necessity of atonement for sins committed in ignorance.

[5] For a short sixteenth-century statement of this view see Cordovero, *Shi'ur Qomah* (Warsaw, 1883), pp. 166–9.

[6] Cordovero, ibid: מרכיבין נפש בנפש מצד שיתוף המעשה. According to the Maggid (*M.M.* 19a. 3) איכא בין עיבור לגלגול דעיבור הוה כד נח רוחא חדא על חד גברא ובהאי אורחא בעיבור יכולין למשרי תרי ותלת כחדא בחד גברא. On *gilgul* v. *'ibbur* cf. also Vital, loc. cit., pp. 192–3, and Scholem, loc. cit., pp. 87 f.

Perhaps the most concise and coherent statement of the doctrine of *gilgul* as held in Karo's circle was made by Solomon Alkabets in his commentary on Ruth.[1] The so-called 'levirate marriage' to which the anonymous kinsman (Ruth iii–iv) could have been obliged provides Alkabets with the occasion for an excursus on metempsychosis.[2] According to Alkabets[3] God

> in his mercy upon His creatures devised devices so that none should be cast out, and instituted the *gilgul*, which is the return to this world. This dispensation is divided into three parts. . . . Those who return (*a*) not on account of their having omitted a religious duty, let alone for having committed a trespass, but solely out of compassion with their contemporaries; such was the case with our master Moses whose soul was not from the present cycle[4] . . . (*b*) to receive punishment . . . and this is the mystery of infants and sucklings that die in their youth.[5] But this applies only to souls that did not repent with perfect repentance.[6] Those who thus transmigrate and yet do not turn to good after three times will henceforth be incarnated in pure and [even] impure animals[7] . . . (*c*) in order to complete certain religious acts.

A completely different reason for *gilgul* is the failure to produce offspring. Souls, like our biological bodies, are arranged in family 'trees'. A soul that has not performed the first commandment, 'Be fruitful and multiply' (Gen. i. 28), has not only lessened 'the divine likeness'[8] but also effectively barred its own return to its celestial family tree. God, in His mercy, has provided for the salvation of the deceased by requiring his surviving brother to marry the widow and thereby enable his reincarnation within his family tree.[9] The

1 שרש ישי (Constantinople, 1561).

2 Already the earliest kabbalists explained the institution of levirate marriage in terms of metempsychosis; cf. Scholem, loc. cit., pp. 69, 89.

3 Op. cit., pp. 81a ff.

4 Moses should not, therefore, have come to this world at all in the present cycle. Moses is the type of the perfect man who consents to transmigrate in order to redeem others. Analogies with similar ideas in other religions (e.g. the notion of Bodhisattvas) are evident.

5 They thereby atone for sins committed in a former existence. Having atoned, they are perfected and there is no reason for them to go on living.

6 Had they repented in their former existence before dying, repentance would have been in lieu of punishment and there would have been no need of *gilgul*.

7 This is pressing literally Job xxxiii. 29: 'three times with *man*'.

8 b. *Yebamoth* 63b.

9 Rebirth seems to be possible only into one's own family tree. Where no brother exists to marry the widow, God has to make other provisions for the rebirth of a man who left no issue.

explanation of Job's suffering must be sought in his former lives:

> And from Rabbi Jacob Berab[1] . . . I heard a beautiful and most acceptable explanation concerning what is said of Elihu,[2] that 'against Job was His [God's] wrath kindled because he justified himself [lit. his '*nefesh*'] rather than God. Also against his three friends was His wrath kindled because they had found no answer and yet condemned Job.' For both sides were right and wrong, since Job was truly a righteous man, though his *nefesh* was not righteous, having sinned in an earlier existence. . . . Therefore was His wrath kindled because he [Job] justified his *nefesh* also and not [merely] his person, in which he would have been right. And against his three friends was His wrath kindled because they condemned Job, though Job was not guilty since [only] his *nefesh* was guilty from an earlier existence, whereas he himself was righteous in his present existence.[3]

This highly interesting passage reveals some of the difficulties of kabbalistic anthropology: the human personality seems to disintegrate into a collection of 'souls',[4] until in the end one is left wondering who, after all, Job was. A similar, though perhaps even more disconcerting, case is mentioned by the Maggid,[5] who attempts to reconcile two conflicting midrashic reports according to which the Prophet Elijah is identical with Phinehas as well as with Joshua. Since the latter two were contemporaries it seems logically impossible to accept both versions even if we were ready to believe in the longevity of either of them. The truth is, we are assured by the Maggid, that the original *neshamah* of Phinehas left him and entered Joshua, whilst Phinehas himself was 'impregnated' by the souls of his two deceased brothers Nadab and Abihu.[6] The net impression one gets from all this is that somehow there is such a thing as an irreducibly individual soul, but that in the concrete human personality or 'self' it always appears united or mingled with other 'soul sparks'. Personality and character may be affected

[1] Cf. above, pp. 87–88, 123–4.

[2] Job xxxii. 2–3. Alkabets's commentary on Job, entitled פצעי אוהב (referred to once by Alkabets himself in אילת אהבים [Venice, 1552], p. 29b), is lost.

[3] Alkabets, op. cit.

[4] On this problem cf. also Scholem, loc. cit., pp. 79–81. One is reminded here of the Buddhist conception of the individual personality as a collection of 'elements'.

[5] *M.M.* 19a. 4.

[6] Cf. *Zohar*, iii. 217a; cf. also Scholem, loc. cit., pp. 86–87.

by these migrating elements, yet it seems to be assumed that the essential soul never loses its distinct, individual identity.

Mention has already been made of Karo's account of the multiplication of 'souls' through the very process of *gilgul*. This theory, incidentally, solves an otherwise insuperable problem in connexion with the resurrection of the body:[1]

Concerning the mystery of *gilgul* you should know that when a *nefesh* is transmigrated it contains part of the body and part of the *ruaḥ* of its former personality; when it is now joined [as a *ruaḥ*] to a second body this joining produces another *nefesh*, and so on with every *gilgul* a new *nefesh* is produced. . . . And all will rise at the time of the resurrection, each body with the *nefesh* that was produced together with it. . . .[2] But the choicest of all is the last body, through which all the others merit [their *tiqqun*], and it will be the first to resurrect, and then all the others will follow it like children following their father.[3]

As regards the other details there is little difference between Karo and Alkabets. The Maggid confirms the fact of *gilgul* into animals. In fact, animals sacrificed on the altar harbour precisely such souls as need the sacrificial act in order to achieve their final release and atonement:[4]

And know that the mystery of the sacrifices is the same as that of metempsychosis, for, when a soul has paid its due, it merits to be sacrificed; and as it is killed the evil side departs completely. . . . Be not surprised that a human soul can transmigrate into a beast, for so Scripture tells us in the Book of Daniel that Nebuchadnezzar was transmigrated into a beast, and not as explained in the commentary of Ibn Ezra,[5] but he was really transmigrated. . . . This is an elementary truth and even the holy *Zohar*[6] did not doubt it, but only doubted whether [human souls] would transmigrate into unclean beasts.

The main reasons for *gilgul* are those already enumerated by Alkabets:

[1] This is one of the oldest problems in the doctrine of *gilgul*; cf. Scholem, loc. cit., p. 79.

[2] Here it appears as if the migrating soul only served as a catalyst for the generation of a new *nefesh*. The Maggid does not really solve his problem.

[3] *M.M.* 18b. 1.

[4] Ibid. 39a. 2. Cf. also Scholem, loc. cit., p. 91, and the gruesome story told by Vital in his *Diary*, pp. 63–64; cf. also the story told by Azikri, op. cit., pt. iii, ch. 7.

[5] *Ad* Dan. iv. 28; Ibn Ezra holds that Nebuchadnezzar went mad and lived like an animal.

[6] Cf. Scholem, loc. cit., p. 92.

Sometimes the righteous who were perfect in their works and committed no mortal sin nevertheless transmigrate in order to acquire further merit, as in the process of refining silver which is refined over and over again. . . . Even so the righteous transmigrate in order to be purified to the utmost; they do not die as infants [in their fourth and subsequent incarnations] after they have been in the world three times without sinning, for there is no danger that they would sin now. . . .[1] But those who have sinned in a previous existence and have subsequently improved their ways, yet [still] require *gilgul* to atone for mortal sins committed or to take away the uncleanness of their impurity, [having been reborn for that purpose, they] die as infants.[2] This prevents them from sinning and their chance of salvation from becoming their undoing. Sometimes the righteous need not be reborn altogether but transmigrate [out of charity] in order to save the generation [with which they live].[3]

In addition to serving humanity by returning to this earth in repeated incarnations, the righteous can redeem sinners by their very death. For the atoning death of the righteous enables the 'naked souls' of sinners—and to be naked is about the worst fate that can befall the soul in kabbalistic eschatology, whose main concern is the proper spiritual clothing of the soul in the hereafter[4]—to re-enter the stream of *gilgul* and to pass from a state of despairing stagnation on to the more hopeful way of purification and salvation.[5]

The Safed kabbalists took an inordinate interest in the *gilgul*-vicissitudes of all kinds of souls: those of biblical figures, talmudic

[1] Having proved their righteousness and strength of character in three previous incarnations, they can now be trusted that their additional lives too will be spent in acquiring further merit; there is no fear that they might spoil their record by sinning.

[2] Cf. the quotation from Alkabets, above, p. 241.

[3] As Moses did; cf. also *M.M.* 17b, 18b. 1. Once, however, the Maggid seems to suggest that Moses had come to the world for the sake of his own perfection (ibid. 55b. 2): ומשה אע"ג דאצטרף בשמיטי' קדמייתא אצטריך לאתגלגלא בהאי שמיטה לאשתלמא, ואע"ג דכתיב ויתעבר ה' בי [למענכם] וגו' דמשמע דלא איצטריך למיתי בגין דיליה . . . But cf. the continuation, ibid. 56a.

[4] Cf. G. Scholem's article mentioned above, p. 238, n. 4. For the concept of 'naked souls' (נשמתין ערטילאין), cf. *Zohar*, ii. 99b ff.; also *Zohar Ḥadash*, 36d; *Tiqquney Zohar*, vi (towards end).

[5] *M.M.* 21a. On the importance of the *ṣaddiq* for the 'naked souls' cf. also ibid. 45a. 2, 61a–b.

teachers, themselves, and their contemporaries.[1] Trying to identify the souls inhabiting their colleagues became a passionate and serious indoor game in sixteenth-century Safed in which the Lurianists, as their writings show, easily won the first prize. Luria himself was considered by his followers as the supreme authority in diagnosing *gilgulim*,[2] but Karo too seems to have been attracted by the subject and the Maggid actually uses his interest as a bait:[3] 'I shall reveal unto thee the mysteries of *gilgul* if thou doest well before me, and I shall reveal the *gilgul* of all thy relatives and friends, and thou shalt see most marvellous things. . . . Therefore always be strong in the fear of the Lord and mortify thyself as much as possible.' The *gilgul* of Karo's wives clearly was a particularly intriguing subject, and the Maggid made his revelations with due solemnity:[4]

And now I have come to inform you of the mystery of this your wife, who she is . . . for I have already informed you that she was a pious scholar [in her former existence]. But if you knew *who* [exactly] she was in her [previous] *gilgul* you would be overawed. Therefore you should treat her with great respect and be ashamed of having intercourse with her for pleasure.

There follows one of the strange 'blockages' which sometimes turned the Maggid's speech into a prolonged stammer:[5]

And you should know, and you should know, and thus he kept saying for more than an hour . . . as if refusing to tell me, until finally he said: And God sent me to inform you . . . but you must not reveal this matter which I want to tell you to any man . . . neither must you write it down in a manner that people can read it. You should know that she has already been through her first and second incarnations. . . .[6] I have now revealed to you his [i.e. her] secret, that he has been reincarnated to receive his punishment.

The same subject is treated elsewhere[7] at greater length, and we learn that there are both male and female souls:[8]

[1] Cf., for example, Vital's *Diary* and *Sefer ha-Gilgulim*; also Scholem, *Eranos-Jahrbuch*, vol. xxiv, pp. 67, 94.
[2] Cf. also above, p. 15.
[3] *M.M.* 1b. 3.
[4] Ibid. 7a. 1.
[5] Cf. below, pp. 261–2.
[6] i.e. his wife was now in her (i.e. his) third and presumably last *gilgul*.
[7] *M.M.* 13b–14a.
[8] A common idea in kabbalistic literature; cf. also Scholem loc. cit., p. 86, and the references in n. 55 ibid.

I have told you . . . the secrets [of the incarnations] of your first two wives and now I have come to reveal the secret of this your third wife. You should know that in her former existence this woman was a male, a pious scholar but miserly with money . . . therefore he was reincarnated into a female [i.e. into an essentially receptive being]. . . . This also explains why she is so very charitable,[1] and she also loves you because you freely spread *Torah*. . . . Since all these things are her *tiqqun*, therefore she loves you,[2] but since she is a male soul, she is not your real mate and you only got her as 'ownerless property', as it were, as the children of Benjamin got the daughters of Shiloh.[3] Because her soul is essentially male she could not bear you children until now, for two males [i.e. male souls] cannot produce offspring . . . but now female soul-sparks have been added to her soul. . . .

Karo himself will not have to return again in *gilgul*[4]

for you shall be privileged to be burnt for the sanctification of God's name. . . . You shall be with the righteous in a very high state and need not be reincarnated again, for you shall 'go thy way [till the end be] and rest [and stand in thy lot at the end of days]', as was said to Daniel [xii. 13], until the resurrection, when you shall rise with the righteous.

The Maggid, we have seen, agreed with those kabbalists who held three incarnations to be an absolute minimum.[5] Only in very rare cases are two births deemed sufficient, and then only because the soul in question has already approached perfection through its transmigrations in a previous cycle (*shemiṭṭah*). This was the case with, for example, Rabbi Akiba,[6] who, in his previous existence, was Jacob's son Issachar. According to rabbinic legend the 'ten martyrs',[7] of whom Akiba was one, died to atone for the unbrotherly behaviour of Jacob's sons towards Joseph. In kabbalistic

[1] Repairing in her present *gilgul* the failings of her former existence.

[2] This is the kabbalistic reason for love: a kind of *Wahlverwandtschaft* based on the soul's need of a helpmate for its specific individual *tiqqun*; cf. also Scholem's remarks on *Seelensympathie*, loc. cit.

[3] Cf. Judges xxi. 16 ff.

[4] *M.M.* 36a. 3.

[5] Cf. above, p. 239. A different view is stated *M.M.* 72b. 2: הן כל אלה יפעל אל פעמים שלש עם גבר . . . ותו דכתיב על שלשה פשעי ישראל וכו׳ דמשמע דארבעה זימנין והכא קאמר תלתא. אבל רזא דמילתא דלגברא דהוה דחיל חטאין מגלגל ג׳ פעמים לזככה יתיה, אבל למאן דלא איהו דחיל חטאין לא מגלגלי אלא תרין זימנין כי היכי דלא יתקלקל בזמנא תליתאה ויצא שכרו בהפסדו. . . . ומאי דכתיב ועל ארבעה לא אשיבנו היינו לציבור.

[6] *M.M.* 55b. 2.

[7] Cf., for example, Midrash *'Elleh 'Ezkerah*.

transformation this came to mean that the ten tribes, i.e. the sons of Jacob minus Joseph himself and Benjamin, were reincarnated in the ten martyrs. According to the Maggid 'Rabbi Akiba was perfected in previous cycles and was reborn in the present cycle only to consummate his perfection . . . so that he was completely perfected after two incarnations only [in this cycle]'. The same is also true of Moses.[1] It thus appears that the soul has to pass through three existences in every world-cycle, and Karo, in fact, expressly accepts the traditional doctrine of cycles and *shemiṭṭoth*[2] which was so emphatically rejected by the Lurianists.[3] The Maggid outlines the theory of cosmic cycles in a short excursus:[4]

The manner of the government of the world is this: each sefirah governs seven thousand years, that is a thousand years or one [cosmic] day for each of its [component sub-]sefiroth. And when the [governing] sefirah arrives [in the seventh millennium] at [the stage represented by] the sefirah *Malkhuth*, which governs the world of separate existences, then the [governing] sefirah [of the cycle] which is now joined to *Malkhuth* ascends to the supernal mother [i.e. *Binah*]. And because she ascends on high [leaving *Malkhuth*, as it were, to fend for herself], things [i.e. the cycle or *aion*] are no longer as strong in the millennium of *Malkhuth* as they were in the preceding six millennia, for the governing sefirah [of the cycle] unites itself [in its action] with each of the [sub-] sefiroth except *Malkhuth*. This is the meaning of [the talmudic saying,[5] 'The world lasts six thousand years, and] one millennium it is waste';[6] that is to say that the *aion* will no longer be as strong as it used to be, which is as much as saying that it is 'waste'. Not that—God forbid—the world will be really destroyed, but it will be 'waste' [i.e. deprived] of its former strength. And this is the mystical meaning of the fallowness of the 'land' which refers to *Malkhuth*.

[1] Cf. above, p. 244, n. 3.

[2] On the beginnings of this doctrine cf. G. Scholem, *MTJM.*, pp. 178–9. For the earliest ideas of the kind in Chaldean and gnostic systems, see the references given by J. Doresse, *Les Livres secrets des gnostiques d'Égypte*, 1958, p. 304.

[3] Cf., e.g., Shlomel Dresnitz's reference, in his first epistle, to the well-known rabbinic saying (*Gen. Rabbah* ix. 2, ed. Theodor, p. 68) that 'God created worlds and then destroyed them': לאפוקי מהסוברים שיש שמיטות ושקודם היה שמיטת החסד ועתה הוא שמיטת הפחד, כל זה אינו אמת ושמעו מרבם שברא הקב"ה עולמות קודם לזה העולם והחריבן, הוסיפו הם מדעתם סברת השמיטות והאמת אינו כך.

[4] *M.M.* 49a. 1.

[5] b. *Sanhedrin* 97a.

[6] i.e. the old speculations about a 'cosmic week' are connected with the kabbalistic doctrine of the seven 'cosmic' sefiroth from *Ḥesed* to *Malkhuth*.

The destruction of which Rabbi Qaṭṭina speaks in the Talmud is thus not to be taken literally. There is no eschatology of cataclysms but an ancient version of the modern physicist's myth of the 'running-down universe'. Every world-cycle consists of seven 'days' of a thousand years each,[1] each being the manifestation of one of the seven lower sefiroth. The last thousand years, corresponding to the Sabbath and to the sefirah *Malkhuth*, signify the liquidation and winding up of the particular cosmic cycle. 'Destruction' and 'Sabbath' are thus equated in the sense of reversion to absolute rest, one is tempted to say 'maximum entropy', after the running down of the cosmic process. With the last sefirah the cosmos expires and returns, viz. 'ascends', tothe womb of the Great Mother, *Binah*, from which the next cycle will then be born. The midrashic expression concerning the destruction of the world is reinterpreted in terms of fallowness (*shemiṭṭah-*) or Sabbath-abeyance[2] of cosmic life as the characteristic mode of existence of each cycle during its last 'day'.

The theory of cosmic cycles thus automatically extends the scope of *gilgul*. There is, however, an even more sweeping extension of this doctrine which converts it from an eschatological-moral dispensation into a cosmic law. 'All things, from the sefirah *Ḥokhmah* down to the very last stone on earth, are subject to a process of change and transformation (*din beney ḥilluf* or *sod ha-shelaḥ*) within the cycle . . . according to a fixed causality.'[3] As Professor Scholem has rightly remarked,[4] 'this doctrine of a general change of forms goes far beyond "metempsychosis" in the normal sense of the word'. The notion seems to make its first appearance in David ben Abraham ha-Laban's *Masoreth ha-Berith*:[5]

This is a profound mystery. . . . The First Cause acts infinitely and its action is infinite . . . and all things descend until they reach the state

[1] Based on Ps. xc. 4: 'For a thousand years in thy sight are but as yesterday'.

[2] The seventh year is described as a 'sabbath of rest unto the land' (Lev. xxv. 4). The analogy sabbath–seventh year–cosmic cycles of seven thousand years is already explicitly made in a statement following that of R. Qaṭṭina, b. *Sanhedrin* 97a: כשם שהשביעית משמטת שנה א׳ לז׳ שנים כך העולם משמט אלף שנים לז׳ אלפים שנה. Proof texts are Isa. ii. 11; Ps. xcii. i, xc. 4.

[3] Scholem, *E.J.*, vol. ix, col. 708.

[4] Ibid.

[5] Written about 1300 and published by Scholem in *Kobez Al-Jad*, N.S., vol. i (1936); cf. also Scholem's introduction, ibid.

of matter, elements, composite bodies, and inanimate matter. Then all things return again full circle and revolve, and *this is the true mystery of re-volution* (*gilgul*). . . .[1] God . . . so disposed that the vegetative soul should become animal, and the animal soul should become rational . . . [like] the bountiful grace of a king that from a knight makes a count and from a count makes a duke. And He disposed thus that all might attain to true and immediate communion with the Primal Light.

This doctrine reached its most extreme expression in what G. G. Scholem has described as the 'radical pan-psychism'[2] of Joseph ben Shalom ha-Ashkenazi of Barcelona (*c.* 1310), the real author of a commentary on *Sefer Yeṣirah* traditionally ascribed to Abraham b. David (RABED). According to pseudo-RABED's commentary:[3]

It is known in the science of the philosophers that there exists a kind of matter which is the substratum of the power of the four elements, and the Greeks called it hylic matter. The existence of this matter is different from that of all other existents . . . wherefore it has been said of this matter that it is neither potentiality nor actuality . . . but all existents below the Supreme Crown (*Kether*) exist by virtue of its existence [!], yet itself does not pass through the processes of transformation or generation and corruption, because it is the beginning of all existence. . . .

'Have the gates of death been opened unto thee? or hast thou seen the doors of the shadow of death?' [Job xxxviii. 17]. Know that death is not the same for all beings; there are different kinds of it and the term is relative, so much so that what is death to one species may be life to another species; e.g. if something vegetable dries up and produces worms, then it has died to its vegetative form and has become one of the animal things . . . and similarly from vegetative to inanimate, and similarly in the world of angels and celestial spheres and planets and fixed stars and even in the world of sefiroth. . . . And know that the whole creation has to pass through the process of transformation, some by eating and drinking, others by the sexual act. . . . Everything that is eaten thereby undergoes the process of transformation. . . . All beings, inanimate, vegetable, animal, and rational, pass through this process of transformation up and down according to [God's] true judgement, 'at

[1] As Scholem rightly points out, if there is a true mystery of *gilgul* there must also be a false one, against which the author's polemic is directed.

[2] *E.J.*, vol. ix, col. 708; cf. also *Eranos-Jahrbuch*, vol. xxiv, pp. 92–94.

[3] *Sefer Yeṣirah* (edn. Warsaw, 1884), pp. 3, 8–9, 15–16.

the commandment of the Lord they abide and at the commandment of the Lord they journey'.[1]

A very similar doctrine is propounded by the Maggid:

> for the esoteric teaching is that all created things permanently revolve from one form into another and thereby they continuously rise to a higher level. . . .[2]
>
> and all things revolve, as I have already said, and the souls too revolve all the time. These revolutions are always for the sake of ascent to higher levels, for the soul's return to this [material] world is also for the purpose of its exaltation. Even when things transmigrate into lower forms it is for their [ultimate] exaltation, for all things [by their very nature] long and desire to adhere to their first cause and therefore they continually revolve. The souls too always revolve until they can rise and adhere to the first cause.[3]

But whereas this statement still seems to echo the views of *Masoreth ha-Berith*, the Maggid also voices a far more radical doctrine when discussing the institution of levirate marriage:[4]

> This is the true kabbalistic teaching: the whole world is based on the mystery of *gilgul*, and all things continually revolve without interruption, like water that always flows until it reaches the sea, and from the sea each river returns to its source and begins to flow again, as before, until it reaches the sea, after which it returns again to its source. . . . Similarly men are born into this world and then go on to the other world [i.e. the hereafter] and then return into this world and so on without interruption, like the aforementioned river. But even as the water that flows in the river is arrested in its flow by canals or by trenches dug in the banks, so also a man who has left no sons in this world but has left a wife is like water stagnating in a canal or trench; through the wife whom he has left behind he is prevented from continuing his revolution though he be a perfectly righteous man.

The difference between this account of levirate marriage and the one given by Alkabets is very instructive. *Gilgul*, we are told here, is not a special dispensation for purging and perfecting the soul, nor is levirate marriage an arrangement whereby the

[1] Cf. Num. ix. 20.

[2] *M.M.* 2b–3a.

[3] Ibid. 3a; cf. also 68a. 1: עוד אמר לי כי סוד אלהי עולם ה׳ הוא רמז על סוד הגלגול כי אלהי העולמות כלם ה׳ ולא ייעף ולא ייגע מלגלגל נשמה מעולם זה לעולם זה ובעולם א׳ עצמו מגלגלו פעמים רבות עד שיצטרף ויתלבן וז״ש אין חקר לתבונתו.

[4] Ibid. 60a. 5.

surviving brother assures the rebirth of the deceased in his own family and thereby enables him to make restitution for his shortcomings. According to the Maggid, *gilgul* is an eternal cycle, though the earlier quotations seem to suggest that it is rather a spiral. Whereas transmigration is usually held to be a painful necessity, the greatest boon being release from the *gilgul*-cycle, the Maggid here reverses the traditional evaluation. The greatest disaster that can befall a soul is to be stopped, blocked, and arrested in the eternal flow of *gilgul*. The man who dies leaving offspring, or who dies without any attachments at all to the world (i.e. not even a widow), can resume the cycle of being without difficulty. However, to leave a wife but no children seems to lead the soul into a kind of *cul-de-sac*, like water that has been diverted from the river-bed into a canal, and special provisions must be made for assuring its further movement. This is a remarkable doctrine indeed, not the least remarkable part of it being the fact that it is not *directly* indebted to pseudo-RABED on *Sefer Yeṣirah*. No doubt the doctrine as such belongs to the tradition represented by *Masoreth ha-Berith* and pseudo-RABED, yet the Maggid's terminology seems to suggest that these texts were not his immediate source.

However, belief in metempsychosis, though congenial to minds of a gnostic or theosophical cast, is not a necessary adjunct of a truly mystical attitude. Quite on the contrary, many of the great systems of philosophical, contemplative, ascetic, and ecstatic mysticism are satisfied with focusing their attention on one earthly life only. This one life is the unique chance of realizing, or possibly of merely preparing, a maximum communion with the divine or—to put the same thing into the language of paradox so greatly favoured by mystics—of dying (to the world or to oneself) in order to come to life with or in God. When finding statements of this sort in kabbalistic literature, one cannot help feeling that they do not really derive from the main stream of gnostic-theosophical kabbalism. They seem rather to belong to a different tradition of mysticism which, of course, the kabbalists absorbed, like so much else, in due course. It is a tradition in which Baḥya ibn Paquda rather than the author of the *Zohar* would seem to be at home and it clearly goes back to Ṣufi, Neoplatonic, and ultimately hellenistic sources. The mystical commonplace *que muero porque no muero* (St. John of the Cross) appears for the first time in Jewish literature in an answer reputedly given by the 'Sages of the South' to Alexander the Great,[1] who had inquired, 'What should a man do in order to live?' They replied, 'He should kill himself.' 'And what should he do in order to die?'—'Cultivate life!' A similar statement is quoted in the popular penitential tract *Sha'arey Teshubah*, by R. Jonah of Gerona: 'Our Sages teach in the tractate *Derekh 'Ereṣ*: If thou wishest not to die, then die before thou diest.'[2]

The Maggid too voices this tradition when he exhorts Karo:[3]

> Let your soul adhere to your Creator and thus death will be unto you a rest. This is the true meaning of what our Sages said, 'He who wants to live should die' . . . and in this way[4] it is like killing oneself. Thereby one truly revives one's soul and the separation from this world will be felt as a profound rest by cleaving to the Creator. For if the soul adhered to the Creator even whilst it was imprisoned in this vile body, how much more will it cleave unto the Creator and be illuminated by the light of life once it has separated itself from matter. . . . And this is the meaning of Abigail's words [1 Sam. xxv. 29] . . . 'the soul of my lord will' necessarily 'be bound in the bundle of life', which is communion with God. This is so of necessity because you [i.e. David] are in union with God all the time even in this world. . . . For since your mind and thoughts are only with God, *of necessity you will adhere to the place on which you always meditate*, but 'the souls of thine enemies', who always meditate on worldly pleasures, 'them shall he sling out as out of the middle of a sling' . . . for it is a natural law that the soul cleaves to the place on which it meditates and concentrates.

There is hardly a trace of kabbalism proper in this passage, and the doctrine of *gilgul* seems to be completely beyond the horizon of its anthropology. On the other hand it contains a most interesting motif of spiritual, or rather psychological, 'idealism'. The actual

[1] b. *Tamid* 32a.

[2] Cf. also the medieval collection of moral and philosophical maxims *Mibḥar Peninim*, ch. 40, and al-Ghazzali's statement (in the Hebrew translation מאזני צדק, ed. Goldenthal, p. 219): והמות והיא לידה שנית. Cf. also Brüll's *Jahrb. f. jüd. Geschichte u. Literatur*, vol. ii (1876), p. 129, and Vajda, *Ibn Malka*, p. 12, n. 2, on this commonplace of medieval literature.

[3] *M.M.* 25b.

[4] i.e. not by committing suicide but by mortifying the flesh.

level of a soul, its objective 'state of grace', as it were, is causally determined by the level of the object of its thoughts and meditations. To meditate on God is to cleave to Him and increasingly commune with Him. The psychological state thus involves and creates a spiritual or metaphysical state.[1] This conception appears like a forerunner of the later and more extreme psychological idealism of the Polish Hasidim who held that their subjective states of *devekuth*, *gadluth*, *qaṭnuth*, &c., were completely identical with and thus also indicative of their objective spiritual condition.[2]

Yet it is in the very nature of kabbalism to stress certain objective aspects of human destiny much more than the subjective interest which the soul quite legitimately takes in its private salvation. Reference has already been made to what might be called the Zoroastrian character of kabbalistic anthropology which conceives of human existence as a dangerous mission on behalf of the divine purpose. Whatever the detailed elaborations of this doctrine, whether it is man's task to heal the disastrous separation within the Godhead caused by Adam's sin (as, for example, in Zoharic kabbalism) or whether it is to repair the even more disastrous and primeval 'fall' known in Lurianic doctrine as the 'breaking of the vessels',[3] man's concern is not merely with his own soul but with an objective reality outside him: the reality of the Life Divine and of the whole cosmos. In pre-Lurianic Kabbalah the conflict between the holy forces of the divine sefiroth and the evil side of the 'anti-sefiroth' is described in a relatively simple, though not always consistent, manner. The moderate or rather 'mitigated' dualism[4] of the kabbalists knows of a demonic anti-world, patterned on an exact analogy with the divine world of holiness to which it is related like the shell of a fruit to its heart or core. To break and discard the 'shell' is the essence of mystico-religious life. In contemplation and in the performance of pious acts the kabbalist

[1] This idealist (or, if we prefer, 'realist') doctrine of meditation is reminiscent of certain Upanishadic utterances, e.g. 'Whatever idea a person is shown, that he sees . . . that he becomes. Possessed of that idea, he realizes it' (*Mandukya Up.*, *Karika*, ii. 29); 'As a person's thought is, so does he become' (*Maitreya Up.*, Schrader, p. 110); 'Man is of the nature of his faith: what his faith is, that is he' (*Bhag. Gita*, xviii. 3).

[2] Cf. also above, p. 52.

[3] Cf. Scholem, *MTJM.*, pp. 265–8.

[4] Cf. Tishby, *Mishnath ha-Zohar*, pp. 285 f., and particularly pp. 292 f.

attempts to save the 'holy side' from the embrace and defilement of the 'other side', which, like a true parasite, draws its very existence, vitality, and strength from its proximity to holiness, the source of all life. To separate and isolate the demonic powers of evil (i.e. the shells) is thus automatically to vanquish and annihilate them.

The view that the rejection or expulsion of the 'shells' from the sphere of holiness is the true meaning and purpose of the commandments of the Law can be found in many kabbalistic writings. Still one may agree with Professor Scholem[1] that this is rather a surprising view to hold for the foremost rabbinic authority of the sixteenth century and the author of the standard code of religious and ritual law, the *Shulḥan 'Arukh*. In a lengthy revelation, communicated the day preceding the eve of the Day of Atonement, the Maggid expatiates on the mystical meaning of the ritual of the scapegoat, explaining it as a symbolic representation of the expulsion of the shell from the world of holiness. Here, it is interesting to note, the Maggid discards the traditional and daring kabbalistic explanation of the rite as a kind of sacrifice to the demonic side (!), a sop, as it were, to the 'shells' in order to keep them quiet and prevent them from attempting to disturb the union of God and Israel on this holiest of days. Karo appears to avoid such close sailing to the winds of dualistic heresy.[2] According to the Maggid's account of the matter, echoing the teaching of the *Zohar*, the world of holiness (i.e. the sefiroth) is surrounded by concentric layers or worlds of *qelippoth* ('shells'). Even as the shells have to be broken or torn away if we want to get to the core of the fruit, so it is necessary for the complete unfolding of the divine world that the world of *qelippoth* too unfold and pass away first. This is the mystery of 'the kings that reigned in the land of Edom before there reigned any king over the children of Israel' (Gen. xxxvi. 31). This verse was interpreted by the *Zohar* and other kabbalistic writings as a mystical statement about the origin of the 'evil side' or 'shells',

[1] 'Tradition und Neuschöpfung im Ritus der Kabbalisten', *Eranos-Jahrbuch*, vol. xix (1950; Zürich, 1951), p. 138.

[2] At least in this particular text. Elsewhere the Maggid seems to accept the kabbalistic idea of bribing the 'other side'; cf. *M.M.* 12b. 1: רזא דתנו שוחד לסמאל וברזא דשעיר המשתלח [!].

but it could also be linked to the doctrine of world-cycles. According to the Maggid's reading of the matter,[1] the verse asserts that in the process of the unfolding of the divine purpose the cycles corresponding to the anti-sefiroth of the 'shell' (i.e. the Kings of Edom) precede those of the holy sefiroth (i.e. the Kings of Israel). Now that the cycles of the 'shell' have passed away and 'the side of holiness is manifesting itself, all our efforts must be directed towards expelling the unclean side from the realm of holiness, and *this is the mystical meaning of all commandments*'.[2] The ritual of the scapegoat exemplifies the rejection and gradual expulsion of the evil side from the sphere of holiness ('the habitations of Israel') to the wilderness. It is characteristic of kabbalistic ways of thinking that when Karo undertakes to explain the ultimate meaning and purpose of religious life he does so by reference to the doctrine of *qelippoth* and to kabbalistic cosmology in general, and without special attention to the human soul. The perspective is definitely not anthropocentric.

The Maggid's anthropology may be neither consistent nor highly original, but it is certainly illustrative of Karo's mystical theology in general. There is a genuine interest in esoteric doctrine, a good knowledge of kabbalistic and ascetic literature, and a psychic disposition for mystical, viz. abnormal, manifestations of a certain kind. But the interest is not central to Karo's life, the knowledge does not become an object of a large-scale systematic intellectual effort and never rises above a homiletic level. Karo's proneness to inspirational possession never produces results that could not have been arrived at as well by the normal, discursive methods of kabbalistic speculation. On the contrary, there is every reason to assume that many of these results were, as a matter of fact, arrived at by normal, discursive methods of speculation. It is difficult, at a distance of four centuries and with insufficient sources, to decide

[1] Other references by the Maggid to the mystery of the Kings of Edom: *M.M.* 14a, 16a. 5, 56a.

[2] *M.M.* 46b. 3–47a. הלא רזא דמילתא דקדושה גניזא בגו קליפה . . . וכמא דאי אפשר למיכל מפירי עד דיתברון קליפייא . . . הכי מקמי דישלוט סטר קדושה שליטא קליפייא. . . . ומכיון דאיתגלי סטרא דקדושה כל אשתדלותא איהי למדחי סטר מסאבו מסטרא דקדושה והאי איהו רזא דפקודייא כלהו . . . (ibid.).

which maggidic communications merely repeated material already consciously thought out by Karo, and which 'revealed' to him ideas and patterns of thought worked out unconsciously. There is, at any rate, the evidence of the Maggid's halakhic statements,[1] which seem to prove, if we may speak of proof in such matters, that the Maggid communicated nothing that had not been thought out and actually committed to paper first. There is no need to assume that the Maggid's kabbalistic revelations follow exactly the same pattern as his halakhic utterances; yet there is enough to show that, in the type of mystical life exhibited by Karo, consciousness and conscious elements play a demonstrably dominant part.

[1] Cf. above, pp. 186–7.

12

THE MAGGID

MORE intriguing, perhaps, than any of the literary and kabbalistic problems connected with the *M.M.* is the figure of the Maggid himself, though perhaps we had better say 'herself'. The problem here seems to be not so much the ultimate interpretation and explanation of this psychological, viz. mystical, phenomenon, but rather the preliminary description and understanding of the identity and nature of the Maggid as they emerge from his own testimonies. Is Karo satisfied to take his experience simply as it comes to him, perhaps with a few theoretical hints thrown into the bargain? Or does he make a serious attempt, conscious or unconscious, to arrive at a systematic or at least consistent interpretation of the phenomenon? The answer yielded by the text of the *M.M.* is by no means as unequivocal as one could wish.

A number of initial facts can be established with certainty and ease even after a cursory examination of the evidence. The maggidic revelations came to Karo at all possible hours: 'the night after the end of the Sabbath, after *habdalah*',[1] 'during the afternoon prayer whilst the reader was reading from the Torah-scroll',[2] 'Wednesday during the afternoon prayer, whilst I was reciting *Mishnayoth*'.[3] The favourite hour, however, seems to have been after midnight, in the early morning—more particularly on Sabbath mornings. The pattern comes out very clearly in a typical passage:[4]

Sabbath night. . . . I had eaten and drunk very little, studied *Mishnah* at the beginning of the night and then slept until dawn. When I woke the sun was already shining and I was grieved, saying to myself, 'Why did I not rise when it was still night so that the *speech* should come to me as usual [!]'. Then I began to recite *Mishnayoth* and when I had read five chapters 'the voice of my beloved knocketh' [cf. Cant. v. 2] in

[1] *M.M.* 31a. 2; 19b. 4. [2] Ibid. 30a. 5. [3] Ibid. 23a. 2.
[4] Ibid. 2a. 2.

my mouth, sounding by itself and speaking thus: 'The Lord be with thee wherever thou goest, and whatever thou hast done or shalt do the Lord maketh to prosper in thy hand [cf. Gen. xxxix. 2–3]. But always cleave unto me, unto my fear, unto my *Torah*, unto my *Mishnayoth*, and not as thou hast done this night. For although thou hast hallowed [i.e. mortified] thyself by [abstaining from] food and drink, yet thou hast slept like a sluggard . . . and didst not rise to recite *Mishnayoth* as thou art wont to do. Thou hast merited that I leave and forsake thee, since by thy prolonged sleep till dawn thou hast added strength to Samael, the Serpent, and the Evil *Yeṣer*. Yet by the merits of the six orders of the *Mishnah* which thou knowest by heart and by the merit of the mortifications and austerities which thou hast practised in former days and also now, it has been decided in the Celestial Academy that I return to speak unto thee as before, not to leave thee and not to forsake thee. Thus have I done, as thou seest, for I am now speaking unto thee as a man speaketh unto his friend [cf. Exod. xxxiii. 11], and thine eyes behold that for many generations no man has reached this high degree of perfection but only some chosen few. Therefore, my son, hearken unto my voice whatever I command thee and devote thyself always, day and night without interruption, to my *Torah*; think of no worldly thing but only of *Torah*, of my fear, and of my *Mishnayoth*.' Then I slept again for about half an hour and awoke with grief, saying, 'Now the speech has been interrupted because I fell asleep', and I recited [more] *Mishnayoth*. [Then] the voice of my beloved [again] knocketh in my mouth, saying, 'Thou shouldst know that God and the whole Celestial Academy send thee [the greeting of] peace and have sent me unto thee to reveal unto thee the works of God.' Thereafter a deep sleep fell upon me and I slept for about half an hour and I awoke, full of grief that he [i.e. the Maggid] had not spoken to me at greater length, as usual. I again began to recite *Mishnayoth* and before I had finished two chapters, the voice of my beloved was knocking in my mouth, saying, 'Though thou hast thought that I had forsaken thee . . . do not think thus.'

This characteristic and representative specimen passage deserves closer analysis and amplification. For the present it must suffice to point out and corroborate some of its main indications. It appears that Karo was wont to recite the *Mishnah* at night but was occasionally overcome by sleep.[1] Nocturnal revelations were for Karo regular and almost 'normal' phenomena ('that the speech should come to me *as usual*'); they usually occurred after reciting

[1] Cf. also 2a, 13a, 22b.

Mishnayoth, though this was not a strict rule (cf. 'during the afternoon prayer'). Very often the Maggid's communications began with severe reprimands for having slept too much or having otherwise relaxed ascetic rules, e.g.:

Sabbath night. . . . I had eaten much and drunk much wine and later drunk too much water. I could not recite *Mishnayoth* at the beginning of the night [being too tired?], but after having slept a little I arose, drank more water, and began to recite [*Mishnayoth*]. But I felt a heaviness in my head[1] as if I had not slept [at all] and went back to sleep. I woke about daybreak and thought that since day had already begun I had been forgotten [by the Maggid] and would not be visited as usual [!]. But behold, the voice [was there] saying, 'The Lord be with thee, etc. . . . Though thou hast thought that I had left and forsaken thee, I have not done so, although thou hast deserved it.'[2]

There can be no doubt that Karo was wide awake when the voice came to him:

I have come to delight myself with thee and to speak in thy mouth, *not in a dream but as a man speaketh with a friend.*[3]

In the early morning of . . . I awoke and could not sleep, so I rose and dressed, said a few prayers, and thereafter he said unto me, 'The Lord be with thee, etc., *I have woken thee in order to speak to thee*, to seek thy face and I have found thee [cf. Prov. vii. 15],[4] behold thy time is a time of love [cf. Ez. xvi. 8].'[5]

In fact, the voice generally came to Karo soon after waking up. Very often Karo fell asleep again after the maggidic manifestation, to wake up a second time and receive further revelations:

Sabbath night. . . . The Lord be with you. . . . Thereafter I slept till half an hour after daybreak. When I woke I was aggrieved that he had not spoken unto me as usual *at length* [!] and I began to recite *Mishnayoth* and hardly finished two chapters when 'the voice of my beloved came' [cf. Cant. ii. 8] and spoke: 'Is it good in thine eyes what thou hast done this night to drink water twice? . . . For this thou hast deserved that I leave and forsake thee, but I shall not do so.[6]

During his speech a deep sleep fell upon me and I slept for more than an hour. When I awoke, I paced up and down in the house reciting *Mishnayoth* till about half an hour after daybreak, then I sat down on

[1] Cf. the quotation from Cordovero above, p. 81. [2] *M.M.* 6b. 4.
[3] Ibid. 36a. 3. [4] Cf. below, p. 277. [5] *M.M.* 71a. 6.
[6] Ibid. 13a. 2.

a chest. But whilst I was still reciting *Mishnayoth*, behold the voice of my beloved knocketh in my mouth and the lyre sounded of itself.[1]

Whatever the kind of waking state that Karo was in on these occasions, he certainly was not asleep. Often a large number of *Mishnayoth* had to be recited before the Maggid manifested himself:

Sabbath night. . . . I rose early as usual in order to recite *Mishnayoth*. I recited about forty chapters, but as it was still night I went back to sleep and slept until the sun shone on the earth. Then I began to recite [more *Mishnayoth*]. I was grieved [at the thought] that I would perhaps not be visited as usual and continued reciting [*Mishnayoth*] until it was said unto me, 'Be strong and of a good courage . . . for although thou hast thought that I had left and forsaken thee [this is not so], though it is what thou hast deserved.[2]

We may assume that as a rule Karo was alone during these visitations. Once or twice the diary reports the sudden cessation of the Maggid's speech because of interruption by strangers: '. . . then people came in and interrupted the speech and he concluded abruptly and departed [with the valediction] "peace be with thee". . . .'[3] '. . . then people came in and interrupted the speech.'[4] A week later the Maggid resumes his discourse where he had broken off: 'Concerning the matter which I discussed with you on the [last] Sabbath when we were interrupted, I shall now give you my love [i.e. proceed with the explanation].'[5] 'I should like to tarry longer with thee, for thy time is a time of love, but the hour of prayer has come. Yet I shall return to this subject, provided thou cleave unto me, unto my *Mishnayoth*, unto my service, unto my fear, and do not separate thy mind from me even for one moment.'[6]

The frequent use of phrases like 'behold the voice of my beloved knocketh in my mouth and the lyre sounded of itself'[7] confirms the automatic character of the phenomenon.[8] The experience

[1] *M.M.* 22b. 2. [2] Ibid. 72a. 3. [3] Ibid. 24a. 3. [4] Ibid. 55b. 1. [5] Ibid. 55b. 2. [6] Ibid. 62a. 1.

[7] והנה קול דודי דופק בפי וכנור מנגן מאליו. This phrase already occurs in Alkabets's Epistle: . . . בהגיענו אל פרשת שמע קול דודנו דופק והתחיל שמעו ידידים . . .

[8] Cf. the quotation from Cordovero, above, p. 81, and also *M.M.* 54a. 5: 'Prophecy means that the *Shekhinah* speaks in the prophet's mouth, though it looks as if the prophet was speaking of himself.'

seems to have been that of an involuntary movement and irresistible automatism of the larynx[1] and lips. The vibration of the lips is referred to once when the Maggid explains:

Therefore cleave unto me, unto my *Torah*, unto my *Mishnayoth*, etc. 'When thou goest it shall lead thee, when thou sleepest it shall keep thee [and when thou awakest it shall talk with thee! cf. Prov. vi. 22]'. 'When thou sleepest [or liest down]'—this is to be understood literally, as it is written [Deut. vi. 7] 'when thou liest down and when thou risest up'. For when thou fallest asleep amid thoughts of the *Mishnah*, then my seven worlds shall keep thee; and when thou awakest after having fallen asleep amid thoughts of the *Mishnah*, then it will speak in thy mouth and thy lips will vibrate.[2]

Here we find a rudimentary attempt at formulating a theory of the maggidic phenomenon. The 'instrumental cause' is the study of the *Mishnah* immediately before falling asleep. This prior recital of *Mishnah* actually converts the 'lying down' (Deut. vi. 7) into a kind of incubation: the sleeper is surrounded and guarded by the seven worlds of the *Shekhinah* and on awakening reaps the mystical fruit of this incubation in the form of automatic speech.[3] This theory, proffered by the Maggid himself, is a remarkable and interesting attempt at self-interpretation though it certainly is far from doing justice to the actual phenomenon. For one thing, the Maggid usually did not speak immediately after Karo's awakening; the impression gained from the majority of entries in the diary is that Karo, after waking up, had to recite *Mishnayoth* for some time before the Maggid would manifest himself.

Other attempts at self-interpretation were forced on the Maggid whenever his behaviour or his communications necessitated special justification. Thus the fluency of the Maggid's discourse was at times interrupted by a curious hesitancy which almost amounted to a stutter.[4] These 'blockages' seem hardly due to particular resistances from the unconscious, as the subject-matter is often trivial enough. More probably the desired information was simply not

[1] בגרוני.

[2] *M.M.* 62a. 5. The ultimate source of this theory seems to be a phrase in the *Zohar Ḥadash* (fol. 28b) which says that the soul ascends at night to study Torah in Heaven and after its return to the body the 'lips move' at day-time.

[3] Cf. also *M.M.* 39a. 1.

[4] Cf. above, p. 245.

yet 'ready': the Maggid hesitated whilst searching for an answer and finally skipped the difficulty by some evasive makeshift manoeuvre. A good example can be found in the long and highly personal communication entitled 'the instruction which he taught him as a father his son'.[1] Conflicts in the Safed community apparently had forced Karo to leave the 'Great Synagogue'[2] and to attach himself to another and smaller congregation. The Maggid now comforts Karo and assures him that these tribulations were ultimately for his own good; but when he tries to give a precise reason for this particular vexation he begins to stammer:[3]

> For although many tribulations will befall you, they serve to purify your soul so that you will be guiltless [i.e. cleansed] of your iniquities. Also the members of the Great Synagogue will suffer even greater tribulations, and the mystery of it is, and the mystery of it is, and thus he kept on saying for more than an hour as if refusing to tell me, until he finally said, 'The mystery of it is that the members of the Great Synagogue have sinned by speaking unseemly words against Heaven . . ., and God's anger, as it were, was roused and [now] He punishes them measure for measure and [therefore] it was decreed that you should not be associated with them for some time.'

On another occasion the Maggid announced that he would reveal to Karo the mystery of his wife's soul as well as her previous *gilgul*, but when he got so far began to stammer and finally delivered himself of some obscure sentences, charging Karo 'not to reveal this thing to any man . . . neither must you write it down in such a manner that others may understand it'.[4] Once the Maggid communicated a complete homily 'according to the plain sense'[5] on the first chapter of *Aboth*. However, 'when he came to the *Mishnah* [*Aboth* i. 17] "all my days I grew up among sages"' he stammered and said 'you cause me to stammer by the wandering [or worldly] thoughts in your mind at the time of prayer, for you do not concentrate sufficiently [on your prayers] . . . .'[6] The same argument also accounts for errors and mistakes generally:[7]

[1] *M.M.* 2a–b.
[2] Probably identical with the בני ק"ק קהל גדול, about whom Moses de Trani complains in his *responsa* iii, nr. 48.
[3] *M.M.* 2b. 1.
[4] Ibid. 7a. 1; cf. above, p. 245.
[5] על דרך הפשט.
[6] *M.M.* 48a. 3.
[7] Ibid. 23a. 2.

for if you find occasionally that what I teach you is not quite correct, you know that already our sages observed that 'sin may interfere [and undo even God's explicit promises'; cf. b. *Ber.* 7*b*]. Even if there is no real sin [of commission], there may be wandering thoughts in your mind that interfere and these cause that not all my words [i.e. prophecies] come true and they also cause me to stammer and prevent me from revealing you everything.

Perhaps the most instructive example of such theorizing about the recipient's influence on the *inspirator* is provided by the Maggid's interpretation of Deut. xxix. 9 ff.[1] The Maggid's exposition is in the usual style of kabbalistic homiletics, but is based on a misquotation of the first verse, which the Maggid glosses as if it read 'ye stand this day [all of you before the Lord your God], your judges, your officers, your elders', whereas, as Solomon Alkabets immediately objected,[2] the correct reading is 'your captains of your tribes, your elders, your officers' [cf. A.V., Deut. xxix. 10]. The Maggid immediately took up the challenge:[3]

Behold the lyre sounded of itself and said: 'Though at times I expound a scriptural verse which does not exist in the form in which I quote it, [this happens] because I quote as it is in your mind. None the less my explanation is true and it is your duty to make it fit the correct reading of the text. This is the meaning of the verse [Job xxxii. 8] 'but there is a spirit in man', that is to say that things are shown to man as they are in his mind,—'and the inspiration of the Almighty giveth them understanding', that is to say that although the [inspired] explanations are true, yet they have to be [re-]interpreted to fit the text.'

The Maggid applies the same principle to the utterances of the prophets and thus practically formulates a theory of inspiration that avoids the more patent difficulties of the verbal inspirationists. The wording of all revelations, so we are told, is subject to individual vagaries and shortcomings; only the general sense is inspired and true. Celestial communications therefore impose a further exegetical duty on the recipient, who has to show that the general purport of the message also fits the correct wording of the sacred text.

[1] i.e. the beginning of the portion *Niṣṣabim*.

[2] This is the most reasonable explanation of the abrupt אז הגיה הר׳ שלמה. Alkabets was either present when the Maggid spoke or read (הגיה!) Karo's notes.

[3] *M.M.* 64a. 3–4.

We have noticed already[1] that the manifestations of the Maggid were audible to bystanders and that Karo himself was awake and conscious:

> You see for yourself the high degree which you have attained before the face of the Lord's people, that *you are spoken to with a loud voice* . . . .[2] And now you see that when I speak to you your eyes are open and you are looking around, and your voice is loudly audible when I speak in your mouth.[3]

It appears that Karo was fully aware of the relative uniqueness of this type of maggidism. In fact, the period during which maggidism in the form of automatic speech flourished in kabbalistic circles was only about to begin and Karo could legitimately look upon himself as an exceptional case. Thus he is assured by the Maggid, 'Your eyes behold that for many generations no man has reached this high degree, except some chosen few.'[4] 'Go and see what you have attained and to what high degree you have ascended that the [inspired] words are spoken in your mouth in this manner.'[5] 'The *Shekhinah* is speaking to you and you have attained what nobody has attained for many generations.'[6] Already in Alkabets's Epistle the singularity of the manifestation was stressed: 'Behold, has a people ever heard a voice speaking [thus] in your midst, "ask thy father and he will show thee; thy elders and they will tell thee" [cf. Deut. xxxii. 7], whether for many centuries such a thing has been heard or seen but you have been found worthy of it.'[7] Similar marks of divine favour to others are either denied or minimized. The Maggid of Rabbi Joseph Taytazak had to be admitted but was pronounced to be of an inferior order.[8] It seems that Taytazak's Maggid manifested himself in automatic writing whereas Karo could pride himself on the audible reception of the divine word.

Having briefly summarized the salient facts we can no longer postpone the obvious question: who exactly is this Maggid who

[1] Above, p. 17. [2] *M.M.* 47b. 2. [3] Ibid. 69b. 1.
[4] Ibid. 2a. 2. [5] Ibid. 65a. [6] Ibid. 36a. 3.
[7] ראו השמע עם קול מדבר בכם שאל אביך ויגדך זקניך ויאמרו לך אם זה כמה שנה שמעו או ראו כדבר הזה ואתם זכיתם.
[8] *M.M.* 34a; 34b. 3; probably also the reference ibid. 9a. 2. Cf. above, p. 118.

speaks of 'my *Torah*, my *Mishnah*, my fear, my love', &c.? What does he mean to be and in what capacity does he introduce himself?

A useful point of departure, from a methodological point of view, would be an investigation into the history and development of the noun *maggid* as a technical term for certain types of revelations. Unfortunately the material on this point is particularly scarce and does not permit any conclusions. As we have seen before,[1] all sorts and manners of revelation and illumination were known in Jewish mystical tradition. Dreams, angelic messengers, manifestations of the prophet Elijah and of the souls of departed saints, inspired intuitions, magically induced infusion of the Holy Spirit, and many other modes of inspiration have been recorded. But not until the sixteenth century does the term *maggid* appear as descriptive of a specific agent of celestial communication.[2] By the time Cordovero and Luria were active in Safed, both the term and the phenomenon were commonplace enough to be mentioned as a matter of course in discussions of mystical practice.[3] As time went on, maggidism increased and in certain periods almost assumed epidemic proportions. But Karo himself still speaks of his Maggid as 'the voice' or, more often, simply as 'the speech' (*ha-dibbur*). Similarly Alkabets, in his Epistle, reports: 'And we heard the voice speaking in the mouth of the *ḥasid*. . . . Later, at midnight, the speech returned a second time. . . . Also on the Sabbath the speech

[1] Above, ch. 4.

[2] Professor E. E. Urbach draws my attention to what may be the earliest example of the use of the noun *maggid* as a technical term. It occurs in Rashi's commentary to b. *Pesaḥim* 105b, on the phrase אנא לא חכימאה אנא ולא חוזאה אנא ולא יחידאה אנא אלא גמרנא וסדרנא אנא. The expression חוזאה is explained by Rashi (both in the commentary attributed to him and as quoted in Rashbam's commentary) 'מגיד'. This seems to suggest that the origin of the term should perhaps be sought in the circles of the German Ḥasidim. It will be remembered that Vital too refers to the subject of *maggidim* as mentioned in the *Sefer Ḥasidim* (cf. above, p. 79) though the word does not occur in any of the extant texts. It is unnecessary to draw attention to the obvious and important distinction that Rashi's *maggid* (= חוזאה) signifies the visionary, viz. the recipient of revelations, and not—as in later usage—the *vox coelestis* or angelic *inspirator*. The actual meaning of the talmudic phrase *Pes.* 105b has been carefully studied and elucidated in a recent Ph.D. thesis (Hebrew University of Jerusalem) on 'The redaction of tractate *Pesaḥ Rishon* of the Babylonian Talmud', by A. S. Rosenthal (pp. 223–52 of the typescript).

[3] Cf. above, pp. 74 ff., 81.

returned to the *ḥasid*.'[1] However, towards the end of his Epistle, when summing up the lesson of the experience, Alkabets already uses the word *maggid* as a technical term.[2] The extant manuscripts of the *M.M.* all bear the superscription *Sefer ha-Maggid*,[3] and the same term is used by Isaiah Hurwitz[4] and, of course, all later writers.

Surprisingly enough not only Alkabets but also Karo's Maggid uses the term on two occasions, though the reference is clearly not to himself. There is no reason at all for assuming that the two references are glosses inserted by the author (Karo) or some later copyist. We may therefore conclude that the term *maggid*, since it was used by the Maggid himself, was already in use in the circle around Karo. The term testifies to the belief in or experience of celestial dictation and reminds us of what has been said before on the subject of automatic writing. For the references in the *M.M.* to a *maggid* clearly have in mind a written source. That certain books were regarded as dictated by a heavenly *maggid* we have already learned from Cordovero.[5] Similar beliefs were apparently held by Karo. His celestial mentor explains the reason for reciting the benediction over the new moon between the 7th and the 15th day of the month as follows:[6]

> If we were to pronounce the benediction over the new moon[7] during the first seven days [of the lunar month], when the outer [i.e. demonic] forces still adhere to her, then we should not be able to separate them again . . . and we should mingle the holy with the profane. Therefore the Maggid has written [!] that the proper time [for the benediction] is from the seventh to the middle of the month.

The reference to a written source is less clear in the second passage, though there too it seems very probable.[8]

Returning to the question of the Maggid's identity, it appears from the evidence already adduced that the speaker is none other than the *Shekhinah* herself. The text of Alkabets's Epistle as well

[1] ונשמע את הקול המדבר בפי החסיד . . . . ואחר כך בחצות הלילה חזר הדיבור פעם שנית . . . . וגם ביום השבת חזר הדיבור אל החסיד . . .

[2] כפי המובן מדברי המגיד.

[3] See Appendix B.

[4] Cf. above, p. 35.

[5] Cf. above, p. 82.

[6] *M.M.* 65b. 3.

[7] In kabbalistic parlance the moon symbolizes the *Shekhinah*.

[8] *M.M.* 46b. 4: וכל מאי דאמר המגיד תלוי בהאי רזא.

as the quotation preserved in the approbation of the Jerusalem rabbinate[1] explicitly state that the speaker was in exile, suffering tribulations, and was lying 'in the dust' whence he, viz. she, expected to be 'raised up' by the pious exercises of the brotherhood. On the other hand this *Shekhinah* did not merely reveal herself as a result of the study of *Mishnah* but was herself identical with the *Mishnah*: 'and he heard the voice speaking from the *Mishnah* herself'[2]—'behold I am the *Mishnah*, the mother which correcteth man, I came to speak to you'[3]—'I am the *Mishnah* that speaketh in your mouth'[4] alongside of 'the *Shekhinah* speaketh to you'[5]—'I am the *Mishnah* that speaketh in your mouth, I am the mother that correcteth her sons, I am called the *Maṭronitha*'[6]—'Verily I am the *Mishnah* that speaketh in your mouth, it is I that dry the sea and wound Rahab,[7] I am the mother that correcteth man, I am the redeeming angel[8] in the mystery of Jacob'[9]—'my *Mishnayoth* are "an ornament of grace unto thy head" [Prov. i. 9], the "ornament of grace" that is the *Maṭronitha*, for all sefiroth attend her.'[10]

Although this *Mother–Shekhinah–Maṭronitha* is usually referred to in the masculine gender,[11] her feminine character is enhanced more than once by unmistakably erotic overtones. A few examples must suffice here: 'I embrace thee and cleave unto thee always'[12]—'through the merit of the *Mishnayoth* I cleave unto thee and kiss thee kisses of love and draw down on thee the thread of the love of Abraham'[13]—'I would find thee without and kiss thee [cf. Cant. viii. 1] with kisses of love as it is written [Cant. i. 2] "let him kiss me with the kisses of his mouth"'[14]—'Lo, I am the *Mishnah* that speaketh in thy mouth, that adorneth itself with excellent ornaments, [to wit] the strings of *Mishnayoth* which thou always recitest, for thou mountest the second chariot.'[15]

[1] Cf. above, pp. 18–19.
[2] Approbation: וישמע את הקול מדבר מתוך המשנה עצמה.
[3] Alkabets's Epistle. [4] *M.M. passim.* [5] Ibid. 36a. 3. [6] Ibid. 16a.
[7] A conflation of different expressions from Isa. li. 9–10.
[8] Gen. xlviii. 16. The term has been a standard epithet of the *Shekhinah* since the early days of Spanish kabbalism; cf. also above, p. 104.
[9] *M.M.* 20b. 2. [10] Ibid. 31b. 1. [11] דבר אלי, אמר אלי, &c.
[12] Ibid. 23b. 4; 39a. 2. [13] Ibid. 64b–65a. [14] Ibid. 66b. 2.
[15] Ibid. 28b. 2. Cf. also what is said of Joseph (!) in Gen. xli. 43; there is an obvious pun on the technical kabbalistic meanings of *Mishnah* and *merkabah*, cf. below on the relation of *Shekhinah–Mishnah–Beri'ah–Merkabah*.

Occasionally the genders and sexes get mixed up, e.g. when the Maggid addresses Karo, 'behold, I am the *Mishnah* that speaketh unto you . . . and you embrace the whole *Mishnah* and she is with you. I tell you now "go thou towards me, my sister, my love . . ., I desire thee and love thee".'[1] Of course, one must not exaggerate the significance of these erotic expressions which are, in part, standard clichés from midrashic literature[2] and even in kabbalistic writings are used of God 'the Holy One, Blessed be He", as distinct from his *Shekhinah*. In fact, the Maggid too uses the selfsame expressions once for the *Mishnah–Shekhinah* and once for the 'Holy One, Blessed be He', e.g. 'when you rise to pray or to study, at the time when God delighteth himself with the [souls of the] righteous in the Garden of Eden,[3] then he delighteth himself also with you and draws down upon you a thread of grace. Then he kisses you with kisses of love and embraces you, and the *Shekhinah* speaketh to you.'[4] But though Karo's relation to the Maggid is not primarily erotic, the erotic overtones are undeniable.

The exact heavenly status of the Maggid is a matter of some ambiguity. As the *Mishnah*, he/she may be considered to be identical with the divine *logos*. In kabbalistic terminology—and this is a commonplace of classical kabbalism—the *Mishnah*, as the embodiment of the 'Oral *Torah*', symbolizes the tenth sefirah *Malkhuth–Shekhinah*, in contrast to *Tif'ereth* ('the Holy One, Blessed be He'), for which the 'Written *Torah*' serves as a symbol. The 'Oral *Torah*' is precisely and almost by definition the speakable or outspoken, i.e. manifest and articulate, mode of the hidden divine Wisdom, and this is also precisely the mode of the *logos* and the *Shekhinah* with regard to the higher, more remote, and less manifest aspects, viz. sefiroth of the Godhead. The symbolic equation *Shekhinah* = *Mishnah* of classical kabbalism goes a long way towards explaining the dual identity of our Maggid. However, against this interpretation of the Maggid as the *Shekhinah* in her quality as an hypostasis of the last and most manifest aspect of the

[1] *M.M.* 68a. 1.

[2] Cf. expressions like הקב"ה מגפפו ומנשקו (particularly frequent in the *Seder 'Eliyyahu*).

[3] i.e. after midnight; a frequent Zoharic motif.

[4] *M.M.* 36a. 3.

Godhead, we must hold the many references in the *M.M.* indicative of a lower status. The Maggid frequently describes himself as a celestial messenger.[1] But messengers there are many, and without disrespect to them it is quite obvious that there are greatly superior types of revelation and of communion with God or the Holy Spirit. One would think that the automatic speech of maggidism is an attempt at emulating and all but equalling Mosaic prophecy, traditionally described by the idiomatic expression 'the *Shekhinah* spoke in his throat',[2] and in fact many of the passages quoted above clearly intend to echo Moses.[3] Yet we find Karo still aspiring to superior forms or revelation. This can only mean that he considered his Maggid as falling short of the highest type of divine *charisma*. Surprisingly enough, this desired higher form is the appearance of the celestial messenger *par excellence*, the prophet Elijah.[4] This desire may be no more than a carry-over from the popular tradition which regarded the apparition of the prophet as one of the greatest spiritual boons. Nevertheless, it seems that the proper way of resolving the apparent inconsistency is in recalling the significance of Moses, Elijah, and others with regard to the *Shekhinah*. The Maggid repeatedly exhorts Karo and prophesies: 'Mortify yourself as I told you, so as to merit to behold Elijah whilst you are awake [i.e. not only in a dream], face to face, and he will speak to you, mouth to mouth, and will give you the salutation of peace. For he will become your teacher and master, and teach you all the mysteries of the Torah'[5]—'I have told you already twice and thrice that you shall see Elijah standing before you whilst

[1] אנא שלוחא דקוב״ה, שדרוני ממתיבתא דרקיעא (*passim*).

[2] שכינה מדברת מתוך גרונו. Mr. J. G. Weiss draws my attention to the fact that this much-quoted phrase is not found in early aggadic texts and seems to occur for the first time in Rashi's commentary on the Pentateuch; cf. also Ginzberg, *Legends of the Jews*, vol. vi, p. 36 (n. 201).

[3] Cf. above, p. 118. Phrases like 'face to face, as a man speaketh with a friend' or 'mouth to mouth' clearly echo Exod. xxxiii. 11, Num. xii. 8.

[4] Cf. also above, p. 22. The description there of the manifestation of Elijah is clearly influenced, at least in part, by Karo's experience of his Maggid. On the manifestation of a *maggid*, followed by the apparition of Elijah as the standard pattern of M. H. Luzzatto's mystical experiences, cf. אגרות רמח״ל *passim*.

[5] *M.M.* 2b. 1. This promise may also be an expression of the ambition to equal Isaac Luria, who was supposed to have learned the supreme mysteries of Kabbalah from Elijah himself.

awake. It is necessary, however, that you fast seven times three consecutive days, and then he will reveal himself to you at the place which you know and there you shall delight yourself with him'[1]—'You already know the high degree to which you have risen in the face of the Lord's people that you are spoken to in a loud voice, and [later] you will also be privileged to behold Elijah, as I told you, provided you amend your ways.'[2] The theoretical background of this ambition appears in another passage where the Maggid explains that the name *'LiYaHV HaNaBY'*, being a compound of the elements *'L*, *YHV*, *H*, and *NBY'*, symbolized the divine supernal ten sefiroth (*YHV*), the *Maṭronitha* which, as a secondary emanation, was composed of the effluence of all the sefiroth (*H*),[3] and Elijah's appearance in bodily form as the representative of the *Shekhinah*:[4]

For by the mystery of the letter *he* [i.e. in Karo's system the secondary *Shekhinah–Maṭronitha*], which is like a body unto the [supernal] sefiroth, Elijah clothes himself in a body and appears visibly in this world. If you want him to appear to you, then meditate these things when lying down [to sleep]. . . . There are thus three degrees [of beholding Elijah]: the one is to see him in a dream; the second is to see him awake and to salute him, but without Elijah returning the salutation; the third is to see him awake, to greet him, and to be saluted by him in return. You shall reach the third degree . . . but Elijah will only come to you by surprise [i.e. when you expect him least[5]].[6]

Elsewhere Elijah, rather like Melchizedek in the *Epistle to the Hebrews*, is described as fatherless and motherless; as a theological type, 'he came to this word solely for the purpose of making known the Divinity of God, and he is the same as Metatron'.[7] This also further clarifies the distinction between Moses and Elijah, for 'our master Moses, though he too died, yet he rose to a degree unattained by other mortals; for God [himself] buried him. This is a supreme mystery, for his body was exalted and purified until he could adhere to the [divine] sefiroth, whereas Elijah's body could only

[1] *M.M.* 19b. 4.
[2] Ibid. 47b. 2; cf. also the quotation above, p. 22.
[3] Cf. Karo's doctrine of the *Shekhinah* as outlined in Ch. 10.
[4] By reading the word נביא in the transposed alphabet א"ת ב"ש.
[5] בהיסח הדעת. [6] *M.M.* 6a. 2. [7] Ibid. 19a. 3.

adhere to Metatron who is the 'servant' [of the Godhead and not the Godhead itself]. You may thus understand the difference between the degree of Moses and that of Elijah.'[1]

Some of the terms used in connexion with Elijah in the preceding quotation can be found elsewhere in connexion with the *Mishnah*. Moreover, precisely as the *Mishnah*, so also Metatron is connected with the *Shekhinah*. The fact that the *Shekhinah* with which Metatron is associated is always the 'lower' *Shekhinah* is of particular relevance for an understanding of the Maggid, since in Karo's system, as we have seen, there is only one *Shekhinah* and this is the 'lower' one. The term *Shekhinah* is simply not used by Karo for the 'supernal *Shekhinah*', viz. *Malkhuth*, or *Keneseth Yisra'el*. The *Mishnah* too is correlated in many texts with Metatron, the Servant, and with the Tree of Knowledge of Good and Evil.[2] In fact, we can now qualify our earlier statement[3] about the original identity tenth sefirah–*Shekhinah–Mishnah*–Oral *Torah* by adding that *Mishnah* and *Shekhinah* remain associated even when demoted from the supernal realm of divine sefiroth. The *Shekhinah* for Karo is no longer the tenth sefirah *Malkhuth* but a secondary, intermediate world (*Maṭronitha—'olam ha-shem*), which can also be described as Metatron and as the Tree of the Knowledge of Good and Evil. Now this is precisely the role of the *Mishnah* according to many kabbalistic texts. Falling back on the more conventional kabbalistic terminology, we might say that both *Shekhinah–Maṭronitha* and the *Mishnah* correspond to the so-called 'World of the Throne' or *Beri'ah*.[4] Bearing in mind the argument of Chap. 10, we are now fully prepared for Cordovero's

[1] *M.M.* 54a. 1.

[2] Cf., e.g. *Reshith Ḥokhmah* (*Sha'ar ha-Qedushah*, ch. 2), pp. 218–19, quoting from the *Tiqquney Zohar*: וייצר ה׳ אלהים את האדם ואיהו עץ הדעת טו״ר.... ודא הוא מטטרון דאיהו עבד דשליט בשית סדרי משנה.... Cf. also above, pp. 219–21.

[3] Above, p. 268.

[4] Or, to be more exact, to *Beri'ah–Yeṣirah* combined, in terms of Karo's system. For similar considerations, but in strictly Lurianic terminology, cf. Jacob Ḥayyim Ṣemah's ס׳ נגיד ומצוה (Constantinople, 1726), fol. 33a: ובקראו במשנה יכוין לשם שד״י שהוא בגימט׳ מטטרו״ן ... כל זה כתוב בס׳ הכוונות. ... והענין כי שתא סדרי משנה הם עתה לגו ... וגם דע כי המשנה מטטרון ביצירה ותכוין להעלות היצירה אל הבריאה והענין כי המשנה היא ביצירה וע״י קריאתך תיכוין שמן אותיות משנה יהיה נשמה ונודע כי נשמה היא בברי׳.

definition:[1] '*Mishnah*: this is [the tenth sefirah] *Malkhuth*. However, she is also called *Mishnah* [the second] in the sense of being next [or second] unto the Queen, for she is like the handmaid of the Queen in the mystery of the Throne and *Beri'ah*, as explained [in a previous chapter]. She is next unto her Mistress, i.e. the *Maṭronitha*.'

Formally at least all this sufficiently accounts for the conflation of the two symbol-clusters *Shekhinah* and *Mishnah*. It does not account, however, for the emphatic and insistent concrete identification of the two in the particular case of Karo's celestial mentor. Here one would have to inquire into the background of the sixteenth-century revival of *Mishnah* study and to ascertain what charismatic or spiritual expectations were connected with it. Unfortunately there are no sources relating to such a revival prior to Karo himself. Elijah de Vidas recommends the study of Mishnah in general terms as a weapon against man's evil *yeṣer*,[2] whereas Isaiah Hurwitz's advice[3] also rings an eschatological note:

> Therefore let thine occupation be mainly the *Mishnayoth*, to study and rehearse them constantly. . . . Blessed is he who comes to know the six orders of the *Mishnah* by heart, for thereby he makes a ladder on which his soul ascends to the highest degree. This is hinted at by the equivalence of the letters of the words *MiSHNaH* and *NeSHaMaH*,[4] and thereby a great [mystical] *tiqqun* is wrought . . . for all salvations for Israel are stirred up in heaven [through the study of the *Mishnah*].

But Hurwitz was, of course, writing a few decades after Karo.

In Safed we know of one great *Mishnah* addict. Conforti tells us[5] that 'at that time there was living in Safed Rabbi Joseph Ashkenazi,[6] called the 'great *tanna*', because he always melodiously recited the *Mishnayoth*'. From Shlomel Dresnitz's Epistles we learn that this *tanna*'s recital of *Mishnayoth* was not only melodious but also by heart: 'one Sabbath night Rabbi Isaac [Luria] entered the house of Rabbi Joseph Ashkenazi, the son-in-law of Rabbi

[1] *Pardes*, שער ערכי הכנויים.

[2] Op. cit., p. 218: סגולת גרסת המשניות להרוג היצה"ר.

[3] Op. cit., fol. 181b: ע"כ רוב העסק יהיה במשניות ללמוד ולחזור אותם בלי ערך ובלי הפסק. . . . ואשרי הזוכה למשנה שיהיו שתא סדרי משנה שגורים בפיו בע"פ.

[4] Cf. above, p. 271, n. 4.

[5] Op. cit., fol. 36b.

[6] See now also G. Scholem's article 'ידיעות חדשות על ר׳ יוסף אשכנזי ה'תנא' מצפת, in *Tarbiz*, vol. xxviii (1958/9).

Aaron Land of Posen, where they were reciting *Mishnah* by heart as was his custom to do.'[1] We have seen that Karo seemed to attach great importance not only to the recital of the *Mishnah* but to his doing so by heart. He is actually praised by the Maggid for renewing the former glory of the *Mishnah* by restoring the latter to her original position of 'Oral *Torah*' (in the literal sense) after having been treated for so many centuries as a text: 'These are the holy days of the month of Nisan, and you have hallowed them even more by studying the *Mishnah* by heart; thus you have restored the crown to its ancient splendour by making [the *Mishnah* again] to be the "Oral *Torah*".'[2] Elsewhere the Maggid implies that devotion to the study of *Mishnah* was comparatively rare: 'God will not take away from you his love and his grace, because of the *Mishnayoth* that you recite. For nowadays they that study her are few, and "there is none to guide her [i.e. the *Mishnah/Shekhinah*] among all the sons whom she hath brought forth" [cf. Isa. li. 18].'[3]

Among Karo's contemporaries and associates, Cordovero evinces no signs of a particular appreciation of the *Mishnah*. The study of *Mishnah* is part of the hierarchically ordered curriculum Scripture–*Mishnah*–Kabbalah, but all talmudic, i.e. halakhic, studies are subsumed under the title *Mishnah*. Cordovero criticizes those who jump to a premature study of Kabbalah without previous study of the exoteric *Torah*; the proper order of study leads through the classes of the *ba'aley miqra'*, *ba'aley mishnah*, and *ba'aley kabbalah*.[4] But there is no doubt that for Cordovero *Mishnah* means talmudic learning in its widest sense.[5] A letter written from Jerusalem in the year 1541 mentions a certain Rabbi bar Rab Ada (?), Chief Rabbi of Jerusalem, who knew the whole *Mishnah* by heart.[6] Study and recital of the *Mishnah* seems to have been rather popular among the saints in Safed, and there are many references to the habit in the rules of the pious brotherhoods printed by Schechter as an

[1] *Shibḥey ha-'Ari*: והיו חוזרים המשניות בעל פה כי כן היה מנהגו תמיד.

[2] *M.M.* 47b. 4.

[3] Ibid. 17a. 4.

[4] *'Or Ne'erab*, pt. i, ch. 6.

[5] Ibid., fol. 17a: אותם האוחזים להם דרך הישר שיש להם חלק במקרא וחלק בגמרא והוראותיה שהם אצלנו כמשנה.

[6] Does the writer perhaps refer to Jacob Berab? For text and discussion see Y. M. Toledano in *HUCA*, vol. iv (1927), pp. 461–2 and p. 463, n. 5.

Appendix to his essay on Safed.[1] Thus we find rules[2] 'at table, before Grace, to recite two chapters [of *Mishnah*] and one Psalm' —'to study as many *Mishnayoth* as is possible every Sabbath night'—'to repeat once a week all the *Mishnayoth* that you know'— 'to learn by heart every week at least two chapters of *Mishnayoth*'. In fact,[3] 'most scholars study the *Mishnah* by heart, some two orders, others three'. The custom seems to have gained ground and to have spread beyond Palestine. Israel Isserl Götz, of Strassburg, the editor of a vocalized text of the *Mishnah*,[4] reports in his preface that the members of the *yeshibah* of Venice knew the *Mishnah* by heart: 'most of them, as well as the other scholars in the city know the six orders of the *Mishnah* by heart.'[5]

The evidence of the testimonies adduced so far does not go beyond Safed and the later period. It seems, however, that Karo's devotion to the study of the *Mishnah* must be dated as early as his European period. In fact, one brief and allusive statement in the *M.M.* actually suggests that the study of the *Mishnah* by heart was cultivated also by Karo's 'rival' Rabbi Joseph Taytazak of Salonica[6] and his circle. The Maggid praises Karo's diligent study of the *Mishnah* and adds 'for although there are others too who know the six orders of the *Mishnah* [by heart], one does not speak to them in the manner one speaks to you,[7] even though you know that you have committed graver and worse sins than they'.[8] The *M.M.* leaves no doubt that Karo's Maggid, though explicitly conceived as the *Shekhinah*, was associated with the *Mishnah* from the very beginning. Also Alkabets records in his Epistle that the first manifestation of the Maggid occurred 'when we had begun to read the *Mishnah* and had read two tractates. Then our Creator privileged us to hear the voice speaking in the mouth of the *ḥasid*.' That this was no accident appears from the account of the proceedings

[1] Schechter, *Studies in Judaism*, 2nd ser. (1908). Now cf. in addition the text printed in Y. M. Toledano, *'Oṣar Genazim* (1960), p. 51.

[2] Schlechter, op. cit., p. 294. [3] Ibid., p. 297. [4] Venice, 1704.

[5] רובם ככולם וחכמי העיר הנ"ל יודעים שיתא סדרי משנה בע"פ.

[6] Cf. above, pp. 118, 264.

[7] Note the identical wording of the passages referring explicitly to Joseph Taytazak, above, p. 118.

[8] *M.M.* 9a. 2: דאע"ג דאיכא אחרינין דידעין שיתא סדרי משנה לא ממלל עמהון כמה דממלל עמך, ואוף דידעת דאית בידך סורחנין תקיפין ובישין מנהון.

of the following night, when 'so great was the joy that we were ten [i.e. a full quorum for liturgical purposes], that [this time] we did not wait until the time for the recitation of the *Mishnah* . . . but immediately as we began reading the Ten Commandments from the Book of Deuteronomy . . . the voice of our beloved knocked . . . .' We may assume, therefore, that by the time of this memorable *Shabu'oth* vigil in Karo's house, the visitations of the Maggid were firmly linked to the study of the *Mishnah*. In this respect no change seems to have occurred in the pattern of Karo's maggidic visitations throughout a lifetime of charismatic experience. In another respect, however, a subtle but significant change does seem to have taken place. It is true that the *Mishnah* was not only the occasion or instrumental cause but also the very agent of the celestial revelations, yet this latter fact is less prominent in the earlier testimonies than in the later. The earlier statements[1] emphasize the identity of the heavenly speaker with the *Shekhinah* whereas the later texts[2] seem to lay the main stress on his identity with the *Mishnah*. And though, as we have seen, *Shekhinah* and *Mishnah* can be identified in terms of kabbalistic symbolism, yet the change in emphasis deserves attention. Revelational experiences after the study of *Mishnah* seem to have been known also to other mystics, and even Vital, who, as a rule, resorted to other methods, does mention in passing his habit of meditating over the *Mishnah* at the time of the afternoon prayer[3] in order to be enlightened concerning mystical questions such as, for example, his previous transmigrations.[4]

The identification of the Maggid as an hypostasis of the *Mishnah* inevitably brings to mind the one faintly similar story recorded in midrashic legend. The story, for which no early source has so far been found, is told for the first time in Al-Nakawa's *Menorath ha-Ma'or*[5] and deserves to be quoted here:

[1] Cf. above, pp. 18–19, 51 n. 4, 103–9.

[2] Cf. above, p. 111. The *Shekhinah* motif is far less obtrusive in most of the *M.M.*

[3] Cf. also references to *M.M.* above, p. 257, nn. 2, 3.

[4] *Sefer ha-Ḥezyonoth*, pp. 54–55 (בעת המנחה נתבודדתי ע"י קריאת המשנה).

[5] Ed. Enelow, vol. iii (1931), pp. 275–6. Aboab quotes the same story from the *Tanḥuma*, but it is not found in any of the extant recensions of this midrash (Enelow, ibid., note).

Once there was a disciple . . . who studied the tractate *Ḥagigah* . . . and he knew no other tractate of the Talmud besides. . . . When he died . . . there came a woman who stood near his corpse and raised her voice in weeping and lamentation . . . like unto a woman mourning her husband. And as this woman wept bitterly and cried, people asked her, 'What is your name?', whereupon she answered, 'My name is Ḥagigah'. But immediately after the burial of the pious disciple the woman disappeared . . . whereupon everybody knew that it was the tractate *Ḥagigah* which had appeared to them in the guise of a woman. . . . And now you may argue for yourself *ad fortiorem*: if this disciple [who knew only one tractate of the Talmud was thus rewarded] . . . how much more so he who studies much *Torah* and raises many disciples.

The purpose of the story is clearly not the glorification of the *Mishnah*, but at least it introduces the personification of a rabbinic text. Karo must have known the story well, for not only is it quoted by contemporary authors[1] but even the Maggid refers to it in one of his most important self-revelatory communications:[2]

Lo, I am the *Mishnah* speaking in your mouth, I am the soul of the *Mishnah* [!] and I and the *Mishnah* [!] and you are united as one. Therefore always return to [the study of] my *Mishnayoth* and never separate your thoughts [from them], even for a single moment. Then I shall always accompany you and never forsake you, neither in this world nor in the world to come. Behold what befell . . . the man who studied the tractate *Ḥagigah* and what was done unto him apart from the [celestial] reward given to him in the Hereafter. Therefore repent and meditate on all my tractates in such manner that they will always be fluent in your mouth.

There is, however, an even bigger surprise in store for those who, like the present writer, believe in the literary background of mystical experiences. There exists a short apocryphal midrash, known as *Marganitha debey Rab*,[3] which contains phrases that are literally identical with the standard openings and greetings of Karo's Maggid. The *Marganitha*, a brief hortatory treatise of ascetic piety, leads up to the following extraordinary climax:[4]

[1] e.g. by Joseph Yabeṣ in his commentary on *'Aboth* (Adrianople, 1555), fol. 5b, and by Karo's younger contemporary Samuel de Ozeda in *Leḥem Dim'ah* (Venice, 1605), fol. 89b. I am indebted for these two references to Dr. H. H. Ben Sasson and Mr. D. Tamar respectively.

[2] *M.M.* 45a. 3.

[3] Printed in *'Or Qadmon* (Venice, 1703) and again in ch. 7 of *Shebeṭ Musar* by Elijah ha-Kohen of Smyrna (Constantinople, 1718), and reprinted by Jellinek, *Beth ha-Midrash*, vol. ii, pp. 120–2.

[4] Ibid., p. 122.

Blessed is he who inclines his ear to hearken to the words of *Torah*, blessed he who every day hears words of *Torah*. The perfect *Torah* of the Lord will stand in front of him whilst he studies the *Mishnah* [!][1] and will address him: 'The Lord be with thee, thou mighty man of valour. Behold I have come to teach thee, therefore have I gone forth to seek thy face and I found thee. Blessed art thou if thou rememberest me, blessed art thou if thou hidest me in thine heart.'

As in the case of the pious student of *Ḥagigah*, the *Torah* appears as an objective, visible manifestation. Unlike the tractate *Ḥagigah*, the *Torah* is here supposed to appear to the student himself and to address him, vouchsafing further and higher knowledge. Neither case is identical with Karo's maggidism, since the Maggid did not appear *to* him but spoke *in* him. None the less the text of the *Marganitha* is of great interest. For although the promised experience is supposed to come about as a result of 'hearing words of *Torah* every day', yet the text shows a significant transition from *Torah* to *Mishnah* and actually provides the wording of the Maggid's standard openings. There can be little doubt that the occurrence of the word *Mishnah* in this text was largely responsible for the Maggid's style. We know that the saints in Safed used to read all available ascetic, hortatory, and penitential tracts, and that the *Marganitha* was one of them. It was incorporated *in toto* by de Vidas in his *Reshith Ḥokhmah*,[2] where it is referred to as the *Marganitha of Rabbi Meir*. Karo must have known the treatise by heart since the Maggid, in one of his exhortations, admonishes him to 'remember what Rab has said in his *Marganitha*'[3] and later enjoins upon him 'to read the *Marganitha debey Rab* every day'.[4]

However, for a fuller understanding of the 'personality' of the Maggid these literary and purely formal links are clearly not enough. In the last resort, the Maggid's character and significance depend on the nature and contents of his messages. These, as has been noted before, conformed to the standard pattern of 'the revelation of the mysteries of the *Torah*' and 'mighty promises' (i.e. personal prophecies). In addition to these the Maggid's

[1] Note the transition from *Torah* to *Mishnah*!

[2] *Sha'ar ha-Yir'ah*, ch. 12.

[3] *M.M.* 49a (last line).

[4] Ibid. 41a. 2. On another occasion the Maggid (ibid. 41b) is satisfied with less: ולמד. . . ומרגניתא דבי רב תרין זמנין בשבוע.

revelations included a third type of message that may well turn out to be decisive for our psychological understanding of the phenomenon. In 1621 Isaiah Hurwitz had reported[1] that the Maggid's words contained 'many exhortations and many virtuous practices and many ascetic rules which he taught him: "eat this, but that you should not eat", forbidding him many permitted foods as if they were [ritually] prohibited ones'. But the Maggid did much more than that. In addition to imposing severe restrictions on Karo—restrictions which, incidentally, were in complete accordance with the ascetic code of the kabbalistic saints—the Maggid also functioned as his bad conscience. A very large part of the Maggid's time is taken up with reproving or even sternly rebuking Karo for minor transgressions of the severe code of ascetic discipline. Time and again he is told that his failings were such that his celestial mentor should have deserted him, were it not for special divine grace and favour.[2] The Maggid's prescriptions include not only extreme continence in food, drink, and sleep but also positive mortifications and frequent fasts,

> and do not enjoy anything of this world as I already instructed thee and as thou didst practise it, in part, this week. Behold, today thou hast terminated a forty days period of fasting, corresponding to the forty days of the formation of the embryo. Although on some days thou didst enjoy things of this world, yet since they were altogether forty days they were [graciously] accepted [by God].[3]

Karo's failings were thus of the usual ascetic kind: occasional indulgence in what would appear to us to be normal quantities of food and drink (mainly water, occasionally wine), oversleeping (probably as a result of too much study), at times relaxing the exclusive preoccupation with and concentration on the Law, the *Mishnah*, and the presence of God, wandering thoughts at prayer, and the incidental enjoyment of the good things of life. As has already been noted, the kabbalistic ascetics were all agreed on the necessity of evolving a technique of performing the various bodily acts and functions prescribed by the Law and required by nature

[1] In the letter mentioned above, p. 35.

[2] Cf. the quotations above, p. 149, and *M.M.*, *passim.*

[3] *M.M.* 30b. 2.

(eating, drinking, marital intercourse) without feeling any pleasure or enjoyment. A draught of cold water simply enjoyed would give rise to severe pangs of conscience and self-castigation. Needless to say that graver lapses such as occasional feelings of anger or pride were not allowed to pass uncensored. This moral and ascetic code being what it was, daily infringements were practically inevitable and the Maggid's reproofs, repeated with unvarying monotony for almost half a century, need not therefore surprise us.

The essentially moral and ascetic purpose of the Maggid's visitations emerges clearly from messages that are not prima facie hortatory. Thus when the Maggid promises revelations concerning the transmigrations of the souls of Karo's relatives and friends, he immediately adds what seems to be the main purpose of an otherwise objectionable pandering to human curiosity: '*Therefore* be strong in the fear of the Lord always, mortify yourself as much as possible, and burn all [worldly] thoughts that come into your mind when you are praying or reciting *Mishnayoth*; burn them in the strawfire of your breath as you recite the *Shema'*.'[1] The lengthy description of Karo's future glory entitled 'The praise of the Rabbi [Joseph Karo]',[2] which falls little short of a megalomaniac's wish-fantasy, is wound up with the practical conclusion: 'God and his Academy have sent me to reveal to you these mysteries, in order that you should behold in which high degree you are and consequently not fall into sin, not even [into the sin] of worldly thoughts. . . . For you should say to yourself, "Is it possible that a man like me, predestined to such high [celestial] honours, should sin by thought?".'[3]

Whatever else the Maggid may be, he certainly also represents Karo's conscience or, in the current psychoanalytical jargon, his super-ego.[4] The last-quoted passage in particular, with its appeal to Karo's better self, should by itself be enough to lead us to a consideration of the super-ego and more especially to that aspect of it which Freud discussed in one of his earliest papers on the subject.[5]

[1] *M.M.* 1b. 3. [2] Ibid. 1b–2a. [3] Ibid. 2a.

[4] The first to have suggested this psychoanalytic interpretation is Dr. M. Perath-Premsela in his brief but illuminating article גלגולי האני העליון in *Gilyonoth*, vol. xxii (1948/9), pp. 185–8.

[5] 'On Narcissism. An Introduction' (first published in 1914).

Considerably deepening certain similar insights by earlier psychologists (e.g. MacDougall's 'sentiment of self-regard'), Freud described the direction, viz. redirection, of part of our libido to the 'self'. This 'narcissistic libido' in its turn undergoes differentiation, and part of it is transferred to our ideal self or 'Ego-Ideal'. The speeches of the Maggid, with their untiring and repetitious reprimands for Karo's failings as well as their excessive confirmations of his unparalleled greatness and future glory are a most instructive example of this redirection or displacement of narcissism. The constant rhythm of 'mighty promises' and severe reproofs (i.e. self-accusations), addressed to the penitent by the hallucinated 'voice of conscience', cannot but bring to mind Freud's observations in his paper on *Mourning and Melancholia*.[1]

Narcissism is, of course, only one of the roots of the super-ego. For there is not only the all-important internalization of parental authority and values, but also the attachment to this introjected image of all the aggression an individual is capable of.[2] The super-ego is thus characterized by the ambivalence of the original parent–child situation: love and need of acceptance (i.e. of safety and protection), the experience of failure and the resultant withdrawal of love, frustration and aggression, punishment and reconciliation. In this respect too the Maggid proved himself a true parent-type super-ego. He clearly represents all the religious and ascetic values cherished and cultivated in Karo's circle, and in the *M.M.* he appears as a strict and uncompromising, yet loving taskmaster. Demanding an unflagging and relentless devotion to the accepted ideals, this super-ego never relinquished its hold on Karo and actually strengthened it by repeated threats of desertion. Like a morally over-ambitious mother, the Maggid constantly threatens withdrawal of his/her presence and love, only to return again and again to the beloved son, comforting, forgiving, and demanding.

If the psychoanalytic interpretation is valid, then the predominantly feminine character of the Maggid deserves further consideration. Freud has shown that the formation of the super-ego

[1] First published in 1917; see *Collected Papers*, vol. iv (1925), particularly p. 152.

[2] Hence the sado-masochistic features of 'conscience', also illustrated by the Maggid.

proceeds by way of introjection and desexualization of the parent images. The super-ego is not simply or exclusively the introjected father-figure, and the process of desexualization may be arrested or modified. The role of the parents in the formation of our 'conscience' is well illustrated by the well-known midrash[1] according to which Joseph had already made up his mind to respond to the advances of Potiphar's wife when, glancing in a mirror, he beheld his father's image looking at him. Similar instances of more recent date have been recorded in psychoanalytic literature.[2] A thief, in the act of stealing, suddenly 'saw' his father sadly looking at him. Another person 'heard' his mother weeping as he entered a brothel. The midrash about Joseph was clearly at the back of Joseph Karo's mind when he was instructed by his Maggid[3] to represent to himself his father's image whenever he was tempted to sin. But in spite of this midrashic echo the maternal features dominate in Karo's Maggid.

Of course, it is a far cry from a super-ego, influenced or dominated by the mother-image, to a full-blown oedipal, libidinous fixation on the mother. If, nevertheless, we venture to suggest that traces of such a fixation are discernible in the Maggid,[4] we must not base ourselves solely on the Maggid's markedly maternal character or on the erotic overtones already referred to. Indirect, though no less valuable, evidence is provided by Karo's attitude of extreme reverence to his wives, as well as by the Maggid's declaration that at least one of them was essentially male since her soul was that of a famous talmudic scholar. We may thus, perhaps, conclude, without overstating our case, that certain elements of the oedipal situation were active in shaping the figure of the super-ego as manifest in the Maggid. As the Maggid exhibits a positive dislike of horseradish,[5] it is, perhaps, a pity that we do not know how Karo's mother felt about this particular vegetable.

[1] b. *Soṭah* 36b, *Gen. Rabbah* lxxxvii. 11 (ed. Theodor–Albeck, p. 1073). According to one version (note ibid., p. 1072) Joseph also saw the image of his mother!

[2] Cf. J. C. Flugel, *Man, Morals and Society* (Penguin Book ed., 1955), pp. 67–68 and the references ibid.

[3] *M.M.* 39a. 2, 40a. 5; cf. above, p. 163.

[4] See Perath-Premsela, loc. cit.

[5] *M.M.* 1a (last §); 6a, 5; 71b. It should be added, however, that talmudic

If our interpretation is not completely mistaken, then Karo is another example of the psychological type of the son whose ambition to achieve great things is fed by the mother, viz. the mother-image. We have already had occasion to point out the element of ambition, flattery, and praise in the maggidic communications in connexion with the halakhic contents of the *M.M.*[1] It will therefore occasion no surprise to learn that homage is paid to Karo by the hosts of heaven,[2] that his writings would all be completed and accepted as authoritative throughout Israel,[3] that he would raise more disciples than any other talmudic scholar for the last five hundred years, and that none but his students would enjoy academic standing.[4] He was destined to be the spiritual chief of Israel,[5] and even to perform miracles.[6] Surely these ambitions were more than the average ideals of even the most distinguished Talmudist and, as we have seen, they were not devoid of eschatological overtones.[7] It is all the more surprising, considering the eschatological mood of the age, that there is so little direct and immediate messianism in either Karo's or the Maggid's utterances. The messianic storm was only beginning to gather, and the kabbalist circle of Taytazak, Alkabets, Karo, and Berab seem to have seen themselves on the verge of the messianic era but not as messianic personalities. Not even Karo's unconscious in its wildest dreams would dare to go that far. It was left to a younger generation of kabbalists to grope hesitantly towards the half-conscious wish-dreaming of a messianic calling.

But whereas super-egos and even oedipal neuroses are fairly normal phenomena, maggidic manifestations are not. For not only is a Maggid more than just a super-ego; the psychoanalytic concepts by themselves do not even explain the fact that a Maggid exists, though they can do much to illuminate his nature and character. To account for the existence of *maggidim* one would need more light than is at present available on the psychopathology

literature supplies sufficient reasons to account for this particular phobia of the Maggid.

[1] Cf. above, p. 186. [2] *M.M.* 3b, 27b–28a, 33a. 3 *et passim.*

[3] Ibid. 4a. 2, 27b. 2, 32b. 3, 34a, 47b. 2.

[4] Ibid. 2b. 1, 16b, 27b. 4; cf. also 71b. 2. [5] Cf. ibid. 39a. 2.

[6] Ibid. 6a, 44a, 57b, 26a, 36a; cf. also above, p. 165.

[7] Cf. above, pp. 53, 95 f., 123 f.

of mysticism and of phenomena of dissociation in general. Since, however, the pathogenesis of these phenomena is still largely unexplored territory, a few brief comments may suffice here.

Even at first sight maggidism resembles certain other well-known phenomena of dissociation, such as mediumistic trances, somnambulism, certain cases of hysteria, and hypnosis. More specifically, the Maggid is reminiscent of the spirit 'guides' or 'controls' of spiritualistic mediums. In fact, Scholem has already shown that maggid-like phenomena were known by the German *ḥasidim* and were accounted for in spiritualistic terms. Inspiration, viz. the Holy Spirit (as distinct from Prophecy proper), was understood as the entrance of another soul into the soul of the mystic. The same would happen, in a negative way, in cases of evil, viz. demonic, possession. This possession or impregnation of the soul was explained in spiritualistic terms and was later combined with the Zoharic theory of *gilgul*, viz. *'ibbur*.[1] There is thus a clear line running from these older spiritualist conceptions to the favourite Lurianic method of seeking illumination from the souls of departed saints[2] on the one hand, and to the theory of maggidism which resorts to non-human spirits (e.g. angels, the *Shekhinah*, and the like) for an explanation[3] on the other. It appears that phenomena of dissociation as psychological processes are indeterminate as far as the precise form of their manifestation is concerned. Their specific form and character (divine voices, angels, spirits, souls of saints or relatives, shamanistic encounters, &c.) are determined by the cultural background of the medium, i.e. by the theoretical background which he or his group provides for the event. Karo's speech automatism is paralleled in many mediumistic trances and differs in this respect from, for example, Moses Ḥayyim Luzzatto's *endophasia*.[4]

One of the most intriguing problems in psychical research which deserves at least passing mention here is the amnesia claimed by a large number of mediums. Considering the doubtful credibility of

[1] On the whole subject see Scholem's remarks in *Tarbiz*, vol. xxviii (above. p. 272, n. 6), pp. 61–62 as well as in *Sabbatai Zevi*, vol. i, p. 65, concerning the common psychological basis of the *dibbuq*- and *maggid*-type of phenomena.

[2] Cf. above, p. 46.

[3] Cf. above, p. 80.

[4] Cf. above, p. 23.

the testimonies of many mediums and the consequent dearth of reliable evidence, it would be premature, at the present stage, to propose definite correlations of mediumistic amnesia with hysteria. It is therefore of some psychological interest to note the fact that the Maggid's revelations were not only remembered by Karo but were hardly ever written down on the spot. As most of the entries in the *M.M.* were communicated on Friday nights, viz. early Sabbath mornings, they could have been written down only after 12–24 hours at the very earliest. The length of the interval possibly detracts from the psychological value of the entries, as it seems to leave too much opportunity for 'secondary elaboration'. The fact itself, nevertheless, affords valuable evidence of Karo's waking consciousness during the visitations of the Maggid.

Even a superficial glance at what we know of Karo's total personality should make it clear that none of the standard psychiatric diagnoses fits his case. His unimpaired physical health and vigour, his intellectual power and creativeness that persisted to his death at eighty-seven, the practical realism manifest in his *responsa* on questions of marriage and divorce, inheritance, and business affairs, &c., which made him the leading halakhic authority of his day, the capacity for leadership that expressed itself in his many foundations of *yeshiboth* and in the raising of a generation of disciples, his sure sense of his own worth and authority coupled with a genuine modesty and avoidance of all quarrels and personal recriminations—all these leave little or no room for the usual alternatives of paranoia, hysteria, or epilepsy. Long-range diagnoses through the centuries, it should be added, are even more doubtful than those uttered at the patient's bedside, and perhaps the most that we may venture to suggest is that Karo probably was an epileptoid type, affected by a chronic hallucinosis but with perfect maintenance of the total personality.

What distinguishes Karo's Maggid from other phenomena of dissociation, viz. mystical phenomena such as apparitions of angels or of the prophet Elijah, is his complex and composite character. Spiritualist experience has taught us that the medium (viz. his unconscious) combines in an amazingly skilful and original manner the most diverse personal elements such as juvenile memories, repressed anxieties or desires, ideals, scraps of information, and the like, and that, moreover, the 'spirit personality' actually develops and changes in accordance with the conceptual and theoretical background in which it is set by the medium. To illustrate this point we may quote from what is perhaps the best known and most thoroughly investigated case in psychological literature. Flournoy's medium,[1] Hélène Smith, had her spirit guide, Leopold, who taught her an entirely new language and script, namely that of the inhabitants of the planet Mars. Flournoy could show that Hélène Smith's understanding of the phenomenon largely resulted from her association with spiritualist circles. The degree to which the unconscious incubation operates under the influence of a specific social pattern or ideology is succinctly formulated by Flournoy's verdict on his medium's association with spiritualist groups: 'Without the spiritualism and the auto-hypnosis of the séances, Leopold could never have developed into a true personality, but would have continued to remain in the nebulous, incoherent state of vague, subliminal reveries, and of occasional automatic phenomena.'[2] We may repeat here what has been said before: the interpretation of the mystical, viz. psychical, phenomenon is itself part of the total creation of the unconscious.

Mutatis mutandis—and in more psychoanalytical language than Flournoy's—we may say of Karo's Maggid that his super-ego provided the focus round which his ideals, ambitions, repressed self-consciousness and self-satisfaction, unadmitted petty jealousies, desire of spiritual power and authority, mystical yearnings, and oedipal fixations crystallized. Unlike the case of Hélène Smith, the total *Gestalt* of the Maggid was determined not by a framework provided by an odd assortment of spiritualist sitters but by a broad, socially dominant pattern of kabbalistic theory and practice. Within this framework, the dynamics of the unconscious could assimilate and fuse such diverse strands as the theory of the *Shekhinah* (viz. Karo's particular version of it), kabbalistic notions of the nature of the *Mishnah*, literary records concerning manifestations of hypostases of parts of the Talmud and their peculiar

[1] T. Flournoy, *From India to the Planet Mars: a study of a case of somnambulism with glossolalia* (1900).

[2] Ibid., pp. 92–93.

mode of address, and the general mystical tradition concerning messengers from the celestial academy. To quote Flournoy once more:[1] 'As regards the faculty of assimilating scanty sources of information, combining them and reproducing them in a living . . . form . . . there is nothing surprising to those who are acquainted—through examples drawn from hypnotic and automatic phenomena—with the fanciful creative abilities of the sub-conscious mind.' The great psychological feat of Karo's personality which distinguishes him not only from Hélène Smith and her kind but also from Luria and other kabbalists was his ability to limit his 'neurosis' to his intimate nocturnal experiences. His charismatic or mystical life did not spill over into his daylight activities. The Karo of the Codes and the *responsa* remained healthy, realistic, and down-to-earth. Whether this thorough dissociation made him a better man or a worse mystic is fortunately beyond the competence of the historian of religion to judge.

[1] *Nouvelles observations sur un cas de somnambulisme avec glossolalie* (1901), p. 207.

EPILOGUE

We have come to the end of our examination of the *M.M.* Our survey was, perhaps, more of a preliminary reconnaissance than a definitive study of the subject. We have found a personal, kabbalistic document concerned with all the problems that agitated sixteenth-century mystical speculation and that found their 'solutions' in the great kabbalistic systems of Safed. The diary permitted a fuller view of the kabbalistic life of the circles of pious scholars that had begun to form in Salonica and Adrianople even before the trek to the Holy Land made Safed into the great centre of the devout brotherhoods. We have learned that kabbalistic life was not restricted to mystical speculations but also involved regular paranormal experiences and celestial revelations of diverse kinds. Karo's case, though distinguished, was not unique or unheard-of. Automatic writing, automatic speech, induced intuitions, various methods of mystical and magical contemplation were practised in this remarkable mystical circle, which, it should be stressed again, consisted not of hysterical or high-strung revivalist enthusiasts but almost exclusively of talmudic scholars of distinction.

This, perhaps, is one of the most remarkable features of the mystical life of Joseph Karo and other learned rabbis. Mystics to whom heavenly secrets are imparted during their ecstasies are known by the hundreds to all historians of religion. Many of them actually initiated new forms of devotion under the inspiration of the Holy Spirit. We need only think, in addition to Alkabets[1] and the Lurianists,[2] of Orsola Benincasa and the blue scapular, or of Marie Alacoque and the devotion of the Sacred Heart. Automatisms too are frequent phenomena and many literary productions owe their existence to this kind of inspiration—from Maria Coronel de Agreda's *Mystica Cividad de Dios*[3] and Mme Guyon's

[1] Cf. above, pp. 52 and 110.

[2] Cf. Scholem's article (referred to above, p. 245, n. 1) in *Eranos-Jahrbuch*, vol. xix, 1950.

[3] Cf. H. Thurston, op. cit., p. 122 ff., and particularly his remarks on pp. 129–30.

commentaries on Scripture,[1] to the automatic writings so assiduously studied in the pages of the *Journal of the Society for Psychical Research.*

We know, in fact, that all sorts of people, whether saints (e.g. Hildegard of Bingen, Katharina Emmerich), poets (e.g. Coleridge),[2] or psychic individuals[3] can pass into states in which their unconscious psychic activity produces results that are quite beyond the normal range of their ideas, knowledge, and capacities. In many of these cases William James's verdict of intellectual deficiency seems remarkably near to the truth. The intriguing feature of similar phenomena among kabbalists is the obvious inapplicability of James's verdict. Their revelations are neither startling nor original, but they certainly betray intellectual effort and capacities. Like the angel appearing in the dreams of R. Jacob the Pious of Marvège,[4] Karo's Maggid reveals mysteries that their recipient had heard, read, explained, or written himself before. The Maggid was an undoubted case of motor (speech) automatism, but everything he said was well within the normal range of Karo's knowledge and intellect, which, needless to repeat, were of a rare calibre. *Mutatis mutandis*, the kabbalistic material tends to bear out Pratt's statement[5] that 'the visions of mystics are determined in content by their belief, and are due to the dream imagination working upon the mass of theological material which fills the mind'. The minds of Karo and his fellow kabbalists were certainly filled with 'theological material'. Had they consciously applied their intellectual powers to kabbalistic problems there would have been no need to reveal the mysteries of *Torah*. These mysteries would have been elucidated just as the 'mysteries' of the *halakhah*, and the mystical urge might have expressed itself in different, less intellectualistic forms. As it happened, the revelation of knowledge counted for more than pure experience, and hence the experience

[1] Cf. Mme Guyon's own testimony in her *Vie*, pt. ii, particularly chs. 2 and 19.

[2] Cf. J. L. Lowes, *The Road to Xanadu* (edn. 2, 1951).

[3] e.g. Dr. Haddock's maidservant Emma, Miss G. Cummins (the 'Cleophas Scripts'), Hélène Smith, &c.

[4] Cf. above, p. 42, n. 7.

[5] J. B. Pratt, *The Religious Consciousness*, 1921, pp. 402 f.

had to take the form of the communication of predigested discursive kabbalistico-theological material.

We have seen that as a scholar and canonist Karo ranked among the greatest. His achievement, though clearly nourished by messianic hopes and personal ambitions, was essentially rational. Nowhere do we find his celestial mentor revealing anything that was beyond his normal intellectual capacities. In halakhic matters the Maggid limited himself to confirming Karo's arguments and rulings. *In cabbalisticis* he revealed mysteries at which Karo would have arrived—and in most cases probably already had arrived—himself by a study of the relevant texts and problems. The problem of the maggidic messages thus became one not of their contents but of their form, i.e. the problem of the dynamics of Karo's unconscious choosing to express itself in a chronic hallucinosis shaped by kabbalistic patterns. Our conclusion was that Karo's mystical states were a means to an end. The means were visible testimonies of divine election and favour in the form of celestial messages according to the conventional kabbalistic pattern of 'mighty promises' and 'revelations of the mysteries of *Torah*'. The end was the maintenance of a psychological equilibrium throughout a life dominated by a tremendous intellectual and spiritual ambition, calling for extraordinary energy and discipline of abnegation in addition to the 'normal' rigours of ascetic piety as imposed by kabbalistic theology. In the kabbalistically transformed mother-image of his celestial mentor Karo found the divine, inspiring, reproving, chiding, encouraging, but above all loving, spiritual agency that on the one hand confirmed his heart's most cherished desires and ambitions, and on the other hand acted as the personified pressure of conscience, urging him to persevere in his ascetic life and in the pursuit of his high aims. Considering Karo's colossal intellectual and social achievement, we are certainly entitled to speak of a psychological equilibrium rather than of a disturbance, and to understand the Maggid's influence as the compensatory function of a complex mother-symbol.

But the tensions that rendered this compensation necessary lie deeper than the surface of the *M.M.* It has been said before that the existence of this strange and disconcerting book in the shadow of the *Shulḥan 'Arukh* is, in a way, symbolic of the hidden complexities of rabbinic Judaism. Perhaps Karo's life may be said to exhibit, on an individual level, what holds true in a larger way of rabbinic Judaism as a whole at a certain stage of its development. For too many years a tendentious and one-sided picture of Judaism as a religion of pure reason and sweet reasonableness has been assiduously fostered and spread. The lack of irrational paradoxes, the absence of manifest absurdities (or so it seemed), and a soberness which knew of no dizzy raptures at the brink of mystical abysses were brandished by apologists as marks of the incontestable superiority of Judaism. To the lovers of paradoxical profundities these vaunted virtues were, of course, only proof conclusive of spiritual poverty. Meanwhile the study of Kabbalah and earlier mystical movements has sufficiently progressed to compel a radical revision of some favourite axioms of the history of Judaism. Still, a good many writers, while grudgingly admitting the new insights, hope to take their sting out of them by declaring the bizarre and bewildering manifestations of myth, mystery, and magic to be secondary, marginal phenomena only. The legal and moral traditions which are central to Judaism, so this revised version goes, are situated in the broad daylight of lucid reason, though at their periphery they may fade into the twilight of dubious emotionalism, obscure theosophy, and apocalyptic messianism. There is a measure of truth in this account, if only for the one decisive fact that mysticism was rarely the undisputed, matter-of-course centre of Jewish self-interpretation. The relation between *halakhah* and mysticism was always one of complementarity or rather of polarity, and it was characterized by all the dialectical tensions which the term implies. Mysticism, whether practised or suppressed, was always viewed with a reserve and caution that bespoke a strong and sure sense of its inherent dangers. This holds true of the *merkabah*-gnosis, of early kabbalism, and again of eighteenth-century Ḥasidism. In fact, sometimes it appears as if the great mystical upsurges were inspired or abetted by non-Jewish influences; their 'Jewishness' consisted in the intensity and eagerness with which certain Jewish circles responded to them, transforming them and making them integral parts of a specifically and characteristically Jewish spiritual life. The precariousness of the transformation was demonstrated more than once by the inherent capacity of these mystical ideas to explode the frame of Judaism into which they had been fitted and to lead straight into antinomianism and heresy. Mysticism could pretend to supplement or illuminate the *halakhah*, perhaps even to offer the ultimate, esoteric understanding of its profounder meaning. It could even revolt against the dominance of *halakhah* and express, in dialectical antithesis, a greater or lesser, implicit and explicit, degree of opposition. But either way it was related to *halakhah* as the central and dominant feature of the religious and social reality of Judaism. Halakhism, on the other hand, could very well exist without taking note of mysticism at all. Even the most enthusiastic evaluation of Jewish mysticism has to take note of the fact that its historical role is, to a large extent, that of an underground current. This underground current could, at times, erupt and flood Judaism as a whole; on such occasions it could even throw up all sorts of things that usually remain hidden beneath the surface. Occasionally it even swept Judaism off its feet, though never for long.

The phenomenology of rabbinic Judaism will have to explain its mysticism as an essential part of its religious life, but precisely as part of its 'shadow' life. The term shadow is used advisedly in this context, for kabbalism clearly represents more than one marginal current in Judaism: it is the complementary, though repressed, side of the other, the better-known and 'conscious' function of Judaism. But the more rigid and dominant the conscious function, the more defective and often negative is the inferior, underdeveloped, and unconscious side. Jewish mysticism seems to bear the distinctive marks of the 'inferior function' in the strict technical sense of Jung's terminology. As such it was never far away from the 'shadow' of Judaism. But even if mysticism is an essential half of Judaism, no useful purpose is served by exaggerating in the other direction and claiming the underground life to be the one real and authentic manifestation of Jewish spirituality.[1]

The sixteenth century was, perhaps, the period of closest union of the two trends. Kabbalah had ceased to be the spiritual discipline

[1] As Martin Buber seems to have done in his earlier writings.

of a religious aristocracy or élite; it penetrated wider circles and finished by dominating Jewish piety everywhere. In Lurianic kabbalism *Halakhah* and *Kabbalah* achieved a maximum symbiosis which remained typical of Jewish piety until the Sabbatean heresy realized the implicit dangers of this 'synthesis'. Karo's circle represents the final development of sixteenth-century non-Lurianic or rather pre-Lurianic kabbalism. *Kabbalah* had already conquered the hearts and the minds of the leading talmudic scholars. In terms of an *unio personalis* in the lives of the rabbis, the mutual permeation and interpenetration of *Halakhah* and mystical theosophy were well-nigh complete. And yet, from a formal point of view, the two were kept strictly apart until the victory of Lurianism. The formal dissociation of *Halakhah* and *Kabbalah* was maintained not only by Karo but also by men like Taytazak and Berab. *Kabbalah* might inspire the mind and provide it with motive power and enthusiasm, but no mystical inroads were allowed on the absolute autonomy of the exoteric, halakhic universe of discourse. This two-track theology, as it may perhaps be called, was a remarkable achievement in that it made the highest demands on the intellectual, reasoning faculties of the rabbinic mind and never permitted mystical enthusiasm to ease the yoke of strict and uncompromising scholarly discipline. The duality of the 'official', halakhic Judaism and its mystical 'shadow' side seems to have reached its most exemplary expression in the period and circle of which Joseph Karo is the most distinguished representative.

It would be an odd accident, fraught with almost symbolic significance, if Joseph Karo, that epitome of talmudic rationality and disciplined thinking, exhibited in his own life the shadow side of rabbinic Judaism: an intense mystical yearning handicapped by a serious emotional immaturity. It found vent in psychical manifestations that welled up from the unconscious and overpowered that part of his personality that was not kept under the strict control of conscious reason. This, as we have seen, was his kabbalistic or 'nocturnal' personality, for the daylight scholar and canonist was kept strictly out of bounds to all mystical messengers. But it is a long way from the desire of mystical life to its genuine fullness. Where mystical phenomena form part of the life of the 'shadow', they are likely to contain more than their share of personal, repressed, and inferior material, and to show more traces of the influence of consciousness than would full-fledged mystics who systematically make mystical life their main business. If Joseph Karo is, perhaps, not the type of the ideal mystic, his life may still be typical of the place of mysticism in the general pattern of rabbinic Judaism.

POSTSCRIPT

AMONG the many studies on sixteenth-century Kabbalah and the history of Safed published since 1962, several are of special relevance to the subject matter of this book. At least two of these should be mentioned briefly here, the one to correct an error in chronology, the other to draw attention to a problem that still requires further investigation.

In chapter 5 (p. 87) I alluded to the much debated question of when and where exactly Joseph Karo could have studied with Jacob Berab, to whom he always respectfully refers as "my great master." The theory that at some time Karo may have studied at Berab's *yeshibah* in Egypt, suggested by Greenwald and mentioned by me (p. 88), has since received the support of D. Tamar (*Kiryath Sefer*, vol. 40 (1964/65), pp. 65–71; reprinted in Tamar, *Meḥqarim* (1970), pp. 195–200). But the major contribution to our knowledge of Berab's activity as a teacher is H. Z. Dimitrovsky's "Rabbi Ya'akov Berab's Academy" (Hebrew) in *Sefunoth*, vol. 7 (1963), pp. 41–102. Dimitrovsky discusses the chronology of Berab's movements to and from Safed (p. 45 ff., especially pp. 49–50), Egypt (p. 43, n. 7), and elsewhere, and he favours the possibility, which I had dismissed as improbable (see above, p. 87), that Karo entered into a disciple-master relationship with Berab after settling in Safed. Karo's arrival in Safed has to be dated 1536 (Dimitrovsky, p. 62, n. 137; similarly, Tamar, p. 70) and not 1537, as I tried to prove on the basis of my datings of the entries in *Maggid Mesharim*. Accepting the date 1536 of course calls into question my carefully computed dates for many of the entries in *Maggid Mesharim* and casts doubts on some of the conclusions I drew from my chronology. The answer seems to be that one should not place too much reliance on the dates given in *Maggid Mesharim*, as these may have been put down incorrectly to begin with, before being further corrupted by copyists. The same point has also been made by Tamar in his review.

In 1968 G. Scholem published an important study of "The Maggid of R. Joseph Taytazak and the revelations attributed to him."

The article was written as a contribution to *Sefunoth*, vol. 11 (pp. 69–112), but for a number of unfortunate reasons the publication of the volume has been delayed, though Scholem's chapter has circulated in a few copies—as a preprint rather than an offprint. The paper discusses at length the phenomenon of Taytazak's *maggid* and its relationship to the disconcerting anonymous work *ha-Mal'akh ha-Meshib*, subjects to which I had briefly drawn attention (pp. 14, n. 1; 46, n. 3; 47; and 118–19). My contention that Taytazak's *maggid* was a case of automatic writing and that Karo regarded his own experiences of automatic speech to be a superior charismatic gift was based on my interpretation of a maggidic communication to Karo (see above, p. 118). Scholem (p. 84) thinks that I "over-interpreted" the wording of the maggidic communication and argues that Karo had no knowledge of Taytazak's *maggid*, although he admits that Taytazak's charismatic life was known to many others and even enjoyed considerable fame. In fact, according to Scholem, it was the charismatic life in Taytazak's circle that attracted Solomon Molkho to Salonica and not (as I had surmised) Molkho's appearance that triggered off a charismatic revival. While Scholem's arguments on this particular question are not conclusive and still leave room for further enquiry, his views on the subject are of sufficient importance and relevance to the present study to merit at least a brief summary and reference.

On pages 18–19, n. 3, I put forward with some hesitation the suggestion that the *maggid*'s wording, borrowing from Ezekiel ii. 6, may imply a punning reference to "Serbs and Slavs," i.e., the Bulgarian population of Nicopolis. From a review by M. M. Halevy (*Revue d'Histoire de la Médecine Hébraïque*, vol. 17 (1964), p. 183) I learned that the pun was less far-fetched than I had thought: in Roumanian parlance, for example, the Bulgarians were often called Serbs, and Church Slavonic was referred to as Serbian (*Sirbi* in old Roumanian).

Among the evidence I adduced for the authenticity of the M.M. was the fact that quotations from the *maggid*'s revelations to Joseph Karo appear in the writings of several kabbalists long before the publication of the first edition of *M.M.*; cf. above p. 15 and the reference to Tamar (now reprinted in *Meḥqarim* (1970), pp. 101–

06), and pp. 34–5. More recently I. Tishby (in *Zion*, vol. 39 (1974), p. 14, n. 10) has drawn attention to more and hitherto unnoticed quotations and references to be found in *Ma'abar Yabboq* by Aaron Berekhya of Modena (Mantua, 1626).

One of our earliest accounts of the Lurianic circle in Safed being Shlomel Dresnitz's epistles, I noted (p. 16, n. 1) that "a critical examination of the value of *Shibhey ha-Ari* as a historical source is still outstanding." A first attempt in this direction has been made by M. Benayahu, *Sefer Toledoth ha-ARI* (1967); but his thesis (cf. also G. Scholem, *Kabbalah* (1974), p. 423) has provoked considerable controversy (cf. Tamar, *Meḥqarim*, pp. 166–93, and I. Tishby, cited above, pp. 12–13) and does not stand up to criticism. Dresnitz's epistles appear to be the earliest account and all later hagiographies are indebted to it.

APPENDICES

INDEX

APPENDIX A

ON THE DATING OF THE ENTRIES IN THE *M.M.*

1. Only few of the entries in the *M.M.* have a complete date, e.g. (5a. 2) 'the year 5296, the eve of Sunday, 4 Nisan', or 'Sabbath night of the feast of Tabernacles, the year [5]308' (48a. 6), or 'the year 5328, the night of Saturday, 19 Ṭebeth' (71b. 2), &c. As a rule the superscriptions do *not* state the year but merely indicate the day of the week and of the month, e.g. 'the night of Sabbath, 23 Ṭebeth', &c.; often the liturgical designation of the week, according to the portion of the Pentateuch read on the Sabbath, is added, e.g. 'the night of the Sabbath, 18 Kislev, the portion *Vayyishlaḥ*'. As the Jewish calendar knows fourteen types of years, recurring in a well-defined though irregular order,[1] the possibilities for any given date can often be narrowed down. Thus, for example, in a year of type i (which occurred in 5279, 5286, 5289, 5306), 18 Kislev falls on a Monday. In fact, 18 Kislev on a Sabbath is only possible in years of type vi and xiii. Even so there are usually too many possibilities left to permit a precise dating, particularly as Karo's maggidic visitations span a whole lifetime.

2. Moreover, the correlation of dates with the liturgical weeks is not always reliable. It has been observed already[2] that the diary has been rearranged to form a kabbalistic commentary on the Bible. If, in the course of a longer communication, the Maggid expatiated on a particular biblical verse, the whole entry was simply attributed to the corresponding weekly portion. For example, the homily on Lev. xxvi. 21 given s.t. *Beḥuqqothay* was certainly not revealed on the Sabbath on which this particular chapter is read. The homily was occasioned by the intimate events reported at the beginning of the entry,[3] and is based on a *double entendre*. The Hebrew word *qeri* ('if ye walk (*qeri*) contrary unto me', Lev. xxvi. 27) also means a seminal emission in rabbinic Hebrew, where it corresponds to the Biblical *miqreh*. Other homilies were prompted by feast days when appropriate chapters from the Pentateuch are read; e.g. the first entry s.t. *Ki Thissa* was not revealed on the Sabbath *Ki Thissa* but on a half-holiday. (On the Sabbath that falls during the half-holiday —*ḥol ha-mo'ed*—of Passover and Tabernacles, a chapter from the portion

[1] For details concerning the calendar, conversion tables, &c., see E. Mahler, *Handbuch der jüdischen Chronologie* (1916).

[2] Cf. above, pp. 25 f.

[3] Cf. above, pp. 138–9.

Ki Thissa is read.) It is perfectly obvious that *Bereshith* never falls in the month of Nisan (cf. *M.M.* 5a and 5b) and that *Vayyesheb*, which is always read on the Sabbath preceding Ḥanukah (25 Kislev), can never fall on 16 Ṭebeth (cf. *M.M.* 13b). The correlation may, however, be presumed to be correct whenever the Maggid uses the words ***parshetha qaddishta da.***

3. The number of possibilities can, however, often be reduced on the internal evidence of the text. Surely all entries containing prophecies of or references to Karo's future residence in Palestine must antedate his actual going there (1537/8 at the latest). Similarly there is a strong presumption for dating all communications prophesying his death at the stake after 1532, the year of Solomon Molkho's martyrdom (cf. above, p. 98). Using this method of elimination, we should be able to ascribe precise dates to some of the more important passages. One example must suffice here. The contents and general tenor of the two entries dated Tuesday, 30 Adar i–*Rosh Ḥodesh* Adar ii, and Sabbath, 4 Adar ii (cf. above, pp. 103 ff.), clearly prove that the communications are consecutive. The command to proceed to Palestine and the reference to martyrdom at the stake suggest some time between 1532 and 1537. The only possible years which fit the given dates are 1533 and 1536.

4. Occasionally there is clear evidence that a number of entries form a consecutive series. An example is given above, pp. 169–70, where it has been shown that the contents of the communications dated from 13 Adar (ii)–5 Nisan 5296 are closely related to Karo's commentary *B.Y.* on *Ṭur Y.D.* chaps. 198–201. This conclusion was further confirmed by an examination of the kabbalistic contents of the same passages (cf. above, pp. 33–34, and Chs. 9–10).

5. However, caution is required in using even the explicit dates furnished by the text. Mistakes and copyists' errors abound and are doubly disturbing when they have to be used, in conjunction with comparative tables and the like, as a basis for further guess-work. Discrepancies between dates as given in the printed editions and in the manuscripts only confirm the suspicion that mistakes of this kind do, in fact, occur. We must not be surprised, therefore, to find that some of the given dates do not fit the calendar at all. Such instances merely emphasize the need for caution; they certainly do not prove, as Rosanes thought they did, that the *M.M.* was a late fabrication (cf. above, p. 31).

6. The study of the *M.M.* has led me to suggest that a major part of the extant text dates from 1536–7. A spurt of intense psychic activity, characterized by frequent maggidic manifestations, seems to have taken place during the months Shebaṭ–Nisan 1536. On the other hand we must consider the possibility that this maggidic activity was in no way extraordinary—according to Karo's standards—and that it is only by

accident that so many of his notes from this period have survived while the rest has been lost.

7. A full discussion and justification of every date put forward in this study would have unduly swelled its size. Enough, however, has been said here to illustrate the principles on which I have tried to determine dates, and to emphasize their tentative character.

APPENDIX B

MANUSCRIPTS OF THE *MAGGID MESHARIM*

(cf. above, pp. 29 ff.)

GROUP A

A 1: New York, Jewish Theol. Seminary, MS. S. 11/158/5514, fols. 1–66.
Title-page: ספר מגיד משרים חלק שני (!).
Parta seconda, Magid Mesarim, parte seconda (scribbled a few times).
Postscript (in square script, 3 pp. after the end): מורי ואלופי רבי אלחנן דוד קרמי מריגגיו.
[Note: did the manuscript belong to a disciple of Elḥanan David Karmi of Reggio (d. 1643; cf. *J.E.*, vol. vii, p. 450, s.v.)?]

A 2: Ibid., MS. 1024 (Catal. Adler, p. 76), fols. 112*a*–136*b*. The manuscript also contains other kabbalistic works, among them a work of Moses Cordovero copied in 1602.
Title: ספר המגיד אל האלהי כמהר"ר יוסף קארו ז"ל.
Postscript: signature of censor *Domenico Scarpetti 1628*.

A 3: Ibid., MS. 39870, fol. 103*a*–127*a*. Fols. 120*a*–125*b* written by a different hand and repeating material already contained in the rest of the copy.
Title: [Rivo or Reggio?] קונטרסי' להרר"י קארו זצק"ל פה רייו.
Ends: חסר כאן.
Colophon: [1584=] פה רייו ע"ש יפ"ש [?] כ"ד למב"י שנת שד"ם לפ"ק.
[Note: ע"ש = *'Ereb Shabbath*, i.e. Friday; יפ"ש may mean יפה שעה 'in a happy hour' (?); למב"י means למנין בני ישראל, i.e. according to the counting of the *'Omer*. The 24th day of the *'Omer* is always on the 9 of Iyyar, and 9 Iyyar 5344 fell, in fact, on Friday *'Aḥarey Moth–Qedoshim*. The reference to Friday actually rules out the alternative reading of the date as שכ"ם. The *gemaṭriah* שד"ם is, of course, merely a device to avoid writing שמ"ד.]

A 4: Ibid., same volume, fols. 128*a*–135*a*. The volume in which A 3 and A 4 are bound also contains other kabbalistic writings.
No superscription; the text ends abruptly.

A 5: London, British Museum, MS. Gaster 434 (Or. 10109), fols. 32*a*–53*a*.

A 6: Ibid., same volume, fols. 114*a*–151*b*.
Ends (fol. 151*b*): בריך רחמנא, followed by signature of censor *fr. Renato da Mod*[a] *1626*.

A 7: Moscow, MS. Ginzburg 334, fols. 54*a*–86 (87)*a*.

Superscription (fol. 54*a*): הגיע לחלקי מיכאל אלישע ממודי׳ יצ״ו
ספר מגיד משרים ובו ביאורי מאורי סודות שנתגלו
לאיש תם הגאון הגדול מוהר״ר יוסף קארו ז״ל
שלי הצעיר אהרן רוויגו יצ״ו
הגיע לחלקי מיכאל אלישע ממודי׳ יצ״ו (fol. 55*a*)
קנין כספי אהרן רוויגו יצ״ו

Postscript: עד כאן מצאתי בריך רחמנא דסייען.

Signed by censor: *fr. Renato da Mod*[a] *1626*.

[Note: the wording of the title in this manuscript is similar to that of the title-page of the printed edition and seems to have inspired the latter.]

GROUP B

B 1: Oxford, Bodleian, Mich. 460 (Neubauer 1822. 1), fols. 1–24.
Title: ספר המגיד של בית יוסף.
Postscript: תם ונשלם.

B 2: Ibid., Opp. 303 (Neubauer 1823. 1), fols. 3–28.
Title: ס׳ המגיד של בית יוסף.
Colophon: מעשה ידי להתפאר במלאכת שמי׳ בסיטרא קדישא מנחם ציון רבינו איש מרגליות מקראץ.

B 3: Ibid., Opp. 447 (Neubauer 1833. 3), fols. 64–78.
Title: העתק מהמגיד של ה״ה מוהר״ר יוסף קארו זלה״ה.
Colophon: עד כאן מצאתי הועתק וכתב שהוא המגיד של ר׳ יוסף קארו ז״ל.

BB: Ibid., Hunt. 577 (Neubauer 1824), 82 fols. (fols. 1–2 missing).
[Note: because of its order and variations this manuscript is one of the most interesting.]

GROUP C

C 1: MS. Sassoon 248 (cf. Catal. *'Ohel David*, vol. i, p. 441).
Title: ספר מוסר ה׳ שהועתק מכ״י של מוהר״י קארו זלה״ה שהיה מיסר ומוכיח ומגיד לי [לו ?] חידושים המגיד בכל שבוע על ח׳ הפרשיות בהיותו בחו״ל בעיר ניקופול על שפת הנהר טונה.

C 2: Jerusalem, MS. Badhab, written 1675; cf. above, p. 27.

Manuscripts not examined (information supplied by Mr. M. Benayahu):

(1) New York, Jewish Theol. Seminary, MS. Schwager 662. (Yemenite MS.)

(2) Ibid., MS. 7949, fols. 41*a*–84*b*. Manuscript begins with ascetic counsels (אזהרות שהיה מזהיר המגיד למרן), exactly as in the printed editions.

Not one of the extant manuscripts contains our whole printed text or anything that is not found in print. The editors of the *M.M.* apparently possessed a manuscript with a much larger text of which the extant manuscripts preserve fragments only. Yet even the manuscript used by the editors presented only a small part of Karo's complete diary (cf. above, p. 37).

APPENDIX C

I. COMPARATIVE CHART SHOWING THE SEQUENCES OF ENTRIES IN THE MAIN GROUPS OF MANUSCRIPTS

The main columns are arranged so as to give a clear picture of the sequences. When an entry in one group of manuscripts corresponds to a completely different number or sequence in another group, the latter is indicated by bracketed numbers; e.g. 32 in Group A corresponds to no. 25 of BB and to no. 13 of B. Although these two numbers obviously appear in their proper places in their respective columns, they are given once more in brackets in the same horizontal line as A no. 32. As this chart is purely formal, i.e. concerned with the relative correspondences of sequences of entries, the corresponding texts in the printed *M.M.* are not indicated.

BB	B	A
1*a*	1	19
1*b*	(4)	(30)
2	2	20
(3)	(5)	21
	3	22
(1*b*)	4	(30)
3	5	(21)
4	6	23
5*a*	7	24
5*b*		
6		25
7		26
8		8
9		9
10		10
11		11
12		12
13		13
14		14
15		27
16		28

BB		B		A			
17						29	
	(1*b*)					30	
						31	
	(25)		(13)			32	
18							
19						33	
20							
21						34	
22		8			15		
		9			16		
		10*a*					
	(5*b*)	10*b*					
23		11			17		
24		12			18		
25		13					(32)
26				1			
27				2			
28				3			
29				4			
30				5			
31				6			
32				7			
33							
34							
35						35	
&c.			(16)			36	
		14				37	
		15				38	
		16					(36)
		17				39	
		18				=	
		19					
		=					

II. COMPARATIVE CHART SHOWING THE SEQUENCES OF ENTRIES IN THE MANUSCRIPTS OF GROUP A

A 1, 5, 6, 7	A 2	A 3	A 4
1	1		1
2	2		2
3	3		3
4	4		4
5	5		5
6	6		6
7	7		7
8	8	1	=
9	9	2	
10	10	3	
11	11	4	
12 } missing in A 5 (6–18)	12	5	
13	13	6	
14	14	7	
15	15	8	
15	16	9 25	
17	17	10 26	
18	18	11 27	
19	19	12	
20	20	13	
21	21	14	
22	22	15	
23	23	16	
24	24	17	
25	25	18	
26	26	19	
27	27	20	
28	28	21	
29	29	22	
30	30	23	
31	31	24	
32	32	28	
33	33	29	
34	34	30	
=	35	=	

A 1,5,6,7,	A 2	A 3	A 4
	36 37 38 39		

APPENDIX D

EDITIONS OF THE *MAGGID MESHARIM*

1. Lublin, 1646 (ת״ו),[1] ed. by Ruben Bingo; incomplete.
2. Venice, 1649 (ת״ט), ed. by Bingo and Eliezer Ashkenazi; consists of supplements to (1).
3. Amsterdam, 1708 (תס״ח), combination of (1) and (2); first complete edition.
4. Zolkiev, 1770 (תק״ל), reprint of (3).
5. Koretz, 1771 (תקל״א).
6. Zolkiev, 1773 (תקל״ג).
7. ,, 1776 (תקל״ו).
8. Polna Neustadt, 1791 (פולנאי עיר חדש, תקנ״א).
9. Lemberg (Lvov) (?), undated.
10. ,, ,, 1850 (תר״י).
11. Vilna, 1875 (תרל״ה). The first edition to show marks of severe editorial bowdlerizing. Thus the frequent references to תשמיש המטה are changed to תענוגות העולם, &c. The quotation from the Talmud (b. *Mo'ed Qaṭan*, 24a) מעשה באחד ששמש מטתו בימי אבלו ושמטו חזירים את גוייתו (ed. Amsterdam 15*b*. 1) is rendered here (fol. 13, col. 1, § 1): מעשה באחד שבקש לו תענוגי העולם בימי אבלו ושמטו חיות טמאות את גוייתו (*sic*!). All subsequent editions follow this one and are therefore unreliable.
12. Vilna, 1879 (תר״מ).
13. ,, 1900 (תר״ס).
14. Piotrkov 1929 (תרפ״ט). Contains many misprints in addition to the inaccuracies noted under (11).
15. (Germany, 1948). A bad photographic reprint of (14). The title-page too is reprinted from (14) and no indication of the actual date or place of publication is given.
16. Jerusalem, 1960. Carefully edited text, based on the first three editions and hence avoiding all later corruptions. No manuscripts have been consulted and the text, therefore, perpetuates the shortcomings (mistakes, lacunas, etc.) of the first editions.

[1] The Lublin edition is referred to in the Amsterdam edition as נדפס בלובלין בשנת ת״ה, but the correct date is indicated by the printer's foreword, which says ותיבנה ירושלים ובית מקדשנו במהרה בימינו לפ״ק אמן.

APPENDIX E

THE WORKS OF R. JOSEPH KARO AND THE DATES OF THEIR FIRST EDITIONS

A. PUBLISHED

Beth Yosef (commentary on Jacob Asheri's Code *Ṭur*), completed 1542; revision completed 1665.
Pt. *O.H.* Venice, 1550 (ש״י).
„ *Y.D.* Venice, 1551 (שי״א); 2nd edn., ibid. 1564 (שכ״ד).
„ *E.H.* Sabionetta, 1553 (אלול שי״ג).
„ *H.M.* Sabionetta, 1558 (printing begun מרחשון שי״ח).

Shulḥan 'Arukh, completed 1555, 1st and 2nd editions, Venice, 1567 (ניסן שכ״ז, תמוז שכ״ז); cf. Steinschneider's note, *Cat. Libr. Hebr. in Bibl. Bodl.* ii, col. 1480.

Bedeq ha-Bayith (glosses, addenda, and corrigenda to *B.Y.*), incomplete (cf. printer's postscript and Azulay, *Shem ha-Gedolim*, s.v.), Salonica, 1605 (שס״ה); 2nd edn., Venice, 1606 (שס״ו).

'Abqath Rokhel (*responsa* relative to *O.H.*, *Y.D.*, *H.M.*), Smyrna, 1795 (תקנ״ה). In the year 1569 the Maggid refers to a book entitled *Quppath ha-Rokhelim* (*M.M.* 61b. 4) and promises Karo that he would live to see it printed. The reference is probably to the same collection of *responsa*, published more than two hundred years after Karo's death under a slightly changed title.

Responsa relative to *E.H.* (edited by Joseph Karo's son, Judah), Salonica 1597 (שנ״ח).

Kelaley ha-Gemara (Talmudic hermeneutics), printed as an appendix to Joshua b. Joseph Halevy's *Halikhoth 'Olam*, Salonica, 1598 (ישמ״ח), 2nd edn., Venice, 1639 (שצ״ט).

Kesef Mishneh (commentary on Maimonides's Code *Yad ha-Ḥazaqah*), Venice, 1574–5 (של״ד–של״ה).

Derashoth (on *M. Aboth* and parts of Scripture), printed in *'Or Ṣaddiqim*, Salonica, 1799 (תקנ״ט).

Talmudic Novellae on the tractates *Qiddushin* and *Giṭṭin*, Piotrkov, 1922 (תרפ״ב).

Maggid Mesharim, Amsterdam, 1708 (first complete edition).

B. UNPUBLISHED

Addenda to *Bedeq ha-Bayith* (cf. printer's postcript to *Bedeq ha-Bayith*).

Commentary on Naḥmanides on the Pentateuch (mentioned by Judah Karo in the introduction to his father's *Responsa* relative to *E.H.*).
Commentary on Rashi on parts of the Pentateuch (see previous note).
Commentary on some tractates of the *Mishnah* (see previous note; also mentioned by Karo himself in *Kesef Mishneh* ad *Ṭum'ath Meth* xix. 5).
Talmudic Novellae (cf. above, A.).

The 'kabbalistic discourses by Rabbi Joseph' in MS. Or. 9161 in the British Museum (cf. *Catalogue of the Hebrew and Samaritan MSS. in the Brit. Mus.*, part iv (1935), p. 157) are certainly not by Joseph Karo. The attribution to Karo, though mitigated by a question mark (ibid., Index, p. 14), is completely unjustified.

APPENDIX F

THE MYSTIC LIFE OF THE GAON ELIJAH OF VILNA

THROUGHOUT our study of Karo's Maggid it has been repeatedly stressed that mystical (including psychical) phenomena were by no means infrequent in Jewish history and that, in fact, many well-known rabbis did have and others did seek maggidic revelations. Chapters 4 and 5 produced ample evidence both of the actual occurrence of charismatic phenomena and of the ardent desire for such in certain circles and at certain periods. It has been suggested that further biographical research will undoubtedly bring to light many more unsuspected cases, in addition to those already discovered by Scholem, Tishby, and others, and that the existence of treatises and manuals such as Vital's or Albottini's prove the widespread desire of pious souls for the gifts of the Holy Spirit. This 'enthusiastic' kind of spirituality, so avid of practical mysticism, is usually set over and against the sternly rationalist and moral type of rabbinic piety. Of course, this alternative type also admits of various subdivisions, from the philosophical-intellectualist piety exemplified by Maimonides to the strictly halakhist devotion which turns faith, *devekuth*, and the moral virtues into articles of *halakhah*. There is, however, still another, if somewhat unusual, possibility. A passing reference has already been made (above, p. 42, n. 2) to a religious attitude which, far from subscribing to the rationalist denial of mystical phenomena, actually takes them in its stride, as it were, but dismisses them as completely irrelevant to the spiritual life.

This view is of sufficient interest in itself to deserve a brief exposition, quite apart from its incidental value as a complement to the material that has formed the bulk of our study of Karo's Maggid. The author of the viewpoint to be set forth here is Elijah, the Gaon of Vilna (1720–97), known, among other things, for his fierce and uncompromising opposition to the Hasidic movement launched by Israel Ba'al Shem Tob. It should not be necessary to waste words on the antiquated and misleading presentation of the conflict between the Gaon and the Hasidim as a clash between talmudic rationalism and kabbalistic mysticism. The anti-hasidic Talmudists were kabbalists too, and the Hasidic founders, to the extent that they were genuine and original mystics, were probably inferior, as kabbalists, to their 'mithnagdic' opponents. The kabbalistic writings of the Gaon Elijah alone exceed in volume those of all his

Hasidic contemporaries put together. We are not concerned here with the precise nature of the battle royal between *Ḥasidim* and *Mithnagdim*; it suffices, for our present purpose, to stress the fact that the conflict between orthodox academic kabbalism and the new Beshtian mysticism must on no account be identified with the opposition rationalism–kabbalism.

But the Gaon Elijah was not only an outstanding talmudic and kabbalistic scholar. The *charisma* of his personality still shines through the awe-struck descriptions of his biographers—'hagiographers' would be more exact—whose rhapsodic and enthusiastic style is reminiscent of Shlomel's epistles *Shibḥey ha-'ARI* or of later hasidic biographies. Moreover, Elijah seems to have enjoyed mystical graces which, had he been a different man or lived in another century, might have made him the equal of Joseph Karo or even of Isaac Luria. In fact, the kabbalistic eminence and 'supernatural' life of the Gaon, who appeared in the public eye mainly as the leading halakhic authority of his age, already suggested to S. P. Rabinowitz (op. cit., p. 233) the otherwise highly questionable comparison with Joseph Karo. His most important disciple, Rabbi Ḥayyim of Volozhin (1749–1821), reports some interesting details of his master's life in his Introduction to the Gaon's commentary on the *Sifra di-Ṣeni'utha*, one of the obscurest parts of the *Zohar* (publ. posthumously, Vilna, 1820). There can be no doubt about the veracity of R. Ḥayyim's reports. The following paragraphs are extracts from his Introduction. The translation is as literal as possible except in the passages in round brackets where I have condensed R. Ḥayyim's text.

'God, in His mercy and to perform His good word that the Law would not be forgotten [from the seed of Israel], sent us a watcher and a holy one, a man in whom there was the spirit of God, our great master, the Gaon and light of the world, whose learning and piety proclaimed his holiness from one end of the world to the other, our pious and holy master and teacher Elijah of Vilna, from whom no mystery was hidden and who illumined our eyes with his holy writings in exoteric [halakhic] and esoteric [kabbalistic] lore. . . . For there are few only that can study the sources of our exoteric *Torah* . . . the Babylonian and Palestinian Talmud . . ., let alone the innermost mysteries of the *Torah* . . . and the writings of the 'ARI. . . . For even the saintly disciples of the 'ARI could not penetrate the innermost depth of the meaning of this holy one of the most high, the 'ARI, except R. Ḥayyim Vital. . . . Until He, for His righteousness' sake, to magnify the Law and make it honourable and to show us marvellous things from His Law, made His merciful kindness exceedingly great over us; and behold one like the son of man came with the clouds of heaven, to him glory was given, unique was this great man, none had been like him for many generations before him . . . all the ways and paths of exoteric and esoteric wisdom were clear to him . . . this is the *gaon* of the world, the *ḥasid* and saint, our great and holy master . . . whose way in holiness always has been to study and meditate and labour with great and incredibly mighty effort . . . and with a mighty and marvellous adhesion [to God] (*devekuth*), and a wonderful purity, until he was granted to penetrate to the full understanding of all things. And in his writings . . . he illumined for us the way . . . which none had been able to tread for many generations.

'And whilst I am speaking of the great and marvellous holiness of the *Torah* of our great master, I am reminded of something that . . . makes my heart burn as a flaming fire, . . . [namely] the rumours [spread] by ignorant and vain men in parts far away, who have never seen the light of his *Torah* and his saintliness . . ., dead flies which cause the fragrant ointment . . . of our great master to send forth a stinking savour, by saying that the holy Rabbi . . . held the 'ARI in low esteem. . . . Others went even farther, . . . saying that also the holy *Zohar* was not found worthy in his eyes . . . let the lying lips be dumb that speak iniquity concerning the righteous. . . . For their eyes can behold . . . this commentary [on the *Zohar*], . . . woe unto the ears that have to hear [such slander], wherefore I found myself obliged faithfully to proclaim to the tribes of Israel his complete and mighty mastery of the whole *Zohar* . . ., which he studied with the flame of the love and fear of the divine majesty, with holiness and purity and a wonderful *devekuth*. And I heard from his holy mouth that he rehearsed the *Ra'ya Mehemna* many and many times . . . until he could count its letters. . . . He also dreamed that our master Moses came to his house and disappeared again. . . .

'Also concerning our holy master, the awesome man of God, the 'ARI, my own eyes have seen the glory of the holiness of the 'ARI in the eyes of our great master, for whenever he spoke of him his whole body trembled . . . and also on his holy writings he meditated (and compared their sources in the *Zohar* . . . until he produced a completely faultless text . . . making the greatest efforts to compare all versions, weighing and counting the letters until he was satisfied that he had established the correct reading . . . and I once heard him say that he would not propose an emendation until he could corroborate it from other—at times even from as many as a hundred and fifty—passages. . . . Concerning the *Sefer Yeṣirah* he said that the 'ARI's text was as good as faultless, but for one mistake that had crept into the printed editions. When I said to him that in that case it should now be easy to create a *golem* [with the aid of the faultless text of the *Sefer Yeṣirah*]), he answered, "Once indeed I started to create a *golem*, but whilst I was engaged on it I saw an apparition above my head and desisted [from the attempt], saying to myself that Heaven wanted to prevent me on account of my youth". When I asked him how old he was at the time, he answered that he had not yet reached his thirteenth year.

'But the most mighty and awesome of his virtues was this, that he did not allow himself to enjoy any good thing but that which he had laboured to acquire through wisdom and understanding . . . and with great effort. And whenever Heaven had mercy upon him, and the fountains of wisdom, the most hidden mysteries, were revealed to him, he regarded it as a gift of God and did not want it. Also when Heaven wanted to deliver unto him supreme mysteries without any labour or effort [on his part] . . . through *maggidim*, masters of mysteries and princes of the *Torah* [i.e. different kinds of angels], he did not desire it; it was offered to him and he refused it. I heard from his holy mouth that many times *maggidim* from Heaven appeared to him, requesting to deliver unto him the mysteries of *Torah* without any effort, but he would not hearken unto them. . . . When one of the *maggidim* insisted very much . . ., he answered, "I do not want my understanding of the *Torah* to be mediated by any [mediators] . . .; my eyes are towards God [alone]: that which He wishes to reveal to me, and the share He wants to give me in His *Torah* through my hard labour [of study, these alone I desire]. He will give me wisdom . . . and understanding, . . . and thus I shall know that I have found favour in His eyes." . . . Once it happened to me that our master sent me to my younger brother—though greater than me in virtue—the pious and saintly *gaon* Rabbi Solomon Zalman, in order to transmit to him his command on no account to admit any angel-*maggid* that might come to him, for he would soon be visited by one. He added that although our master the *Beth Yosef* [i.e. Joseph Karo] had a *maggid*, this was more than two hundred years ago when the generations were in a proper [spiritual and moral] condition and he [Karo] himself resided in the Holy Land. But today, when there was so much looseness, and more particularly outside the Holy Land, it was impossible that [a celestial revelation] should be [all] holy of the holiest without any admixtures. More particularly revelations without *Torah* were an abomination to him and he would not consider them at all.

'He went even further than that and said that the wonderful insights obtained by souls during sleep, when the soul ascends to enjoy supernal delights in the celestial academies, were not highly esteemed by him. For the important achievement is what a man acquires in this world through his labour and efforts in choosing the good and devoting his time to the study of *Torah*, for thereby he pleases his Creator. . . . But the insights obtained by the soul during sleep, without labour and without [exercising] choice and free will, this rather belonged to the category of rewards which God grants a man [already] in this world by way of anticipation of the Hereafter. The implication of his words was that he experienced such ascents of the soul every night . . . and one of his disciples confirmed to me that he had actually heard him admit this. . . .

'Once, on the first day of Passover, two of his senior disciples were sitting near him—and they knew that it was his holy habit to rejoice exceedingly in the gladness of the Lord, rejoicing in the most marvellous manner on the festival days as we are commanded by the Law. But when they saw that his rejoicing was not as full as was his wont, they asked him about it. At first he refused to answer, but when they insisted he could no longer refrain himself and said, "I must needs tell it to you, though it is not my way to do so; but by fulfilling the verse 'if there be anxiety in the heart of man, let him tell it to others' [I may hope to relieve myself and thus be able to rejoice more fully on this holy day]. For last night [the Prophet] Elijah visited me—if I remember rightly my informants did say in his name that it was Elijah, but possibly it was some other messenger from the celestial academy [parenthesis of Ḥayyim of Volozhin]—and revealed awesome things . . . and in the morning, because in the excess of my joy I immediately meditated upon them before reciting the [prescribed] benediction over the study of *Torah*, I was punished and forgot everything. . . ." Then they comforted him and wished him, "May God make good to our master his loss". Some time later one of them asked him whether what he had lost had been returned to him (to which he answered, "Yes, . . .) even as I know why it was taken from me, I also know why it was revealed to me a second time. . . ."

'To him these things were as "natural", and he did not require any special meditations or *yiḥudim*. And forsooth, this stands to reason, since all his words and thoughts . . . were given only to the study of *Torah* . . . and everything he did was with a marvellous holiness and piety. Man is shown [in his dreams] according to what is in his heart [cf. b. *Ber*. 55b]; so what need was there in his case for special meditations and *yiḥudim*? He used to say that God had created sleep to this end only, that man should attain the insights that he cannot attain, even after much labour and effort, [in his waking state] when the soul is joined to the body, because the body is like a curtain dividing [man from the spiritual world]. But during sleep, when the soul is out of the body and clothed in a supernal garment . . . one reveals to her [these insights].

'Truly, from all his . . . wonderful deeds, as well as from what I have seen with my eyes in his writings, it appears that . . . holy mysteries were revealed to him by the Patriarch Jacob and by [the Prophet] Elijah. In other places where he wrote in a general way that "it had been revealed unto him" I am not quite sure whether these were waking revelations or ascents of the soul to the celestial academy during his sleep. There can be no doubt that he certainly experienced ascents of the soul every night . . . as said before; but concerning the revelations in his waking state I have nothing certain from him, for he kept these things secret . . . and the little that I know about it is what he would tell us incidentally, on rare occasions, in the course of our conversations. However, from one amazing story which I heard from his holy mouth I inferred that he also had great revelations when awake. My father in heaven is a witness that once I heard from his holy mouth that there was a man in Vilna who dreamed dreams, awesome dreams that frightened all who heard them, for he told everyone his innermost thoughts and deeds so that people greatly feared him. [Once] he was brought before [the Gaon] and said to him: "Rabbi, permit me to say one thing to your honour. A fortnight ago Thursday you sat in this place and expounded these and these verses from the portion *Ha'azinu* [Deut. xxxii] and Rabbi Simon bar Yoḥai was sitting at your right hand and the 'ARI at your left hand." Our master was amazed whence this mortal knew all this, and said, "But I remember that [on that day] I even sent my servant away from the house [so that nobody should know]." Then our master said to him, "It is true that I expounded awesome mysteries on that occasion", and as he said this his face waxed very pale—which shows that these must have truly been wonderful things and exalted mysteries, worthy of being expounded in the presence of Rabbi Simon b. Yoḥai. Then our master looked at the dreamer and recognized that he was suffering from melancholia, and melancholics do at times have correct and true dreams. Then he ordered his servant to chase the man away.

'But in truth, all these wonderful things are not wonderful at all in my eyes . . . for this is *Torah* and this is its reward. . . . We have a tradition from the *Tanna* Rabbi Me'ir [cf. the so-called 6th chapter of *'Aboth*] to the effect that [he who studies *Torah* for its own sake] "is vouchsafed many things" . . . ["many things"]—this is a hint at those wonderful things and exalted revelations. . . . And our eyes have seen how all these gifts [listed by Rabbi Me'ir and in the Baraitha of Rabbi Pinḥas b. Ya'ir] were fulfilled in our master. . . . To him permission was granted . . . to behold the inner light, . . . the most exalted and hidden mysteries, . . . and all the celestial gates were open to him . . . as our Sages have said [b. *Soṭah* 49a], "he who studies *Torah* even in distress . . . the curtain will not be closed before him", for he [by studying the *Torah*] communes with God—for God and the *Torah* are one.'

INDEX